DEUTERONOMY

Brazos Theological Commentary on the Bible

Series Editors

R. R. Reno, General Editor
Creighton University
Omaha, Nebraska

Robert W. Jenson
Center of Theological Inquiry
Princeton, New Jersey

Robert Louis Wilken
University of Virginia
Charlottesville, Virginia

Ephraim Radner
Wycliffe College
Toronto, Ontario

Michael Root
Lutheran Theological Southern Seminary
Columbia, South Carolina

George Sumner
Wycliffe College
Toronto, Ontario

DEUTERONOMY

T E L F O R D   W O R K

BrazosPress
a division of Baker Publishing Group
Grand Rapids, Michigan

© 2009 by Telford Work

Published by Brazos Press
a division of Baker Publishing Group
P.O. Box 6287, Grand Rapids, MI 49516-6287
www.brazospress.com

Printed in the United States of America

Library of Congress Cataloging-in-Publication Data
Work, Telford
    Deuteronomy / Telford Work.
       p. cm.—(Brazos theological commentary on the Bible)
    Includes bibliographical references and indexes.
    ISBN 978-1-58743-098-5 (cloth)
    1. Bible. O.T. Deuteronomy—Commentaries. I. Title. II. Series.
  BS1275.53.W67 2008
  222′.15077—dc22
                                                        2008041846

Quotations of Deuteronomy are adapted from the World English Bible, an adaptation of the American Standard Version in the public domain (ebible.org/web).

Scripture quotations labeled NRSV are from the New Revised Standard Version of the Bible, copyright ©1989, by the Division of Christian Education of the National Council of the Churches of Christ in the United States of America. Used by permission. All rights reserved.

Scripture quotations labeled RSV are from the Revised Standard Version of the Bible, copyright 1952 (2nd edition, 1971) by the Division of Christian Education of the National Council of the Churches of Christ in the United States of America. Used by permission. All rights reserved.

Scripture quotations labeled NJPSV are from the New Jewish Publication Society Version ©1985 by the Jewish Publication Society. All rights reserved.

CONTENTS

SERIES PREFACE

Near the beginning of his treatise against Gnostic interpretations of the Bible, *Against the Heresies*, Irenaeus observes that Scripture is like a great mosaic depicting a handsome king. It is as if we were owners of a villa in Gaul who had ordered a mosaic from Rome. It arrives, and the beautifully colored tiles need to be taken out of their packaging and put into proper order according to the plan of the artist. The difficulty, of course, is that Scripture provides us with the individual pieces, but the order and sequence of various elements are not obvious. The Bible does not come with instructions that would allow interpreters to simply place verses, episodes, images, and parables in order as a worker might follow a schematic drawing in assembling the pieces to depict the handsome king. The mosaic must be puzzled out. This is precisely the work of scriptural interpretation.

Origen has his own image to express the difficulty of working out the proper approach to reading the Bible. When preparing to offer a commentary on the Psalms he tells of a tradition handed down to him by his Hebrew teacher:

> The Hebrew said that the whole divinely inspired Scripture may be likened, because of its obscurity, to many locked rooms in our house. By each room is placed a key, but not the one that corresponds to it, so that the keys are scattered about beside the rooms, none of them matching the room by which it is placed. It is a difficult task to find the keys and match them to the rooms that they can open. We therefore know the Scriptures that are obscure only by taking the points of departure for understanding them from another place because they have their interpretive principle scattered among them.[1]

---

1. Fragment from the preface to *Commentary on Psalms 1–25*, preserved in the *Philokalia* (trans. Joseph W. Trigg; London: Routledge, 1998), 70–71.

As is the case for Irenaeus, scriptural interpretation is not purely local. The key in Genesis may best fit the door of Isaiah, which in turn opens up the meaning of Matthew. The mosaic must be put together with an eye toward the overall plan.

Irenaeus, Origen, and the great cloud of premodern biblical interpreters assumed that puzzling out the mosaic of Scripture must be a communal project. The Bible is vast, heterogeneous, full of confusing passages and obscure words, and difficult to understand. Only a fool would imagine that he or she could work out solutions alone. The way forward must rely upon a tradition of reading that Irenaeus reports has been passed on as the rule or canon of truth that functions as a confession of faith. "Anyone," he says, "who keeps unchangeable in himself the rule of truth received through baptism will recognize the names and sayings and parables of the scriptures."[2] Modern scholars debate the content of the rule on which Irenaeus relies and commends, not the least because the terms and formulations Irenaeus himself uses shift and slide. Nonetheless, Irenaeus assumes that there is a body of apostolic doctrine sustained by a tradition of teaching in the church. This doctrine provides the clarifying principles that guide exegetical judgment toward a coherent overall reading of Scripture as a unified witness. Doctrine, then, is the schematic drawing that will allow the reader to organize the vast heterogeneity of the words, images, and stories of the Bible into a readable, coherent whole. It is the rule that guides us toward the proper matching of keys to doors.

If self-consciousness about the role of history in shaping human consciousness makes modern historical-critical study critical, then what makes modern study of the Bible modern is the consensus that classical Christian doctrine distorts interpretive understanding. Benjamin Jowett, the influential nineteenth-century English classical scholar, is representative. In his programmatic essay "On the Interpretation of Scripture," he exhorts the biblical reader to disengage from doctrine and break its hold over the interpretive imagination. "The simple words of that book," writes Jowett of the modern reader, "he tries to preserve absolutely pure from the refinements or distinctions of later times." The modern interpreter wishes to "clear away the remains of dogmas, systems, controversies, which are encrusted upon" the words of Scripture. The disciplines of close philological analysis "would enable us to separate the elements of doctrine and tradition with which the meaning of Scripture is encumbered in our own day."[3] The lens of understanding must be wiped clear of the hazy and distorting film of doctrine.

Postmodernity, in turn, has encouraged us to criticize the critics. Jowett imagined that when he wiped away doctrine he would encounter the biblical text in its purity and uncover what he called "the original spirit and intention of the authors."[4] We are not now so sanguine, and the postmodern mind thinks interpre-

2. *Against the Heresies* 9.4.
3. Benjamin Jowett, "On the Interpretation of Scripture," in *Essays and Reviews* (London: Parker, 1860), 338–39.
4. Ibid., 340.

tive frameworks inevitable. Nonetheless, we tend to remain modern in at least one sense. We read Athanasius and think him stage-managing the diversity of Scripture to support his positions against the Arians. We read Bernard of Clairvaux and assume that his monastic ideals structure his reading of the Song of Songs. In the wake of the Reformation, we can see how the doctrinal divisions of the time shaped biblical interpretation. Luther famously described the Epistle of James as a "strawy letter," for, as he said, "it has nothing of the nature of the Gospel about it."[5] In these and many other instances, often written in the heat of ecclesiastical controversy or out of the passion of ascetic commitment, we tend to think Jowett correct: doctrine is a distorting film on the lens of understanding.

However, is what we commonly think actually the case? Are readers naturally perceptive? Do we have an unblemished, reliable aptitude for the divine? Have we no need for disciplines of vision? Do our attention and judgment need to be trained, especially as we seek to read Scripture as the living word of God? According to Augustine, we all struggle to journey toward God, who is our rest and peace. Yet our vision is darkened and the fetters of worldly habit corrupt our judgment. We need training and instruction in order to cleanse our minds so that we might find our way toward God.[6] To this end, "the whole temporal dispensation was made by divine Providence for our salvation."[7] The covenant with Israel, the coming of Christ, the gathering of the nations into the church—all these things are gathered up into the rule of faith, and they guide the vision and form of the soul toward the end of fellowship with God. In Augustine's view, the reading of Scripture both contributes to and benefits from this divine pedagogy. With countless variations in both exegetical conclusions and theological frameworks, the same pedagogy of a doctrinally ruled reading of Scripture characterizes the broad sweep of the Christian tradition from Gregory the Great through Bernard and Bonaventure, continuing across Reformation differences in both John Calvin and Cornelius Lapide, Patrick Henry and Bishop Bossuet, and on to more recent figures such as Karl Barth and Hans Urs von Balthasar.

Is doctrine, then, not a moldering scrim of antique prejudice obscuring the Bible, but instead a clarifying agent, an enduring tradition of theological judgments that amplifies the living voice of Scripture? And what of the scholarly dispassion advocated by Jowett? Is a noncommitted reading, an interpretation unprejudiced, the way toward objectivity, or does it simply invite the languid intellectual apathy that stands aside to make room for the false truism and easy answers of the age?

This series of biblical commentaries was born out of the conviction that dogma clarifies rather than obscures. The Brazos Theological Commentary on the Bible advances upon the assumption that the Nicene tradition, in all its diversity and

5. *Luther's Works*, vol. 35 (ed. E. Theodore Bachmann; Philadelphia: Fortress, 1959), 362.
6. *On Christian Doctrine* 1.10.
7. *On Christian Doctrine* 1.35.

controversy, provides the proper basis for the interpretation of the Bible as Christian Scripture. God the Father Almighty, who sends his only begotten Son to die for us and for our salvation and who raises the crucified Son in the power of the Holy Spirit so that the baptized may be joined in one body—faith in *this* God with *this* vocation of love for the world is the lens through which to view the heterogeneity and particularity of the biblical texts. Doctrine, then, is not a moldering scrim of antique prejudice obscuring the meaning of the Bible. It is a crucial aspect of the divine pedagogy, a clarifying agent for our minds fogged by self-deceptions, a challenge to our languid intellectual apathy that will too often rest in false truisms and the easy spiritual nostrums of the present age rather than search more deeply and widely for the dispersed keys to the many doors of Scripture.

For this reason, the commentators in this series have not been chosen because of their historical or philological expertise. In the main, they are not biblical scholars in the conventional, modern sense of the term. Instead, the commentators were chosen because of their knowledge of and expertise in using the Christian doctrinal tradition. They are qualified by virtue of the doctrinal formation of their mental habits, for it is the conceit of this series of biblical commentaries that theological training in the Nicene tradition prepares one for biblical interpretation, and thus it is to theologians and not biblical scholars that we have turned. "War is too important," it has been said, "to leave to the generals."

We do hope, however, that readers do not draw the wrong impression. The Nicene tradition does not provide a set formula for the solution of exegetical problems. The great tradition of Christian doctrine was not transcribed, bound in folio, and issued in an official, critical edition. We have the Niceno-Constantinopolitan Creed, used for centuries in many traditions of Christian worship. We have ancient baptismal affirmations of faith. The Chalcedonian definition and the creeds and canons of other church councils have their places in official church documents. Yet the rule of faith cannot be limited to a specific set of words, sentences, and creeds. It is instead a pervasive habit of thought, the animating culture of the church in its intellectual aspect. As Augustine observed, commenting on Jeremiah 31:33, "The creed is learned by listening; it is written, not on stone tablets nor on any material, but on the heart."[8] This is why Irenaeus is able to appeal to the rule of faith more than a century before the first ecumenical council, and this is why we need not itemize the contents of the Nicene tradition in order to appeal to its potency and role in the work of interpretation.

Because doctrine is intrinsically fluid on the margins and most powerful as a habit of mind rather than a list of propositions, this commentary series cannot settle difficult questions of method and content at the outset. The editors of the series impose no particular method of doctrinal interpretation. We cannot say in advance how doctrine helps the Christian reader assemble the mosaic of Scripture. We have no clear answer to the question of whether exegesis guided by

8. *Sermon* 212.2.

doctrine is antithetical to or compatible with the now-old modern methods of historical-critical inquiry. Truth—historical, mathematical, or doctrinal—knows no contradiction. But method is a discipline of vision and judgment, and we cannot know in advance what aspects of historical-critical inquiry are functions of modernism that shape the soul to be at odds with Christian discipline. Still further, the editors do not hold the commentators to any particular hermeneutical theory that specifies how to define the plain sense of Scripture—or the role this plain sense should play in interpretation. Here the commentary series is tentative and exploratory.

Can we proceed in any other way? European and North American intellectual culture has been de-Christianized. The effect has not been a cessation of Christian activity. Theological work continues. Sermons are preached. Biblical scholars turn out monographs. Church leaders have meetings. But each dimension of a formerly unified Christian practice now tends to function independently. It is as if a weakened army had been fragmented, and various corps had retreated to isolated fortresses in order to survive. Theology has lost its competence in exegesis. Scripture scholars function with minimal theological training. Each decade finds new theories of preaching to cover the nakedness of seminary training that provides theology without exegesis and exegesis without theology.

Not the least of the causes of the fragmentation of Christian intellectual practice has been the divisions of the church. Since the Reformation, the role of the rule of faith in interpretation has been obscured by polemics and counterpolemics about *sola scriptura* and the necessity of a magisterial teaching authority. The Brazos Theological Commentary on the Bible series is deliberately ecumenical in scope, because the editors are convinced that early church fathers were correct: church doctrine does not compete with Scripture in a limited economy of epistemic authority. We wish to encourage unashamedly dogmatic interpretation of Scripture, confident that the concrete consequences of such a reading will cast far more light on the great divisive questions of the Reformation than either reengaging in old theological polemics or chasing the fantasy of a pure exegesis that will somehow adjudicate between competing theological positions. You shall know the truth of doctrine by its interpretive fruits, and therefore in hopes of contributing to the unity of the church, we have deliberately chosen a wide range of theologians whose commitment to doctrine will allow readers to see real interpretive consequences rather than the shadow boxing of theological concepts.

Brazos Theological Commentary on the Bible has no dog in the current translation fights, and we endorse a textual ecumenism that parallels our diversity of ecclesial backgrounds. We do not impose the thankfully modest inclusive-language agenda of the New Revised Standard Version, nor do we insist upon the glories of the Authorized Version, nor do we require our commentators to create a new translation. In our communal worship, in our private devotions, in our theological scholarship, we use a range of scriptural translations. Precisely as Scripture—a living, functioning text in the present life of faith—the Bible is not semantically fixed. Only a modernist, literalist hermeneutic could imagine that this modest fluidity is a liability. Philological precision and stability is a consequence of, not a basis for, exegesis. Judgments about the meaning of a text fix its literal sense, not the other way around. As a result, readers should expect an eclectic use of biblical translations, both across the different volumes of the series and within individual commentaries.

We cannot speak for contemporary biblical scholars, but as theologians we know that we have long been trained to defend our fortresses of theological concepts and formulations. And we have forgotten the skills of interpretation. Like stroke victims, we must rehabilitate our exegetical imaginations, and there are likely to be different strategies of recovery. Readers should expect this reconstructive—not reactionary—series to provide them with experiments in postcritical doctrinal interpretation, not commentaries written according to the settled principles of a well-functioning tradition. Some commentators will follow classical typological and allegorical readings from the premodern tradition; others will draw on contemporary historical study. Some will comment verse by verse; others will highlight passages, even single words that trigger theological analysis of Scripture. No reading strategies are proscribed, no interpretive methods foresworn. The central premise in this commentary series is that doctrine provides structure and cogency to scriptural interpretation. We trust in this premise with the hope that the Nicene tradition can guide us, however imperfectly, diversely, and haltingly, toward a reading of Scripture in which the right keys open the right doors.

R. R. Reno

AUTHOR'S PREFACE

This volume is dedicated to the students of my spring 2005 Westmont College course on theological interpretation of the Bible:

Nick Baer	Stephanie Kremmel	Micah Ralston
Meredith Burns	Casey Massena	Kate Retzer
Julieanne Faas	Amanda Mathison	Tarah Roberts
Danielle Garcia	Connor Murphy	Jennifer Salemann
Natasha Gettings	Alison Noseworthy	Lindsey Smith
Kelly Hardenbrook	Luke Oliver	Matt Tyler
Ryan Hoxie	Flavia Onofrei	

You and I came together unsure that we could ever pull off decent treatments of a book like Deuteronomy. We worked together through our textbooks all semester, terrified of the approaching task of preaching a passage "theologically." And you came through! Your final projects were the best collection of biblical interpretations I have ever had the privilege of hearing. Think of this book as *my* final project. I'm honored to place it alongside yours (and sorry it ended up too large to feature selections from your interpretations). May they be just the beginning.

> Assemble the people, the men and the women and the little ones, and your foreigner who is within your gates, that they may hear, and that they may learn, and fear YHWH your God, and do all the words of this Torah—and that their children, who have not known, may hear, and learn to fear YHWH your God as long as you live in the land you go over the Jordan to possess. (Deut. 31:12–13)

ABBREVIATIONS

General

+   indicates a term that could or should be translated inclusively to allow the reader to judge whether and how to respect gender inclusivity

→   indicates a cross-reference to commentary on passages in Deuteronomy

NJPSV   New Jewish Publication Society Version

NRSV   New Revised Standard Version

RSV   Revised Standard Version

Biblical

Acts	Acts	Gal.	Galatians
Amos	Amos	Gen.	Genesis
1 Chr.	1 Chronicles	Hab.	Habakkuk
2 Chr.	2 Chronicles	Hag.	Haggai
Col.	Colossians	Heb.	Hebrews
1 Cor.	1 Corinthians	Hos.	Hosea
2 Cor.	2 Corinthians	Isa.	Isaiah
Dan.	Daniel	Jas.	James
Deut.	Deuteronomy	Jer.	Jeremiah
Eccl.	Ecclesiastes	Job	Job
Eph.	Ephesians	Joel	Joel
Esth.	Esther	John	John
Exod.	Exodus	1 John	1 John
Ezek.	Ezekiel	2 John	2 John
Ezra	Ezra	3 John	3 John

Jonah	Jonah	2 Pet.	2 Peter
Josh.	Joshua	Phil.	Philippians
Jude	Jude	Phlm.	Philemon
Judg.	Judges	Prov.	Proverbs
1 Kgs.	1 Kings	Ps.	Psalms
2 Kgs.	2 Kings	Rev.	Revelation
Lam.	Lamentations	Rom.	Romans
Lev.	Leviticus	Ruth	Ruth
Luke	Luke	1 Sam.	1 Samuel
Mal.	Malachi	2 Sam.	2 Samuel
Mark	Mark	Song	Song of Songs
Matt.	Matthew	1 Thess.	1 Thessalonians
Mic.	Micah	2 Thess.	2 Thessalonians
Nah.	Nahum	1 Tim.	1 Timothy
Neh.	Nehemiah	2 Tim.	2 Timothy
Num.	Numbers	Titus	Titus
Obad.	Obadiah	Zech.	Zechariah
1 Pet.	1 Peter	Zeph.	Zephaniah

INTRODUCTION

On putting up. Now I know why it defiled one's hands to hold the scrolls of the holy scriptures that were kept in the temple (Beckwith 1990: 39–45, 62–63): it burns the skin.

Deuteronomy is a wonder. Like no other biblical book, it is a template for the two-volume canon of Old and New Testaments. It is the seal of the Pentateuch and the gateway from the patriarchs⁺ to the Former and Latter Prophets. Its narrative framework for the covenant's rules and regulations sets the Psalms and Proverbs and all other wisdom within Israel's life of grace. Its blessings, curses, and sobering song are both the raw material and the essential storyline of apocalyptic. And all these revelations converge on the Messiah on its distant horizon, whose signs and wonders, prophesying, sufferings, and new life will restore and amplify the covenant's blessings after faithlessness has run its cursed course.

Why then do Christians ignore it so? Jews traverse it every year with joy, but Christians seldom enter it at all—especially the thicket of ordinances at its heart. For us it seems a dark and forbidding forest. Or we make it out to be a petrified forest, a dead monument to an age that Christ has put away for good, and good riddance.

Yet the church calls Deuteronomy holy scripture, inspired and useful for teaching, reproof, correction, and training in righteousness (2 Tim. 3:16). The apostles and their churches certainly found it so; it is one of the most quoted books in the New Testament. Along with the end of Isaiah and the Psalms, it is the font of Paul's Christian imagination. In naming it canonical, we claim that it perfects and equips the people of God (3:17), and we bundle Deuteronomy with the Bible's other books and print copies by the billions.

It is one thing to call a book biblical, and another thing to treat it that way. To excuse our reticence to engage Moses's last words, we have needed to invent rationales for treating Deuteronomy the way we do. These only harden our distance from the canonical voices for whom Deuteronomy was so much more prominent.

If we cannot read the story of Moses's last words in the same power as did the prophets, priests, and sages of ancient Israel and the apostolic church, then it is hard to claim that we and they share the same faith, at least in much depth.

This theological commentary is a recovery project. I think Christians need to put up or shut up. We need to read Deuteronomy as a volume in the canon of the church of Jesus Christ, and to do it well. We need to interpret *all of it* in ways that honor both the gospel and Deuteronomy itself. We do not need to do this just to show others that it can be done. We need to do it because we must stand under Deuteronomy's testimony as the word of God in order to know and respect the Father's will, as our Lord Jesus Christ has done.

The fourfold apostolic sense of scripture. Theological commentaries—an intentionally underdetermined genre at present (see Rowe and Hays 2007)—could do all this in a variety of ways. My approach here focuses on one main goal: to form and discipline a contemporary apostolic imagination by reading every passage of Deuteronomy according to the sensibilities of the New Testament church.

Richard Hays concludes that the New Testament writers share three common "root metaphors" that function as lenses focusing the canonical texts' diverse details (1996: 194–95). These summarize the biblical story and guide readings of the Bible's individual texts. He distills three "focal images" that he calls "community, cross, and new creation":

> The church is a countercultural community of discipleship, and this community is the primary addressee of God's imperatives.
> Jesus' death on a cross is the paradigm for faithfulness to God in this world.
> The church embodies the power of the resurrection in the midst of a not-yet-redeemed world. (1996: 196–98)

I do not think it is coincidental that these three focal lenses suggest the three spiritual senses of the fourfold allegorical method of medieval exegesis, often encapsulated in Augustine of Dacia's jingle:

> The letter teaches events,
> Allegory what you should believe,
> Morality teaches what you should do,
> Anagogy what mark you should be aiming for. (de Lubac 1998: 1)

The medieval church was following up on the apostolically formed instincts of the patristic era. There is no sudden departure from the faith of the apostolic communities that knew Jesus and his authorized ambassadors, no massive apostasy into "early Catholicism" or whatever one wants to call the consolidated subapostolic faith. There is instead an imperfect but profound sense, exploited in the masterful storytelling of Irenaeus of Lyons in *Against Heresies* (de Lubac 1998: 154; cf. Hays 1996: 199), that every chapter and verse of the whole story of God in Jesus Christ means what it means in light of that whole story, and vice versa.

So Hays's three lenses along with something like a critical literal sense can work in contemporary biblical scholarship as the fourfold sense did in the Middle Ages, guiding readers into a more accurate, clearer, and fuller sense of the import of biblical texts and forming an apostolic imagination in ourselves in the process. The so-called literal sense of a passage is its *plain* sense in its immediate literary and perhaps historical context. The allegorical sense is its meaning in light of the advent of the Messiah in whom we are to *believe*. The anagogical sense is its significance for the eschatological age that stirs in Israel's return from exile, approaches in the kingdom of God, and culminates in the Son of Man's *hoped*-for return to judge all things and make them new. The tropological or moral sense is its guidance for the church that signifies that kingdom and respects its law of *love*.*

These are not Platonistic or Christian impositions! They follow trajectories that are already prominent in Israel's scriptures. Ecclesiology, the proper life of the people of God, is of course a driving focus of Tanakh. Eschatology not only suffuses the prophets but describes the futurology of the Torah and the hopes and dreams of the writings. And deliverance is a memory not just fixed in Israel's Egyptian past but fueling trust that YHWH will send an anointed one, a *mashiach*, to restore the nation's blessings and relocate it in its promised global and cosmic context. What distinguished the first Christians' interpretations of Israel's scriptures was not the presence or even prominence of these concerns, but the conviction that all three were being fulfilled through Jesus the son of Mary. That conviction informed a distinctively Christian biblical hermeneutic—an "apostolic hermeneutic." Its various forms—from the focal lenses and voices of the New Testament to the fourfold allegorical method to liturgical syntheses and folk preaching—inspire and structure this commentary.

I have arranged my observations on each passage roughly according to the four senses. (Please disagree charitably if you do not agree with a particular classification. I have treated the senses as broad semantic domains rather than rigid categories to keep them flexible, and even then one sense is not always easy to isolate from others.) With space limited, I have rarely offered an observation on every sense of every passage. Moreover, comments devoted to the plain sense are often missing or very brief. This is not because I regard the plain sense as unimportant—it teaches us *and* grounds all the others—but because so many fine commentaries already concentrate on the plain sense, often exclusively. These serve Deuteronomy's readers (and have served me) exceptionally well, and I rarely have much to add.

---

*Indeed, the specific form of love that characterizes the *ekklēsia Israel* answers Hays's objections in rejecting "love" in the abstract as an adequate focal image, and the specific form of hope that waits for the kingdom meets his similar objections to "liberation" and "freedom" (1996: 200–204). The particulars of Christology, eschatology, and ecclesiology keep faith, hope, and love from diffusing into abstractions no longer determinatively informed by the canon's content.

Inspired by the Talmud, I had unrealistically hoped to set my comments alongside rather than under the biblical text, in five columns. This format would have the virtue of leading the reader back and forth from the commentary's senses and the text, rather than just *away* from the text to our contemporary worries and debates, as the conventional format subtly does. It would also have been confusing to most readers, and astronomically expensive to publish. I have retained the five-column format only on the first page to give readers a visual sense of my strategy, then reverted to a one-column format in which my observations on the four senses follow the text. I have usually ordered the senses thus: *plain* (literal or historical) sense, *faith* (christological), *hope* (eschatological), *love* (ecclesiological). This is neither Hays's order nor the traditional medieval order. Instead it follows both the order of the Pauline theological virtues of 1 Cor. 13 and the narrative order of the creeds, which begin with creation in the first article, follow salvation christologically from the Son's first advent to his last in the second article, and end in the third article's explicit ecclesiology. I have reordered observations where it would serve to unite distinct senses into a passage's broader lesson. At any rate, I do not consider the order of the senses to be terribly significant, since each sense informs the others.

The claim that *all* scripture is God-breathed is a genuine apostolic conviction. As a test of the fact—which many would call a dogma, others a hypothesis, and some just a convention—that Deuteronomy belongs in the canon of Christian scripture, I offer a Christian interpretation of every passage. This has been a wonderful discipline for me, if sometimes intimidating and rather fatiguing. It has helped me see how Paul and other New Testament writers read Deuteronomy, why churches found answers there when they came to the text with their most urgent questions, and where Moses's voice reverberating through centuries of subsequent history tutored these later voices in the first place—especially the prophet like him. I cannot certify that I have offered *good* Christian interpretations of each passage, nor do I expect readers to find them all plausible, but I have knocked on all of Deuteronomy's doors, and every time I have come away satisfied.

Many professional biblical interpreters share a disdainful attitude toward allegory. This is a pity, not least because it trains us to be perplexed by the Bible's own metaphors, symbols, types, and allegories. Certainly there are many bad allegories out there, and they should warn us away from doing allegory badly. Allegorical exegesis is never supposed to be *fanciful* exegesis. But neither is literal exegesis, and there are enough examples of fanciful literal readings in contemporary biblical scholarship and theology to feed a lifetime of popular disdain toward modern theologians, biblical scholars, and pastors. I have been impressed and edified by both skillful allegorizing and skillful literalizing and wish only to improve skills in both. My dream is that preachers, liturgists, teachers, and students in particular would find these observations useful in developing sermons, hymns, lessons, and intuitions drawing on Deuteronomy.

Sacrifices. One can do only so much in a commentary. Dedicating this one to the task of "disciplining an apostolic Deuteronomic imagination" has meant sidelining other, truly worthy, pursuits, including some that qualify as theological commentary.

The broad rhetorical sweep of Deuteronomy, "the theology of the Deuteronomist," and relationships between Deuteronomy and the rest of the Pentateuch, the rest of the Tanakh, postbiblical Jewish interpretive traditions, and specific schools of Christian theology—all take a backseat to intertextual relationships between Deuteronomy and the New Testament as they resonate in the present. This will disappoint readers for whom these other topics matter more.

To professional biblical scholars who want to see more attention to historical context, critical scholarship, and secondary literature than the occasional observations I have incorporated here: please do not take my inattention as ignorance (though sometimes it is), let alone disdain. To source critics and redaction critics who wish I had concentrated on Deuteronomy's "sources," literary critics on its themes and major structures, historicists on its correlation (or lack of correlation) with real historical events, and so on: I involved such questions and insights here and there, but chose not to focus where so many others do. Old Testament theologians will lament the relative paucity of references to other Old Testament texts; their scholarship already develops these relationships much more extensively than relationships between the Testaments, and I commend interested readers to the fine work of these theologians—from Abraham Heschel to Walther Eichrodt and Gerhard von Rad to Samuel Terrien and Brevard Childs.

Jews will search for rabbinic sources here and find barely any; here I say only, rather sadly, that the distinct trajectories of apostolic and subapostolic exegesis and rabbinic and Hellenistic Jewish exegesis set our two traditions on very different courses, with divergent central questions. I would like someday to be equipped to enter into the informed and mutually enriching conversations between these two traditions. My task here is to fortify the Christian side of that conversation so that Christian readers can more adequately represent it and so that Jewish readers can perhaps understand better why we read Torah as we do.

Some in all these circles will tire of Jesus, the eschaton, and the church showing up again and again in every passage. They will suspect that my approach imposes a foreign agenda onto the text. Does it really? Or does it respect what Markus Bockmuehl calls "the explosively 'totalizing' theological assertions that writers like Paul and the evangelists state or imply in practically every sentence" (2006: 46)—assertions altogether warranted given the developments since the days of Moses?

Finally, my fellow theologians will wish I had appealed much more often to the towering voices in the history of the church, from Augustine and Chrysostom to Thomas Aquinas to Luther and Calvin, as well as to theology's many contemporary voices from across the confessional and theological spectrum. Those resources are already at hand—one can write a dissertation on the history of any one influential passage's interpretation—and I have not wanted to offer a history of exegesis or a compendium of other people's readings. Instead, I have aimed to assimilate a style of exegesis that yielded our New Testament, once dominated our common theological tradition, and guided these very theological authorities to the readings their disciples so prize, but that has been driven underground or intimidated into near silence in modern academic theology. For meanwhile, the church's old traditions of spiritual reading have lived on in folk traditions, unofficial networks, stubborn preachers, confessional loyalists, mystics, artists, and liturgists, and other movements and denominations that don't really give a damn—well, maybe a damn—about what credentialed theologians think; and it looks as if these traditions will continue to flourish with or without us. As a theologian who has learned far more from this motley assortment of experts than I am supposed to admit, I have prioritized the voices of the masters who seem to have taught the best of them: the writers of the New Testament. I am sitting at their feet in the hope that I might inherit the inheritance they themselves inherited from the once itinerant, now ascended and seated royal sage who "opened their minds to understand the scriptures" (Luke 24:45 NRSV).

My debts and debtors. This is not to say that the Bible has been my only teacher. Far from it! I can express profound gratitude to a number of people at the same time that I commend them to you. Richard Hays embodies a faithful and powerful, if uneasy, synthesis of critical biblical scholarship and apostolic reading. Geoffrey Wainwright shows habitual rationalists like me that worship has informed the deepest instincts of the church's biblical interpreters. He also introduced me to my favorite contemporary theological commentary: Lesslie Newbigin's *The Light Has Come* (1982). Miroslav Volf and Stanley Hauerwas have mentored me in theological interpretation just by teaching, writing, and living. John O'Keefe and Rusty Reno represent patristic exegetical habits in a way that has transformed my students' and my appreciation for precritical interpretation. Robert Alter is a master of Hebrew narrative and poetry whose literary instincts are a godsend and an inspiration to students wearied by the artificialities of some styles of biblical criticism, while Richard Bauckham and Marianne Meye Thompson analyze scriptures historically and theologically in ways that simultaneously honor the gifts of contemporary critical insight and expose its vices. Reuven Hammer's translation and commentaries in *The Classic Midrash* (1995), Hammer's edition and translation of *Sifre* (1986), and Abraham Joshua Heschel's *Heavenly Torah* (2005) all display the vanishing (and, among many Christians, vanished) art of reading Israel's Bible as what Peter Gomes calls "the lively oracles of God."

While my approach here differs from the conventional critical commentary form, I owe a vast debt to critical commentaries on Deuteronomy and the whole Torah. Contemporary Jewish commentaries are particularly rich, treating the Torah both as a text of ancient Israel and as a living covenant. Jeffrey Tigay's JPS Torah Commentary (1996) is a treasure—a goldmine of critical, literary, and traditional exegesis. If you read a critical commentary alongside this one (and you should), Tigay's is an excellent choice. Robert Alter's *The Five Books of Moses* (2004) and Richard Elliott Friedman's *Commentary on the Torah* (2001) offer two delightful translations of the Masoretic Text, along with commentaries engaged with both scholarly and contemporary Jewish questions. Among other one-volume commentaries I have found Richard D. Nelson's Old Testament Library commentary (2002) and Walter Brueggemann's Abingdon Old Testament Commentary (2001) repeatedly helpful. We are truly God-blessed to live in an age with such voices.

My greatest debt of gratitude goes to Robert Jenson and Rusty Reno, who entrusted me with one of the volumes in their pathbreaking Brazos Theological Commentary on the Bible, and to Brazos Press for publishing the series. It is a privilege even to be able to *read* the holy scriptures. To have as one's career the task of reading the Bible better and helping others do the same is the work of a teacher, and that is grace upon grace. To be able to write a commentary, let alone a theological commentary on the blueprint of the whole canon, is just *awesome*. And I mean that in both the literal sense of the word and its southern Californian spiritual sense.

Rodney Clapp stayed patient and encouraging in the face of my ambitious (read: unworkable) ideas. Thanks, Rodney, for both the justice and the grace.

In the midst of her graduate school education, Danielle Garcia volunteered to read a draft of this whole volume and offered very helpful comments, suggestions, and observations of her own. George Sumner did the same, sending me a valuable list of corrections and pointers. My Westmont colleague Tremper Longman III read a draft of this book's early chapters, caught some truly embarrassing errors, and offered some much appreciated encouragement. With patience and care, David Aiken edited the manuscript, made a number of improvements, and caught a slew of inconsistencies. Joshua Nunziato did his usual splendid job compiling indexes. Sincere thanks to all of you. The howlers that remain are all my own.

Commentary format. My format aims to compress a lot of information conveniently and efficiently. Here is an explanatory legend:

[1:1]Passages are reproduced or altered from the World English Bible. [2]References to passages (6:4) and to notes on passages (→6:1–3) are embedded in the text or the commentary.

Plain Observations on the plain sense of the passage pertain to its literal or critical meaning, in its literary or historical context. Boldface words in the commentary on all four senses are reproduced or slightly adapted from vocabulary in the passage.
Faith Observations on the allegorical sense pertain to faith, ultimately in the person and work of Jesus Christ.
Hope Observations on the anagogical sense pertain to hope of the eschaton that stirs in Israel's return from exile, that approaches in the kingdom of God, and that culminates in the Son's return to judge and renew all things.

Love Observations on the moral or tropological sense of love concern guidance for the church, which signifies that kingdom.

While this is my usual ordering of the senses, observations may be listed in a different order that serves some dependence or progression across them.

Issues of translation. I have reproduced Deuteronomy from the World English Bible, an adaptation of the American Standard Version that has been placed in the public domain (ebible.org/web). While it retains a bit more of the awkward pomp of traditional biblical English than I usually prefer, it is literal enough to be useful for close readings and economical to reproduce. I have sometimes altered the text and punctuation for readability or where I have disagreed with the translation. The World English Bible's "Yahweh," usually rendered LORD in English, is YHWH here.

Translations of other biblical books sometimes follow the RSV, sometimes the NRSV, sometimes the NJPSV, sometimes my own translation—whatever accurate version lay at hand at the time.

Gendered nouns and pronouns present a stubborn problem in contemporary English. Contemporary translations often translate pronouns inclusively and circumvent awkward sexist language. This strategy comes at the price of sometimes distorting the underlying language or obscuring important terminology, as well as alienating readers of both sexes for whom the old-fashioned English inclusive masculine is intuitive and inoffensive. I know of no translation convention that has been wholly successful. So I translate Hebrew and Greek gendered terms that could or should be translated inclusively nowadays into the English inclusive masculine, while marking them with a superscript plus symbol ($^+$). Since YHWH is beyond gender, I have done the same with pronouns referring to God, the Father, and the Holy Spirit (but not the incarnate Son). This allows the reader to judge for himself$^+$ (read: "for himself or herself") whether and how to respect their inclusivity. Words that seem to refer only to males or only to females are not so marked. The superscript notations will grate on those who prefer inclusive masculines, while the masculine language will grate on those who prefer explicitly gender-inclusive English. I hope this device is irritating enough to everyone to communicate just how difficult it is to handle this translational dilemma in a way that satisfies more than one camp at a time.

Westmont College
Rosh Hashanah 5768 / September 2007

DEUTERONOMY 1

Plain Classic Jewish tradition rests on both the written Torah of the Pentateuch and the oral Torah given to Moses at Sinai. But Deuteronomy's opening verse, and others such as 4:2, construe oral Torah as the contents of Deuteronomy itself. **These words** are Moses's authoritative spoken interpretation of what was received at Sinai and what it means for his people. Deuteronomy sets them in a narrative frame from some future (monarchical? exilic?) age or ages. So do the prophetic, rabbinic, apostolic, and academic frames that follow. These settings did not originate on Sinai, nor do they need to. Teaching has always gone beyond mere transmission to involve (and so legitimate) understanding, wisdom, imagination, and courage. Deuteronomy's narrator possesses all of these, and more: determination that refuses to stop repeating the message until Israel really does learn and fear (→31:9–13); vision that assembles Israel's origins, immediate past, immediate future, possible as well as determinate legacies, eschatological horizon, and present day in a panorama so stunning that it practically orders the whole Jewish *and* Christian Bible; and a burning love for YHWH, Israel, holiness, the vulnerable, the nations, the land, and the traditions that carry these from their old homes across and near the Jordan to all who ache for the promises to be fulfilled.

Faith Jesus has not just fulfilled Moses's original **words**, whatever they may have been; he has fulfilled *the scriptures* (→32:40–43). He did this by trusting them, in life and death, as his Father's words to him as **all Israel's** Spirit-anointed Son. He bequeaths **these** fulfilled holy writings (Luke 24:27, 44–45) on all who preach his name (24:46–47) in the power of the Father's Spirit

1:1a These are the words Moses spoke to all Israel

(24:48–49). He has not retired Moses's words from YHWH's service but has *unveiled* them for **all** to see and heed (cf. Deut. 32:35 and 28:64, echoed in Luke 21:20–31; →30:1–5).

Faith Moses's divinely authorized **speech** yields Deuteronomy's whole narrative. Likewise, the church does not need to pin every holy tradition in the time the apostles spent with Jesus before his ascension in order to honor his charge to teach all he has commanded his disciples (Acts 1:2), or to respect that **these** canonical scriptures of the Old and New Testaments are the God-breathed **words** with which they have done so.

Hope The final verse of Numbers (36:13) sets the stage for Deuteronomy. The close of the interval between exodus and entry is the setting of this teaching. Deuteronomy is both a conclusion and an introduction—an end to the old and a beginning for the new. The Apostle Paul treats it as an introduction written especially for us "on whom the ends of the ages have come" (1 Cor. 10:11 NRSV). Its New Testament analogue is the Gospels' saga—a veritable Pentateuch of the disciples' calling, failure, remediation, restoration, witness, and pneumatic preparation for Jesus's long mission (Acts 1:8a). Deuteronomy is advice for a people preparing for their big event, from the sage who led them to it. We are that people (→34:10–12).

Hope In this fullness of time our sage is among us even more truly than **Moses** in his day (→1:1b). Christ is YHWH, Moses, Joshua, and Israel all in one. He takes on every role in a play with a cast of thousands (Gal. 3:15–4:7). He has seen us through our trials, has persevered despite our doubt, has suffered for our folly, has prevailed when we have drawn back, has put us in our right minds, has restored us to our task, and has commanded all of us to enter into his Father's and his fathers' inheritance with the time his Father has given us (Acts 1:7).

Love With story, command, law, song, pleading, and silence, Deuteronomy probes the depths of the relationship between the bride and our bridegroom. Diligent readers will find its pages a mirror in which we can see who we truly are, in all our depravity and all our promise, and learn how to act accordingly (Jas. 1:23–24). Moses did not speak just to Israel's appointed leaders (cf. Deut. 1:9–18) or to one generation (→1:19; →27:9–10), but to a collective identity that exceeds both. Jesus's disciples too were charged to take his words to **all Israel** and then to all the earth (Acts 1:8b). Neither the gospel nor the Torah is for just a few—for only peoples in the ancient Near East, gnostic elites, professional clergy, religious eras or subcultures, or the spiritually disposed. It orders the whole lives of whole fellowships: families, cities, tribes, inner consciences, and ages. "Repentance and forgiveness of sins" (Luke 24:47 NRSV)—"peace and mercy" (Gal. 6:16a)—are offered not in only one place or age, but to "all who walk by [his] rule . . . the Israel of God" (6:16b RSV).

1:1bbeyond the Jordan in the wilderness, in the Arabah opposite Suph, between Paran and Tophel, and Laban, and Hazeroth, and Di-zahab.

Faith The geography moves southward through the Sinai Peninsula, as if to recall the first years following Sinai. Many of these places are likely settings for earlier words from Moses. Deuteronomy is a final summary of what Moses has been teaching all along. He does not suddenly become Israel's teacher at the conclusion of his life, like a parent determined to compensate all at once for years of inattention. John 2:22 reveals similar continuity in Jesus's teaching.

Hope Deuteronomy's readers are not with Moses **in the wilderness**. Nor are we farther east in Babylonian exile, as modern critical reconstructions intimate. Deuteronomy sets us in the promised land (→2:10–12). It takes us as Canaan's residents back to the long train of events that fulfilled God's promises and forward to the long train of our own catastrophic failures to respond faithfully—without ever surrendering our rightful place of residence.

Love Suph has traditionally been understood as the Sea of Reeds or Red Sea, though critics now differ. The exodus is now far away, worth only (perhaps) a secondary mention in this introduction! First Cor. 10:1–2 reflects this priority: Israel was transformed "in the cloud and in the sea." The wilderness was literally a death and rebirth for Israel, with Sinai its point of departure (Deut. 1:2). Deuteronomy labors to develop and harvest the fruit of that baptismal transformation among its readers.

1:2 It is eleven days from Horeb by the way of Mount Seir to Kadesh-barnea. **3a**In the fortieth year, in the eleventh month, on the first day of the month,

Hope Israel has taken **forty years** to travel the short distance from Sinai to the southern threshold of Canaan. The wilderness punishment and rehabilitation costs one generation its entry into the master's joy and delays another's. Nevertheless, after forty years Israel has made it. Sin's frustration is never total and never final. The long time we take to fulfill the will of the Father can always become a short time if we stop resisting. Wesleyan Arminians and sanctificationists can appreciate God's impatience and expectation of these **eleven days**, just as Lutherans and Calvinists can appreciate God's patience and determination in those forty years.

Love The northward journey from Sinai to Canaan through the Negev would have been faster than Israel's roundabout journey following the debacle at **Kadesh-barnea** (1:26–28). Yet entering Canaan through **Seir**-Edom and across the Jordan yields the additional blessing of land for Reuben, Gad, and half of Manasseh (3:12–17). Where sin increased, grace abounded all the more (Rom. 5:20).

Faith Jesus takes the harder and longer route. His **forty days** without food or drink are not southward at Sinai (Exod. 34:28), but eastward in the wilderness

(Luke 4:2). Rather than ascending immediately to face the glory of the Father, he follows the Spirit into the wasteland and faces the devil on our behalf.

> **1:3b**Moses spoke to the sons⁺ of Israel according to all (→4:1–2) YHWH had given him in commandment to them,

Faith In Exodus's scenes of lawgiving, God is the trustor and Moses the trustee (e.g., 19:3–25). That scene returns when the disciples, like Moses, climb the mountain to receive the Lord Jesus's teaching (Matt. 5:1–2). In Deuteronomy the roles shift: Moses is the trustor and Israel is the trustee and beneficiary. This scene returns with Jesus in the wilderness heeding Moses's words (→6:13–16 and →8:1–5 in Matt. 4:1–11) and later when he instructs his disciples to teach along with him in their cities (10:5–7; 11:1). So is Jesus a divine authority or a human one? A prophet, or more than a prophet (11:9)? Emmanuel is both. At once trustor, trustee, and beneficiary, Jesus speaks Torah *and* hears it *and* passes it along. Torah is God's commandment of Christ (→30:11–16 in Rom. 10:4–9) for instructing the apostles, and through him and them all of God's people (→25:4 in 1 Cor. 9:1–14).

Hope Moses's instruction is set in a season of intense expectation. Like a confirmation homily and like Jesus's last words to his disciples just before his passion in John 14–16, his long review orients God's people to what is coming soon.

> **1:4**after he had struck Sihon the king of the Amorites, who lived in Heshbon, and Og the king of Bashan, who lived in Ashtaroth, at Edrei (2:24–3:11). **5a**Beyond the Jordan, in the land of Moab (29:1),

Plain Despite the paragraphing of many translations, a flashback begins in 1:4 that runs through the end of Deut. 3 and sets the stage for Deut. 4.

Faith Who **struck** these kings, Moses or YHWH? The antecedent is ambiguous both grammatically and theologically. YHWH alone is credited for these victories (3:24); however, Israel under Moses (3:3) and later Joshua (3:28) can also be named as conquerors. Considering only one of these the antecedent does not respect the cooperative character of this work of Israel's sovereign lord. Nor does it respect the unity of divine and human through which Joshua's namesake will defeat sin and death.

Hope Of all the many events of the wilderness wanderings, why make **Moab** the setting and subject of the first discourse? Because these strikes conclude the age of Israel's frustration after its failure to trust YHWH to fight. Though minor compared to, say, Sinai, they are proleptic fulfillments that rekindle hope in an otherwise unpromising present. Similar smaller-scale events early in the Gospels and Acts anticipate the crucifixion, resurrection, and ascension at the center of Jesus's story. Dismissing either set of preliminaries as insignificant or fixing on them as climactic is eschatologically mistaken.

Love **Heshbon**, **Ashtaroth**, and **Edrei** are the Transjordanian homelands of two-and-one-half tribes of Israel. For them these victories are not just foreshadowing.

Likewise, for the paralytic of Mark 2:1–12, Jesus is bringing salvation, not just setting the stage for even greater things. Some in the story receive their most tangible benefits long before the story's climax. They deserve recognition as goals of grace rather than just signs of greater grace. Yet they must appreciate that grace *does* increase—to heed the rest of Deuteronomy, as it were. Otherwise they are liable to remain content with their lesser blessings and forget the kingdom's other beneficiaries and greater blessings.

> **1:5b**Moses began to explain this Torah, saying:

Plain In Deuteronomy the **Torah** is not five written texts but the content of God's commandments (4:2), decrees (4:45), laws, and rules (4:1) as interpreted through Moses and delivered in a book to the Levites (→31:9–13).

Faith **Moses** draws on his skill, experience, and wisdom to **explain** God's instructions. He is not just a relayer of God's words but their authoritative interpreter. His tactics include reworking, simplifying, and changing what look like earlier traditions (e.g., Exod. 18:13–26 and Num. 11:14 in Deut. 1:9–15; and Num. 20:1–13 in Deut. 1:37). These are his prerogatives, as long as he acts faithfully. In committing his **Torah** to writing and canonizing it as part of *the* Torah—which Jesus himself respects as God's word to him—Israel and the church acknowledge his faithfulness and distinguish biblical prophecy from the kind that dominates in Islam, where the Qur'an's human traits can be treated as marginal if not embarrassing.

Love The term **began** has the sense "determined." The passage highlights both Moses's effort as a teacher and his courage (cf. Gen. 18:27, 31). It is one of Deuteronomy's many signs of Moses's fierce love of his people. These are constitutive virtues for a rabbi. So it is no surprise to find similar efforts and attitudes in Saul of Tarsus and especially in Jesus, who "began" (*ērxato*, using the same word as Deut. 1:5 Septuagint) to explain his fulfillment of Isa. 61:1–2 at the synagogue at Nazareth before his congregation cut him off (Luke 4:16–22).

> **1:6**YHWH our God spoke to us in Horeb, saying: "You have lived long at this mountain (2:3): **7a**turn and take your journey,

Faith Israel's time at Sinai did not give Israel the courage to conquer its fears at Kadesh-barnea (1:22–28), and more time would not have helped. Retreat for spiritual preparation is necessary but not sufficient for a life of faith, and more is not always better. Excess is one of the spiritual abuses that Jesus warns his disciples (Matt. 6:7–15) and Paul warns the Corinthians about (1 Cor. 12–14).

Hope Sinai is a stop, not a destination. A mystic might consider Sinai the pinnacle of Israel's experience with God, but YHWH prefers Israel to have a good home. In fact, Israel must **turn** and go in order not to turn away again from God (→1:40; →1:46–2:1; →10:6–11). Likewise, for Jesus's witnesses Jerusalem is the point of departure for their travels to the end of the earth (Luke 24:44–49; Acts 1:6–11). The land is critical at all points of both missions.

Love God did not say: "**You have lived long** *with me*." No sacred space contains YHWH (Isa. 66:1–2 in Acts 7:44–50). The Holy Spirit accompanies Israel and later Israel's Messiah as the leader of its wilderness journey (cf. Luke 4:1).

> **1:7b**and go to the hill country of the Amorites, and to all the places near there, in the Arabah, in the hill country, and in the lowland and in the Negev, and by the seashore, the land of the Canaanites (Num. 13:29), and Lebanon, as far as the great river, the river Euphrates.

Faith The **Amorites** live in the heart of future Israel, but **the Arabah** is Edomite territory, the **Negev** is a desert waste, the coastal lands are Philistine, and **Lebanon** and the **Euphrates** become troublesome borders. God is calling Israel to a life of trust in *all* situations—better or worse, richer or poorer, sickness or health.

Hope Some of **the places** on this itinerary are on the way; others belong to the promised land; others name its farthest boundaries. At the outset of the journey God discloses a future narrative whose shape is greater than just a migration or even a homecoming. "I go to prepare a place for you" (John 14:2 NRSV).

Love Israel's interactions with neighbors are ultimately more noteworthy than its domestic life. Israel is a witness not only of YHWH's love of the patriarchs but for YHWH's power beyond Israel's borders (Mal. 1:5) and **the great river** (Rev. 9:14).

> **1:8**Behold, I have set the land before you: go in and possess the land YHWH swore to your fathers, to Abraham, to Isaac, and to Jacob, to give to them and to their seed after them (→4:36–39; →11:8–15; →34:1–4)."

Faith Only as Israel heeds God's word to turn toward **the land** is it set **before** them.

Love As a God of not the dead but the living (Matt. 22:32), he[+] not only remembers the patriarchs but continues to set their names at the center of his[+] mercy on their descendants (→2:4–5; →5:8–10). Likewise, the Father's blessings on disciples today are blessings on the Living One (Rev. 1:17–18).

> **1:9**I spoke to you at that time, saying: "I am not able to bear you myself alone (→31:1–8). **10**YHWH your God has multiplied you, and behold, you are this day as the stars of the sky (Gen. 15:5; →26:1–11; →28:58–63a) for multitude. **11**YHWH, the God of your fathers, make you a thousand times as many as you are, and bless you, as he has promised you! **12**How can I myself alone bear your encumbrance, and your burden, and your strife? **13**Take wise men of understanding and experience according to your tribes, and I will make them heads over

you." **¹⁴**You answered me and said: "The thing that you have spoken is good to do."

Faith Moses's inability cannot be logistical; he has already led Israel out of Egypt to Sinai with YHWH providing spiritual food and drink (Exod. 16–17 in 1 Cor. 10:3–4), and it is only eleven days to Canaan. The problem is deeper. Moses is worried not about the Canaanite threat (Deut. 1:29–30) but about Israel's internal dynamics. His concerns are well placed; the next story reveals that Israel's group psychology is its own worst enemy and that he is caught up in it himself (→31:1–8). So it is in Paul's churches (1 Cor. 10:5–13): they have Christ's provision (10:16–17; 11:26) and even the Spirit (12:1–13) but lack decency and order (14:40).

Love God had been fulfilling the old **promises** even while Israel was crying out in captivity (Heb. 11:12–14). The nation's numbers now loom as a threat to fulfillment's next stage. The peril of grace is a pervasive Deuteronomic and biblical theme. Wisdom yields prosperity that numbs and distracts (Luke 12:13–21; Rev. 3:17–18). Free grace tempts the justified to sin freely (Rom. 6:1). Family puts loyalty before lordship (Luke 14:26; →1:26–28). Moses's solution is not to resist the grace (e.g., postponing children and reducing family sizes, as both ascetics and the wealthy do today), but to welcome the further blessing of wisdom for handling it. Yet in Deuteronomy's narrative this move fails (1:22–28), because all the wisdom, understanding, and experience in Israel's structures of justice only constrain rather than overcome its internal disorder and **strife** (→4:9–10). Only love "bears all things, believes all things, hopes all things, endures all things" (1 Cor. 13:7 NRSV). The wilderness generation has shown precious little of it, and its lovelessness destroys it. Its saga is Torah for us "on whom the ends of the ages have come" (10:11 NRSV), because lovelessness is deadly in any generation and any age.

> **¹:¹⁵**So I took the heads of your tribes, wise men and experienced, and made them as heads over you, captains of thousands, and captains of hundreds, and captains of fifties, and captains of tens, and officers, according to your tribes. **¹⁶**I commanded your judges at that time, saying: "Hear the cases between your brothers⁺, and judge righteously between a man⁺ and his⁺ brother⁺ and the foreigner with him⁺. **¹⁷ᵃ**You shall not show partiality in judgment; you shall hear the small and the great alike; you shall not be intimidated, for the judgment is God's.

Faith Moses establishes a consensual and just political order for the brief journey to the promised land under his leadership, which is not unlike the arrangement for life in the land (→16:18–17:1). Respect for the reality of God's just reign underpins **wise** discernment, fair **judgment**, and courageous action. Instead, unchecked and self-serving subjectivity paralyzes Israel in the next passage, and corruption erodes landed Israel from within.

Hope The ban on intimidation has the form of a commandment but the hint of a prophecy. The wicked who have "no fear of God before their eyes" (Ps. 36:1 NRSV in Rom. 3:18) do not **intimidate** those who know YHWH's saving judgments (Ps. 36:6). Those who rest their hope in God's determinations, like Joshua and Caleb in the following verses, are "more than conquerors through him who loved us" (Rom. 8:37 NRSV).

Love Why does it follow from **God's judgment** that **brothers**[+] (fellow Israelites; →2:4–8) and **foreigners** should be treated impartially? The nations' deities are supporters of clan loyalty and champions of the already great, but Israel's God is associated with impartiality because of who he[+] is: the God of love before whom *all* are beloved neighbors.

> **1:17b** And the case that is too hard for you, you shall bring to me, and I will hear it." **18** I commanded you at that time all the things you should do.

Hope After Jesus's ascension Peter gets the church's political affairs in order and waits in the city for the Holy Spirit to come and lead his witnesses to the ends of the earth (Acts 1:15–26).

Love Moses maintains his leadership under the new system as supreme judge; in the land leaders will bring cases to the central authorities (→17:8–13). Paul appoints leaders in churches he is leaving but still intervenes from afar when necessary (1 Cor. 6; Gal. 1). Judgment "begins with us" in God's household (1 Pet. 4:17). A disordered or overwhelmed Israel is not fit as a missionary of God's power either in or out of the promised land. Justice and holiness within God's fellowships are both goals and grounds of future hope. So Peter's treatise on Christian mission in our time of wandering concludes with a command for just and humble church leadership (5:1–11).

Love *Sifre Deuteronomy* 2.10 on 1:3 calls Deuteronomy Moses's parting rebuke to Israel. If Deuteronomy is a rebuke, it is one delivered out of fierce dedication to the welfare of its audiences. This passage hints at Moses's full commitment to Israel's total political and spiritual readiness for its new life and his patience through **all** its failures. Training both these leaders and their people at the journey's outset is an even more important political task than hearing difficult cases; and forty years later, Moses's pastoral ambition remains undiminished (→4:1–2). The prophets, the apostles, and their common Messiah share this gift of the long-given Spirit of fellowship and use it proportionately (Rom. 12:6–8).

> **1:19** We traveled from Horeb, and went through all that great and terrible wilderness you saw, on the way to the hill country of the Amorites, as YHWH our God commanded us. And we came to Kadesh-barnea.

Faith Moses's audience has not literally **seen** or **come** (1:35), but through tradition the sight, arrival, and memory are truly theirs (→26:1–11). However, this is not the only way to read Moses's use of pronouns. The converse is also true: through living tradition, past and future generations are included along with the present one in Moses's *whole* audience. This device extends through 2:1. Living and dead alike tell and hear, as well as resist and accept, the good news of God.

Hope Another demonstrative pronoun reminds the audience of how intimidating the first days of their journey from Sinai were. If Israel made it through **that great wilderness** as God commanded, how much more could they have fulfilled God's command to cross this border and possess the land! We too stand on an eschatological borderland between having been justified and someday being saved (Rom. 5:9–10). Cooperation with Israel's faithful God makes suffering a factory of endurance, then character, then hope that does not disappoint (5:3–5).

Love The last tale in 1:9–18 prepares for the one that begins here at **Kadesh-barnea**. Success (reaching the border) and failure (drawing back) are juxtaposed to focus present and future audiences on the life-and-death consequences of how they respond to these words (→30:11–16). As mentors build up the inexperienced by reminding of minor past successes **on the way**, so prophets and psalmists pass on to their audiences a legacy of triumph as well as defeat. Tempering each with the other is a key to telling the truth in love (Eph. 4:15). Here Moses coaxing Israel into the land prefigures the apostles, evangelists, prophets, pastors, and teachers who raise up the body of Christ to full stature (4:11–13).

> **1:20**I said to you, "You have come to the hill country of the Amorites, which YHWH our God is giving us. **21**Behold, YHWH your God has set the land before you. Go up, take possession, as YHWH the God of your fathers has spoken to you. Do not fear or be dismayed."

Plain At this point Moses is still allowed to enter.

Faith The divine assurance **not** to fear pervades the Bible from Genesis (15:1) to Revelation (1:17). Often it precedes good news of a deliverance or a mercy that hearers might be too intimidated to grasp. Its uses in Deuteronomy (3:2, 22; 7:18; 31:8) give a variety of warrants for Israel not to fear, but all converge on God's trustworthiness. Moses has learned this firsthand, so he does not softly suggest—"let us not fear" or "let us go up"—but commands. Unlike the rest, Joshua obeys his command to **take possession** rather than fearing (1:38). Joshua's messianic namesake follows his example, entering the land obediently and thus victoriously on behalf of his people (Phil. 2:8–10). In turn, with the exceptions of the angels in the Gospels' infancy narratives and 1 Pet. 3:14, Jesus is the only one in the New Testament who tells us not to fear.

Hope What Moses does **fear** is God's anger (9:19 in Heb. 12:21). That is not the place to which we **have come** in Christ (12:18–20), but to Jesus and his church and to the joy of the new covenant's every fulfillment (12:22–24).

Love "There is no fear in love, but perfect love casts away fear; for fear involves punishment, and whoever fears has not been perfected in love" (1 John 4:18, my translation). Israel's downfall and ours (Heb. 12:25) is unreciprocated love.

At the threshold of the gift **God has set before** us we turn away in fear (Deut. 1:28). Its new opportunity and ours is the grace of a truly reciprocal love in the Father's beloved and loving Son. "We [can] love because he first loved us" (1 John 4:19 NRSV).

> **1:22**You came near me, all of you, and said:"Let us send men before us, that they may search the land for us, and bring us word of the way by which we must go up, and the cities to which we shall come." **23**The word pleased me well, and I took twelve men from you, one man for every tribe. **24**And they turned (→1:6–7a) and went up into the hill country, and came to the Valley of Eshcol, and spied it out. **25**They took of the fruit of the land in their hands, and brought it down to us, and brought us word and said: "It is a good land that YHWH our God is giving us."

Faith The account in 1:22–45 condenses memories or traditions from Num. 13–14 to offer a contrary narrative, rooting the desire for spying out the land in the people rather than YHWH. For instance, contrary to Num. 13:1–2, in Deuteronomy the Israelites ignore the chain of command just established and go to Moses as a group. Here we meet the kind of threat that Deut. 1:12 alludes to and that Exodus and Numbers repeatedly chronicle. The multitude of Israel threatens order when it becomes a foolish and frustrating mob. A fickle crowd will similarly deal injustice rather than wisdom to Jesus (Luke 23:18–25).

Faith Whether out of eagerness or overconfidence, Moses relaxes his own procedure. In accepting the people's recommendation (cf. Num. 13:17–21), he earns a share of the blame for the debacle that follows (Deut. 1:37). His efforts to retroject a semblance of order into the situation with **twelve men** are ineffectual. Discernment is a communal office.

Faith Moses expects the spies to find evidence of God's goodness, and they do. **Eshcol** is an especially fruitful valley. Despite the dubious nature of the mission, God still leads the spies to the best land. This makes Israel's dismay that much more egregious.

Hope Israel did not spy out the "great and terrifying wilderness" (1:19). God has led the way until now. With the land finally in view, the nation suddenly feels the need for others to go **before** them. Why? As 1:41 confirms, Israel thinks war is its own affair—for YHWH to assist rather than lead, let alone win on his+ own. Spiritual food and drink are one thing; battle against earthly cities and appropriation of territory is another! The Constantinian church drew a similar dichotomy, seizing the sword from God's hand and assuming his+ blessing for its ambitions. In reaction, today's postcolonial church exhibits 1:22's cagey timidity, spying out prospects and pursuing only the campaigns it thinks easy. Neither triumphalism nor defeatism is a sustainable alternative to hope.

Love Used three times in this brief passage and once shortly afterward, **word** holds together the good words of all the people, Moses, and the spies. Moses highlights the news that is encouraging, yet Israel uses the same report to rebel against the word of YHWH (1:26). In →26:1–11 Moses offers a more reliable way of combining produce and testimony to train Israel's narrative imagination and protect its inheritance.

> ^{1:26}Yet you would not go up, but rebelled against the mouth of YHWH (→1:7b) your God. ²⁷And you murmured in your tents, and said: "Because YHWH hated us he⁺ has brought us forth out of the land of Egypt, to deliver us into the hand of the Amorites, to destroy us. ²⁸Where are we going up? Our brothers have made our heart to melt, saying:'The people are greater and taller than we. The cities are great and fortified up to the sky. And moreover we have seen the sons of the Anakim (→2:10–12) there.'"

Faith "Let me first say farewell to those at my home" (Luke 9:61 NRSV). Moses's plan backfires when the logic of tribal self-protection overpowers Moses's authority (→1:9–14). The report in Deuteronomy makes no mention of dangers, only that the land is good (1:25). Compared to Num. 13:27–33, Moses all but splits the report into two: a good word according to him and bad news according to the crowd. So the people's rebellion against God is rebellion against Moses and vice versa.

Hope The people do not take the matter to their leaders or to Moses for judgment (cf. 1:17), but grumble and panic in private. Israel's faithless heart leads it in the opposite direction of God's good news, missing the way to hope and melting in social disorder, despair, and nostalgia for slavery. Lack of trust estranges from God (Rom. 5:1), breeds discord with God, bars his⁺ grace, perceives trial as **hate**, **murmurs** in secret, and turns suffering into bitter disappointment (cf. 5:1b–5).

Love The people make no mention of the goodness of the land or the way of YHWH. With every phrase their analysis becomes more and more dire. By ignoring God's promise and presence they see only hazards. So they infer that **Egypt** was their security and God is their enemy. The deepest theological chasm seems to separate the theology of these two parties: faith, hope, and love versus distrust, despair, and hatred. Each side fixes on the evidence that confirms its convictions. Today believers and skeptics read the signs of the times in the same opposing ways.

> ^{1:29}Then I said to you, "Do not dread or be afraid of (→4:9–10) them. ³⁰YHWH your God who goes before you, he⁺ will fight for you, just as he⁺ did for you in Egypt before your eyes, ³¹and in the wilderness, where you have seen how YHWH your God bore you, as a man does

bear his son, in all the way you went until you came to this place." ³²Yet despite this word (→1:22–25) you did not believe YHWH your God, ³³who went before you in the way to seek you out a place to pitch your tents in, in fire by night to show you by what way you should go and in the cloud (→31:14–18) by day.

Faith It is God, not a party of spies, who really **goes before** Israel (1:22). And YHWH bearing Israel as a **son** is no mere analogy but a figure of Christ (→8:1–5). Indeed, YHWH has found places for the very **tents** in which the Hebrews murmur (1:27), providing even the room in which we doubt. YHWH above, his⁺ tabernacling son, and his⁺ revealing fire image the Spirit-led Son on the Father's mission to recover the lost.

Faith To ignore the evidence of God's favor and the assurance of his⁺ prophets is to **disbelieve** God himself⁺. The risen Jesus rebukes his faithless disciples on the road to Emmaus with an appeal to Moses, the prophets, and all the scriptures (Luke 24:25–27).

Hope Moses takes the word **way** from the people's original request for spies (1:22) and repeats it three times to try to recall them to their original stated purpose: not to assess the risks and rewards of their venture but to discover the way of fulfillment. Unlike Israel, Moses sees consistency rather than discontinuity in God's dealings on either side of the border. There is no dichotomy between providence in nature and providence in human affairs. He reminds them that **Egypt** was not a refuge but an oppressor. Divine wisdom, not human ingenuity, lifted Israel out of captivity and has sought the whole way to this point. Wisdom still leads the way and will overcome all the natural and social obstacles that lie ahead.

Love Committing God to **fight for** Israel poignantly reasserts God's love after the people's accusation. Yet this word turns out to be presumptuous. These things do not take place until this generation has passed away (3:22; 31:1–8). By comparison, Jesus assures his own rebellious generation that it will not pass away before his victory (Luke 21:17–19, 31–32), and he and his apostles indeed begin restoring them to justice within days of his resurrection (24:46–47; Acts 2:40).

¹:³⁴YHWH heard the sound of your words and was angry, and swore, ³⁵"Surely not a man⁺ of these men⁺ of this evil generation shall see the good land I swore to give to your fathers, ³⁶except Caleb the son of Jephunneh (Num. 13:6, 30; 14:6–10; →33:7). He shall see it, and to him will I give the land he has trodden on, and to his children, because he has wholly followed YHWH."

Faith Caleb literally "fully went after" YHWH. The imagery is spatial. Caleb trusts that God goes before him (1:30). His blessing, later extended to the next generation (→11:22–25), is that he will inherit all that he has stepped on (cf. 2:5)—all God has led him to.

Hope **The land** is **good**, but even the tone of the Hebrews' **words** is **evil**. Their **generation** will be denied, but Caleb's generations will inherit the promise. Moses wants his present audience to see what Caleb saw, walked, proclaimed, and now awaits.

Hope Not one except one? Following a generality with a particularity is a common device in the Torah. The *klal shehu tzarich lifrat* rule of later rabbinic exegesis extends the rule of the particularity to the generality. All who wholly follow YHWH are eligible for Caleb's blessing. For instance, his **children** would inherit the **land** with the rest of the descendants of Caleb's generation anyway. Their mention here is not superfluous, but an intensified blessing on account of God's approval of Caleb. As with God's curse of Eve (Gen. 3:16, 20), God embeds hope for all in an emphatic condemnation of all (→1:37–38). Paul follows the logic in drawing out the universal consequences of Israel's rejection and acceptance (Rom. 11:12, 30–32).

> [1:37]Also with me YHWH was angry because of you (→4:21–24), saying: "You also shall not go in there (→32:48–52). [38]Joshua the son of Nun (→33:12–17), who serves you, shall go in there. Strengthen him, for he shall secure it (→31:1–8) for Israel.

Faith Why does Moses not stand above this judgment? He has encouraged Israel rather than joining in the tribes' murmuring. However, he did not discern the root of Israel's wish to look ahead into the land; he approved the plan; he chose the surveyors; and his response to their rebellion was equal parts prophetic word, denial of the deeper problem that needed addressing, and wishful thinking. He shares responsibility for Israel's failure. Deuteronomy testifies to Moses's determination not to make the same mistake twice, for "he learned obedience through what he suffered" (Heb. 5:8 NRSV).

Faith Meanwhile YHWH's confidence passes to **Joshua**. On first impression this seems to be a cruel personal humiliation: the great Moses, God's servant (3:24; 34:5), will decrease, and his mere servant will win the victory. The truth is the opposite: God will salvage Moses's work by raising up a worthy servant. The kingdom's great ones and especially its Savior **serve** not just God but all, even sinners (Matt. 20:25–28).

Hope In Numbers, Joshua is named only later (Num. 27:12–23), so these verses are out of the natural sequence of events. As God has contrasted Moses's generation with Caleb and his posterity, he[+] contrasts Moses with Joshua, who will be the leader of Israel that Moses can no longer be. Throughout Israel's story God raises up new leaders when the old ones are too compromised (→32:48–52). With so much blood on his hands, David receives the promise of a son of peace to build the temple he longs for (1 Chr. 22:8–10). God chooses Matthias in the place of the apostle Judas Iscariot, who chose a place of his own (Acts 1:24–26). The last Adam's righteousness atones for the first Adam's trespass (Rom. 5:18). Joshua is God's providence for Moses and all of Moses's charge.

Love Like a lame-duck politician, Moses's new task is to prepare his successor (so 3:21; cf. 3:28). However, this does not diminish Moses's power or significance. Moses's new supporting role for Joshua magnifies his work. Israel's later infidelities reverse Joshua's conquests (1–2 Kings), but until all is accomplished the Torah will still stand (Matt. 5:17–18). Even Jesus calls for his disciples to stay and **strengthen him** as he prepares to win them their legacy (26:38). Even the smallest assistance in his name has eternal consequence (10:40–42).

> **1:39**Moreover your little ones, who you said should be a prey (Num. 14:1–4), and your sons, who this day have no knowledge of good or evil, they shall go in there. And to them I will give it, and they shall possess it.

Plain **Sons** are those not old enough to be warriors (2:14), that is, those under the age of twenty. The Talmud makes this the age of moral accountability. Students' maturation between entering college and graduating illustrates its wisdom.

Faith Ironically, the parents' desire to protect their infants and children from the land's enemies would corrupt them into the same disbelief and heresy (1:27). The one "who loves son or daughter more than me is not worthy of me" (Matt. 10:34–39 NRSV).

Hope The kingdom is the future arriving in the present. So it belongs to such as these **little ones** (Matt. 19:14).

Love The most profound test of faith involves releasing one's own children to the costly call of discipleship. Our culture resists that sacrifice. We rationalize our hesitation as instinct, prudence, deference to individual spiritual conscience, and even love. But it is really a lack of trust. It breeds contempt for God the Father who carried and **gave** his[+] only Son (1:31; 8:5; Rom. 8:32). It divides God's fellowship and would sell our **little ones** into slavery to the present age. Jesus assures his disciples of his profound identification with believing children (Matt. 18:5), fierce protection of them (18:6), and steadfast care of them (18:10–13). In Matthew's literary context it is familial love, not the usual lust or greed, that is a particularly powerful temptation to sin against the Father's will (18:7–9, 14). Father Abraham, who would cut off even his only son, is the Father's kind of parent (Gen. 22:1–19).

> **1:40**And you, turn, and take your journey (1:7; →2:1) into the wilderness by the way to the Sea of Reeds."

Faith Without God's confidence that it can take and hold the land he[+] has given, Israel is now spiritually vulnerable to its enemies in the land and needs the protection of the terrifying **wilderness** (Gen. 3:21; 4:15).

Hope Israel is still facing the land—but in dread rather than hope. God now commands them to turn back on **the way** they came. To the suspicious this could sound as if he⁺ has granted their muttered wish to return to slavery, but he⁺ really intends a baptismal renewal and retraining in their own identity.

Love **And you** means everyone, against most translations' "but you," meaning everyone else. After all, Joshua and Caleb must endure forty years of delay for which they were not responsible. The innocent suffer guilt's consequences too. The time will be well spent as Joshua receives the strength he needs to lead a better prepared Israel into its inheritance. "So Jesus also suffered outside the gate in order to sanctify the people through his own blood. Therefore let us go forth to him outside the camp" (Heb. 13:12–13 RSV).

> **1:41**Then you answered me, "We have sinned against YHWH. We will go up and fight, according to all YHWH our God commanded us." Every man of you put on his weapons of war and presumed to go up into the hill country. **42**YHWH said to me, "Tell them, Do not go up or fight; for I am not among you (31:17); lest you be struck before your enemies."

Plain **Every man**? Were even Caleb and Joshua caught up in Israel's war fever (→1:34–36)?

Faith The word **all** God has **commanded** is poignantly ironic. Israel now has two contradictory divine directives (1:21 and 1:40). Selective memory lets them couch their presumption in the language of obedience. If eisegesis reads into the Bible what the interpreter wants to find, "ectogesis" crosses out what the interpreter wishes were not there. Moses will prohibit both in →4:1–2. Like savage wolves, sinful teachers restore what has been superseded, supersede what still stands, overlook the inconvenient, and fix on the desirable. The problem is endemic in contemporary biblical studies, theology, and pastoral preaching. Children of guilty Catholics, trembling Lutherans, dour Calvinists, and zealous Wesleyans have become breezy universalists who, under the guise of faith, presume God's refusal to condemn. True exegesis trusts, heeds, and teaches the whole counsel of God (Acts 20:26–32). And by obeying Deut. 1:40 the next generation will eventually become ready to obey 1:21 and fulfill God's whole counsel.

Faith The mob swings in an instant from defeatism to triumphalism (→1:22–25). Why the change? The Anakim are as tall as ever (1:28). Perhaps the **presumptuous** Hebrews now construe God as having commanded them to believe in themselves. Or perhaps God's rebuke has exposed insecurity and provoked them to arrogant self-defense. In Num. 14:42–44 the departing Israelites **go up** without the ark of the covenant, as if to prove they are capable of victory on their own. Here the soldiers **put on** their **weapons** without the spiritual preparation necessary before holy war (Deut. 20:1–4). They trust in their own strength and strategy and in God's unconditional solidarity with the oppressed. Either pride or shame could lead to this bizarre shift in group psychology, but not humility. "'Lord, where are you going?' . . . 'Where I am going, you cannot follow me now; but you will follow afterward.' . . . 'Lord, why can I not follow you now? I will lay down my life for you'" (John 13:36–37 NRSV).

Love Israel's remorse and God's warning are a devastating display of mutual spiritual estrangement. The people's going up is no longer a partaking in God's victory. Even their repentance and confession are not genuine—not from the Lord. The Spirit remains over the Hebrews as judge and protector, but the Spirit is **not among** them either to conquer or to convict (cf. John 16:8). The contrast with the kingdom's powerful arrival in the Spirit-anointed Son is absolute (Luke 11:20–22). The correlation of divine presence, self-knowledge, and community strength continues in the conquest (Josh. 7:1–15), in the time of the judges (Judg. 10:6–16), and from the beginning to the end of the monarchy (1 Sam. 28:4–19; 2 Kgs. 24:18–25:7). It extends all the way to the apostolic present (Matt. 28:16–20; 1 Cor. 11:27–32; Jas. 3:13–4:10; Rev. 3:1–6; cf. 3:7–13).

> **1:43**So I spoke to you, and you did not listen; but you rebelled against the mouth of YHWH, and were presumptuous, and went up into the hill country. **44**The Amorites (Num. 14:41–45; Deut. 25:17–19) who lived in that hill country came out against you and chased you as bees do and beat you down in Seir even to Hormah. **45**You returned and wept before YHWH, but YHWH did not listen to your voice or give ear to you.

Plain Israel **rebelled** earlier in word (1:26) and now rebels in deed (Matt. 21:28–32).

Faith Israel finally does "turn and travel"—in retreat (1:40). Moses delivers a relentless succession of humiliating images. Rather than being carried into its inheritance like a father's son (1:31), Israel is chased and beaten like a panicked child (→28:20–26), and the army travels the last leg of its journey alone to the border and cries. It weeps out of profound sadness, not just defeat (Judg. 20:26; 21:2). **Hormah** is south of the hill country but still north of Kadesh-barnea. Here the word plays cruelly on its root *cherem*, the giving over to YHWH of the land taken in conquest. Self-deprecating accounts like these fill the pages of both Testaments. They testify to a people whom the prophets have taught to boast only in the things of its weakness (2 Cor. 11:30) and so only in the Lord who delivers in the midst of their own disasters (Jer. 9:22–23 in 1 Cor. 1:31).

Hope How will **that hill country** become "this good land" (4:22)? The audience's physical location does not change in the course of Moses's address. What changes is our spiritual location and thus our eschatological location. Sanctification will have once again placed the land within reach.

Love **The mouth of YHWH speaks**, and the people **do not listen**; the people **weep** but YHWH stops his⁺ **ears**. Deuteronomy warns of even worse alienation in the future (→31:14–18). Ruptures such as these call for a different kind of communication: absence and silence that will restore attentiveness (such as Paul's declaration of excommunication in 1 Cor. 5). Likewise, the long sequence of miscommunication between Jesus and his disciples comes to a head when Peter rebukes Jesus for speaking of the Son of Man's suffering and rejection, and Jesus in turn rebukes him as an adversary (Mark 8:31–33). Mystified disciples can be quiet, take up our crosses, and follow behind—or expect our shunning to be reciprocated on judgment day (8:34–38).

DEUTERONOMY 2

1:46 So you stayed in Kadesh many days, according to the days you stayed there. **2:1**Then we turned and took our journey into the wilderness by the way to the Sea of Reeds, as YHWH spoke to me. And we encircled Mount Seir (→1:2–3a) many days.

Faith The people loiter at the border where they sought and received the spies' report (1:19), as if paralyzed by regret about the past and by reluctance about the future. They are neither in the land nor beyond the edge of the wilderness. Between rebellion and obedience lies the sloth of disbelief. Many spend our lives here, indecisive (cf. Josh. 24:14–15), "hopping between two opinions" (1 Kgs. 18:21 NJPSV), at the gate but not going through it (Matt. 7:13–14), hearing the word but not doing it (7:21–27), forgetting who we are (Jas. 1:22–25), "neither hot nor cold" (Rev. 3:15 New International Version), not actively obeying and thus passively disobeying. Finally the people obey and **turn** their backs on the land they refused. The Gospel of Mark ends with an apostolic **turn and journey** back through collective failure in order to discover the Savior's true identity: "He is going before you to Galilee; there you will see him" (Mark 16:7 RSV).

Hope Israel spends **many days** in mourning and tedium, against which the earlier episode stands out and the near future looms. Yet this unremarkable time is where the work of regeneration takes place. The people demonstrate in the book of Joshua that they have become far more capable (if still imperfect) over those decades (→34:8–9).

Love First-person plural verbs, absent since 1:19, return only after the people stop stalling, turn, and retrace their steps in repentance. They and Moses are one people again. There is no mention here of either the remedial education or the troubles that follow in Num. 15–25—it would interrupt the flow of the narrative here anyway—but only prophetic companionship in the decades of wandering.

²:²YHWH said to me, ³"You have encircled this mountain long enough (1:6). Turn northward.

Faith Nearly thirty-eight years elapse in a rhetorical instant, and the story starts over. Fresh starts occur throughout the economy of salvation in a string of typological events. This one overtly suggests the departure from Sinai, **this mountain**, and foreshadows return from exile in Babylon, which itself is a foretaste of Israel's messianic restoration.

Hope Some remain from the generation that failed at Kadesh-barnea (cf. 2:14–18). For them, going north is not a futile journey but an opportunity to anticipate a future for their children. They can die in faith, without having received the promises yet seeing and greeting them from a distance (Heb. 11:13), like Simeon and Anna when the baby Jesus was presented at the temple (Luke 2:22–38).

Love The way **northward** into the land is different this time because its travelers are untested. The last generation's trials strengthened it for leaving Egypt (4:34), but not for entering Canaan. The kinds of trials that intimidated that generation now face this one as it approaches the border. This is still the way for a father to carry a son (cf. 1:31): a way of paternal discipline that produces proof of sonship, holiness, righteousness, and healing (8:3 and Prov. 3:11–12 in Heb. 12:5–13); endurance, maturity, and perfection (Jas. 1:4); and genuineness of faith (1 Pet. 1:7)—the way of inheritance of a whole kingdom (Luke 22:28–30).

²:⁴Command the people, saying: 'You are about to pass through the land of your brothers⁺ the children of Esau, who dwell in Seir (1:2–3a); and they will be afraid of you. Take good heed to yourselves therefore; ⁵do not contend with them; for I will not give you any of their land, no, not so much as for the sole of the foot to tread on (11:24), because I have given Mount Seir to Esau for a possession (32:8; 2:5).

Love The Edomites will fear Israel (Exod. 15:14–16) not necessarily for its military prowess, but perhaps for the size of the tribes and their livestock (cf. Num. 22:3–4). But why then do the Moabites not share that fear (Deut. 2:9)? Perhaps Edom fears El, the Canaanite god whom the Israelites know as YHWH (→33:2). At any rate, someday in Christ common faith will dissolve, not underwrite, ethnic and economic animosity and exclusion (Gal. 3:28; cf. Ps. 137:7).

Hope The conquest is not exploitation, imperialism, or any of the activities these overused words are meant to suggest (→2:6–9). In yet another sign that Deuteronomy is not just about the welfare of Israel, **brother**⁺ nations are remembered according to the patriarchal promises they received in Genesis (also Deut. 2:9, 12, 19 and →1:8). Moreover, Edomites may someday join the assembly of Israel (→23:1–8). Indeed, through Abraham's seed this blessing extends to all families of the earth (Gen. 12:3). Even if Deuteronomy is centered on Israel and broadens only to include its neighboring peoples, its scope is no less cosmic than Genesis (→32:40–43).

2:6 You shall purchase food of them for money, that you may eat, and you shall also buy water of them for money, that you may drink. **7**For YHWH your God has blessed you in all the work of your hand. He⁺ has known your walking through this great wilderness. These forty years YHWH your God has been with you. You have lacked nothing." **8**So we passed by from our brothers⁺ the children of Esau, who live in Seir, from the way of the Arabah road from Elath and from Ezion-geber. We turned and passed by the way of the wilderness of Moab. **9**YHWH said to me, "Do not bother Moab or contend with them in battle, for I will not give you of his land for a possession, because I have given Ar to the children of Lot for a possession."

Faith Shifts from first-person to third-person are common in Hebrew biblical narrative. Is YHWH's narrative voice merging with Moses's (→33:1–5)? Or is Moses interpreting YHWH's words with a gloss (→1:5b)? Either way, this is one of the times when YHWH's assurances need human mediators. A generation living on manna and water could stand to hear that it has **lacked nothing** only from someone who has shared its condition. Similarly the assurance that the Father gives all necessities to those who do not worry about them (Matt. 6:25–34; Luke 12:22–31) would sound comically naïve if it did not come from the one who both multiplied loaves and laid down his life for us, or from his apostles who have known little as well as plenty and are godly and content with only food and clothing (Phil. 4:11–13; 1 Tim. 6:6–10). Christ even became a curse for the cursed (Gal. 3:10–14), God parting from God for everyone (Heb. 2:9); **God has been with** Israel even in punishment and alienation (Ps. 139). Even so (assuming Moses is narrating), the subject of these clauses is **you**, not "we," because Moses knows the people's perilous temptation to grumble. Jesus uses the same device in John 6:49 when reminding the Pharisees of the same events. It is not sociological exclusion or anti-Judaism, but prophetic rebuke.

Faith Normal economic times are foreign to this wilderness generation. It must learn that confessional practices include business practices. Israel is called to **purchase** with care and justice in their dealings with neighboring rival **brothers⁺**, as well as aliens (1:16). This displays gratitude that properly acknowledges God's **blessings**, while greed and covetousness embody ingratitude, which signifies disbelief (5:21). Fair dealings in prosperity are the corollary of the kingdom's standard of reciprocal forgiveness in debt (e.g., Matt. 18:23–35).

Hope Relations are cooler with **Moab**, north of Edom, which is ethnically more distant from Israel. Yet God still commands "respect to whom respect is due" (Rom. 13:7 NRSV). Moab is not a land marked for conquest. The church's obligations toward all who have not accepted or have even refused Christ's reconciliation share this passage's cordiality: honor, righteous commerce, and patient witness (1 Pet. 2:11–17).

Hope Israel **passes** by on the way to its own land and its richer produce. Moses will acknowledge the wanderers' present hardship and brighter future only later (Deut. 8), when Canaan's temptations to forgetfulness rather than these lands' temptations to covetousness are more immediate.

Hope In 2:4–23 the emphasis is on fulfillment in the past, for the future depends on it. Deuteronomy's audience is (or once was) settled in its new home (→1:1b). Why should God's promises to Abraham and Jacob be durable if God's promises to Lot and Esau are not? **Lot's possession** (Ruth 4:13–17 in Matt. 1:5) is a sign of hope that even Israel's apostasies will not revoke its gifts and call (Rom. 11:29; →19:14; →29:22–24).

> **2:10**(The Emim lived there before, a people great and many, and tall as the Anakim. **11**These also are accounted Rephaim, as the Anakim, but the Moabites call them Emim. **12**The Horites also lived in Seir before, but the children of Esau succeeded them; and they destroyed them from before them, and lived in their place, as Israel did to the land of his possession, which YHWH gave to them.)

Plain These are peoples with intimidating, even superhuman, histories. Scary descriptions run throughout 2:10–23. **Emim** is taken as "fearsome ones" in Jewish tradition; **Anakim** are the giants of 1:28; most importantly, **Rephaim** are giants who had possessed these lands in the distant past (Gen. 14:5), of whom Og of Bashan is the last (Deut. 3:11). Rephaim have the additional advantage of sharing their name with "the dead" (Isa. 26:14). All these are feared by Israelites, Edomites, and Ammonites alike (Deut. 2:20–21).

Plain The anachronistic reference to Israel's conquest of Canaan reinforces the deliberate setting of Deuteronomy in the land (→1:1b). Whatever these flourishes may reveal about the date of Deuteronomy, they are hardly the inadvertent editorial slips some take them to be, and Deuteronomy is not a "pious fraud."

Faith This route is a guided tour for strengthening Israel's faith. If God displaced these fearful people **before** to make room for Edom and Moab (→3:11), how much more will God displace mere Canaanites when Israel inherits its **land**!

Hope The parentheses in Deut. 2–3 offer primordial histories, other peoples' names for Israelite lands (according with Num. 32:38–42), and repeated references to the Rephaim of Gen. 6:1–4 from a later commentator, who places Israel's travels in a universal human and superhuman context (→2:16–23). These editorial touches imply a broader story that stretches back to Genesis's beginning and forward to some later audience's present (2:22; 3:14). As Genesis's creation story includes Moses's Sabbath, so Moses's Torah echoes Genesis's first things. Deuteronomy is not a freestanding book but an episode in YHWH's unfolding epic of all things (→1:1a). Each depends upon the other for its full significance. The intercultural place-names also respect that this broader story deserves a wider audience than just Israel. With these labels, holy writ is already beginning to be translated into the languages of the nations.

> **2:13** "Now rise up and cross over the brook Zered." We went over the brook Zered. **14** The days in which we came from Kadesh-barnea until we crossed the brook Zered were thirty-eight years, until all the generation of the men of war were consumed from the midst of the camp, as YHWH swore to them. **15** For the hand of YHWH was against them to destroy them from the midst of the camp, until they were consumed.

Faith As Israel buries the last of the exodus generation, a call from God interrupts, commanding the children of the wilderness to **rise and cross over** Moab's southern boundary. There is no resistance to the call this time. Israel **goes over** through faith in the power of God (Col. 2:12). This passage is the first evidence of a revival, a Great Awakening, that has quietly happened in the midst of a troubled generation's demise. Trust waxes and wanes; it does not simply grow or die over the course of either the life of a person or the span of a people. Jesus interrupts the Sabbath with a similar call to rise up at the pool of Bethsaida to a man alone and paralyzed for **thirty-eight years**, and he picks up his mat and walks (John 5:5).

Faith **Men of war** (of military age) is a deliberately awkward description of a generation distinguished mainly by being defeated and dishonorably discharged. Jesus teases James and John by dubbing them "Sons of Thunder" (Mark 3:17). They had been called to follow him second (1:16–20) but want to be first in his kingdom. Jesus's commission is not to the accumulation of power but baptismal service to others (10:35–45).

Hope "Where there's death there's hope!" God has the courage to put to an inglorious death that which is incompatible with Israel's new identity as a raised and free people (Col. 3:5–6).

Love God is **against them** as objects of wrath (Col. 3:6), yet also with them (Deut. 2:7) as objects of corporate renewal (Col. 3:7–11). Baptismal death and rebirth are not just metaphors. Christian initiation is a figure of the real end and new beginning of Israel at the edge of the wilderness.

> **2:16** When all the men of war were consumed and dead from among the people **17** YHWH said to me, **18** "You are this day to pass over Ar, the border of Moab (29:1). **19** And when you approach the people of Ammon, do not bother them or contend with them, for I will not give you of the land of the children of Ammon for a possession, because I have given it to the children of Lot for a possession." **20** (That also is accounted a land of Rephaim. Rephaim lived there before, but the Ammonites call them Zamzummim: **21** a people great and many, and

tall as the Anakim; but YHWH destroyed them before the Ammonites, and they succeeded them and settled in their place, [22]as he[+] did for the children of Esau, who dwell in Seir, when he[+] destroyed the Horites before them; and they succeeded them and lived in their place even to this day [→2:10–12]. [23]And the Avvim, who lived in villages as far as Gaza, the Caphtorim, who came from Caphtor, destroyed them and lived in their place.)

Plain This passage nearly repeats 2:9–12, with several significant departures. It uses Israel's label **Ammonites** for Moabites and mentions the Moabite name for **Rephaim**. Finally, 2:23 adds an account of the Philistine invasion from Crete (Gen. 10:14) in which the language of divine action is notably absent. (On the **Avvim** see Josh. 13:3.) Why repeat these parenthetical explanations? In written text they break the action just as it is getting started. But in oral storytelling they build suspense.

Hope Adding **Caphtorim**, Philistines, to the list brilliantly foreshadows a theme that comes not just later in Deuteronomy but that extends all the way into the Davidic monarchy. As the mention of Lot and Esau reaches back toward the horizon of a vast primordial saga of promises long ago delivered, the mention of the Philistines points toward that saga's contemporary horizon. This climactic year in Israel's history is also the beginning of another epic stage in the story. At the same time, setting these peoples in the same list as **Ammonites**, **Rephaim**, and **Horites** lends a tone of assurance to help Israel through the trials of every age (→3:12–17).

Love The plural imperatives in 2:18–19 now shift to singular (→2:26–30). Israel again moves as one toward its goal.

Love What of the fate of the dispossessed and disappeared **Rephaim**, **Horites**, and **Avvim**? Do they matter? All nations matter (Ps. 72; Isa. 66:18–21; Mark 13:10); but they last only through the nation of God's choosing—and that nation lasts only through faith (→32:22–25). The people are grass that withers and flowers that fade, but the word of YHWH to Zion, Jerusalem, and Judah stands forever (Isa. 40:6–11). And in that one word and among that elect people stand all peoples and tongues in their only true security (Jer. 3:17; Acts 17:22–31; Rom. 11:17–24; Rev. 7:9). Indeed, in refusing to call the Philistine settlement a divine conquest, Deuteronomy draws back from divinizing all such settlements and universalizing election.

[2:24]"Rise up (2:13), take your journey and pass over the Valley of the Arnon. Behold, I have given into your hand Sihon the Amorite (→2:26–30), king of Heshbon, and his land. Begin: possess it, and contend with him in battle. [25]This day I will begin to put the dread of you and the fear of you on the peoples who are under the whole sky, who shall hear the report of you, and shall tremble and be in anguish because of you."

Faith In 1:20–22 and 1:29–33 Moses delivers a message of reassurance to Israel, but it is not enough. Here YHWH is delivering a message of victory to Moses, and it is. God's determination is decisive. Yet this generation is also readier. There is no need to dwell on belief or doubt (cf. 1:32) among the strong who show their faith by their works (Jas. 2:18). Moses obeys, the people follow quietly and calmly without his coaxing and arguing, and God is confident. So the people's faith is decisive too. There must be both a giver and a hand to receive. The Son is the ultimate worthy receiver of the Father's gifts in the Spirit (Rev. 5:12–13).

Faith The contest with **Sihon**, like the contest with Pharaoh and the Spirit's descent at Pentecost, makes YHWH's name resound among all the **peoples** (Exod. 9:16; Acts 2:5). Even holy war is mission, as the news of victory spreads.

Hope "Behold, he is coming with the clouds ... and all tribes of the earth will wail" (Rev. 1:7 RSV). **Possession** and **contention** are two stages in redemption: entry arouses opposition that is joined and defeated. Jesus's career follows this Israelite pattern of faithful witness, birth from the dead, and rule of the kings of the earth (Rev. 1:5). So does his persecuted church (7:9–17). By grace through his suffering, the nations' **fearful** wailing turns to rejoicing and healing (19:6–7; 22:2; →4:9–10).

Hope That Israel is handed the **king** and **his land**, not just one or the other, is an important feature of holy war and conquest. Christ both binds and plunders God's enemies (Mark 3:27). The defeat of spiritual enemies without the reclamation of their possessions is an otherworldly gnostic distortion, whereas the appropriation of territory without the defeat of its powers and principalities is a this-worldly Constantinian distortion. Egypt's firstborn are struck and its households plundered. The conquest narratives anticipate a truly incarnational salvation that tells the good news of total victory and whole deliverance. And in the end the pattern culminates with Satan destroyed (Rev. 20:10) and both his[+] former heavenly domain (12:8) and present earthly domain (12:9) renewed (21:1).

> **2:26**I sent messengers out of the wilderness of Kedemoth to Sihon king of Heshbon with words of peace, saying: **27**"Let me pass through your land: I will go along by the highway, by the highway, I will turn neither to the right hand nor to the left (→28:7–14). **28**You shall sell me food for money, that I may eat; and give me water for money, that I may drink: only let me pass through on my feet, **29**as the children of Esau who dwell in Seir, and the Moabites who dwell in Ar, did to me; until I shall pass over the Jordan into the land YHWH our God gives us." **30**But Sihon king of Heshbon would not let us pass by him; for YHWH

your God hardened his spirit, and made his heart obstinate, that he⁺ might deliver him into your hand, as at this day.

Faith **Kedemoth** is an area already within Sihon's boundaries (Josh. 13:18). Israel has already obeyed God's order to cross in Deut. 2:24.

Faith YHWH hardens Sihon's **spirit** as God had **hardened** Pharaoh's heart in Egypt (Exod. 7:3). Does God destine wickedness by somehow making us unreceptive to his⁺ mercy? That prospect raises severe moral problems regarding God's goodness, the gospel's genuineness, and the scope of God's will for redemption. None of these occasions of hardened rejection (including Isa. 6:9–10 in Mark 4:10–12; 6:51–52; Acts 28:23–28; Rom. 11:25–29) shows God hardening through means other than the word itself. The message to **Sihon** is similar but not identical to those to Edom and **Moab**. Including these other kingdoms in the message raises the stakes. It might be a bluff. Or it might establish Israel's good faith. Or it might give Sihon the chance to distinguish himself over against his passive neighbors to the south—or to defeat his neighbors' conspiracy to allow an invading army to march to his doorstep—or to punish Israel's presumptuous entry by driving Israel back out of his territory and into his neighbors'. Divine words of peace like these arouse their own opposition—not by the will of the enemies who hear them but by the will of the one who speaks them in power. The living and active agent is the word of God that opens hearts to judgment (Heb. 4:12–13). Edom and Moab can tolerate an offer of peace from a kindred people on their way to take over someone else's country, but not the king of a people who shares no such genealogy and whose kin live in that country (Deut. 1:20). Like Pharaoh, unbelieving Israel, and Jesus's own Markan disciples, Sihon rejects God's peace because of who he is when confronted by who God is.

Hope Moses's diplomatic provocation is not only foreseen but deliberate, that YHWH might deliver **Sihon** to Israel. By appealing to **this day**, Moses drives the point home: **Heshbon** anticipates the imminent victory over the Amorites **in the land**. These are the same people who had Israel terrified of being delivered into their hands (1:27).

Love Moses's confrontation with **Sihon** has echoes of his exchanges with Pharaoh (Exod. 6–10), but Moses has come a long way from being afraid that the king will not listen to him (6:30). Now he so identifies with his people that he simply speaks on their behalf—to let the people pass is to **let** him **pass**—even though he knows he will not complete his journey with them. The identification of Moses and Israel begun in Deut. 2:24 continues in the next verses.

> ²:³¹YHWH said to me, "Behold, I have begun to deliver up Sihon and his land before you. Begin: possess (2:24) that you may inherit his land." ³²Then Sihon came out against us, he and all his people, to battle at

Jahaz (→3:1–2). ³³YHWH our God delivered him up before us; and we struck him, and his sons, and all his people.

Faith Moses is the one (→2:26–30) to begin the second stage of the conquest (→2:24–25). God's step of giving (**I have begun**) calls for his reciprocal step (**begin**) of taking in order to inherit (**you** is singular). Will Moses grasp what God has put in his hand (2:24) in order to inherit it? Jesus's parables similarly portray the kingdom of God as something to enter and acquire in order to inherit.

Faith In this account, deliverance is given and taken as neatly as the crossing in 2:13. **Sihon's** army is quickly removed as an obstacle to Israel's inheritance.

Hope YHWH's call for Moses to **inherit** is a poignant promise. What inheritance does Moses receive when he cannot enter the promised land? As a Levite (Exod. 2:1–10), his inheritance is not land but YHWH (→18:1–8). So God's promise is genuine.

> ²:³⁴We took all his cities at that time, and offered every inhabited city, with the women and the little ones; we left none remaining: ³⁵only the livestock we took for a prey to ourselves, with the spoil of the cities we had taken. ³⁶From Aroer, which is on the edge of the valley of the Arnon, and from the city that is in the valley, even to Gilead, there was not a city too high for us (1:28); YHWH our God delivered up all before us: ³⁷only to the land of the children of Ammon you did not come near; all the side of the river Jabbok, and the cities of the hill country, and all YHWH our God commanded.

Faith **Offering** the Amorites to YHWH goes against Israel's material advantage: the people are not made slaves, mates, or vassals, but **only the livestock** (→25:4). Nevertheless, the inherited **spoil** of the land's **cities** is the point of the victory. "Do not rejoice . . . that the [demons] submit to you, but rejoice that your names are written in heaven" (Luke 10:20 NRSV).

Faith **Offered** means *destroyed*—by *cherem*, an act of worship that devotes something to God and thus removes it from the realm of human use (Lev. 27:28). *Cherem* either permanently dedicates a good thing to God's purpose or permanently removes an obstacle to that purpose. The Son's baptismal and cruciform career is not the abolition of *cherem* but its final realization. The Amorites' future, not just their present, given up to God in the execution of their **women** and **little ones**. Jesus sets aside marriage and thus a genealogy of his own. He surrenders his life and legacy to his enemies and to the Father; and he calls his disciples to surrender not others but themselves to the same cruciform and living future (Matt. 16:24–26).

Hope This scene of *cherem* (→2:24–25; →20:10–18) is not sensationalistic, but it is horrific. From Noah's flood through Babylon being cast into the sea, God's reservation to himself⁺ through destruction inspires fear in all who take it seriously. Whether the stories in Deuteronomy and Joshua remember literal events or portray purely symbolic ones (the historical persistence of Amorites in the region and the somewhat different account in Num. 21:21–32 do not indicate that **none** actually **remained**), they still announce that God himself⁺ forecloses any future for humanity beyond his⁺ own. Along with many other unpleasant and increasingly discarded truths of Christian faith (e.g., natural evil, exclusive salvation, excommunication, divine violence, eternal condemnation, hell), we ought to find these stories abhorrent—and thus hear and heed their message, which spans the canon and all Christian history, of God's utter rejection of us apart from the economy of salvation in Israel, Christ, and church. "All have turned aside" (Ps. 14 in Rom. 3:12). The mission that culminates in Jesus reconciling all things to God cannot tolerate that which does not tolerate him (Mark 8:38). An age that no longer tolerates that fact no longer respects the reconciler or perceives the reconciliation.

Love Relinquishing good things and removing bad things in God's covenantal domain are necessary features of life in Christ. Buried with Christ in baptism, members of his body live or die not to themselves but to the Lord of the dead and the living (Rom. 6:3–4; 14:7–9). "Put[ting] to death the deeds of the body" brings victorious life in the Spirit (8:13 NRSV). Like **Heshbon's** scalable **cities**, they no longer have power over us (8:1–11), and the baptized must "show them no mercy" (→7:2–5).

DEUTERONOMY 3

3:1 Then we turned, and went up the way to Bashan: and Og the king of Bashan came out against us, he and all his people, to battle at Edrei. **2**YHWH said to me, "Do not fear him; for I have delivered him, and all his people, and his land, into your hand; and you shall do to him as you did to Sihon king of the Amorites, who lived at Heshbon."

Plain Whereas Jahaz (2:32) does not appear to have been Sihon's capital, **Edrei** is one of Og's two capital cities. This difference, combined with the compressed narrative of 3:1–7 compared to 2:26–37, intensifies the action. Israel is immediately victorious against **Og**, and at the heart of his realm.

Hope The deliverance of **king**, **people**, and **land** is threefold because the enemy is personal, social, and local. Each of these three distinct aspects is singled out in the treatment that follows (3:3–12a).

Love Delivering Bashan **into** Moses's **hand** is one of the long string of events that bring Israel out of Egypt (5:6) and into its destination (6:1). Repeating the elements of 2:26–37 in 3:1–7 confirms the pattern of God powerfully at work, displayed already in Esau's and Lot's possessions, that Moses is encouraging Israel to continue to respect across the Jordan. Repeated accounts of victories in the later chapters of the collected prophets and the earlier chapters of the four Gospels and Acts have a similar effect. Such acts of loving faithfulness warrant Israel's faithful love in return (6:5).

3:3 So YHWH our God delivered into our hand (→3:8–10) Og also, the king of Bashan, and all his people: and we struck him until none was left to him remaining. **4**We took all his cities at that time; there was not a city that we did not take from them; sixty cities, all the region of Argob, the kingdom of Og in Bashan. **5**All these were cities fortified with high walls, gates, and bars (→28:49–52); besides the unwalled towns a great many. **6**We utterly destroyed them, as we did to Sihon king of Heshbon, utterly destroying every inhabited city, with the women and the little ones. **⁷**But all the livestock, and the spoil of the cities, we took for a prey to ourselves.

Faith Such a thorough victory stands in poignant contrast to Israel's imperfect conquest within the land (Josh. 9; 15:63; Judg. 1). God's record beyond Israel's borders wins greater renown for his⁺ name (Mal. 1:3–5; →2:24–25) than in Canaan. The same is true in the Gospels: Jesus's astounding works of power in Gentile territory compare ironically with his failure (or refusal) to do similar works in his hometown.

Hope These **sixty cities** will be numbered among Solomon's holdings in Bashan (1 Kgs. 4:13; cf. 1 Chr. 2:23).

> **3:8**We took the land at that time out of the hand of the two kings of the Amorites who were beyond the Jordan (→1:1b), from the valley of the Arnon to Mount Hermon **⁹**(the Sidonians called Hermon Sirion, and the Amorites called it Senir) (→2:10–12); **¹⁰**all the cities of the plain, and all Gilead, and all Bashan, to Salecah and Edrei, cities of the kingdom of Og in Bashan.

Faith In contrast to 3:3, Moses's summary stresses Israel's active role in **taking** (literally "gleaning" or "harvesting") the land. Emphasis on the divine initiative returns in 3:18. Either style is appropriate to the nature of the task (→3:18–20).

Hope Mentioning the Gentile names of towering **Hermon** (cf. 4:48) underlines its intercultural significance. Indeed, in Israel's imagination its significance transcends even human cultures: the sons of God landed upon it and there made their oath in pursuit of the daughters of men (1 Enoch 7 on Gen. 6:1–4), and the Song of Solomon's lover woos his beloved from its slopes (Song 4:8). Now it belongs to Israel in a sign that the ages are shifting from promise toward fulfillment.

> **3:11**(For only Og king of Bashan remained of the remnant of the Rephaim; behold, his bedstead was a bedstead of iron; isn't it in Rabbah of the children of Ammon? Nine cubits was its length, and four cubits its breadth, after the cubit of a man [→2:10–12].)

Plain A man's **cubit** compares to the longer royal cubit—or perhaps an even longer Oggish one.

Faith Having a **bed** of then-rare **iron** reveals Og's power. The relic is a museum piece whose existence evokes awe at the formidable enemy whom God had delivered to Moses.

Hope The last **remnant** of the giants of old (Gen. 6:4) is given into Moses's hand. In context, this closure becomes a sign of future closure—as Israel in the land remains faithful to Torah and completes its conquest, or Israel in exile awaits its eschatological restoration and returns to the land (like the other editorial inserts, this verse is an expansion from a later time), or the Israel of God (Gal. 6:16) awaits Jesus's return in glory to judge and perfect all creation.

Love Commentators are right to be alarmed at the violence in these "texts of terror," but we should also note the element of justice in them. The **Rephaim** are legendary products of cosmic evil, whose kingdoms took root and persisted from the time of Noah until they were dispossessed by conquest. As the flood was a fresh start for a land filled with violence, so the conquests are opportunities for fresh starts for the domains of that violence.

> **3:12**This land we took in possession at that time. From Aroer, which is by the valley of the Arnon, and half the hill country of Gilead, and its cities, I gave to the Reubenites and to the Gadites: **13**and the rest of Gilead, and all Bashan, the kingdom of Og, I gave to the half-tribe of Manasseh. (All the region of Argob, even all Bashan, is called the land of Rephaim. **14**Jair son of Manasseh took all the region of Argob, to the border of the Geshurites and the Maacathites, and called them, even Bashan, after his own name, Havvoth Jair [cf. Num. 32:41], to this day [→2:10–12].) **15**I gave Gilead to Machir. **16**To the Reubenites and to the Gadites I gave from Gilead even to the valley of the Arnon, the middle of the valley, and the border of it, even to the river Jabbok, which is the border of the children of Ammon; **17**the Arabah also, and the Jordan and the border of it, from Chinnereth even to the sea of the Arabah, the Salt Sea, under the slopes of Pisgah (→33:1–5) eastward.

Plain The repetition of 3:12a is not redundant but demonstrative, in the style of the whole book (1:1a). Moses is preaching on the very land he is describing.

Faith "Freely you have received; freely **give**" (Matt. 10:8, my translation). God gave these lands into Moses's hand (Deut. 2:24; 3:2). Now Moses is responsible for assigning the lands east of the Jordan to Reuben, Gad, and half (cf. 1 Chr. 27:20–21) of Manasseh. Jesus, having received all things from the Father (Matt. 11:27; 28:17–18), shares them with his righteous ones as he will (25:14–15).

Hope Mentioning **the Geshurites** adds another ominous note to the narrative; Geshur supplies tragic twists in the story of the house of David (Josh. 13:13; 2 Sam. 3:3; 13:1–18:18; 1 Chr. 2:23). Moreover, **Jair's** name for **Bashan** sticks **to this day**, but not forever; these two-and-one-half tribes are "trimmed" from Israel in 2 Kgs. 10:32–33. Deuteronomy narrates the conquests bittersweetly (→2:16–23), just as the prophets narrate their disasters hopefully. In these and other ways biblical literature avoids the opposite evils of triumphalism and despair.

Love The list of names is tedious only for those for whom it means nothing. Like the mountains, prairies, and oceans white with foam in Connie Francis's "America the Beautiful," they call for the affirmation that only experience can create, only investment can appreciate, and only love can enliven. We who do not share that experience (or, given Deuteronomy's exilic audiences, mourn its absence) can at least be polite guests who enjoy the joy of others, putting up with our loved ones as they ramble on about the things they love. Better yet, we can accept their invitation to become interested, invest for ourselves, and come to appreciate their importance to us—just as Moses's commentator does in supplying the expansion in 3:13b–14. The fruit of such efforts is even deeper love (6:5–6).

> 3:18 I commanded you at that time, saying: "YHWH your God has given you this land to possess it: you shall pass over armed before your brothers the sons of Israel, all the men of valor. 19 But your wives, and your little ones, and your livestock—I know that you have much livestock—shall live in your cities that I have given you, 20 until YHWH gives rest to your brothers, as to you, and they also possess the land YHWH your God gives them beyond the Jordan: then you shall return every man to his possession that I have given you."

Plain Numbers 32 gives these tribes' **livestock** as the reason for remaining east of the Jordan. God's special treatment of these tribes respects their special character and needs. Needing bread, they do not receive stone (Matt. 7:9).

Faith The bequest includes both divine and human elements. The **land** is God's provision, the **cities** are Moses's distribution.

Hope **The Jordan** symbolizes the eschatological divide of old and new, with blessings on each side that belong to the greater work that spans the ages. As the seven thousand faithful in Elijah's day are a remnant for the sake of all and for the Lord of all (cf. Isa. 37:31–32), so God's special favor here on the two-and-one-half tribes only confirms God's ultimate favor on all Israel. And if the firstfruits of Israel in the present is holy, so is the rest (Rom. 11:13–16).

Hope Moses is obviously addressing armies of **men**. Indeed, his constructed audience is male for the whole of Deuteronomy. Yet much is also inclusive (e.g., 5:17). What is the contemporary reader to make of this? When are women's relationships to the Torah, to Moses, or to God too different from men's to generalize with gender-neutral language? The New Testament respects power imbalances in gendered and intergenerational family relationships (Eph. 5:21–6:9) even while rejoicing that God has adopted females as well as males as eschatological "sons" or heirs (Rom. 8:14–17; Gal. 4:4–7) and betrothed the whole church as a bride (Eph. 5:32; 2 Cor. 11:2). Both of these relationships are already prefigured in the old covenant (Hos. 11 and Hos. 1–4 respectively). In the end all these relationships describe all of us because, like the Ten Commandments and the whole complex of ordinances that follows, they involve all of us. The whole church leads, the whole church follows, and the whole church waits for our soldiers' return.

Love It is not enough for the **brothers** who have already inherited to join their kin in conquest; having already received benefits, they are to lead. As God's hired workers quit and earn their pay only together at the end of the day, so here too these tribes rest only when all rest (Josh. 22:4). The last are first and the first last (Matt. 20:1–16). The conquest is not self-service, but radical mutuality: communion.

Love That Moses stresses that these brothers are **Israel's sons** shows that communion does not come easily or naturally. The eastern tribes need reminding that they belong to a nation greater than themselves; the tribes going west need assurance that their blessing is on the way. We must continually remind one another of our status as brothers and sisters in Christ. Otherwise we will shirk our obligations (Matt. 25:40). The sacrament or ordinance of communion does just this: it reminds us that Jesus the firstfruits from the dead has still gone before us to complete the Father's mission for his brothers' and sisters' sake. He sits in glory, but he does not rest (John 5:17).

> **3:21** I commanded Joshua at that time, saying: "Your eyes have seen all that YHWH your God has done to these two kings: so shall YHWH do to all the kingdoms where you go over. **22** You shall not fear them; for YHWH your God, he⁺ it is who fights for you."

Faith **Joshua's** strength comes from his faith; his faith draws on his witness; his witness testifies to all YHWH has done; his testimony confers the blessing of being an **eye**witness upon those who have not **seen** yet have believed (John 20:29), so that through him all Israel becomes a witness (Josh. 24:1–28). Accordingly, **you shall not fear** (→1:29–33; →4:9–10; →31:1–8) is plural, a commandment for all the people.

Hope Moses repeats the assurance he gave to Israel after the debacle at Kadesh-barnea (1:29–30). Now Moses directs it at **Joshua**, in order to strengthen him as God commanded (1:38). In Joshua, Moses's old promise to all Israel will finally come to pass (31:1–8). The comparison of the last **two kings** with **all the kingdoms** to come is another *qal wahomer* ("light to heavy"—if this, how much more that) move that takes an event in the past or present as a sign of greater future fulfillment (→3:18–20).

> **3:23** I begged YHWH at that time, saying: **24** "My Lord YHWH, you have begun to show your servant your greatness, and your strong hand: for who is a god in heaven or on earth that can do according to your works, and according to your mighty acts? **25** Please let me cross over and see the good land that is beyond the Jordan, this good hill country, and Lebanon."

Plain The construction **who is a god?** is sometimes taken as a vestige of Israel's henotheistic heritage when it worshiped its one god among many. But here it primarily echoes the triumphant language of Moses's song in Exod. 15:11. Moses's excitement is growing, even uncontainable. Passionate moments like these tend to get him into trouble—murdering the Egyptian (2:11–12), striking the rock (Num. 20:10–11), and now getting carried away by conquest.

Faith Forty years (and most of the Pentateuch) is quite a **beginning**! Is Moses minimizing all that has happened so far (cf. 3:26)? Rather, he is weighing it in the proper context of its fulfillment (→3:21–22). Luke describes his gospel as "all that Jesus began to do" (Acts 1:1 RSV) as a prelude to what comes next. As Jews need to know where the Torah leads—to the subsequent life of Israel—so the church needs to know where the Gospels lead—to the subsequent life of the church.

Faith Yet Luke immediately shows the danger of this proper interpretation: the tendency for people in the middle of the story to get caught up in their own expectations. The disciples ask Jesus, "Will you at this time restore the kingdom to Israel?" (Acts 1:6 RSV). They have already seen the "**works** of power, wonders, and signs" of Jesus of Nazareth (2:22, my translation) and heard forty days of his teaching on the promise of the Father (1:3–5). But they interpret them impatiently, rather than as the Father's patient will and better plan. So does Moses, who wants not just to **cross the Jordan** but to travel the whole extent of the land to **Lebanon** at its northern border. To set the disciples straight Jesus must do what he does repeatedly in his career, and what God does next with Moses (→3:26–27): he breaks the momentum by making them wait (Acts 1:7–11). Momentum is the enemy of faith, which grows in the space between saving events.

Hope Moses is correct that YHWH has **begun** something new, but his usage is presumptuous. Moses is indeed the servant of YHWH (34:5). But the **servant** to whom YHWH has begun **to show** his⁺ greatness is Joshua. This clever prayer is an attempt to usurp Joshua's role as the witness who will get Israel its legacy and to "receive what was promised" (Heb. 11:39 NRSV) rather than waiting patiently in faith for something better (11:40). Whereas in, say, Islamic eschatology Muhammad's triumph and swift success are paradigmatic for the results of faith, in the Old and New Testaments triumph is distributed across the ages and realized only through suffering and in the fullness of time (Rom. 8:12–27). Deuteronomy finds such expectations to be greed masquerading as hope.

Hope The parallelism between **greatness** and **works**, between God's **strong hand** and **mighty acts**, is not merely decorative. Both combinations allude to two stages of salvation: first the deeds, then the victory. What is reaped must first be sown; the building stands on its foundation. Jesus's obedience yielded his exaltation (Phil. 2:5–11); the servants' investing yields their commendation (Matt. 25:19–23). The separations between salvation's two stages reveal God as their only common agent. The prophets foretell, the Messiah fulfills—and the Spirit is glorified. Paul plants, Apollos waters—and God gives the growth (1 Cor. 3:5–9). God intends Moses to sow but Joshua to reap, to show that YHWH, not Moses, is Israel's deliverer.

Love Moses's praise of **Lord YHWH** (a traditional address for a prayer of petition) is not love but a pretext for begging for **the good land** that God has denied him (→1:37–38). If God granted this request, no one but Moses would be served.

Contemporary churchgoers who gather not for adoration or service to the fellowship but for their own "worship experiences" have fallen into the same narcissistic trap. Even in calling on the Lord they place themselves at the center of things.

> **3:26**But YHWH was angry with me for your sakes (→4:21–24), and did not listen to me; and YHWH said to me, "You have much. Speak no more to me of this thing. **27**Go up to the top of Pisgah, and lift up your eyes westward, and northward, and southward, and eastward, and see with your eyes, for you shall not go over this Jordan.

Faith Most translate **you have much** as "enough!" in a way that parallels the "long enough" in 1:6. Richard Elliott Friedman notes that the language is also the same as Korah's complaint in Num. 16:3 that Moses and the other leaders "have much" (2001: 573). Moses must learn to be content (Phil. 4:11).

Hope Yet God addresses Moses's longing with the gift of hope. He[+] reminds Moses—in fact he[+] commands him—to **lift up** his **eyes** in all directions and **see** his people's future. "Many prophets and righteous people longed to see what you see, but did not see it" (Matt. 13:17 NRSV). Moses's **going up** the mountain will have to substitute for Israel's "going up" to inherit the land (Deut. 1:21). YHWH's alternative to Moses's proposal maintains the integrity of Moses's testimony as eyewitness to the God who brought Israel out of Egypt (5:6). He is the prophet of exodus, Torah, and wanderings rather than conquest and settlement (→3:23–25; →32:48–52). His testimony to YHWH will be characterized by its own incompleteness—just as the witness of the Twelve trails off in the course of Acts and Paul's testimony to God's power is framed in his own weakness and postponed deliverance (2 Cor. 12:7b–10).

Hope YHWH's stern final reminder that Moses **shall not go over** leaves him contemplating all he has received, all he has not, and the nearby boundary that separates the two. The combination is duplicated at the scene's poignant fulfillment in →34:1–4. It will be where God's and Moses's relationship culminates.

Love Some translators use "cross with me" to capture the Hebrew pun with "cross" in 3:25. In begging to cross the Jordan, Moses crosses the line and crosses YHWH. The parallels between this scene and the earlier scene at Kadesh-barnea in which Israel and YHWH do **not listen** to one another (→1:43–45) suggest just how fraught the situation is. Something is fundamentally amiss in Moses's heart (→3:28–29). He is on the verge of making the same mistake at the border that Israel made at the border a generation ago. As his confidence in YHWH's judgment falters, his own ability to lead YHWH's people teeters with it. Hanging in the balance are the Torah he is due to explicate, the succession to Joshua, and this generation's rest. Given the stakes, truly it is for the **sake** of all Israel (cf. 1:37) that God rebukes Moses and refuses to lead him into temptation. His[+] firm discipline keeps another curse from postponing his[+] blessing.

3:28 But commission Joshua, and encourage him, and strengthen him; for he shall cross over before this people, and he shall secure for them the land you shall see." **29**So we stayed in the valley by Beth Peor.

Plain **Beth Peor**, near Moses's burial place (→34:5–7), has tragic overtones (→4:3–4) that make for an ominous epitaph to the whole episode in 3:23–29. This is another subtle indictment of Moses's temptation and a fitting transition to the next stage in the discourse (→4:44–49).

Faith God's quick response reveals the political desire within Moses's formal request (→3:23–25). God uses the same language he used a generation ago (1:38): **Joshua** "before Moses" will be Joshua **before this people** as their leader and Moses's imminent successor.

Faith Moses does not immediately obey; instead he and Israel linger as they (and we) normally do after a rebuke (→1:46–2:1).

Hope In →34:8–9 and Num. 27:12–18, Joshua's commissioning indicates God's prior commissioning of him with his Spirit. Under him Israel will finally succeed in entering **the land**, and Moses's own legacy and aspirations for his people will be secure.

Love God repeats the charge he gave to Moses at Kadesh-barnea (→1:37–38). The rest of Deuteronomy is Moses's faithful response. Moses's term as a leader is ending, but his role as an **encourager** and **strengthener** has continued. His teaching (→4:1–2) sustains Joshua and all the people as they prepare to cross—as well as the prophets and exiles who await restoration, Jesus in the wilderness as he prepares to accomplish that restoration, and the apostolic church as it announces his reign to the world at the ends of the ages.

DEUTERONOMY 4

4:1 Now, Israel, hear (→6:4; →4:29–30) the statutes and the ordinances (Exod. 15:25–26) I teach you, to do them; that you may live, and go in and possess the land YHWH, the God of your fathers (→4:31), gives you. **²**You shall not add to the word I command you or reduce it, that you may keep the commandments of YHWH your God I command you.

Faith Israel **may live**, in contrast to those who perished. Deuteronomy is an invitation to the children of a disordered generation—thus to every new generation, including the Messiah's—to hear, learn, do, live, and receive.

Faith The structure of 4:2 is extremely perceptive. The law lasts so Israel will **keep** it. Revision is rebellion (Rev. 22:18–19). So dissatisfaction with Torah indicates that its hearers are unfaithful, not that it is no longer "holy, just, and good" (Rom. 7:12). Baal Peor illustrates this (→4:3–4), Israel's subsequent canonical history confirms it, and Augustinian theology in particular sharpens it. Much so-called reform from then to now is neither true progress nor true fidelity but revision borne of disrespect.

Hope Doing Torah to **live** and **possess the land** is a major theme in Deuteronomy. Deuteronomy 4 is its heart and central thesis; Deut. 1–3 leads up to it and Deut. 5 onward develops it. Disobedience at Beth Peor brought death (Num. 25:1–9); obedience from Beth Peor will maintain life. Israel is not to enter now and obey later; obedience precedes inheritance, because obedience is more basic to life itself. This theme extends through the prophets and writings and beyond. "Do this, and you will live," confirms Jesus (Luke 10:25–28 NRSV).

Hope Yet obedience does not earn inheritance. God is still the benefactor. The sequence here is neither "cheap grace" nor "works righteousness," but faithful reception in hopeful expectation.

Love *Choq* (**statute**) has the connotation of a proscription or regulation, and *mishpat* (**ordinance**) a judgment or law. However, the categories are broad and overlap. When they come together they have the same idiomatic feel as "rules and regulations." Moses's paradigmatic role in Deuteronomy is that of their **teacher** (→3:28–29).

Love If revision is rebellion, obedience respects God's love of the patriarchs and so loves the **fathers** as well, maintaining the right relationships necessary to the life of a people.

> **4:3**Your eyes have seen what YHWH did because of Baal Peor; for all who followed Baal Peor, YHWH your God has destroyed them from your midst. **⁴**But you who clung to YHWH your God are all alive this day.

Faith As the golden calf ironically illustrates Israel's tendency to acculturate idols even as the Spirit of YHWH writes the commandments above on Sinai, so the episode from Num. 25:1–5 illustrates the same tendency right after the Spirit upon Balaam prophesies against Moab above on **Peor** (Num. 22–24; →4:9–10). As YHWH **destroyed** below Sinai, so also below Beth Peor (Exod. 32:25–28; Num. 25:9). The failures of trust that Moses recalls in Deut. 1–3 are not Israel's most profound or most destructive weaknesses.

Love The man of the second creation account **clings** to his wife as one flesh (Gen. 2:24). The covenant is Israel's union with God. This fellowship can endure no fornication (1 Cor. 6:12–20 on Gen. 2:24) or partnership with idols (1 Cor. 10:6–22 on Num. 25:1–9). We who are one with Christ cling to him (→11:22–25) through fellowship in his covenantal body and blood and so live (1 Cor. 10:16–17; 11:24–30).

Love From Deut. 4 onward, the text has shifted from lesser to greater matters— from conquest and inheritance to covenant, obedience, and instruction. Yet Israel treats residency in the land as more fundamental than fidelity to YHWH. In effect, it seeks to hold onto its world at the price of its **life** (Matt. 16:24–26). In the prophets and in exile, Israel finally awakens to the commandments' true significance and puts love of God before love of self and so saves its own life (John 12:25).

> **4:5**Behold, I have taught you statutes and ordinances, even as YHWH my God commanded me, that you should do so in the midst of the land you go in to possess. **⁶**Keep therefore and do them; for this is your wisdom and your understanding in the eyes of the peoples, who shall hear all these statutes, and say: "Surely this great nation is a wise and understanding people." **⁷**For what great nation is there, that has a god so near to them, as YHWH our God is whenever we call on him⁺ (→33:26–29)? **⁸**What great nation is there, that has statutes

and ordinances so righteous as this whole Torah that I set before
you this day?

Faith As Moses **taught** what **YHWH commanded**, so "the words that you gave
to me I have given to them, and they have received them and know in truth that
I came from you" (John 17:8 NRSV).

Faith Perspective shifts from the eyes of Israel (4:3) to the **eyes of the peoples**
and back (4:9). Israel's obedience is life-giving as well as life-keeping: "As you have
sent me into the world, so I have sent them into the world" (John 17:18 NRSV).
Mission is an essential theme to include in the midst of God's judgment on the
nations through Israel's conquest. Without a clear distinction between conquest
and obedience, mission would be collapsed into imperial assimilation, and exile
would be an excuse for apostasy. The heavenly wisdom of Torah, not Israel itself
or its earthly holdings, converts the nations. This is unforgettably demonstrated
and the verse fulfilled in the most surprising way when Israel is stripped of its
earthly holdings and sent abroad with only the Torah to discover its true identity
and mission (→31:9–13; →4:26–30). The necessary juxtaposition of obedience,
conquest, and mission points to the Righteous One whom the unrighteous reject
and so doom themselves (Matt. 11:11–24), whom the Father hands all things
(11:25–27), and whom the weary approach for rest (11:28–30).

Love Idols are intrinsically **near** to their makers and worshipers: as Émile Dur-
kheim shows, they are in effect a projection of social identity. How could YHWH,
who infinitely transcends the creation, be nearer? Because idols estrange their
servants from their own image of God, leading them further and further from
who they truly are into the void of falsehood. With idols so apparently near
and YHWH so apparently far, mission will succeed only as the **people** embody
YHWH's **wisdom**. Only thus can the nations see YHWH with Israel—a proxim-
ity of a whole different order—and believe. "Sanctify them in the truth . . . that
they may all be one . . . so that the world may know that you have sent me and
loved them" (John 17:17–23 NRSV).

Love The Torah's wisdom and understanding of God become perceptible and
accessible only when **done**. Israel's wisdom and holiness manifests itself before
the nations as justice. Injustice in the land thus betrays every reason for Israel to
be there in the first place (Amos 5). Jesus's appeal is not just his signs or his words
but his **righteous** deeds (Matt. 11:19b).

> ⁴:⁹Only watch yourself, watch yourself well, lest you forget the things
> your eyes saw, and lest they depart from your heart all the days of
> your life, and make them known to your children and your children's
> children; ¹⁰the day you stood before YHWH your God in Horeb, when
> YHWH said to me, "Assemble for me the people, and I will make them

> hear my words, that they may learn to fear me all the days they live on the earth, and that they may teach their children."

Faith Confession is evangelism. "Go therefore and **make** disciples, . . . **teaching** them to observe all that I have commanded you" (Matt. 28:19–20 RSV). "I passed along to you as of first importance what I had received" (1 Cor. 15:3, my translation). "Continue in what you have learned and firmly believed, knowing from whom you learned it" (2 Tim. 3:14 NRSV). **Hearing**, guarding, remembering, **teaching**, **learning**, and **fearing** are distinguishable but inseparable acts. Passing down Israel's witness is the form of its vigilance, the shape of its remembrance, and the embodiment of its respect. A generation that does not teach the next ones—and ours seems to have taken the task less seriously than many previous generations—abandons, forgets, and disrespects both its redeemer and its own self.

Faith Whatever we **fear** is our master. The previous generation feared the Amorites and so disbelieved YHWH and perished (1:29). The present generation is forbidden to fear them (3:22) and commanded to fear YHWH. Faith fears YHWH alone. But fear of those who fear YHWH is a step on the road to faith (2:25).

Faith The account of Baal Peor in Num. 25 concerns the two acts that most profoundly threaten Israel's future: idolatry and intermarriage. Each encourages the other. Neither is compatible with an Israel that **teaches** Moses's Torah to its **children** and grandchildren. This chapter at the heart of Deuteronomy focuses on both (→4:3–4; →4:25–26). Leviticus 18–20, Romans 1, 1 Corinthians 6–11, and many other texts in both Testaments concern these two intertwined facets of apostasy.

Faith Both forgetfulness and fearfulness are totalizing. They eventually claim our whole character and our whole story. A tiny sin is a grave danger because it grows to empty one's whole heart (Gen. 3–6); a tiny share of faith is sufficient because it grows to fill it (Matt. 17:20).

Hope Like Deuteronomy's narrator (→34:10–12), Moses assumes a future whose signs and wonders do not compare with the sights of the past forty years. Israel's journey from Egypt to **Horeb** into Canaan is the canon of its teaching for all future generations. Nevertheless, memories of its return from exile under David's Righteous Branch will someday eclipse the memories from Moses's day (Jer. 16:14–15; 23:5–8).

Hope Conversely, hearts full of the past depend upon the real presence of the future. A community without catechumens dissolves spiritually long before it disappears physically. The two greatest forces of Christian renewal in the former Soviet bloc have been parents and grandparents who quietly catechized their children and grandchildren and evangelicals who reached out to those who had not heard. Their orientation to the future preserved their integrity under decades of pressure.

Love Moses sought the strength he needed by ordering and then informing Israel's polity (→1:15–17a). Now he strengthens Joshua by strengthening Israel under his **watch**. This proves to be a more durable approach.

4:11 You came near and stood under the mountain; and the mountain burned with fire to the heart of the sky, with darkness, cloud, and thick darkness. **12**YHWH spoke to you out of the midst of the fire: you heard the voice of words, but you saw no form; you heard only a voice. **13**He⁺ declared to you his⁺ covenant, which he⁺ commanded you to perform, the Ten Commandments; and he⁺ wrote them on two tables (→5:22) of stone. **14**YHWH commanded me at that time to teach you statutes and ordinances, that you might do them in the land you cross over to possess. **15**Watch yourselves well (4:9); for you saw no kind of form on the day YHWH spoke to you in Horeb out of the midst of the fire,

Faith While the terms in this passage describe Sinai, some also echo the first days of Gen. 1's creation narrative. They link this passage to →4:16–20.

Faith Neither the **darkness** nor the **fire** was a form of God. God is neither sheer power (as some theologies of glory suppose) nor the absence of sheer power (as some romanticizations of weakness and kenotic Christologies suppose). Neither positive (kataphatic) nor negative (apophatic) theology, nor even some analogical synthesis of both, is adequate as divine form. God identifies only with the **speech** at Horeb. After admonishing Israel not to forget what its own eyes have seen, Moses describes a vivid scene (cf. Exod. 19:16–21) in which the most significant detail is what Israel's eyes did not see. The scene is similar to Elijah's experience in the cave (1 Kgs. 19:11–13). The lesson is one that the Fourth Gospel takes to heart: the **form** of God is none other than the Word. Any substitute is a radical departure from the Word who has become flesh and dwelt among us. So the worship of God in spirit and truth cannot mean prostration before either power or powerlessness, but only reception and obedience to God's voice.

Hope **Stone**, signifying permanence, is often used in ancient Near Eastern agreements. In coming days the **covenant** will be written not in stone but in flesh and blood made imperishable (Heb. 9; →5:22). "Christ has died, Christ has risen, Christ is coming again."

Love This account respects the traditional distinction between the Decalogue as written by God and the rest of the Torah as interpreted by Moses (→9:9–11). The former is the **covenant** proper, the latter its implications. Israel **came near** enough to see YHWH come before their eyes and to hear that God is addressing them and not just Moses (Exod. 19:9–11). All this confirms Moses's authority as a teacher (19:9): to be qualified to **teach** any subject is to have been formed in the presence of what is taught in order to bear it to others.

4:16lest you corrupt yourselves, and make yourself an engraved image in the form of any figure, the likeness of male or female, **17**the likeness of any animal that is on the earth, the likeness of any winged bird that flies in the sky, [18]the likeness of anything that creeps on the ground, the likeness of any fish that is in the water under the earth (5:8); [19]and lest you lift up your eyes to the sky, and when you see the sun and the moon and the stars, even all the array of the sky, you are drawn away and worship them, and serve them, which YHWH your God has allotted to all the peoples under the whole sky. [20]But YHWH has taken you, and brought you forth out of the iron furnace, out of Egypt, to be to him[+] a people of inheritance, as at this day.

Faith The elements in 4:16–19 draw heavily on the vocabulary and imagery of Gen. 1's final days of creation (→4:11–15). The previous passage and the current one thus draw together creation and Sinai to develop a theology of worship that associates the voice at Sinai with none of God's many creatures and Israel with none of the other nations. Israel is to be holy as God is holy (Lev. 11:44–45), teaching the words of the holy voice and remembering the acts of the speaker. Deuteronomy resolutely refuses a natural theology that would associate God with nature or associate his[+] covenant people with the peoples (→4:32–35). Theology's distinction from both natural and social science is in these aspects absolute.

Faith Yet these are not the terms used in Gen. 1:26 of making humanity in God's **image** and **likeness**. God does not make idols; misplaced human worship and servitude do. God has forged Israel out of the oppressive **furnace** of **Egypt** to serve him[+] as his[+] heirs, and absurdly Israel is tempted to forge oppressive **images** and serve its own **inheritance**. Idolaters refuse to be made by another; they try to be the makers. The ultimate demonstration of this will also be the most surprising: when the Spirit conceives the very Word of God in human flesh, the Son and heir is rejected by his own people (John 1:10–14) and yet is brought forth from the tomb to confirm his righteousness (Acts 17:31). The image of the invisible God exposes, overthrows, and redeems idolaters by offering himself as the incorruptible object of their own corruption (Col. 1:15–20; Ps. 16 and Ps. 132 in Acts 2:23–36).

Faith God does not countenance Gentile idolatry here, let alone ordain it, as some commentators suppose (though →32:7–9). Rather, these creatures are for the benefit of all **the peoples**, for humanity as a whole (Gen. 1:26–28; 2:20; 6:1–7). In **serving** them Israel would forsake the God who has taken it from among all peoples to be his[+] covenant **people**. This is precisely what happens to Israel in the land (Deut. 31:16; 1 Sam. 8:4–8).

Hope Teleology untangles this confusing combination of affirmation and negation of creation. These idols' prototypes are not evil but good. However, idolatry misconstrues the relationship between them and the Father who made them through the inheriting Son in the **inherited** Spirit. Tragic irony inevitably follows: the man and the woman in the garden already had divine likeness (Gen. 1:26), but desired to be like God (3:5, 22; →32:15–18). Suppressors of the truth exchange the revelation of the invisible God's glory for the senseless worship of the things that are made and so exchange gratitude for debasement (Rom. 1:18–28). The idols that tempt Israel are material they already enjoy as YHWH's heirs, and this Torah is their trustee while in the Son they come of age (Gal. 3:15–4:7). In worshiping the creation they will renounce their claim and become its slaves—as do the Gentiles who serve the elements as if they were gods, despite God's will to adopt them into Abraham's blessing with the Son's Spirit (4:3–11). Idolatry is hope inverted—eschatology in reverse that can lead only back to *nihil*, to the nothingness God abolished in speaking creation into being.

> **4:21**Furthermore YHWH was angry with me for your sakes, and swore that I should not go over the Jordan, and that I should not go into that good land that YHWH your God gives you for an inheritance. **22**For I must die in this land; I must not go over the Jordan; but you shall go over and possess that good land. **23**Watch yourselves, lest you forget the covenant of YHWH your God that he⁺ made with you and make yourselves an engraved image in the form of anything YHWH your God has forbidden you. **24**For YHWH your God is a devouring fire, a jealous God.

Faith This chapter treats idolatry as practically the fundamental sin. Our age treats idolatry as a far less serious offense than crimes against fellow human beings. After all, "an idol is nothing in the world" (1 Cor. 8:4 King James Version). A **covenant** with these priorities seems stilted and even inhumane. Why in the heart of Deuteronomy does it loom so large? Because the covenant is grounded in God's deliverance of Israel, and images evoke powers that have always opposed that deliverance (→31:14–18). The offense of idolatry is not primarily metaphysical but salvation-historical. Idols receive the misplaced trust of a people who hope other than in salvation that has arrived in Israel, Jesus, and the church. For Israel to serve them is to **forget** the exodus and Sinai covenant, the definitive signs of YHWH's mercy and compassion for his⁺ people, and even to take Egypt's side against them. That is why idolatry is inhumane, why aniconic traditions not grounded in respect for God's irrevocable covenant with Israel (e.g., atheism, nihilism, and Islam) are not inherently good, or even necessarily improvements upon idolatry, and why idolatry in the patriarchal narratives (Gen. 31:19–35) and among Gentiles who have not yet heard the good news of Jesus Christ (1 Pet. 4:3–6) comes in for somewhat milder criticism.

Hope If God's **anger** is the stick, the **goodness** of the promised **land** to which Moses is pointing from beyond the Jordan is the carrot. This introduces the covenant's device of blessings and curses in Deut. 27–28. As the Sinai covenant anticipated the idolatry soon to infect Israel below the mountain (Exod. 20; 32), so Moses anticipates Israel's next failures. These warnings are providential, addressing weaknesses before we are aware of them (so Gen. 2:16–17).

Hope **Devouring fire** and **jealous God** evoke the imagery of the Sinai **covenant** (Exod. 19:18; 20:5) and are to be interpreted according to that context. In forsaking its covenantal obligations, idolatrous Israel enters in God's mercy (→4:31) into the threat of judgment (→28:27–34; →29:16–21; →32:22–25) and the consciousness of YHWH's jealousy. This refreshes Israel's memory of exodus and Sinai, as oppression reminds them of Egypt's blast furnace (Isa. 48:10; →4:16–20). In refreshing Israel's memory of Sinai, God's devouring fire and jealousy are signs not only of imminent destruction but of subsequent deliverance (Ezek. 16:38–43 [cf. 23:25 and 36:6]; Zeph. 1:18 [cf. 3:8]; Zech. 1:14 [cf. 8:2]). They remind faithless Israel of its original hope as God's only son and restore it to the path of its father's salvation. The same logic drives the practice of discipline in the church (1 Cor. 5). Christ the Passover lamb has been sacrificed; discipline awakens fear of judgment to restore hope in something better than the present and holiness that brings betterment already.

Love Moses again associates Israel with God's **anger** at him (1:37–38; →3:26–27). Only now do we discover the *full* reason. He is not scapegoating or blame-shifting, as he never denies the occasion for God's anger that audiences know from Num. 20:10–11. Rather, he understands God to have made him an object lesson for their benefit. As a convict shares his story with young people to scare them away from a life of crime, so Moses tells Israel, "I blew my opportunity to enter this land, and God made me an example for you. Now don't blow yours." God's love for Israel is so profound that he has not withheld even Moses as the object of his discipline—and Moses's love for his people is so fierce that he grasps this and uses it to protect them. Far from being an unwilling victim of a wrathful God here, Moses has already laid down his life on idolatrous Israel's behalf (Exod. 32:31–32), and it turns out that YHWH has accepted the offer in a kinder and more fruitful way.

> ⁴:²⁵When you shall father⁺ children, and children's children, and you shall have been long in the land, and shall corrupt yourselves, and make an engraved image in the form of anything, and shall do what is evil in the sight of YHWH your God, to provoke him⁺ to anger, ²⁶I call heaven and earth to witness against you this day, that you shall soon utterly perish from off the land you go over the Jordan to possess; you shall not prolong your days on it, but shall utterly be destroyed.

Faith The trope of environmental witnesses, common in ancient Near Eastern covenants, follows brilliantly on the natural theology of →4:16–20 and announces the climactic confession of 4:39. Egypt's magicians demonstrate what makes idolatry so wrong: it tries to manipulate created powers to seize their redeemer's power. The **heaven and earth** that God made and populated testify to the absurdity and evil of Israel's serving images of any of their array and to the proper consequence that Israel should be removed from its rightful place in the cosmos when it misplaces the things of that cosmos (cf. Jer. 10:1–16; →30:17–20). Heaven and earth are apocalyptic prophets (Matt. 24:7, 29) who **witness against** Jesus's persecutors on the day of crucifixion with darkened skies and an earthquake (27:45, 51).

Hope The (chiastic) elements in this passage stack ironies on top of ironies to confirm the futility of idolatry. The practice is intrinsically self-contradictory. We will compromise in order to defer to or protect our **children** or **children's children** but **shall utterly be destroyed**. We **shall have been long in the land** yet **shall not prolong** our **days**. We will **make an engraved image of anything** in God's creation but raise **heaven and earth to witness against** us. When this generation's memories have faded and its descendants have been raised in ignorance, the future generations who find idolatry irresistible will learn anew that it is an eschatological dead end.

Hope Given the survivors mentioned in the next passage, some interpreters take God's promise of destruction as hyperbolic. A better reading is eschatological. That present generation will be **utterly destroyed**, as the whole faithless generation was overthrown in the wilderness (1:35). However, a future remnant will remain to begin anew in a more distant future (1:36). The sequence resembles baptismal death and resurrection (→2:13–15).

Love The idiom **evil in God's sight**, common in Deuteronomy (9:18; 17:2; 31:29) and the rest of the Deuteronomistic corpus and picked up in Jeremiah (7:30; 18:10; 32:30; 44:22), has a poignantly ironic literal sense. YHWH witnesses Israel's heartbreaking adulteries as if behind a two-way mirror that Israel itself has put between them. The practices of prophetic conviction and penitential confession are essential to the well-being of God's community because they cast light on God's side of the mirror, reveal his[+] all-seeing presence, restore the mutuality of the relationship, and dispel both God's anger and the fellowship's folly. "You tolerate that woman Jezebel," Jesus tells the Christians of Thyatira. "I gave her time to repent, but she refuses to repent of her fornication. Beware, I am throwing her on a bed, and those who commit adultery with her I am throwing into great distress, unless they repent of her doings; and I will strike her children dead. And all the churches will know that I am the one who searches minds and hearts" (Rev. 2:20–23 NRSV).

Love This apostasy is not just a failure of parents to catechize their children (cf. 6:7). It is a life of "*apo*-chesis" in which parents train their children away from purity. Apochesis is endemic in our day when tradition is mistrusted, cultural revolution exalted, experimentation treated as expression, and youth glorified for its own sake. Here it is a result of the parents' **corruption**.

> 4:27YHWH will scatter you among the peoples, and you shall be left few in number among the nations, where YHWH shall lead you away. 28There you shall serve gods: the work of men's[+] hands, wood and stone, which neither see nor hear nor eat nor smell.

Hope This passage is the antithesis of →4:5–8. Idolatry will seem to undo all of God's redeeming work. Yet the next passage shows something else: the beginning of a great reversal in which **YHWH shall lead** Israel back not just to the scattered and confused world of peoples in Gen. 11, but back beyond it to the restoration of all creation in Gen. 1–2. Israel in exile will regress to a captive and ignorant people (Exod. 1–2) whose wise ones (e.g., Daniel and Nehemiah) will impress their rulers as Joseph impressed Pharaoh (Gen. 39–41) and gain their permission to return to the land that Joseph and the clan of Jacob had left (Gen. 28–38)—**few in number** (34:30) and stripped of the glory of the house of David. Dwelling in the midst of foreign nations, it will bring forth a new and final patriarch who is the heir of Abraham and his promises (Gen. 12–24). With his Spirit Jesus will gather the peoples that heaven's judgment had scattered (Gen. 10–11). In baptism he will take on the consequences of the flood's judgment on a world filled with violence (Gen. 6–9). In graciously enduring persecutions he will end fratricide and tribal rivalry (Gen. 4). In becoming a curse for us he will break the curse of Adam, Eve, and the serpent (Gen. 3). Returning to the ground from where we were taken he will arise imperishable, and us in him, as the forever restored images of God dwelling in the edenic new Jerusalem (Gen. 1–2). Moving forward in reverse is not a New Testament imposition on the Tanakh (Law, Prophets, and Writings) but is already its own grand shape.

Love Moses highlights idols' impersonality. The prophets condemn world-denying spirituality that supposedly attends to God at the expense of our neighbors (Matt. 23:23–24). They also condemn God-denying relationships that supposedly attend to neighbors but without glorifying God (23:13–15). Serving things as **gods** breaks both fundamental commandments at once (23:16–22), directing love to insensate things. Idolatry is antisociality that ultimately depersonalizes the idolater (Ps. 115:4–8). Wealth and power are no more sensate than engraved images, and coveting them is no less destructive of real community. "You cannot serve [both] God and mammon" (Matt. 6:24 RSV). Joshua's generation will indeed find idols an occasional snare (Josh. 7), but the land itself, its cities, and its fruit will become the more profound lure (Deut. 6:11). By linking the two threats, Moses brings the resources we have for fighting each temptation to the service of fighting the other. The most fundamental resource, of course, is the person-making fellowship that keeps the commandments of loving God with all we are and loving neighbors as ourselves. The healthy life of the body of Christ keeps all good things in their proper places.

> [4:29]But from there you shall seek YHWH your God, and you shall find him[+], when you search after him[+] with all your heart and with all your self. [30]When you are in oppression, and all these things are come on you, in the last days you shall return to YHWH your God, and hear his[+] voice:

Faith God's discipline will have allowed Israel to begin **searching** with its whole **heart** and **self**. Sinners seek in response to God's prior (or "prevenient") grace of judgment. Growing crowds can hear Jesus's same charge to "**seek**, and you will **find**" because his authority to teach has aroused their trust and sense of need (Matt. 7:7 RSV; 7:28–8:1). They knock only after he has shown them the door.

Hope Israel's assimilation to the theological cultures of the nations will lead to the dispersion that will finally reverse the assimilation of →4:27–28. Then the invitation to fulfill this oracle will be extended to all peoples (Isa. 55:6), and the covenant they will enter will be an everlasting one (55:3). **All these things** and **in the last days** are eschatological catchphrases indicating a further restoration than Israel's incomplete return from exile in Ezra and Nehemiah (→30:1–5). Only at the end of this sequence will Israel **return** to the obedience Moses calls for in 4:1 (cf. Rom. 11:25–32).

Love Sometimes **heart** and **self** are extended to heart, soul (self), and might (→6:5) to express total commitment. Such commitment finds several champions in the next few centuries, such as Joshua (Josh. 22:5), David (1 Kgs. 2:4; Ps. 16:9 by attribution), and Solomon (1 Kgs. 8:48), but few exemplars, most notably Josiah (2 Kgs. 23:25; 2 Chr. 34:31). Luke allusively describes the apostolic church as finally receiving the gift Moses promises here: "The whole group of those who believed were of one **heart** and **soul**" and lived out that love with an unembarrassed witness to the Lord's resurrection and profound self-sacrifice for one another's welfare (Acts 4:32 NRSV).

> **4:31**for YHWH your God is a merciful God; he[+] will not fail you, or destroy you, or forget the covenant of your fathers that he[+] swore to them.

Plain The exhortation in 4:31–40 finishes what the echo of 4:1 in 4:30's "hear his[+] voice" started: a concluding push for Israel to take Moses's Torah seriously (→4:40).

Faith How could YHWH **fail**? Israel has failed God! Yet in the covenantal economy YHWH is still responsible for fulfilling promises made to the fathers, which fall to the Son. "If we have died with him, we shall also live with him; if we endure, we shall also reign with him; if we deny him, he also will deny us; if we are faithless, he remains faithful—for he cannot deny himself" (2 Tim. 2:11–13 RSV).

Love The same assurances and calls to covenantal faithfulness are extended to the "aliens and sojourners" serving Jesus Christ "among the Gentiles." "Once you were not a people, but now you are God's people; once you had not received mercy, but now you have received mercy" (1 Pet. 2:10 NRSV; →4:21–24).

> **4:32**For ask now of the days that are past, which were before you, since the day that God created man[+] on the earth, and from the one end of the sky to the other, whether there has been any such thing as this great thing is, or has been heard like it? **33**Did ever a people hear the voice of God speaking out of the midst of the fire, as you have heard, and live? **34**Or has God tried to go and take him[+] a nation from the midst of another nation, by trials, by signs, and by wonders, and by war, and by a mighty hand, and by an outstretched arm, and by great

terrors, according to all YHWH your God did for you in Egypt before your eyes? [35]It was shown to you so that you might know that YHWH, he[+] is God (1 Kgs. 18:39). There is no one else besides him[+].

Faith Having focused his audience on the future in 4:25–31, Moses now shifts back to the **past**. Both ages testify to the God of all. Creation's panoramic imagery frames a point related to that of 4:15–20: no people's rival salvation-history can compare to Israel's. This is true even of the peoples whom YHWH allotted land (2:4, 9–12). The grace they have received does not affirm their theologies. Deuteronomy's opening chapters are resources for a robust account of human social plurality that honors what belongs exclusively to Israel (teleological knowledge of God and God's purposes), to many through Israel (benefits and opportunities from God's covenant faithfulness to the patriarchs and the Messiah), and to all peoples (the blessings of God the **creator** of all, corollary insights, and lasting significance in God's ultimate purposes).

Faith What Israel **might know** is "that Jesus is the Christ, the Son of God, and that believing you might have life in his name" (John 20:28–31 RSV). Prior grace is a condition for responsive faith (→4:29–30).

Hope Isaiah advances Moses's argument in terms of the **signs** and **wonders** of Israel's improbable return from exile in Isa. 45:20–25: "There is **no** other god **besides** me, a righteous God and a Savior." This in turn is appropriated in Phil. 2's hymn of universal recognition of the exalted Jesus (2:5–11). From Egypt to Canaan, from Canaan to Babylon, from Babylon to Jerusalem, and from Jerusalem to the ends of the earth the peoples are coming to glorify the Father.

Love YHWH is known as **God** not in sheer miracles but in the community that bears his[+] name as his[+] creation, deliverance, and beloved. Each image here is one of particularity in generality: **humanity** before earth and sky, a living **people** before the peoples, and **a nation** before its host nation. Israel bears the name of the only God to all those who do not.

[4:36]Out of heaven he[+] made you hear his[+] voice, that he[+] might instruct you: and on earth he[+] made you see his[+] great fire; and you heard his[+] words out of the midst of the fire. [37]Because he[+] loved your fathers, therefore he[+] chose his[+] seed after him[+], and brought you out with his[+] presence, with his[+] great power, out of Egypt; [38]to drive out nations from before you greater and mightier than you, to bring you in, to give you their land for an inheritance, as at this day. [39]Know therefore this day, and lay it to your heart, that YHWH, he[+] is God (→4:32–35) in heaven above and on the earth beneath (→4:25–26); there is none else.

Faith In Exod. 19:18–20 God descends to speak to Moses; in 20:22 God has spoken to him from heaven. There is no inherent discrepancy, only affirmation that YHWH reigns everywhere (→30:11–16). Here Moses firmly connects the imagery of creation (**heaven** and **earth**) and of redemption (**voice** and **fire**) to insist that all creation is a forum for God's economy of salvation.

Faith The theophanies of exodus and Sinai are pedagogical to their core.

Hope Every exodus of every generation, including the gathering in of God's chosen ones from the corners of the earth (Mark 13:27), is grounded in this original divine love. Every future promise lies secure in the character of the triune **God**.

Love God **brought** Israel **out** without employing an angel or some other inter-mediary (Heb. 1:3–14), whereas in Num. 20:16 God sends an emissary to free Israel. Hebrews 1:3–14 respects both by distinguishing between the emissaries and the Son/Savior whom the emissaries worship and serve.

> **4:40**You shall keep his⁺ statutes, and his⁺ commandments I command you this day, that it may prosper you, and your children after you, and that you may prolong your days in the land that YHWH your God gives you forever.

Faith The drama that unfolds between **this day** and the last day, anticipated by the material following Deuteronomy's **statutes and commandments**, shows that Torah obedience alone is not what secures the arrival of the eternal blessing God promises, but the faith of Jesus Christ for those who believe (Gal. 3:21–24).

Hope This conclusion drives home Moses's exhortation in 4:1. The eschatological development in this chapter (→4:29–31) adds a dimension of future finality to 4:1's elements, casting Moses's Torah as instruction primarily not for his contemporary audience but for those living near and in Israel's end-times (1 Cor. 10:11).

Love Moses reworks the elements of 4:1 with a sense of benediction. As wrath gives way to mercy, so warning comes as well-wishing (→28:27–34). Torah is Moses's benediction for every generation—in and out of the land, on all sides of the kingdom's arrival, never to pass away (Matt. 5:18; Luke 16:17).

> **4:41**Then Moses set apart three cities beyond the Jordan toward the sunrise; **42**that the manslayer⁺ might flee there, who kills his⁺ neighbor unawares, and did not hate him⁺ in time past; and that fleeing to one of these cities he⁺ might live: **43**namely, Bezer in the wilderness, in the plain country, for the Reubenites; and Ramoth in Gilead, for the Gadites; and Golan in Bashan, for the Manassites (2:24–3:17).

Faith Moses does what he still can, given the restriction of his authority to this side of the Jordan. He will command the rest (19:1–13) after assuring Israel that God will provide the authorities to accomplish it (18:9–22). Joshua will oversee the founding of the other three cities (Josh. 20). Moses heeds the calling he has received to "prove what is the will of God" (Rom. 12:2 RSV), however wide or narrow the scope of that calling may be. "Having gifts that differ according to the grace given to us, let us use them" (12:6 RSV). Moses's faithfulness anticipates Paul's under similar circumstances. Paul is commissioned as Christ's apostle to the nations (1:5), though his heart is for Israel (9:3; 10:1). Like Moses, his authority does not extend into Judea or Samaria, and his policies are distinct from the policies in Judea and Samaria set by the church in Jerusalem (Acts 15:1–29; 21:17–26). Yet he still sees his mission in terms of the whole mission of God, involving the salvation of all Israel in fidelity to the promises made to their fathers (Rom. 9:6–8; 11:26–29). He understands both the partial character of his role and its significance to the whole (12:3–5; →1:37–38).

Love At first this passage seems oddly placed, but it is intentionally opposed with Moses's ordering Israel into hundreds and fifties at the outset of the journey in the wilderness (1:9–18). As Moses gave Israel a political administration for its wanderings, so now Moses gives Israel a political administration for its settlement—with a difference: now he respects his diminishing role and sets up only the three **cities** that are east of the **Jordan** rather than all the six mentioned in Num. 35:6–15.

Love Israel's own internal strife remains a great enemy (1:12) outside as well as within the land. It is essential that God's fellowship make provision to defuse it so that the fellowship's complex whole does not fracture. Mercy is an essential spiritual gift (Rom. 12:8) that keeps each tribe from descending into compensatory violence of the kind that soon nearly exterminates the tribe of Benjamin (Judg. 19–21). The unity and proper ordering of the churches in Paul's jurisdiction—and any other, and among jurisdictions—is essential to the **life** and well-being of the churches of all places. God's good rationing of spiritual gifts draws us together to present our "bodies as a living sacrifice" (Rom. 12:1) in which we will not think too highly of ourselves (12:3) but "love one another with brotherly⁺ affection," "outdo one another in showing honor" (12:9–10)—and "never avenge [ourselves], but leave it to the wrath of God" (12:19). When things go wrong, God's good provision of justice and mercy keeps God's beloved people from flying apart. It "overcome[s] evil with good" (12:21—all quotations from RSV).

> 4:44This is the Torah that Moses set before the sons⁺ of Israel: 45these are the testimonies, and the statutes, and the ordinances Moses spoke (→1:5) to the sons⁺ of Israel, when they came forth out of Egypt, 46beyond the Jordan, in the valley by Beth Peor, in the land of Sihon king of the Amorites who lived at Heshbon (→3:12–17), whom Moses and the sons of Israel struck, when they came forth out of Egypt. 47They took his land in possession, and the land of Og king of Bashan, the two kings of the Amorites, who were beyond the Jordan toward the sunrise; 48from Aroer, which is on the edge of the valley of the Arnon, even to Mount Sion (that is, Hermon) (→3:8–10), 49and all the Arabah

beyond the Jordan eastward, even to the sea of the Arabah, under
the slopes of Pisgah (→33:1–5).

Faith **Moses** does not hold **Torah** over us, force it upon us, withhold it from us, or even leave it distant from us, as abusive or intimidated teachers do. Instead he brings it to us and lays it down in front of us, showing it to be ours and inviting us to take it up as our own—as adolescent Jews do in bar mitzvoth and bat mitzvoth, as adolescent Christians do in confirmation, and as new believers do in catechism.

Faith This passage's proper nouns belong mainly to Deut. 1–4 rather than Deut. 5–28. This passage concludes the scene of Moses's first sermon (1:4–4:43) and turns it into the narrative setting of Moses's second sermon (5:1–29:1). The highlights of the first four chapters become the backdrop of Deuteronomy's major address. Moses's Torah is not just rules and regulations (4:1) but includes his own narrative **testimony** (1:6–3:29). The Jewish canon of instruction, like the Christian canon after it, includes a variety of genres all working together to teach, convict, correct, and train (2 Tim. 3:16), so that its audiences may be completely equipped for every task (3:17).

Hope Everything in the years between leaving Egypt and the conquests across the Jordan drops out of this condensed narrative—even Sinai. The effect is one of uninterrupted movement and onrushing fulfillment. "The time is fulfilled, and the kingdom of God has come near; repent, and believe in the good news" (Mark 1:14b–15 NRSV).

DEUTERONOMY 5

^{5:1}Moses called to all Israel, and said to them: Hear, Israel, the statutes and the ordinances I speak in your ears this day, that you may learn them, and be careful to do them. ²YHWH our God made a covenant with us in Horeb. ³YHWH did not make this covenant with our fathers, but with us, even us, who are all of us here alive this day.

Plain Deuteronomy 5–11 is an extended prologue to the laws for Israel enumerated in Deut. 12–26. The prologue's interpretation therefore governs the terms by which the laws themselves are to be understood and applied. Several sections articulate a series of reasons for the laws of Deut. 12–26. Together they comprise a Mosaic theology of Torah. Deuteronomy 5 focuses on Israel's inability to face God at Sinai after the Decalogue is delivered. God's further commandments are the product of Moses's intercession on our behalf.

Faith Hearing, **learning**, **care**, and **doing** are all required if any of them is finally to matter. From Exodus through Numbers, Israel holds God's instructions, but God's instructions do not yet hold Israel. Having *recorded* God's revelation, Israel now has to *receive* it. Success depends not only on Moses taking God's good news to his people but on them taking God's good news to heart. The state of the hearts God sets out to reach makes reception a rocky process involving misunderstanding, rejection, conversion, intensive retraining, and commitment to the long process of deepening. Similarly, it is only at the end of Matthew's Gospel that Jesus's people are ready to "go . . . and make disciples . . . teaching them to observe all that I have commanded you" (Matt. 28:19–20 RSV), beginning over with others the process that they themselves have been undergoing.

Hope In pleading for the present generation to embrace the covenant given to its immediate ancestors (→11:1–7), Moses exposes the distinction between trust in the patriarchal promises and obedience to Sinai's words. The prophets identify it too (Isa. 51:1–6; 63:15–19), and Paul develops it at length. Israel's latter generations are fulfilling promises to the former generations of patriarchs (e.g., Gen. 12:7; 15:4–6, 12–14, 17–20; 17:15–16). The nature of those promises demands observance of both the original Passover generation and all that follow it. Yet Paul does not find Abraham to be our forefather by obedience (Rom. 4:1). His paternity extends beyond the generations blessed with Torah to include the uncircumcised too (Gen. 17:4–8; 22:17–18; Rom. 4:9–12). "The promise to Abraham and his [seed], that they should inherit the world, did not come through the law but through the righteousness of faith" (4:13 RSV).

Love All Israel includes every member in every generation down to the present.

Love Moses's emphatic appeal to **all here alive** exposes another subtle distinction that is developed by the prophets (Jer. 31:31–34; Ezek. 11:19) and then further by the apostles. His appeal that the covenant is given to the living is somewhat ironic given that the Sinai generation has died in the wilderness. Does not the Torah give life? It does (Deut. 30:16)—but not eternal life (Rom. 7:9). "The law is binding on a person only during his⁺ life" (7:1 RSV). This does not mean that the Torah is void, for the son of David lives (1:3–4), and through the body of Christ even the dead live (7:4). But as Christ belonged not to the Torah but the Torah to Christ, so we belong to Christ and serve the Torah of the spirit of life (8:2) rather than the old written code (7:6). In Christ, living Israel's relationship to living Torah is transformed.

> **5:4**YHWH spoke with you face to face on the mountain out of the midst of the fire **5**(I stood between YHWH and you at that time, to report to you the word of YHWH: for you were afraid [Exod. 19:16] because of the fire, and did not go up onto the mountain), saying: **6**"I am YHWH your God, who brought you out of the land of Egypt, out of the house of bondage.

Faith Moses's reassurances did not calm Israel's **fear** (Exod. 20:19–21). The first commandments keep God-fearers from imposing a distance between God and us that we fill with less frightening substitutes. There is no practical alternative but to trust in the one we fear (→9:18–21) and so to learn that the fire is purifying love that ultimately devours fear (→4:24). Jesus's coming will overcome that aniconic distance and replace the spirit of cowardice with one of power, love, and self-discipline (2 Tim. 1:6–7).

Hope "Where the Spirit of the Lord is, there is freedom" (2 Cor. 3:17 NRSV). As a warrant for the commandments that follow, the reminder that **YHWH brought** Israel **out** operates at several levels. As narrative theologians often note, it locates the commandments not in some self-evident or natural moral structure to the universe or to humanity but in the economy of salvation of Israel that brings its Messiah and his church. It also reminds Israel that this covenant rests on a prior relationship of benefits that makes Israel responsible for how it responds. The commandments are appropriate for the life of freedom that Israel has entered. It further functions to interpret the goal of the commandments not as submission for submission's sake, maintaining justice between "the soul and its God," but for the well-being of God's people. The one who blessed this people with exodus from bondage and a land to settle in brings this further blessing in the commandments.

Love Exodus 13:3 also parallels **Egypt** with **the house of bondage** on the night of the Passover. The pairing bears Jewish liturgical as well as salvation-historical significance. Death entered every house in Egypt (12:30) except for houses observing YHWH's Passover commandment (12:46).

Love **Face to face** is person to person—**with you** rather than just "to you." The encounter on Sinai is a true exchange between giver and receiver as two (collective) subjects. Its covenant is a personal relationship. Moses's interposition authorizes him to speak on YHWH's behalf—as he does in Deuteronomy—and commits the other Israelites to receive his **word** as for them too. In this interpretation of the Sinai scene, Israel is not so much below as behind Moses receiving the word of YHWH through him. The second-person singular verbs of the commandments (→5:7) address Moses and through him each Israelite and all Israel together; and while only Moses has known YHWH face to face (→34:10–12), in Moses all Israel and its people have known YHWH too. The coming prophet like Moses (→18:15–19) also hears the Father's words of Torah as addressed to him, through him, and from him, so that in him they can be renewed for everyone who is in the Son.

> **5:7**You shall have no other gods before me.

Plain As an idiom, **have** can connote possession. **Other gods** may be "had"—owned—if not by a person then by the institution or group that constructs them. YHWH is not a possession or a construction, but constructs and possesses Israel as an inheritance (4:20). To have other gods is thus to try in vain to reverse the terms of divine-human relationships.

Faith It is significant not only what God commands, but that God commands at all. A god with no instructions is only a servant or a stranger, not a master. YHWH sets rules that reflect the terms of his⁺ relationship with Israel. Many in the West ignore those demands and construct religiosities of mildly benign and infinitely tolerant presence—as Israel did under the divided monarchy until foreign oppressors swept theirs away. Having made even more profound demands on his disciples, Jesus is either another prohibited god or the God of Israel. The many who wish away God's demands would turn Jesus into something more convenient—neither a false god nor the Lord but a prisoner of their imaginations. The prophetic histories suggest that capturing Christ will end in the capture and exile of his captors, who will lack the sense even to understand what is happening (32:16–18).

Faith God speaks the first two commandments in the first person, grammatically linking them to the preamble in 5:6: "I brought you out . . . you shall have no other gods **before me**." The one who identified himself⁺ to Abraham, Moses, and Pharaoh commands our full allegiance (→6:4). Fidelity infinitely transcends mere henotheism and even monotheism. "Whoever loves father or mother more than me is not worthy of me" (Matt. 10:37 NRSV).

Hope God holds the future; other gods do not even have a future to be held. Turning our backs on the God of Israel and serving others' doomed gods forecloses our own future. Deuteronomy warns of a day when Israel will have betrayed its redeemer, fallen back on gods that embody the dark hopes of its neighbors, "forgotten the rock that bore you," sacrificed to demons, and entered again into slavery (→32:15–18). The result will be an Israel on the brink of dissolution and cultural extinction. Only when God pours his Spirit on its descendants will they again identify with YHWH—and on that day even strangers will seek adoption and gain a future (Isa. 44:4–5). The other gods will have brought only shame (44:9–10). The proper interpretation of this remarkable saga will be as inescapable to the other nations as it already is to Israel: "There is no other rock" than YHWH (44:8).

Love "There is no God but one.... There are many **gods** and many lords" (1 Cor. 8:4–5 NRSV). In all the world of powers, no other god brought these tribes out of the house of bondage. To Pharaoh they were a commodity and a threat. To the other nations they were someone else's problem, if they were anything at all. Even Israel could not see itself except in shame—that is, except in the eyes of the many gods and many lords who mask the evil one. "He had no form or majesty that we should look at him, nothing in his appearance that we should desire him" (Isa. 53:2 NRSV). No one else championed these wretched slaves as a people to be loved. Because God alone is love for the loveless, only YHWH is Savior, only YHWH is creator, only YHWH is God. Only in YHWH can Israel see itself as beloved. Only through YHWH's eyes for Israel can the other nations see the gods and lords as the charades they are and come to know themselves as enslaved, beloved, and free.

> **5:8**You shall not make an engraved image for yourself, or any likeness of anything that is in heaven above, or that is in the earth beneath, or that is in the water under the earth: **9**you shall not bow yourself down to them or serve them; for I, YHWH, your God, am a jealous God (→4:21–24), punishing fathers'+ guilt on the children, and on the third and on the fourth generation of those who hate me; **10**and showing loving-kindness to thousands of those who love me and keep my commandments.

Faith Some traditions take this commandment as the second part of the commandment against other gods (→5:7). Both approaches honor aspects of the Hebrew parallelism. The two prohibitions are certainly close, but the prior commandment focuses more on other peoples' gods, this one on Israel's own innovations. This commandment penetrates more deeply into the heart of the transgressor and the deep grammar of the transgression.

Faith These are all the locations God made on the first three days of creation and populated with creatures on the second three (Gen. 1). Everywhere we look we encounter powers that intimidate or entice us. Yet in each of these three arenas we also encounter a **servant** in human **likeness**—in preexistence and ascended glory, in birth and burial, and in baptism respectively—to whom "every knee should **bow**, in heaven and on earth and under the earth" for the invisible Father's glory (Phil. 2:10 RSV).

Faith These manufactured images are not necessarily "other gods" of other peoples, which the previous commandment already forbids (→5:7), but products of Israel's own distrustful imagination. Their qualities of lifelessness, fruitlessness, helplessness, and senselessness betray the hearts that conceived them. The only divine image that lives is not engraved but incarnate, full of the Spirit of life, a fruit-bearing vine, helper of the helpless, and penetrating in his acuity—the polar opposite of these futile substitutes, the only begotten and therefore definitive sign of his Father's heart.

Hope In a culture without a solid conviction of an afterlife, **children** and grandchildren are its eternity. Apostate parents effectively disinherit their children. Since heeding God secures blessings on children despite the curse of sin, rejecting God cuts them off from those mercies and consigns children to the curse. Shrewdly, Israel's jealous God appeals to paternal instinct to warn of idolatry's consequences. If a generation will not remain faithful for its own sake, perhaps it will do so for the sake of the descendants who will bear its names. When the **fathers** disobey anyway (→31:24–30), it falls on a son and servant of Israel to bear their **punishment** and turn them from their ways (Acts 3:12–26).

Hope Parents struggle mightily to shape just one or two generations of descendants in limited ways. Beyond them, matters are simply out of our hands. God's **kindness** to us, however, is different. Because it unites heaven and earth in holy fellowship, it extends into the future far beyond even our potential to imagine (7:9). Faithfulness stores treasure in a heaven whose permanence fills all futures. The only sure way to bless the children of our **thousandth** generation is to obey their and our eternal God.

Love Is idolatry really **hatred**? Is obedience really **love**? These associations grate on contemporary sensibilities. Are religious rituals really so significant? It becomes clear that they are when we take into account the commandments' narrative background: "I am YHWH who brought you out of Egypt" (→5:4–6). Consider the analogy of a celebrity or a businessman who dumps the wife who supported him through times of hardship, tears apart his family and scars his children, and remarries someone young and glamorous. This is what Israel does when it settles in the land God gives it and then turns to idols. Spurning our Savior after receiving such grace is the contemptuous betrayal of a hateful heart. The one reliable sign of true love is loyalty that respects God's matchless wisdom and honors his+ will. "We are in the true one, in his+ Son Jesus Christ. He is the true God and eternal life. Little children, keep yourselves from the idols" (1 John 5:20–21, my translation).

5:11 You shall not take up the name of YHWH your God in vain, for YHWH will not hold him⁺ guiltless who takes up his⁺ name in vain.

Faith Oaths invoking deities were common in the ancient Near East as elements of contracts, testimony, and ordinary discourse; **in vain** means abusively, falsely, or emptily, as in an insincere oath (cf. 5:20). To use a **name** is to rely on a relationship. The commandments exclude certain understandings of the covenant relationship. Here God denies unconditional allegiance to a group—what sociologists call "tribalism" and liberation theologians call "solidarity." Israel may not presume that God will automatically affirm the swearer by virtue of the covenant relation—"my country right or wrong," as it were. This does not change with the Messiah's advent. "Many will say to me, 'Lord, Lord, did we not prophesy in your name, and cast out demons in your name, and do many deeds of power in your name?' Then I will declare to them, 'I never knew you; go away from me, you evildoers'" (Matt. 7:22–23 NRSV).

Hope Participation in a people, a class, a cause, a heritage, or even a divine covenant is not self-justifying. Only God justifies (Isa. 50:8; Rom. 8:33). God promises poetic justice for those who swear by his⁺ name. Since they appeal to the prospect of judgment, God will render it. The meaning we have given the word "God" will be judged and put on display for all to contemplate (Isa. 48:1), "for why should my name be profaned? My glory I will not give to another" (48:11 NRSV). The findings will be mixed. "The name of God is blasphemed among the Gentiles" because of the presumption of many (52:5 in Rom. 2:24 NRSV). Yet a righteous servant "walks in darkness and has no light, yet trusts in the name of [YHWH]" (Isa. 50:10 NRSV; cf. 50:8 in Rom. 8:33–34). Whoever speaks against this Son of Man will be forgiven (Matt. 12:32a), with the result that "my people shall know my name" (Isa. 52:6 NRSV; cf. Rom. 10:15). However, the promise in this commandment retains its dark edge even in the new covenant. Not all have obeyed his good news (Isa. 53:1 in Rom. 10:16). The Holy Spirit's blasphemers are not **held guiltless** either now or forever (Matt. 12:32b). Having given our accounts of God in our speech, "each of us shall give account of himself⁺ to God" (Isa. 49:18 in Rom. 14:10–12 RSV).

Love Exploiting God's **name** is a galling way to mistreat the redeemer who offered his⁺ name as assurance that he⁺ would stop the exploitation of the Hebrews (Exod. 3:13–17). In trading on God's reputation, the blasphemer occupies the position of disbelieving Pharaoh in that showdown (4:28–5:2; 7:8–13): he⁺ mistreats God's people, refuses to fear God, hardens his⁺ heart against God's wonders, and is overthrown. Ananias and Sapphira learn this when they lie to God (Acts 5:1–11). The best defense against our own insincerity is to deny the evil one every opening and let our fellowship with God speak for itself by simply saying "yes" or "no" (Matt. 5:37).

5:12 Observe the Sabbath day, to keep it holy, as YHWH your God commanded you (→5:16). **13**You shall labor six days, and do all your work;

14but the seventh day is a Sabbath to YHWH your God, in which you shall not do any work, you, or your son, or your daughter, or your male servant, or your female servant, or your ox, or your donkey, or any of your livestock, or your stranger who is within your gates; that your male servant and your female servant may rest as well as you. **15**You shall remember that you were a servant in the land of Egypt, and YHWH your God brought you out of there by a mighty hand and by an outstretched arm: therefore YHWH your God commanded you to keep the Sabbath day.

Faith **Observance** connotes religious practice. Many Christian theologies distinguish among moral, political, and (no longer binding) ceremonial law within the Torah. But the **Sabbath** commandment is no less ceremonial and no less binding than the ones that come before it, and no less political and moral than the ones that follow.

Faith In Exodus the fourth commandment is grounded in God's creation (Exod. 20:11). Here (and in Jesus's ministry [Luke 13:10–17]) it is grounded in redemption. Despite the derivation of **Sabbath** from the word for cessation, the point of Sabbath practice is not cessation but holiness. "It is lawful to do good on the Sabbath" (Matt. 12:12 NRSV). The rule of circumcising sons on the eighth day supersedes the Sabbath day (John 7:23) because entering the covenant comes before keeping the covenant. Joshua's army circled Jericho on a Sabbath (Josh. 6:14–15). Priests honor the covenant with acts that otherwise would "profane" the Sabbath (Num. 28:9 in Matt. 12:5). Jesus observes the Sabbath with work that does his Father's will (John 5:17, 30) and so **keeps it holy**. In restoring the Sabbath to its intended purpose in the context of the covenant, "the Son of Man is lord of the sabbath" (Matt. 12:8 NRSV).

Faith "The **sabbath** was made for man+" (Mark 2:27 RSV), but not simply for health or social benefits. It is a sacrificial memorial **to YHWH** the provider and a sign of trust in God's providence. Faithfulness requires the discipline to complete all one's **work** in **six days**. The Son of Man (2:28) even saw to it that "all was now finished" on the cross before Sabbath fell (John 19:28–30), and he waited to rise until the Sabbath had passed (20:1). YHWH virtually forced Sabbath observance on a disobedient Israel by supplying manna that would not cooperate with their sin (Exod. 16:26–28). Israel's Sabbath faithfulness is currently habituated but still untested. When the manna stops falling, the people will be faced with renewed temptation to work to increase their gain (cf. 16:22–30), to become the industrious counterparts of the wicked servants who desert their posts when the master is away (Luke 12:42–47).

Hope The first thing humanity does after its creation is **rest** (Gen. 1:26–2:3). Instituting the **Sabbath** moves Hebrew society from slave-**work** to rest—a temporary respite from the Adamic curse (3:17–19). Jesus moves his people further from the first things to the last things by making the Sabbath a time of healing and new creation—signifying a lifting of that curse. He does not abolish the practice but fulfills it. So the last hope for restored humanity is to enter God's rest (Heb. 4:1–11) by believing in the Son.

Hope **The seventh day** is not the Lord's Day, the first day of the week (1 Cor. 16:2), which commemorates Jesus's resurrection in gathered worship. Most Christian traditions have shifted the **Sabbath** to Sunday. The few that have not have typically shifted their times of Christian fellowship to the seventh day. But the Sabbath and the Lord's Day gathering were distinct in the New Testament church (Luke 23:56–24:1; 24:33–36). Jesus's activities on the Sabbath do restore it under his lordship (Mark 2:28), and Christian Sabbath practices do signify the arrival of his kingdom, but without somehow relocating the seventh day to another day of the week.

Love The commandment includes **livestock** mainly for the sake of the servants who would work them (but →25:4). Our "capital"—offices, staff, machinery, and so on—must rest if we are really to rest too. But rest is not an excuse for neglecting the needs of others. Caring for capital involves support that continues even during **Sabbath** rest (like the "work" of leading livestock to water or rescuing them; 22:4 in Luke 14:5).

Love Sabbath-keeping looks back to rest from servitude and includes "the least of these," even the **stranger** and the sick, in that blessing. Sabbath practice is therefore missional. It invites Jew and Gentile, slave and free, **male** and **female** into the common life of God's redeeming providence (cf. Gal. 3:23–28; →23:15–16).

> **5:16**Honor your father and your mother, as YHWH your God commanded you, that your days may be long, and that it may go well with you in the land YHWH your God gives you.

Faith If naming YHWH rightly respects the category of guilt, this commandment respects that of **honor**. Honor regulates behavior through prestige and shame rather than vindication and condemnation. It relies on social rather than juridical structure in a covenant involving both.

Faith Honoring parents is distinct from obeying them (→21:15–21), especially when children have broken faith with their parents (2 Kgs. 22:13) or when parents have failed to bring them up in the Lord's Torah (Eph. 6:4). Then, like King Josiah, the grandchildren may have to violate their parents' confused expectations in order to restore family honor (2 Kgs. 22:20). The prophets so honor the patriarchs by rejecting the ways of their apostate ancestors. They endure rejection to restore their **wellness** and greater lineage. This is of course Jesus's way of honoring his generations (Matt. 1:1–17). "I have come to set a man against his father, and a daughter against her mother" (10:35 NRSV). The Father's only Son "came to his own home, and his own people did not accept him. But to all who received him . . . he gave power to become children of God" (John 1:11–12 NRSV margin).

Faith In Deuteronomy, **as YHWH your God** has **commanded you** is appended to Exod. 20's versions of both positive commandments but not the eight negative ones. Affirmative commandments require more reinforcement and structure than negative ones, especially in times of personal and social change. As the absence of manna in the land will be a temptation to overwork, so this generation's success in entering the land after the last generation's failure will be a temptation to arrogance. Both commandments fight the sins of adolescence, as a person—or a people—tests its new independence and learns its limits.

Hope Longevity is the first promise with a commandment (Eph. 6:1–4). The past holds the future. Conversely, a generation that does not honor its ancestors is overthrown. Jesus condemns the hypocrisy of a Pharisaic "tradition of the elders" that lets children neglect their parents (Mark 7:1–13). This kind of "honor" dishonors God (Isa. 29:13 in Mark 7:6–7), prompting him⁺ in Isaiah to overthrow their innovations and send his⁺ salvation to uncovenanted peoples (Isa. 29:14–21). Jesus immediately fulfills that promise (29:18 in Mark 7:31–37) and confirms the consequences of keeping or breaking this commandment.

Hope Familial **honor** belongs in a **land** that after all is ancestral (Num. 36:9).

Love Many place this commandment at the head of the second tablet, but it also belongs at the foot of the first. The first five commandments feature associations with **YHWH**. We come from God, and we come from our parents. They are our personhood. Their wisdom is our treasure (Prov. 1:8–9). To abandon the providential family structures of God's creation is to abandon ourselves to nothingness, alongside the self-hating prodigal son and then the self-loving good son (Luke 15:11–24). And to embrace the kingdom of God is more than a reentry into God's providence: it is adoption into the triune God, "for whoever does the will of my **Father** in heaven is my brother and sister and mother" (Matt. 12:50 NRSV). This relativizes the family structures that sometimes tyrannize family members (Luke 15:25–32). The genealogies of the Old Testament end with Jesus the seed of Abraham (Matt. 1:1–17) because he shares his Spirit of sonship and final inheritance. Jesus's final act before giving up his Spirit is to give the beloved disciple a **mother** to honor and give her a son to be honored by (John 19:25–27). Joining together this family of grace, in which the whole church is contained, finishes his work (19:28).

5:17 You shall not murder,

Plain The final commandments are linked with "nor" (or "and"), giving them a fluidity and coherence (Mark 10:19; Rom. 13:9) that is missed when they are considered in isolation.

Plain The Hebrew verb for **murder** by itself has a wider range than English equivalents. It can refer to unintentional killing, premeditated killing, accidental death, and legal execution. The categories are also less easily distinguished than they appear. Manslaughter, neglect, and execution sometimes amount to murder—as in the stories of Moses (in some Jewish legends and in the Qur'an), Joseph, and Jesus respectively. However, the backdrop of Exod. 21–23; Num. 35; and elsewhere warrants a more precise translation here. The commandment criminalizes all taking of human life apart from the standards of justice made clear through the whole of Israel's story and jurisprudence.

Faith In Noah's days the earth was filled with violence (Gen. 6:13), and the murder continues to the last days (Rev. 9:21). Throughout the Bible's bloody narrative, murder is associated with unbelief (Rom. 3:10–18). It is the resort of the calculating, the callous, and the desperate. From Abel to Zechariah (Luke 11:49–51) and "from . . . John the Baptist until now the kingdom of heaven has suffered violence" (Matt. 11:12 NRSV). Standing firmly in the tradition of Israel's persecuted prophets and heading a new tradition of Christian martyrs is Jesus, murdered while Barabbas is set free. His resurrection is the definitive testimony of God's rightful life overturning wrongful death. Jesus "died for our sins according to the scriptures" (1 Cor. 15:3 NIV).

Hope **Murder** is the ultimate in what sociology and psychology call "othering." Someone's very life becomes an unbearable offense. Murder becomes habitual (Rom. 1:29–31) because the problem lies in the debased mind of the murderer. Jesus roots murder in anger (Matt. 5:21–22), which is perverted hope (Rom. 1:32). Pharaoh (Exod. 1:8–22) and Moses (2:11–15) embody two alternate paths for murderous lives: futile vengeance and covenantal repentance.

Hope To **murder** another is to issue the Son of Man's command on judgment day: "Depart from me" (Matt. 25:41 NRSV)—as if we were the judges. Only God and God's appointed agents (Rom. 13:4) have that role. Setting ourselves up in their place is idolatrous. The irony doubles when the Judge is the victim, but grace doubles with it (Acts 17:30–31). Murder's opposite is mercy, which bestows renewed life on the unbearable through living relationship: "You are my people" (Hos. 2:23 NRSV).

Love The commandments as a whole are not God's highest aspirations for humanity but minimal requirements for a functioning society. The rest of the Old Testament offers a more penetrating analysis of the distant goal toward which they point, and Jesus famously radicalizes commandments in the Sermon on the Mount. However, the greatest radicalization of this commandment is not to resist anger but to love our enemies (Matt. 5:43–48). This reflects the gospel's agenda of shifting humanity from depravity to sanctification—from sin to mere abstinence from the narrower definitions of idolatry, fraud, rebellion, **murder**, adultery, theft, and envy and finally to the embrace of God, integrity, family, and others. Church life offers society more than these bare social minimums, shifting its aspirations from not being murdered to guarding hearts against malice, living safer lives, and abandoning cruel and unusual punishment (and perhaps eventually capital punishment). The shift from the commandments to "the royal law of love" (Jas. 2:8–13), from judgment to mercy, happens not through coercive governmental policymaking but by making the kingdom's grace freely available through the gracious ministries of Jesus's church to lawbreakers, law-abiders, law-enforcers, and lawgivers alike.

5:18neither shall you commit adultery,

Faith The primal interrelationships among murder, **adultery**, theft, lying, and coveting here (→5:17) are developed repeatedly in the New Testament (Matt. 5–7; Gal. 5:19–21). We know them directly in the multiform destruction that adultery and the rest bring to all human relationships. Abraham's fear of the violence of adulterous hearts leads twice to a threat of unwitting adultery with Sarah that almost frustrates the promise (Gen. 12:11–12; 20:11). Both times, God must intervene (12:17; 20:3–7). Further sinning—in Abraham's case, lying by speaking half-truth—will entangle us only further. Only the righteousness of faith saves (Hab. 2:4 in Rom. 1:17). Likewise, Hosea condemns (northern) Israel for seeking to save themselves through infidelities that leave them ruined (Hos. 1–8), then promises deliverance through a "faithfulness [that] comes from me" (14:8 NRSV). Christ's advent delivers all nations from bondage to all evil, including sexual evil (John 4; 8:10–11; 1 Cor. 5:7–8).

Hope In the Torah's ancient Near Eastern context, **adultery** was sex between a married woman and anyone besides the husband, who all but owned her (→22:22–30). As Israel abandoned polygamy, recovering the monogamous character of male and female humanity in the image of the triune God, adultery became any violation of marital exclusivity by either spouse.

Hope In the present age we suffer dissatisfaction (Rom. 8:16–25). Where the dissatisfaction is sexual, **adultery**, fornication, divorce, and perversity are forms of impatience (Matt. 15:19; 1 Cor. 5) that embody sexual despair, and chastity and abstinence are forms of patience (Song 3:1–5) that embody sexual hope. Cultures that capitulate to impatience—such as Israel and Judah in the waning days of their monarchies, first-century Rome, and the sex-obsessed libertines and puritans on every continent today—reap destruction: "The rest of humankind, who were not killed by these plagues, did not repent of . . . their fornication" (Rev. 9:20–21 NRSV). On the other hand, cultures that embrace patience with ourselves and with each other (1 Cor. 7:1–16, 25–40) discover the goal of this commandment in the kingdom: apostolic contentment and fruitful relationship in all circumstances (2 Cor. 12:9–10; Phil. 4:11–13) that finds enough to satisfy present needs even while looking forward to far more (John 2:1–11). "I saw the holy city, the new Jerusalem, coming down out of heaven from God, prepared as a bride adorned for her husband" (Rev. 21:2 NRSV). The abolition of adultery and the perfection of chastity, then, is not a desexed heart free from desire but a community life omnipotent with Christ's strength.

Love The **adulterous** do not know jealousy as the adulterated do. Neither the acquisitive eroticism of philanderers nor the desperate eroticism of love-starved adulterers can appreciate YHWH's jealousy for Israel (4:24)—a love that makes and keeps promises, waits for maturity, bears with failures, suffers from rejection, punishes transgression, and rejoices in reunion. The hard discipline of sexual faithfulness, whether in or out of marriage, awakens our appreciation of the bridegroom's love and thus our own love of the bridegroom and one another. "The Spirit and the bride say, 'Come.' . . . Let everyone who is thirsty come. . . . Come, Lord Jesus!" (Rev. 22:17–20 NRSV).

5:19neither (→5:18) shall you steal,

Plain The missing object of the verb is traditionally construed as property (as in Exod. 22:11). Some scholars maintain that the object is personal, turning **stealing** into kidnapping or enslaving (as in Deut. 24:7). Given that the objects of the tenth commandment are both persons and property (→5:21), there is room for an open-ended and even an expansive implied object here.

Faith A cluster of words describes our possible relations that involve possessions: on the one hand, creating, giving, having, sharing, withholding; on the other hand, taking, receiving, lacking, **stealing**, destroying. Alone among these, stealing necessarily fails to trust in God's providence. (Some taking is not stealing—for instance, gleaning the remnants of fields in 24:21.)

Faith Different economic visions value these relations differently. Capitalism prizes creating, having, and withholding, tending to view takers with more suspicion than givers and to glorify havers over lackers, whereas socialism prizes sharing and taking, tending to view creators with more suspicion than stealers and to glorify lackers over havers. The eighth commandment withholds blanket pronouncements on these visions. It does, however, condemn any practice or vision that condones theft, whether as banditry, exploitation, appropriation, sloth, seizure, or any other form.

Faith The original sin was a theft in a garden (Gen. 3:6). In the parable of the wicked tenants in the vineyard (Luke 20:9–19), Jesus's is another. The Father has given the Son all things to hold; the Son has held onto them in spite of the tenants' crimes. He will come again to destroy the robbers of his realm, reclaim his own, and hand them back to the Father, along with those with whom he has shared them in the Spirit.

Faith In the community of the resurrection, as in the exodus community, the most common thievery is **stealing** oneself. "You were bought with a price; therefore glorify God [with] your body" (1 Cor. 6:20 NRSV).

Hope "[YHWH] has greatly blessed my master [Abraham], and he has become wealthy; he has given him flocks and herds, silver and gold, male and female slaves, camels and donkeys" (Gen. 24:35 NRSV). "Woe to you who are rich, for you have received your consolation" (Luke 6:24 NRSV). Eschatology reconciles these two narrations of possessions. Our property embodies our future expectations. In the days of the prophets and apostles, wealth embodied impoverished expectations (Isa. 5; Rev. 3:17–18). "Where your treasure is, there your heart will be": either in the land of thieves or in the Father's kingdom (Luke 12:33–34 NRSV). Theft embodies the worst of future expectations: a cynical and destructive parasitism that kills the host on which the thief depends. Cultures of theft—corruption, organized crime, rapacious greed, proletarian revolution, machine politics, the welfare state, slavery, fascism, and family tyranny—are eschatologies of death, signified in the thieves crucified alongside the Savior and doomed to their fate apart from repentance and restoration (Luke 23:39–43).

Love Greed loves oneself over one's neighbor; **stealing** indulges greed (Matt. 15:19) to love oneself at the direct expense of one's neighbor. The final commandments all cultivate direct and indirect consideration toward one's neighbor. If they fall short of the Golden Rule (Matt. 7:12) in profundity, they surpass it in specificity. Reading them together in light of God's kingdom and righteousness in Jesus Christ reveals the *telos* of not stealing. The practice of giving in secret (6:2–4) is a sign of the truest fulfillment of this commandment: a community leaving earthly value for Christ's sake (19:29) and freely offering to him and one another our treasure (6:2–4), the good news (10:8), and our lives (16:25; 20:28). We find in our sinful hearts the antithesis of this vision in the apostle Judas Iscariot's handing over his own master for payment—stealing his Lord's freedom and life in exchange for money (26:14–16). Grace utterly defeats theft when the two meet in Christ's passion.

> 5:20neither shall you testify in vain (→5:11) regarding your neighbor,

Plain The context is judicial, the sin perjury. **Regarding** is not simply "against" as in some translations. False witness favoring one's **neighbor** is equally forbidden (16:19–20).

Faith Genesis 2 treats language as a trust; Gen. 3–4 portrays the twisting of language into a power wielded against God and fellow human beings; and Gen. 11 portrays the frustrating of ambitions through God's confusing of language. Abuse of language makes human societies low-trust environments for information: "Their throat is an open grave, they use their tongues to deceive" (Ps. 5:9 in Rom. 3:13 RSV). The practices of witness and discernment (→19:15–21) cultivate higher-trust environments for gleaning reliable information from low-trust environments. When these are abused, witness becomes prophetic. Prophecy is a community's last social resource for emancipation from lies (→31:16–22). False prophecy corrupts even that way of truth-telling (→18:15–22). As these measures resort to greater and greater—yet still failing—emergency measures to conserve truthfulness in a world of sin, it would seem as if the power of the lie has triumphed (Zech. 10:2) and the father[+] of lies reigns (John 8:44). Yet Jesus of Nazareth is God made into our neighbor, and with the Father and the scriptures as his witness (5:31–40) along with the Spirit and his disciples (15:26–27), our heavenly neighbor's truthfulness is confirmed in all circumstances (16:1–15).

Love Language's inherent relationality makes it basic to humanity's personal nature. God calls for personal integrity not mainly for the sake of the witness but for God's name (5:11) and then for **neighbors**, putting truthfulness in the service of others before oneself. This makes language truly personal and ultimately ecclesial rather than merely powerful—and enables its speakers to deliver God's good news (Rom. 1:9). If a world of lies is also a world of evil, violence, arrogance, and ignorance of God (3:10–18; Col. 3:5–9), then a people of covenantal testimony is a fellowship of blessing, peace, humility, and Holy Spirit (Rom. 12:11–18) whose citizens speak truth, whether harshly or gently, as one body of Christ and members one of another (12:5; Col. 3:10–11).

Hope In Christ's kingdom false witness is no longer to be believed or tolerated (Zech. 13:2–3). All the church is a judiciary, a collective witness to the resurrection and its implications on the world and a collective jury inheriting the Spirit of conviction (1 Cor. 6:2, 11). Submitting to one another's truth-telling (6:1, 4) characterizes a community of sincerity and truth (5:8) ready for the day on which we will give an account, for "we are to judge angels" (6:3 NRSV). Conversely, resorting to the wisdom of outsiders defeats the ones commissioned (6:7–11) to expose the world's foolishness (1:20, 30). The promise of this commandment is fulfilled in a cloud of witnesses with testimonies of mission, evangelism, prophecy, worship, discernment of spirits, judgment of sin, assurance of forgiveness, teaching apostolic traditions, encouragement of the weary and wavering, and prayer even for enemies and persecutors.

> 5:21 neither shall you covet your neighbor's wife+, neither shall you desire your neighbor's house, his+ field, or his+ male servant, or his+ female servant, his+ ox, or his+ donkey, or anything that is your neighbor's."

Plain The final commandment is a whopper, convicting hearts rather than just actions (→27:26). The Hebrew verbs for **coveting** and **desiring** are distinct but the meanings similar. In Exod. 20:17 **covet** is used in both cases, so that the second use explains the first. Exodus's form of the tenth commandment is adapted to Israel's earlier nomadic life, whereas this version is adapted to life settled in the land.

Faith Theological tradition is divided over whether these should be one commandment or two. Would combining them not objectify and depersonalize the spouse, turning him or her into property? Yet covetousness does precisely that. It depersonalizes all parties. Forbidden desire fantasizes a relationship in denial of actual relationships (such as marriage and parenthood) that constitute persons as the persons they are. Coveting another's spouse abstracts the coveter, the coveted one, and the spurned spouse(s) (and every other concomitant relation, from parents and in-laws to siblings, children, and neighbors) from their actual circumstances and thus denies their personhood.

Faith The Decalogue is patriarchal, addressed to men rather than women (→5:18; →22:22–30). The form of this commandment is thus contextualized both to Israel's surrounding economy and to its internal social structure. In the filial rather than patriarchal structure of the body of Christ, all are "sons" or coheirs (Gal. 4:5), even daughters and servants (Acts 2:17–18), and none but the Lord himself⁺ is a father or a master (Matt. 23:9). While our structures are still informed by gender (Eph. 5:21–6:9), the kingdom's commandments are for all in Christ, in whom "there is no male and female" (Gal. 3:28, my translation). "Fornication and all impurity or covetousness must not even be named among you, as is fitting among [holy ones].... No... one who is covetous (that is, an idolater) has any inheritance in the kingdom of Christ and of God" (Eph. 5:3, 5 RSV).

Hope One world of envy is domestic. When relationships are measured by the personal fulfillment they bring, family members become annoyances, disappointments, and impediments to self-realization. Similarly, alternative arrangements—a new start in another marriage, city, or social class—become irresistible temptations. Another world of envy is public. Flux is a feature of life in a living world. How do we respect it faithfully? Our culture accepts and even encourages the pervasive desire to win employees and capital (donors, markets, votes, colleagues, authority, strategic alliances, parishioners, pastors) from competitors and increase power and productivity both in one's own enterprise and in its neighborhood. Insofar as the motive and principle of that sensibility is covetousness, it undermines the very relationships of those it seeks to help. Weakening one business, political party, school, or church in order to supply resources to another can strengthen the fittest and ultimately the whole, but it also reinforces the vice that divides the whole against itself. Paul describes the kingdom differently (Rom. 14:17–18): the strong bear with the weaknesses of the weak, the weak do not hinder the strengths of the strong, and all build one another up to please the neighbor and offer hope to all (15:1–4).

Love Unlike the prohibition against stealing (5:19), this prohibition against envy stresses the **neighbor**. The goal is not just to possess the thing itself but to usurp the neighbor's life. Envy twists community into a means of discontentment and even a kind of torture. "Those who want to be rich fall into temptation and are trapped by many senseless and harmful desires that plunge people into ruin and destruction" (1 Tim. 6:9 NRSV). One takes hold of "the life that really is life" (6:19 NRSV) only by shunning selfishness and forsaking the goal of acquiring the neighbor's life. "There is great gain in godliness combined with contentment" (6:6 NRSV). Jesus construes envy as fraud (→25:13–16). In his dominion one gains not only freedom from envy but gains one's neighbor, now as a friend and loved one. The Lord's fellowship rejoices in each other's blessings and shares them freely (not the spouses as such, of course, but the spouses as friends—an impossibility in cultures of envy) because it sets its hope only in the God who supplies them (1 Tim. 6:14–18). As a result, the one who leaves behind solitary possessions for holy fellowship gains all of them back a hundredfold, along with eternal life.

5:22 These words YHWH spoke to all your assembly on the mountain out of the midst of the fire, of the cloud, and of the thick darkness, with a great voice: and he⁺ added no more. He⁺ wrote them (cf. Exod. 24:12; 34:1–28) on two tables of stone, and gave them to me.

Faith Many contemporary characterizations of religion notwithstanding, this covenant is neither a human initiative nor even a human response to divine initiative, but a new creation. God is the trustor of the Torah, Moses the trustee, and all the **assembly** (*ekklēsia*) of Israel the beneficiary. Likewise the Father is the trustor, Christ the trustee, and his body the beneficiary of the Holy Spirit (Eph. 1:11–14, 22–23).

Faith The Torah that follows in the rest of Deuteronomy will merely expand upon the already adequate commandments here. In Deuteronomy the Ten Commandments are the head from which God grows the body of Torah (cf. Eph. 4:15–16). They alone are written in stone and placed in the ark (→10:1–5; →31:9–13) because the rest follows. The Decalogue is for Mosaic application, priestly maintenance, royal appropriation, prophetic renewal, and messianic transformation rather than the supplementation, distortion, qualification, and supersession to which false prophets and teachers have constantly subjected it.

Hope Sinai's intimidating backdrop becomes apocalyptic imagery when the Torah's giver promises to speak again to judge the covenant's children and their enemies and so usher in a new age (Rev. 11:15–19). Meanwhile, its scene is replayed at Joshua's commissioning (→31:14–18) and especially the transfiguration (Luke 9:28–36), where the prophetic word is confirmed in the glorified Son (2 Pet. 1:17–19). He is the leader of God's new exodus (Luke 9:31) and the Son of Man who will return to judge the living and the dead (9:26–27).

Hope Stone suggests permanence, but in both historical and eschatological perspective it has proven to be too transitory for God's eternal words. The first tablets were broken (9:17); the second were hidden or lost. By contrast, the word of YHWH remains forever (Isa. 40:6–9; 1 Pet. 1:23–25a). Ironically, the right eternal medium for it turns out to be flesh (→4:11–15)—indwelt with the Spirit of God (Ezek. 36:25–28) and awaiting resurrection to eternal life (37:1–14). This is because God's words are not merely written or passive but living and active (Heb. 4:12). The blocks of material that follow the commandments begin the commandments' legacy and life. Through the hundreds of implications of the covenant in Moses's preaching, from the many rules to the blessings and curses to the eschatological warnings and promises at the end of Deuteronomy, the covenant begins to shape the maturing hearts of Israel. Torah's legacy culminates in "the good news that was announced to you" (1 Pet. 1:25b NRSV).

Love The **two tables** are sometimes understood as two copies, similar to the modern practice of making two copies of a contract, but they are traditionally understood as two volumes. Here Moses reveals the inner structure of the Decalogue: the first set or table more directly defines one's relationship with God;

the second one's neighbors (but →5:16). The first concerns the Almighty; the second offers a grand tour of life's powers: family, death, sex, possessions, truth, and desires. The first runs "don't, don't, don't, do"; the second runs "do, don't, and don't, and don't, and don't, and don't." Moses appends the phrase "as YHWH your God commanded you" to both "do" commandments. As the first table's prohibitions find practical embodiment in the affirmation of Sabbath practice, so the affirmation of honor to parents implies the second table's prohibitions, whose violations would bring shame not only on the sinner but on his or her family. The two practices together structure a faithful life: "You shall each revere his⁺ mother and father, and keep my Sabbaths: I am YHWH your God" (Lev. 19:3, my translation).

> **5:23**It happened, when you heard the voice out of the midst of the darkness, while the mountain was burning with fire, that you came near to me, even all the heads of your tribes, and your elders; **24**and you said: "Behold, YHWH our God (→5:27) has shown us his⁺ glory and his⁺ greatness, and we have heard his⁺ voice out of the midst of the fire: we have seen this day that God does speak with man⁺, and he⁺ lives.

Faith The "wise and knowledgeable people" of 1:13–15 perceive in the wonders of Sinai God's **glory and greatness** through God's speech and help their whole nation know God as powerfully revealed through his⁺ words. Receiving God's covenant in this way opens Israel's relationship with God and thus its life to the new possibilities that follow in Moses's storytelling and teaching. And every new step of faith makes further changes possible. "The Word became flesh and dwelt among us, full of grace and truth; we have beheld his glory. . . . The [Torah] was given through Moses; grace and truth came through Jesus Christ" (John 1:14, 17 RSV).

Hope Hebrew *adam* (**man**) can here be rendered universal and thus gender inclusive (so NRSV). Yet the traditional reading elegantly leads into the next verses, which make clear that Israel's other leaders mean it to refer only to Moses (→5:25–26), almost as if he were a new Adam.

Love There is a bittersweet distancing here between God and Israel's leaders. Even as Sinai smokes in front of them, they approach Moses rather than God. Wandering Israel has moved from ignorance and distrust of God to presumptive and false intimacy at Kadesh-barnea and now to a wary respect. It is a sign of progress in the tortuous relationship between God and Israel that will be repeatedly redefined and renegotiated along the way to its fulfillment.

> **5:25**Now therefore why should we die? For this great fire will consume us: if we hear the voice of YHWH our God (→5:27) any more, then we shall die. **26**For who is there of all flesh, that has heard the voice

of the living God speaking out of the midst of the fire, as we have, and lived?

***Faith* Who of all flesh?** Moses, of course. While Israel's leaders could have taken Moses's human life as a sign that the Spirit's fire may be poured out on all flesh and everyone made a prophet (Joel 2:28–29), instead they are "jealous for [Moses's] sake" (Num. 11:29) and wish to restrict divine access to him alone. Their willingness to put him forward on their behalf does not prove they are sure of his safety, though it does conveniently keep them out of danger.

Hope Despite the passage's promising start (5:23–24) and acceptable conclusion (5:27), it nevertheless includes this troubling middle. Moses's interlocutors are right that God is a devouring **fire**, but only to whose who draw back (Heb. 12:18–29). Having just learned that *adam* may speak with YHWH and live, they still primarily associate YHWH with despair rather than hope. They will prefer to forge more manageable gods from their own fires (→9:15–17). This makes Moses's teaching task primarily theological: he must locate Israel's fear (and introduce love; so 6:5) within the whole life-refining economy of Israel's unmaking and remaking. The fear of YHWH is the beginning of wisdom (Ps. 111:10), but only the beginning. We must "fear and love God" (Luther).

***Love* As we have** is a telling comment. Israel's leaders admit that they, and all Israel, have already seen God's great glory and lived. God is known only at God's initiative, but he⁺ wills all to see him⁺ face to face and live forever (Rev. 22:4). We are the ones who set limits on God's availability, as if this would save our lives. The commandments lead all to the tree of life and the heavenly city (22:14).

> ⁵:²⁷Go near, and hear all that YHWH our God shall say: and tell us all that YHWH our God shall tell you; and we will hear it, and do it."

Faith Israel's response still suggests the "obedience of faith" (Rom. 1:5) that trusts in advance and inherits eternal life (Luke 10:28).

Hope While God adds nothing further to the Decalogue (5:22), Israel's leaders still expect further communication. Living relationship with God awaits not only a prolongation of the present but an open future.

Love Moses uses the phrase **YHWH our God** often in Deut. 1–6 and Deut. 29. So far Israel has only used it once, presumptuously, at Kadesh-barnea (1:41). Here Israel finally uses it faithfully. Proper use of the name of YHWH is sinking in (→5:11). Deuteronomy 6 habituates this through the Shema (→6:4) and envisions generations who associate their relationship with God with the covenant (6:20). The phrase finds a home in Israel's worship of both obedience (Ps. 99) and repentance for disobedience (Dan. 9; Jer. 3:19–25).

> ⁵:²⁸YHWH heard the voice of your words, when you spoke to me; and YHWH said to me, "I have heard the voice of the words of this people, which they have spoken to you: they have well said all that they have

spoken. [29]Who would put such a heart in them, that they would fear me, and keep all my commandments always, that it might be well with them, and with their children forever!

Faith God distinguishes the people's **words** from their **heart**. What they **say** is right, but not what they will do (cf. Matt. 23:3). So God will honor their words and provide a way eventually to reform Israel's heart into one of love and commitment (Deut. 6:5–6; 10:12, 16; 11:13, 18; 13:3; 26:16; 28:47; 30:2, 6, 14; 32:46). The difficult grace of God's discipline, through which Israel's Messiah triumphs in faith, can put in us such a new heart and turn what we say into what we actually mean.

Hope The words **forever** and **always** hint at apostasy after a time of obedience (31:16–22).

Love Moses shows Israel the compassion in God's **heart** for them. The covenant's blessings and curses are not a tyrant's utilitarian means to achieve Israel's obedience. Instead, Israel's obedience should display a **heart** that can receive God's love and intended blessings. A leader like Moses who loves both parties would reveal such a disparity in the two parties' intentions only to resolve it.

[5:30]Go tell them, Return to your tents. [31]But as for you, stand here by me, and I will tell you all the commandment and the statutes and the ordinances you shall teach them, that they may do them in the land I give them to possess."

Faith A stark and even humorous juxtaposition banishes Israel to isolated shelters of cloth while Moses **stands** (for forty days!) to learn the whole Torah in YHWH's fiery presence. Moses now has God's sole authorization to learn and teach. The Sermon on the Mount is set similarly (→1:3b), with a key difference: while like Moses the disciples come into Jesus's presence to hear his teaching (Matt. 5:1–2), the Lord allows the crowds to overhear (7:28–29). The Torah and the prophets have prepared the way of the Lord (Isa. 40:3 in Matt. 3:3) so that the people can see God's glory together (Isa. 40:5). When Sinai's fire descends on the gathered church, the instruction formerly at the mountaintop now takes place wherever God's ambassadors go with his[+] good news.

Hope The point of all the rules that follow the Decalogue is **possession** of the promised **land**. This is secured by the Son's obedience and extended to include all things (1 Cor. 3:22). This fulfillment simultaneously contextualizes, relativizes, and intensifies the significance of the instruction that follows as the preliminary formative work in an ultimately far greater project involving every tribe, tongue, and nation.

[5:32]You shall do as YHWH your God has commanded you: you shall not turn aside to the right hand or to the left (→28:7–14). [33]You shall walk in all the way YHWH your God has commanded you, that you may live, and that it may be well with you, and that you may prolong your days in the land you shall possess.

Faith These verses epitomize the first ten chapters. They bridge all that has come before with all that follows, setting the instruction from Deut. 6 onward in the historical and theological circumstances of Israel on the other side of the Jordan at the end of its wilderness wandering. The previous history of failure now links to the coming stress on success. In times of accusation this sequence can be reversed (cf. 9:9–12).

Faith Moses urges Israel to **do** what they have just promised to do (5:27). The people's underlying weakness is not disobedience but mistrust in God and inordinate trust in others and self. This "theology of glory" is what will yield disobedience. God's covenant is not primarily rules but a **way**, a life that yields life (30:15–20). The way to Israel's faith and the life it brings means the undoing and replacement of that misplaced trust.

Hope It is currently popular to think of one's exclusive allegiance to a tradition as somehow giving up a fullness available through respect for plural traditions. Moses frames Israel's choice far differently. To follow other gods is to **turn aside** and give up **all** that God offers. Those who look longingly to the left and right are not complementing deficiencies at the center but only failing to seek the perfection at its end.

DEUTERONOMY 6

^{6:1}Now this is the commandment, the statutes, and the ordinances YHWH your God commanded to teach you, that you might do them in the land you go over to possess; ²that you might fear YHWH your God, to keep all his⁺ statutes and his⁺ commandments I command you, and your son, and your son's son, all the days of your life (→5:28–29), and that your days may be prolonged. ³Hear therefore, Israel, and do it; that it may be well with you, and that you may increase mightily, as YHWH, the God of your fathers, has promised you, in a land flowing with milk and honey.

Faith The vocabulary is catechetical and repetitive (→1:8; →4:1; →4:9–10). To readers used to compact arguments, the repetition of familiar phrases seems only to add to the tedium of all this material. One easily imagines audiences drifting in and out as they hear the same words over and over again. Yet it is an effective style of preaching and teaching. Deuteronomy 6 casts the covenant's commandments as the *remembrance* necessary for gaining and keeping God's fulfilled **promises**. Moses's repeated themes here pierce through audiences' inattentiveness, and the specifics that audiences focus on develop those stresses in specific, sustainable, and memorable ways. Churches with seemingly redundant and even rambling hour-long sermons often have congregations that are more theologically literate and more committed than churches with tidy, linear homiletics.

Hope **Flowing milk and honey** were first heard of in God's appearance to Moses in the burning bush (Exod. 3:8). Practical growth and prosperity have been God's covenantal goals from the beginning. But the promises are also warnings. Fulfillment will bring temptations to which Israel will surrender (Deut. 31:20; Jer. 32:21–23). Much will be required where much has been given (Luke 12:48).

Hope The final preposition **in** is routinely inserted in English translations, but it is not present in the Hebrew. (The Septuagint inserts "to give" in order to make sense of the passage.) The text could literally mean that God has promised Israel to *be* **a land flowing with milk and honey**. After all, these commodities do not simply exist; they must be received and cultivated. Without a faithful population to do it, the land and people will fail. In God's old and new creation each depends on the other (Gen. 1:28; Mic. 4:3–4). Israel could even prefigure a "land" that is a community flowing with the Holy Spirit (→11:8–15).

Love Where **you** is plural in 4:9, here it is singular. The earlier passage concerns the catechetical responsibility of Israel as a whole, and this one concerns that of each of its families. Each supports the other. The nation depends on the faithfulness of its families and vice versa. Christ the son of David son of Judah ultimately takes on the covenant of his whole people on behalf of its lost sheep (Matt. 15:24), freeing all to become his own glorious legacy.

> **6:4**Hear (4:1), Israel: YHWH is our God (→5:27); YHWH is one:

Faith The Shema is often spoken, but it must be *heard*. Confessors must not only confess but **hear** one another's confession. The primary audience of third-person confessions is not **God** but others. We need to listen to our neighbors because faith does not originate in uncorrupted hearts and wills of our own, as Pelagius supposed. It comes from outside, raised by the God who assigns it (Rom. 12:3) and given freely among the depraved through the Spirit (12:4–8). And whereas the audience for this confession is God's covenant people **Israel**, the audience for Christian creeds is limited only by the scope of atonement: "for us and for our salvation," "our sins," and so on. Christian confession is global mission as well as family catechesis.

Hope The implied verbs are usually rendered in the English present tense, but God's promises to be Israel's God are often future (Exod. 29:45; Jer. 31:1; Ezek. 34:24; Zech. 8:8; Rev. 21:7). The Shema bears the same hope. God's unity is eternally active, not statically passive, being. This is displayed most starkly in the economy of salvation. Sin among the people who bear God's image besets God with the dilemma of judgment versus mercy—setting God against himself[+] in a sense. The dilemma is resolved in the mission of the Son, who suffers the world's loss of fellowship with God. Through his unity with the Father for the world, God can truly become ours, we can become God's, and we can become **one** as the Son and Father. In John 17 the indicative verbs of divine unity in 17:11 and 17:21 are also implied rather than stated—and delivered in a context as futuristic as it is present.

Love The claim is above all one of relationship. Covenant with Israel makes **YHWH our God**. The Shema logically coheres like the three articles of the creeds: its soteriology is its ecclesiology is its theology. The economy of salvation in Jesus Christ does not overturn this conviction—the triune God is not three Gods—but deepens appreciation of its coherence to the point that God's "our-ness" is God's very essence: the Father's love of the Son in the Spirit unto all who love is simply who God is (1 John 4:7–21).

6:5and you shall love YHWH your God with all your heart, and with all your self, and with all your might.

Hope Israel's **heart, self**, and **might** are not intrinsic qualities, but gifts from God. Moses has already reminded Israel that its right heart will not come from itself (→5:28–29), that Israel's "heart and self" are inseparable (→4:29–30), and that its might owes entirely to God (→3:23–25). So doing the Torah's commandments requires the character that the Torah itself is to cultivate. If Israel fails to keep the Torah it will lose its capacity to love, identify with, and obey the Torah. "The very commandment that promised life proved to be death to me. For sin, seizing an opportunity in the commandment, deceived me and through it killed me" (Rom. 7:10–11 NRSV). Wayward Israel will dissolve—as it does under the monarchy—unless and until it is restored through God's bestowal of a new character and capacity to love. And as Deuteronomy itself promises in →30:6–10, indeed in the last days "God has done what the [Torah], weakened by the flesh, could not do" (Rom. 8:3 NRSV).

Love Heart, **self**, and **might** are not three components of a tripartite human nature as Hellenists and gnostics supposed and some still maintain, but three ways of naming both a whole people and a whole person (Babylonian Talmud, tractate *Berakoth* 61b). (Hebrew *nephesh* carries different connotations than the casual sense of "soul," especially here.) To Israel's one God (→6:4) we owe our whole devotion. This is not an analytical inference from a generically monotheistic cosmology; a first cause with some other character might be an enemy or an irrelevance. The love of God is the specific eternal reality from which Israel originates and into which Israel is invited.

Love Can **love** be commanded? Modern emotivism treats moral authenticity as outward expression of independent inner consciousness. Commanded love seems to violate the "inside out" direction of true love. But in fact love is fruit of the Spirit (Gal. 5:22; →30:6–10). It is brought into the human heart. The commandment to love is then a promise to receive in faith, and with it our full identity as moral agents in God's image. "God's love has been poured into our hearts through the Holy Spirit that has been given to us" (Rom. 5:5 NRSV). Deuteronomy 6–11 and then Deut. 12–16 will treat the love of God at length as a life of receptivity to God's past, present, and future.

6:6 These words, which I command you this day, shall be on your heart (32:46);

Faith Israel can gain the heart and self and strength with which to love God by keeping God's **words on its heart**. Here and in the following chapters Moses urges Israel to have Torah rather than the ways of the nations as its nearest neighbor so that the Sinai covenant will be "my heritage forever . . . the joy of my heart" (Ps. 119:111 NRSV). Torah is to be Israel's "good treasure of the heart," out of which comes good (Luke 6:45 NRSV).

Hope The true abundance of Israel's heart will be the **words** of the Lord Jesus that it will hear and do and so survive every flood (Luke 6:47). Sinai's further goal for "the children of promise" (Gal. 4:28 NRSV) is a heart prepared to receive the Spirit of the Son (4:1–7).

> **6:7**and you shall impress them on your children, and shall talk of them when you sit in your house, and when you walk by the way, and when you lie down, and when you rise up. **8**You shall bind them for a sign on your hand, and they shall be for symbols between your eyes. **9**You shall write them on the doorposts of your house, and on your gates.

Faith **Impressing** connotes recitation for memorization, sometimes in a liturgical context (→31:9–13). Forgetfulness is a chronic condition of mortal humanity. A generation easily comes to presume its wisdom or forget it. Parents fail to pass on the lessons of history. That YHWH is revealed in exodus and Sinai makes Torah not propaganda to spread but memory to refresh and pass along; the practices of 6:7–9 help realize 6:6 in order to fulfill 6:4–5.

Faith Holy scripture is authorized by Moses speaking for God. Israel's most direct fulfillment of this command is Deuteronomy itself, then by extension Torah, then Tanakh with its words of the prophets and psalmists, then the New Testament with its words of Jesus and his apostles. The life of Israel is the **written** words of scripture.

Faith Sin as well as death vitiates God's memory. The Gentiles put their trust in the mark of their beast (cf. Rev. 13:16–17), but the tefillin that Israel's men wear on their **hands** and foreheads **symbolize** life ordered by covenantal trust in its deliverer from evil.

Faith The greatest danger to God's words is not that anything superior would overpower them but that careless trustees would lose or corrupt them. So Israel is called not to shout, force, or defend them with any power of its own, but simply to keep the commandments of God and so persevere (Rev. 14:9–12).

Hope As Moses commends God's words to Israel on the border of the promised land to honor God's deeds on both sides of the Jordan, so Israel is to inscribe God's words along the thresholds of its homes and cities. No boundary restricts or delimits the scope of God's economy. Mezuzot turn the potential distractions of landed prosperity (→6:10–12) into occasions to remember and reflect on the future as well as the past.

Love Oral and written tradition are one while remaining distinct: Moses's words are written and recited, but **talked** about in every setting of everyday life. Oral Torah is interpretive, interactive, and expansive written Torah. Both are God's instruction through Moses. Each is the life of the other, and neither the stable **written** and memorized forms nor the changing conversational and inculturated forms are redundant or dispensable.

6:10 When YHWH your God shall bring you into the land he[+] swore to your fathers (1:8; 30:20), to Abraham, to Isaac, and to Jacob, to give you, great and goodly cities you did not build, **11**and houses full of all good things you did not fill, and cisterns you did not dig, vineyards and olive trees you did not plant, and you shall eat and be full, **12**then beware lest you forget YHWH, who brought you forth out of the land of Egypt, out of the house of bondage.

Faith Israel's failure to remember its past contradicts God's faithfulness to remember his[+] promises. A forgetful people misrepresents the faithful God it proclaims, first by hypocrisy, then by apostasy. Nevertheless, its sheer existence remains a witness to a God it no longer understands (→29:22–24). "See, your house is left to you, desolate. For I tell you, you will not see me again until you say: 'Blessed is the one who comes in the name of the Lord'" (Matt. 23:38–39).

Hope If receiving the **land** were the point of the pentateuchal narrative, the whole story would be concluded at Josh. 21:43–45. But Israel's freedom, law, and possessions serve still greater goals. Israel must remember in order for YHWH to be its **God**—to maintain the relationship that the land and its properties symbolize and support.

Hope **Landed** Israel faces the temptation of all who are provided for: not to honor or give thanks to their providers (cf. Rom. 1:20–22). Like prosperous children ignorant of their parents' sacrifices—or like the prodigal son—Israel forgets that the blessings it inherits are blessings. American Christians today often take for granted forgiveness on demand, the coherence of the universe, the consistency of human knowledge, the rule of law, rare personal freedoms, the wide availability of education, basic sustenance and even extraordinary prosperity, financial credit at reasonable rates, historically unusual levels of social respect for others, and the like. These are not simply given, but a social harvest from the soil of cultural folk wisdom and two millennia of the sowed and tended word of God. Like Israel in Deuteronomy, we live in an unusual present. When we refuse to consider its origins we miss its significance and jeopardize our future.

Love Through a quirk of human psychology, or perhaps the noetic consequences of sin, we remember plans and promises more clearly while they are unfulfilled. The regression in tribal focus and solidarity from Joshua to Judges illustrates the temptation to drift and fragment in settled times (→32:15–18). The body of Christ is no temporal coalition of opportunity or defense, but a fellowship of unconditional neighborly love. The eternal consequence of the passion it recalls and the hope it awaits can keep it from **forgetting** its mission to love one another to the end (John 13:1, 34–35).

6:13 You shall fear YHWH your God; and you shall serve him[+], and shall swear by his[+] name (5:11). **14**You shall not go after other gods, of the gods of the peoples who are around you; **15**for YHWH your God in your midst is a jealous God; lest the anger of YHWH your God be kindled against you, and he[+] destroy you from off the face of the earth. [16]You shall not try YHWH your God, as you tried him[+] in Massah.

Faith Israel is not just to "accept," "believe that," or even "believe in." Those conventional terms of religious loyalty are too weak for the relationship that YHWH has forged. What many now consider extrareligious dimensions of life—for example, the familial, political, economic, and intellectual—are just as covenanted as the conventionally religious. So those powers that operate outside the field of the conventionally religious are still **other gods**. The covenant's radical terms exclude any loyalties that would rival it. Not only may Israel not **fear**, **serve**, or **swear by** these objects of ultimate commitment, but it may not even **go after** them in pursuit of either religious or secular loyalties. Thus Jesus cites Deut. 6:16 against the temptation to throw himself down from the temple to prove God's allegiance (Matt. 4:5–7; Luke 4:9–12) and cites Deut. 6:13 in refusing the temptation to receive the devil's political authority over the kingdoms of the world (Matt. 4:8–10; Luke 4:5–8; →6:17–19; →33:8–11).

Faith God has been testing Israel these forty years to prove and improve it as a father his son (→8:1–5). For Israel to **try YHWH** instead—like all, skeptics and apologists alike, who would force the Lord to submit to our unredeemed wills and rationalities—is insubordination. We cast ourselves as idols when we judge God, "but when we are judged by the Lord, we are disciplined so that we may not be condemned along with the world" (1 Cor. 11:32 NRSV).

Hope The sustained spatial imagery here is significant both literally and allegorically. Israel is an earthly sign of YHWH's presence in the **midst** of the nations. Yielding to the temptation to envy and **go after** their **gods** necessarily turns away from the God in *their* midst, ignoring or doubting that YHWH is *present* among them (Exod. 17:7). This denial of God in God's own presence is the most blatant apostasy. At **Massah** God's solution to Israel's failure to trust was *providential presence* on the stricken rock at Horeb (17:6). That memory may now guide Israel through a season where God's presence is less obvious but no less real. Pursuing other gods will provoke God to rekindled jealousy (→4:21–24), which would overthrow them **from the face of the earth**. These warnings (and a hint of the spatial imagery) pertain also to Christians who "hear his[+] voice" but might "fall away from the living God" (Heb. 3:7–4:2 RSV on Exod. 17:1–7).

Love Massah's rock from which life-giving water issued was Christ (1 Cor. 10:4), and the destruction of those who tested God there warns Christians to beware any temptation and shun any idolatry that might corrupt Christ's body (10:9–18). "The table of demons" is every public and domestic order that seeks its welfare anywhere but the cross on which God is truly and fully in our midst.

[6:17]You shall diligently keep the commandments of YHWH your God, and his[+] testimonies and his[+] statutes he[+] has commanded you

(→6:1–3). **¹⁸**You shall do what is right and good in the sight of YHWH; that it may be well with you, and that you may go in and possess (→5:30–31) the good land YHWH swore to your fathers, **¹⁹**to thrust out all your enemies from before you, as YHWH has spoken.

Faith The rules of Torah are not arbitrary, let alone bad, as antinomians so often suppose, but "holy and just and good" (Rom. 7:12 NRSV). Their holiness, justice, and goodness manifest God's. They are the heavenly Father's will for Israel's **wellness** on the earth (Deut. 12:28). Jesus appeals to Deut. 6 and Deut. 8 in the wilderness and in the land as the heir of those blessings and the embodiment of their holiness, justice, and goodness and so thrusts out all God's enemies from before him through the power of the word **YHWH has spoken** (Matt. 4:10–11, 23–25; Luke 4:13–14, 31–44). His salvation and ours is won through Jesus's faithfulness to Torah, not in spite of it or in some other way.

6:20 When your son asks you in time to come, "What do the testimonies, the statutes, and the ordinances, which YHWH our God has commanded you mean?" **²¹ᵃ**then you shall tell your son,

Faith The covenant assumes that future generations will need not only to know the commandments (→6:7–9) but to understand what they **mean**. Torah must get inside us, but we must also get inside it. The **ordinances'** fundamental character is not self-evident but depends on the narrative of God's faithfulness to the patriarchs, the Hebrew slaves, the wandering tribes, Canaan's settled inhabitants, and exiled Jews (→6:21b–25; →8:11–14a). Successful catechesis assimilates both halakah (rules) and haggadah (story) in a way true to both.
Faith The **son** feels a living relationship with YHWH (**our God**) but not yet with Torah (**commanded you**). This "generation gap" dangerously distorts the character of God, Israel, and their covenantal relationship. This happens **in time to come** when the unconditional royal promises to the house of David crowd out the blessing and curses of the Mosaic covenant, and in the church when "cheap grace" displaces grateful discipleship (→6:21b–25).
Love Israel's primary catechetical responsibility is paternal, with the priesthood and other institutions in both supportive and extraordinary roles. Apostolic fellowship transcends (Matt. 8:21–22; 10:34–38), transforms (Col. 3:18–21), honors (1 Cor. 7:13–16; 2 Tim. 1:5), and creates (John 19:25–28; Phil. 2:22) families rather than annihilating them. So the teaching office is more diffuse in the church than in patriarchal and tribal Israel, and familial in both earlier and new ways.
Love This is brilliant pedagogical technique. The father waits to teach Torah's reasons until the peculiarities of its **testimonies, statutes,** and **ordinances** have aroused his son's curiosity (or perhaps his irritation). Then the **son** will be properly receptive to the saga. By contrast, much Christian education robs the gospel of its power by divorcing the rules of Christian life from the story of Jesus, confusing the two, substituting one for the other, or ordering them in a way that misrepresents

the intrinsic suspense of the good news. In the apostles' experience, Christ's crucifixion, resurrection, and subsequent explanation bring unforgettable clarity to a frustratingly obtuse sequence of experience, teaching, apprenticeship, and failure. Their rhetorical effect is to move the apostolic audience in permanent, life-changing ways.

> 6:21b"We were Pharaoh's bondservants in Egypt: and YHWH brought us out of Egypt with a mighty hand; 22and YHWH showed great and awesome signs and wonders on Egypt, on Pharaoh, and on all his house (→34:10–12), before our eyes; 23and he+ brought us out from there, that he+ might bring us in, to give us the land he+ swore to our fathers. 24YHWH commanded us to do all these statutes, to fear YHWH our God, for our good always, that he+ might preserve us alive, as at this day. 25It shall be righteousness to us that we do all this commandment before YHWH our God, as he+ has commanded us."

Hope The anomaly of a relationship with YHWH apart from the terms of Torah (→6:20–21a) is removed here by catechesis that shows the son both halakah (rules) and haggadah (story) and corrects the son's misperception. In the fullness of time, the problem of generations with different settings than that of Moses's original audience is resolved through a change in the covenant's terms and a corresponding eternal change in the character of the relationship (Heb. 8:6–13; 9:15–28; Rom. 7:1–6). This change does not abolish our need to know and teach the meaning of Torah, but recasts and amplifies its significance in eschatological retrospect.

Hope This passage appeals to **this day**, but it does not appeal to "this land" or otherwise locate the father and son in Canaan. The point of Torah in every age and location is not just habitation in the **land** but everlasting goodness and eternal life.

Faith Israel's Torah observance will not earn possession of the **land**, for in the Torah itself any such saving act is understood to be a gift of sheer grace (→9:4–5). Rather, observing God's whole commandment attests to **righteousness** of God that is otherwise manifested and disclosed (Rom. 3:21–22). Grace, faith, and works relate in this way: God's reign bears the fruit of righteousness in the Spirit (Jas. 2:20; Rom. 14:17). Only an obedient life respects the Father's kingdom and righteousness (Matt. 6:33) and does "justice" to his+ grace (Phil. 1:9–11).

Love Israel experiences God while being built into God's covenant people. They are *beloved* for the sake of the **fathers**. They are *witnesses* for YHWH having **showed** his+ **signs and wonders**. They are *free* for being **brought out** of slavery and *heirs* for receiving **the land** of promise. God's whole *mitzvah* is the right life for such a people. Likewise, the right way to observe God's whole *mitzvah* is *as* such a people. Only then will we appreciate its true meaning. This comes fully to pass in the life, death, and resurrection of the Messiah, who came to accomplish the fulfillment of the Torah and the prophets (Matt. 5:17–18). Jesus calls all to do and teach these commandments in the kingdom of heaven with **righteousness** that exceeds the teachers of his day (5:19–20). As beloved in him, witnesses of him, free in him, and heirs in him, his followers are uniquely positioned to do so.

DEUTERONOMY 7

^{7:1}When YHWH your God shall bring you into the land where you go to possess it, and shall cast out many nations before you, the Hittite, and the Girgashite, and the Amorite, and the Canaanite, and the Perizzite, and the Hivite, and the Jebusite, seven nations greater and mightier than you;

Faith Stephen uses the phrase **seven nations** as shorthand in Acts 13:19, suggesting that this phrase is well known. Their specification here from **Hittite** to **Jebusite** (adding the obscure **Girgashite** nation to the list in Exod. 23:23) articulates the particular rather than unconditional character of God's acts. This fixes concrete events in Israel's memory (Josh. 6–8; 10–12) while leaving room for memories of specific failures such as falling for the Gibeonites' deception (Josh. 9). The effect is humbling rather than triumphalistic. An analogy might have George Washington list future American military victories in which Vietnam becomes conspicuous in retrospect by its absence.

Faith **Greater and mightier** is an important clue to the meaning of the chapter (→7:2–8). These are Pharaoh's very thoughts about Israel (Exod. 1:9). Israel's psychological insecurity (Deut. 7:17) makes these neighboring principalities a temptation God must **cast out** (→24:6–7). Israel has already learned that it cannot do so on its own (1:41–45), for "apart from me you can do nothing" (John 15:5 NRSV).

Hope Deuteronomy's exilic readers look back on this assurance as fulfilled and so may find hope for the challenges of their day: "You will take up this taunt against the king of Babylon: . . . You are **cast out**" (Isa. 14:1–4, 19 NRSV). So can the apostles: "'Father, glorify your name.' Then a voice came from heaven, 'I have glorified it, and I will glorify it again.' . . . Jesus answered, 'This voice has come for your sake, not for mine. Now is the judgment of this world; now the ruler of this world will be driven out'" (John 12:28–31 NRSV; →9:4–5). These victories call for not just gratitude but strengthened resolve.

7:2and when YHWH your God shall deliver them up before you, and you shall strike them; then you shall utterly destroy them: you shall make no covenant with them or show mercy to them. **³**Neither shall you make marriages with them; your daughter you shall not give to his⁺ son, nor shall you take his⁺ daughter for your son. **⁴**For it will turn away your son from following me, that they may serve other gods: so the anger of YHWH would be kindled against you, and he would destroy you quickly. **⁵**But you shall deal with them like this: you shall break down their altars, and dash their pillars in pieces, and cut down their Asherim, and burn their engraved images with fire (cf. Exod. 23:32–33; 34:12–16).

Plain Israelites would turn **from following** YHWH, not Moses. There are several similar shifts in Moses's preaching (cf. 11:8–15).

Faith God's providence for settled Israel, like God's mercy on all who enter his⁺ approaching kingdom, calls for cooperation and trust (→20:10–18). In driving the world's intimidating powers out from before insecure Israel, God gives his⁺ people a new standing in the land of promise—justifies them, so to speak. Now Israel must accept its new standing by **striking** these obstacles and putting away their temptations—so that it may be sanctified.

Love "Whatever does not proceed from faith is sin" (Rom. 14:23 NRSV). God warns here that a "strong" generation's fear and greed will ensnare the "weak" one that follows it. His⁺ Torah provides for those of little faith more wisely than their own leaders. Likewise, "we who are powerful ought to bear with the failings of the weak, and not to please ourselves . . . that we may have hope" (Rom. 15:1, 4, my translation).

Love "Among the Gentiles those whom they recognize as their rulers lord it over them, and their great ones are tyrants over them. But it is not so among you" (Mark 10:42–43 NRSV). These dangers to Israel are sources of conventional social power. Intimidated (and/or attracted and seduced) by these nations' greatness and might (→7:1), Israelites will be tempted as Pharaoh was to harness them for their own purposes, eventually turning Israel into an empire, a client state, or a pagan society. Ridiculous as it sounds, Israel is not dominating the nations it destroys. **Covenanting, showing mercy**, and **marrying** from its position of temporary advantage would be futile efforts to master, manage, and exploit them. These would only **destroy** Israel **quickly**, contradicting its justification and obscuring God's alternative future for the nations. Israel will have to pursue the **fire** of "the purgative way" of spirituality that sets aside what is incompatible with God's lordship, even to its apparent strategic disadvantage (Matt. 5:29–30; →7:16–21). We "take no part in the unfruitful works of darkness, but instead expose them" (Eph. 5:11 NRSV).

Love **Deal with** whom? The nearest and best antecedent is the **other gods**. The spiritual underwriters of the nations' power must be deposed as well—by destroying their **altars** and **images**. Israel's battle is not primarily "against flesh and blood" but "against the principalities, against the powers, against the world rulers of this present darkness, against the spiritual hosts of wickedness in the heavenly places" (Eph. 6:12 RSV). Our materialistic age dismisses and demythologizes these only to serve them more profoundly. Paul's churches **strike** the powers God has set **before** them with swords not of metal but of the Spirit of God's word, freeing the devil's slaves with God's good news; and they defend themselves against the devil's methods with the church's weaponry of spiritual virtue (6:13–17). Joining their mission, we follow the Lord Jesus, who subdued every unholy power in the land with his own flesh and blood (2:13–15). Through him we are not less than conquerors, but more (Rom. 8:37).

> **7:6**For you are a holy people to YHWH your God: YHWH your God has chosen you to be a people for his+ own possession, above all peoples who are on the face of the earth. **7**YHWH did not set his+ love on you, or choose you, because you were more in number than any people; for you were the fewest of all peoples: **8**but because YHWH loves you, and because he+ would keep the oath he+ swore to your fathers, has YHWH brought you out with a mighty hand, and redeemed you out of the house of bondage, from the hand of Pharaoh king of Egypt.

Love Trying too hard to make ourselves lovable makes us repulsive. "Knowledge puffs up, but love builds up" (1 Cor. 8:1 RSV). God is not a shrewd investor who chooses what already appraises well (→7:2–5); God is a gracious Father who elects and **loves** the unknown, unloved, and even uncreated. "If anyone imagines that he+ knows something, he+ does not yet know as he+ ought to know" (1 Cor. 8:2 RSV). God's people are of no intrinsic worth apart from his+ creating, redeeming, and sanctifying grace. "But if one loves God, one is known by him+" (8:3 RSV). **A holy people to YHWH** sets aside the world as an object of security, opportunity, and anxiety and lives joyfully as **his+ own possession above all peoples** (8:5–6). The relentless logic of Christ's victorious grace undoes humanity's chronic calculus of temporal advantage and disadvantage, of sexual selection and political association (→22:22–30), of pride and shame—and ultimately of hate (7:10)—and creates a beloved and loving fellowship that understands fully and is fully understood (1 Cor. 13:12), to the Lover's glory (1 Pet. 2:12). "Once you were not a people, but now you are God's people.... Abstain from the desires of the flesh" (2:10–11 NRSV).

> **7:9**Know therefore that YHWH your God, he+ is God, the faithful God, who keeps covenant and loving-kindness with them who love him+ and keep his+ commandments to a thousand generations (→5:8–10), **10**and requites those who hate him+ to their face, to destroy them: he+

will not be slack to him⁺ who hates him⁺, he⁺ will requite him⁺ to his⁺
face. ¹¹You shall therefore keep the commandment and the statutes
and the ordinances I command you this day, to do them.

Faith God does not put up with a tolerable level of faithlessness like a permissive parent, a tolerant pagan god, or a faraway emperor. Such laxity could only characterize completely different parties than YHWH in **covenant** with Israel. Nor will God refrain from stopping the relational rot that results from spurning him⁺. The consequences of grasping for conventional social power rather than living in God's **loving-kindness** are immediate, even if they are not immediately manifest. Unrighteousness (→6:21b–25) breaches the covenantal relationship, distorts Israel's self-understanding, garbles its knowledge of God, corrupts its holiness, and betrays its mission. Disasters begin to cascade right away. They may appear negligible at first, like Achan's appropriating a few of the devoted things of Ai (Josh. 7), David's concealed tryst with Bathsheba (2 Sam. 11), or Ananias and Sapphira's insincerity (Acts 5). But they grow just as "a little leaven leavens the whole lump" (1 Cor. 5:6 RSV). Torah's clear contrast, blessings, and restorative justice (5:7; 5:12–13 on Deut. 17:7) echo spiritual theology's "illuminative way."

> ⁷:¹²Because you listen to these ordinances, and keep and do them, YHWH your God will keep for you the covenant and the loving-kindness he⁺ swore to your fathers: ¹³and he⁺ will love you, and bless you, and multiply you; he⁺ will also bless the fruit of your body and the fruit of your ground, your grain and your new wine and your oil (→24:17–22), the increase of your livestock and the young of your flock (→28:49–52), in the land he⁺ swore to your fathers to give you. ¹⁴You shall be blessed above all peoples: there shall not be male or female barren among you, or among your livestock. ¹⁵YHWH will take away from you all sickness; and none of the evil diseases of Egypt, which you know, he⁺ will put on you (→28:20–26), but will lay them on all those who hate you.

Hope The blessings of faithfulness outweigh to the point of absurdity the desired social advantages of associating with Israel's powerful Canaanite neighbors. By forsaking the precarious advantages that Pharaoh had sought (→7:1), Israel will enjoy the prosperity, health, and fertility promised to its ancestors, while its enemies will reap the exodus's curses on God's opponents.

Hope The good life described here seems too good to be true. Moses might be exaggerating in an obvious way to make his point equally obvious: YHWH is the only way to go. Even so, such hyperbole pales in comparison to "the glory that is to be revealed to us" (Rom. 8:18 RSV) described in the prophets and glimpsed in the ministry of Jesus with the son born to Zechariah and Elizabeth, water turned to wine, the chronically ill healed and raised, loaves multiplied, lost sheep found, land and kin multiplied a hundredfold, justice in the promised land, opponents fallen and eaten by worms, and above all the seed of Abraham risen and ascended. Papias reported apostolic predictions that when God's blessings on Jacob were finally fulfilled, "a grain of wheat would produce ten thousand ears, and that every ear would have ten thousand grains, and every grain would yield ten pounds of clear, pure, fine flour" (in Irenaeus, *Against Heresies* 5.33.3).

Love The parallelism of Israel **keeping** and God **keeping** respects the mutuality at the heart of the covenantal relationship. Israel's faithfulness maintains rather than produces God's **love** and its **blessed** life (→7:6–8). However, the mutuality is not symmetry. Israel is emphasized in both actions. Its fidelity and YHWH's fidelity are both **for** Israel's sake.

> **7:16**You shall consume all the peoples YHWH your God shall deliver to you; your eye shall not pity them. Neither shall you serve their gods, for that will be a snare to you. **17**If you shall say in your heart, "These nations are more than I; how can I dispossess them?" **18**you shall not be afraid of them. You shall well remember what YHWH your God did to Pharaoh, and to all Egypt: **19**the great trials your eyes saw, and the signs, and the wonders, and the mighty hand, and the outstretched arm, by which YHWH your God brought you out. So shall YHWH your God do to all the peoples you fear. **20**Moreover YHWH your God will send the hornet among them, until those who are left, and hide themselves, perish from before you. **21**You shall not be scared of them; for YHWH your God is in your midst, a great and awesome God.

Hope While **hornets** are plaguing Israel's enemies from within their midst, God is delivering from **within** Israel's **midst**. Their covenantal unity, the goal of spiritual theology's "unitive way," is as basic to Israel's relationship with God as is Israel's partitive refusal of wickedness and its illuminative growth in wisdom through living the Torah. Israel leaves and shuns the darkness to know the source of the illumination by which it walks. Its pilgrimage from slavery to establishment images the saints' inheritance of the kingdom.

Hope Our age cheers the liberation of Israel's exodus but abhors the destruction of its conquest. (It is no surprise that our era also prefers justifying grace to sanctifying grace; →7:2–5.) However, the eradication of Canaanite **nations** is continuing what the contest with Pharaoh started. God's resettlement of Israel is a simultaneous judgment "against all ungodliness and wickedness" (Rom. 1:18 NRSV; →9:4–5) among all the nations from Egypt to Israel (→7:25–26) to Canaan. This makes Israel's salvation a new beginning for Gentiles too (Mic. 4–5; →32:40–43). Being grafted into Israel, they can come to share in its new standing and new character (Rom. 11:13–24).

Love **Pitilessness** seems as troubling a commandment as mercilessness (7:2) and gives rise to Marcionite distinctions between the "God of wrath" of the Old

Testament and the "God of love" of the New. However, the context of each command is revealing. God's reassurances in 7:18–21 speak to Israel's insecurities, not to the fate of those it might supposedly pity. That is because Israel's so-called pity would be displacing its fear that **these nations are more than** it can dispossess, just as Israel's mercy would be manifesting its underlying opportunism (→7:2–5). Here God is neither commending nor prohibiting genuine and sacrificial love of another, of the kind Jesus displayed in loving his enemies and commanding his disciples to do the same (Matt. 5:43–48). Rather, God is forbidding his[+] people to act out of discouragement, just as Jesus commands his disciples to remain faithful to their character as undiluted salt (i.e., not culturally assimilated) and shining light (i.e., not driven underground) under the threat of persecution (5:11–16). In this sense Moses's old instructions and Jesus's new instructions fundamentally cohere, even if the former involved systematic violence and the latter involves systematic nonviolence.

> [7:22]YHWH your God will cast out those nations before you by little and little: you may not consume them at once, lest the animals of the field increase on you. [23]But YHWH your God will deliver them up before you, and will confuse them with a great confusion, until they are destroyed. [24]He[+] will deliver their kings into your hand, and you shall make their name perish from under the sky: no man shall be able to stand before you, until you have destroyed them.

Faith Demoralized and panicky armies fail internally, practically defeating themselves. The Canaanites' apparent strength is as much a psychological fiction as is Israel's apparent strategic weakness. In a world dominated by lies, illusions, foolishness, and bluster, much so-called strength is just the opportunity to exploit the weaknesses of others. The Spirit overpowers deception prophetically with truth, among the nations now and someday in faithless Israel (→29:25–28).

Faith The "perished" **names** of some Canaanite **kings**, from Og and Sihon in Deuteronomy (e.g., 1:4) to whole lists in Joshua (e.g., Josh. 10:3), are in fact canonically preserved. The irony is that their people are no longer their legacy. Worldly rulers seek immortality in the memory of their peoples. But their names are now consigned to become mere historical pointers, like Pontius Pilate's name in the creeds of the church, for in Christ the earth's peoples are now God's legacy (Rev. 21:3). Those kings who do enter the new Jerusalem will bring along their treasure to glorify only the Lord God Almighty and the lamb (Rev. 21:22). "I will make the nations your heritage," the Father tells his[+] anointed Son, so "be warned, O rulers of the earth" (Ps. 2:8, 10 NRSV).

Hope The kingdom may come in an instant, as at the flood, the exodus, the resurrection, and Christ's return across the skies. Or it may be transformed **little by little**, even imperceptibly, as a mustard shrub grows (Luke 13:18–19), as yeast transforms flour (13:20–21), and as life under Torah matures Israel in the wilderness. The master's new servants are entrusted with "little" to gain experience and prove themselves, so that one day they might come to rule over whole cities (19:11–27). So Israel inherits Canaan at a rate it can "grow into."

Love In the maturing life of Christian discipleship the threatening **animals** are the habits of immaturity that are not sinful, but are still imperfect (1 Cor. 13:8–12). These wild beasts are not Israel's fundamental challenge or ours; but their numbers are best kept low as God's people grow to inherit all in store for them and so attain "the measure of the full stature of Christ" (Eph. 4:13 NRSV). The trials of communities that inherit windfall success and corresponding responsibilities, from the fourth-century Roman Empire to today's young megachurches, suggest the wisdom of sustainable church growth and patience in sanctification.

> ^{7:25}You shall burn the engraved images of their gods with fire. You shall not covet (5:21) the silver or the gold that is on them, or take it for yourself, lest you be snared in it; for it is an abomination to YHWH your God. ²⁶You shall not bring an abomination into your house, and become an offering like it. You shall utterly detest it, and you shall utterly abominate it, for it is an offered thing.

Faith Augustine famously regarded rhetoric as "Egyptian **gold**" for enriching the church's preaching ministry. Are some traditions, disciplines, and practices not Egyptian gold but "Canaanite gold" to be shunned entirely? Some are (→18:9–14). Moreover, Israel turned even the common objects plundered from Egypt (Exod. 12:35) into a golden calf (Exod. 32). The abomination of Canaan's idols is not the precious metal itself but the blasphemous stories that perverse hearts make it tell—whether as **gods** or as **offerings** plundered from YHWH and reworked for personal gain (→7:2–5).

Hope Reclaiming false gods is literally playing with **fire**. An Israelite family may not take on even lingering aspects of a forbidden future without foreclosing its own (Josh. 7; Judg. 8:22–27). Our hope for life with God is purely covenantal. Election is neither unconditional ethnic preference (for Canaanites such as Rahab confess YHWH and find mercy) nor guaranteed salvation (for God's chosen people can and do become *cherem*, **offerings**; →2:34–37), but a mission of living witness to an unattainably different future. "What if God . . . has endured with much patience the objects of wrath that are made for destruction . . . to make known the riches of his⁺ glory for the objects of mercy?" (Rom. 9:22–23 NRSV).

Hope The combination of **silver** and **gold** is prominent in the prophets' condemnations of idolatry (e.g., Isa. 2:7; Jer. 10:1–16; Ezek. 7:19–22; Dan. 11:8; Zeph. 1:18; →8:6–10). That resourcefulness can be idolatry is counterintuitive, to say the least, in a culture like ours so used to searching for and realizing overlooked value in things and in people. Nevertheless, Christ-like hope trusts enough in the new creation to **detest** the depreciating value of the old creation offered up for its sake. "Alas, alas, the great city, where all who had ships at sea grew rich by her wealth! . . . Rejoice over her, O heaven, you saints and apostles and prophets! For God has given judgment for you against her" (Rev. 18:19–20 NRSV). In the end, the only astute resourcefulness is singular fidelity. "On finding one pearl of great value, he went and sold all that he had and bought it" (Matt. 13:46 NRSV).

Love Both **coveting** and **detesting** concern affections as well as actions. The **abomination** is the forbidden object (7:26), but indirectly and syntactically the antecedent can include covetousness, theft, and being snared. The transgression involves topics of four of the ten commandments: gods preferred to YHWH, (formerly) engraved images, stealing, and coveting. Two come from each tablet, demonstrating the interrelationships among the commandments and their relevance to the mission of God's people. "For the love of money is a root of all kinds of evil, and in their eagerness to be rich some have wandered away from the faith and pierced themselves with many pains" (1 Tim. 6:10 NRSV).

DEUTERONOMY 8

8:1 You shall do all the commandment that I command you this day, that you may live, and multiply, and go in and possess the land YHWH swore to your fathers. **2**You shall remember all the way YHWH your God has led you these forty years in the wilderness, that he⁺ might humble you, to test you, to know what was in your heart, whether you would keep his⁺ commandments or not. **3**He⁺ humbled you, and allowed you to hunger, and fed you with manna, which you did not know, nor did your fathers know; that he⁺ might make you know that man⁺ does not live by bread only, but by everything that proceeds out of the mouth of YHWH does man⁺ live. **4**Your clothing did not grow old on you, neither did your foot swell, these forty years. **5**You shall consider in your heart that as a man chastens his son (1:31), so YHWH your God chastens you.

Plain Moses returns again and again to the connection between obedience and life. Each time he develops its implications in a slightly different direction involving one more reason, lesson, or promise. These passages are not repetitions but variations. Little by little (→7:22–24) they fill out the significance of Israel's covenantal life.

Faith Because both hard times and good times can last for generations (as in America today), **remembering all** of Israel's past is essential. It puts every season in proper perspective, lest God's forgetful people lapse into either despair or complacency. We always recall that "he suffered, died, and was buried" and that "on the third day he rose from the dead."

Faith God's providence **in the wilderness** included the loving provision of mysterious food and drink and the loving discipline of deprivation. These prefigure both "abundance and want" (Phil. 4:12 RSV) in the land (→8:6–10). There is not one god of abundance and another god of want, but one God who blesses and curses. Both forms of providence teach us to put our whole trust in God for

everything or every word (*kol dabar*) of life. "I have learned, in whatever state I am, to be content" (Phil. 4:11 RSV).

Hope The goal of just discipline, even mortal discipline (Exod. 32:25–28), is future welfare (32:29; 33:1–6). Timidity aborted Israel's first foray into the land (Deut. 1:26–28), and presumption its second (1:41–45). Both failures highlighted a serious deficiency of character. So God has raised a new generation in radical hardship and sustenance **to test** and prepare Israel for a powerful term in the land. After **forty years**, Israel passes the tests to **keep his⁺ commandments** it had once defied. Later Elijah returns to this path when Israel veers into another age of idolatry (1 Kgs. 19:1–9): his forty days of solitary hardship end with angelic sustenance (bread baked on rock, water for life) and divine assurance that the faithful are not alone (19:7, 9, 11–18). God simultaneously humbles and promises Elijah that his disciple and his king will defeat the idolatry. All these images crystallize in God's new mercies on the newly anointed Messiah. Having assimilated humility's lessons for God's internally exiled **son** Israel, Jesus suffers the devil in the wilderness for forty days and defeats him⁺ with the word that man⁺ does not live by bread only (Deut. 8:3 in Matt. 4:1–4 and Luke 4:1–4) but by all God provides—in his case, the Holy Spirit resting on him (3:21–22). Following him and sharing his indwelling Spirit as well as his mission, the "church militant" necessarily inherits the Father's discipline of his⁺ Son so that the "church triumphant" will inherit the Son's glory (Rom. 8:17).

Love "God wills that we know that he⁺ keeps us even ever alike, secure, in weal and in woe, and as much loves us in woe as in weal" (Julian of Norwich, seventh Showing). If God's strictness manifests itself in **hunger** and **manna**, God's affection peeks through in Moses's observation that Israel's **clothing did not grow old** or its **foot swell**. The kingdom's small signs of perseverance among the trials and plagues of this age indicate God's resolve to bring his⁺ good work to completion (Phil. 1:6; →32:4–6).

> **8:6**You shall keep the commandments of YHWH your God, to walk in his⁺ ways, and to fear him⁺. **7**For YHWH your God brings you into a good land, a land of brooks of water, of springs, and underground water flowing into valleys and hills; **8**a land of wheat and barley, and vines and fig trees and pomegranates; a land of olive trees and honey; **9**a land in which you shall eat bread without scarceness, you shall not lack anything in it; a land whose stones are iron, and out of whose hills you may dig copper. **10**You shall eat and be full, and you shall bless YHWH your God for the good land he⁺ has given you.

Faith By listing at length the specifics of Israel's prosperity, Moses turns each into a discrete sign of God's faithfulness as well as a warning of the risk of Israel's unfaithfulness in return (→28:15–19). Consider by analogy a listing of what the average American takes for granted: thriving economy, affordable natural resources, safe and healthy meat and vegetables and fruits and starches, quiet and safe apartment or house, bright and comfortable clothing for every season, medical services, dental services, reliable court system, free public education, financial security for retirement, car and fuel to power it, audio and video players, refrigerator, stove, water heater, washer and dryer, computer, cell phone. . . .

Faith Israel tithes each of the seven *Bikkurim* at the Feast of Weeks (→16:9–12). Torah does not condemn wealth, but only the perversions of faith and fellowship that can come from it. By ignoring its lessons, contemporary Christianity has fallen into modern materialism's false dilemma of wealth as guilt and vice or as **blessing** and virtue. Only radical fidelity can carry us through prosperity's temptations and so keep prosperity a blessing.

Hope "When they were satisfied, he told his disciples, 'Gather up the fragments left over, so that nothing may be lost.' So they gathered them up, and from the fragments of the five barley loaves, left by those who had eaten, they filled twelve baskets. When the people saw the sign that he had done, they began to say, 'This is indeed the prophet who is to come into the world'" (John 6:12–14 NRSV).

Love Gold and silver are notably absent from Moses's list of commodities (cf. 8:11–14a; →7:25–26). Practical plenitude, not garish opulence, is God's intention for **landed** Israel. Such modesty befits the church, not only in its material adornments (1 Tim. 2:9; 1 Pet. 3:3–4) and displays of wealth (Jas. 1:9–11; 2:1–7) but also in its displays of spiritual gifts (1 Cor. 14:22–25). Paul treats the practice of *glossolalia* as demanding more modesty, especially before strangers who could confuse it for pagan ecstasies, than "the higher gifts" (12:17–31; 14:20–25).

> **8:11**Beware lest you forget YHWH your God, in not keeping his[+] commandments, and his[+] ordinances, and his[+] statutes, which I command you this day: **12**lest, when you have eaten and are full, and have built goodly houses, and lived therein; **13**and when your herds and your flocks multiply, and your silver and your gold (→8:6–10) is multiplied, and all that you have is multiplied, **14a**then you exalt your own heart, and you forget YHWH your God,

Faith Israel's **forgetfulness** is not intellectual (→31:19–23) but practical. Its Torah practices, both halakic and haggadic, are its memory of the power of God (→32:7–9). They are for training each generation to know it arises out of the Torah's past and aims toward its promised future (→6:20–21a). **Keeping God's commandments** must not be twisted to serve some other goal—for instance, self-righteousness—or it goes demonically wrong. "You are wrong," Jesus told the scribes and Pharisees, "because you know neither the scriptures nor the power of God" (Matt. 22:29 NRSV).

Faith Having forgotten the way we have come and concentrated only on our present circumstances, we are left with the apparent problem of accounting for those circumstances. Two possibilities will come to Israel: its own efforts and

mysterious outside forces, that is, the gods that Israel knows through contact with its surrounding peoples. These alternatives will still seem to leave room for a god who blesses and curses, but either for reasons unknown and undisclosed or in exchange for worship and respect. Without the memory of where Israel has actually come from, the logical clues will lead to materialism or pagan mysticism, with or without a theistic veneer. This is the general spiritual state of the West. The metaphysical contrast between materialism and paganism may be vast, but the moral contrast is less stark than it appears. Both cosmologies make us moral agents whose task is either to manipulate the world through our force of will or to influence the world through our power of persuasion. Both set our destiny in harnessing the courage—"the **heart**"—somehow to make the most of our circumstances (→8:17–18). Both contrast absolutely with Israel's call to love YHWH with all its heart (6:5). Again, prosperity itself is not the problem, but the corporate amnesia of unfaithfulness.

Hope Because God's action in the world is ordered not just toward present circumstance but ultimately toward the realization of the Father's will in the Spirit through the Son, it takes a narrative shape. The tragic results of Israel's amnesia demonstrate that to forget the way we have come (→8:1–5), that is, Israel's story, is simply to **forget YHWH**. Preferring cultural convention for the strange specifics of God's actual economy of salvation and the life it has won for us in the name of relevance is rapidly evacuating contemporary Christian memory in our own time and demonstrating the same thing.

> 8:14b who brought you forth out of the land of Egypt, out of the house of bondage; 15 who led you through the great and terrible wilderness, fiery serpents and scorpions, and thirsty ground where there was no water; who brought you forth water out of the rock of flint; 16 who fed you in the wilderness with manna, which your fathers did not know; that he+ might humble you, and that he+ might prove you, to do you good at your latter end:

Faith God had put Israel in both **Egypt** and the **wilderness**, as the Spirit would lead Jesus into the wilderness, and thus exposed God's people to these hardships. Here they are remembered providentially—even the serpent plague (also Num. 21:4–9 in John 3:14)—along with the list of miraculous deliverances, **water out of the rock** and mysterious **manna**, and an allusion to the earlier list of future **goods** (→8:6–10). Paul reflects on a similar list in his own christomorphic ministry (→8:1–5).

Hope "Recall the former days when, after you were enlightened, you endured a hard struggle with sufferings. . . . Therefore do not throw away your confidence, which has a great reward. For you have need of endurance, so that you may do the will of God and receive what was promised" (Heb. 10:32–36 RSV).

Love You means not any one generation, since the slaves have died in the **wilderness** and the children of abundance have not yet been born, but the generations together, some of which have known nothing but hardship and others nothing but prosperity. As unfair as this diversity of experience is, it tells one story of one God, whose one Son brings all things together for the sake of his one church. "My God will supply every need of yours according to his⁺ riches in glory in Christ Jesus. To our God and Father be glory for ever and ever" (Phil. 4:19–20 RSV).

> **8:17**and say in your heart, "My power and the might of my hand has gotten me this wealth." **18**But you shall remember YHWH your God, for it is he⁺ who gives you power to get wealth; that he⁺ may establish his⁺ covenant he⁺ swore to your fathers, as at this day.

Faith This passage's materialists and pagans (→8:11–14a), even the theistic ones, ultimately succumb to their own hearts' self-glorification and imagine that they are the lords of their own great or small or missing fortunes. Though they imagine themselves to be in control, in fact their self-image depends utterly on their precarious circumstances. They may appear to be confident, but introspectively they are anxious. A society of such convictions swings from arrogance to despair and back as its fortunes inevitably change. It acts on its illusions and insecurities by dominating and repressing its neighbors. Paul's conclusion in Phil. 4:13 that all things are possible (→8:14b–16), forged by a life of witness that remembers Christ through imitation (Phil. 1:29–30; 3:17–21), shows the far more durable strength of those who **remember YHWH**.

Hope The ultimate goal of **wealth** is not the comfort of its trustees but the glory of its benefactor and the sake of its true beneficiaries. We tell our stories with our personal, ecclesial, and social possessions. But God's judgment tells God's story, sometimes contradicting the narratives of our hearts. "You shall see the difference between the righteous and the wicked, between one who serves God and one who does not serve him⁺. See, the day is coming, burning like an oven, when all the arrogant and all evildoers will be stubble; the day that comes shall burn them up, says [YHWH] of hosts, so that it will leave them neither root nor branch. But for you who revere my name the sun of righteousness shall rise" (Mal. 3:18–4:2 NRSV).

Hope The lands east of the Jordan that have already been bestowed are signs that this promise is already being fulfilled (→8:19–20).

Love Wealth's true beneficiaries are God's beloved (here the **fathers**), not necessarily the wealthy themselves. Only those who **remember** will recognize them *as* beloved beneficiaries and live and love accordingly. Since God's promises to Abraham include descendants beyond number (Gen. 13:15–16) and whole nations (17:4–7), the land's productivity for Abraham's sake (13:14–15; 17:8) is for the improvement of *all* those descendants and nations. To the rich man of Jesus's parable Abraham said: "Child, remember that during your lifetime you received your good things, and Lazarus in like manner evil things" (Luke 16:25 NRSV). Prosperity cannot degenerate into greed while God's gracious **covenant** is truly understood and honored. And once God's covenant is remembered and refreshed in Christ's kingdom, greed is driven out by a return to true prosperity: "Make friends for yourselves by means of dishonest mammon so that when it is gone, they may welcome you into the eternal tents" (16:9 NRSV margin).

> **8:19**If you shall forget YHWH your God, and walk after other gods and serve them and worship them, I testify against you this day that you shall surely perish. **20**As the nations that YHWH makes perish before you, so you shall perish; because you would not listen to the voice of YHWH your God.

Faith Moses concludes this chapter's prong of his argument by condensing it: to miss the preamble to the Decalogue (5:6) is to miss the rest of the Decalogue, and vice versa. **Forgetfulness** is a mortal sin. The great seriousness of Moses's **testimony** formula suggests a foreshadowing of future judgment upon the present generation (30:17–20). Both the covenant's blessings (→8:17–18) and its curses (2:14) have already been arriving. Jesus's preferred apocalyptic formula in the Gospel of John is "amen, amen, I say to you."

Hope This oracle will come to pass even before such a generation's literal mortality, because the **you** in all these statements will cease to be a lived reality. What connects the patriarchs to the slaves to the wanderers to the landed is at once the continuity of God's faithfulness, of which Israel may not be aware, and the continuity of Israel's memory of God and its implications. Without covenantal memory, future generations will not appreciate the connections they have (→6:20–21a) and will disown it. Deaf and blind Israel (29:3 in Rom. 11:8) will still be among the "you" of Moses's whole audience, but fatally unaware of it. Dead to their own identity as the people of God, they will join **the nations** that **perish** in their rebellion against the reign of God and God's anointed (Ps. 2). God's ignorant, idolatrous people will be capable of only resurrection or destruction.

Hope A community that stumbles over worldly things cannot be trusted with heavenly things. "If then you have not been faithful with the dishonest wealth, who will entrust to you the true riches? And if you have not been faithful with what belongs to another, who will give you what is your own?" (Luke 16:11–12 NRSV).

DEUTERONOMY 9

9:1 Hear, Israel: you are to pass over the Jordan this day, to go in to dispossess nations greater and mightier than yourself, cities great and fortified up to the sky, **2**a people great and tall, the sons of the Anakim (→2:10–12), whom you know, and of whom you have heard say: "Who can stand before the sons of Anak?" **3**Know therefore this day, that YHWH your God is he⁺ who goes over before you as a devouring fire (→4:21–24; →5:25–26). He⁺ will destroy them, and he⁺ will bring them down before you: so you shall drive them out, and make them to perish quickly, as YHWH has spoken to you.

Faith In the power that conquers its enemies, Israel is to recognize and acknowledge its God. Yet Israel's subsequent history suggests a more mysterious pattern of recognition. The Canaanites are not in fact uniformly routed from the land. They do not perish quickly. Israel does gain a standing in the land, though neighbors near and far rapidly seduce and paganize it, soon ending its tenure in Canaan. How is Israel supposed to recognize and acknowledge God in *that* course of events? Deuteronomy 27–33, developed in the rest of the biblical canon, holds the complex answer to Israel's vexing question. The Deuteronomistic historian appeals to God as the dispenser of curses on sinners as well as blessings on the chosen. The Chronicler focuses on Israel's long historical trajectory back into the land as a sign of God's resolve on behalf of Israel. The prophets reflect on all this to interpret a foreseen future beyond the coming disasters. And in the signs and wonders of the career of Jesus of Nazareth the evangelists see that future arriving as the Lord **goes over** the Jordan **before** his people and brings down every rival and enemy so fully that he is revealed as the very word **YHWH has spoken to** Israel all along.

Faith Both Israel's victories and its sins (→9:12–14) can come **quickly**—and do (Josh. 6–7).

Love The strong of the world seem invincible and their domination irresistible. Yet when YHWH acts, it is they who can no longer **stand** (Jer. 49:17–20). When the sixth seal is broken, "the kings of the earth" (cf. Ps. 76:7–9) will beg for shelter "from the face of him+ who is seated on the throne, and from the wrath of the Lamb; for the great day of their wrath has come, and who can stand before it?" (Rev. 6:15–17 RSV; cf. Mal. 3:1–2). They are defeated not by greater worldly strength or mere destructive power but by another kind of power altogether: the wrath of a lamb(!) slain to ransom a new kingdom for God from every nation (Rev. 5:9–10). What ends the reign of the **Anakim** is not sheer destruction but the lamb's salvation, shelter, and leadership of those who suffer (7:10; 13–17). "**Who can stand before** his+ indignation? . . . [YHWH] is good . . . ; he+ protects those who take refuge in him+. . . . He+ will make a full end of his+ adversaries" (Nah. 1:6–8 NRSV).

> **9:4**Do not say in your heart, after YHWH your God has thrust them out from before you, "For my righteousness YHWH has brought me in to possess this land," because YHWH drives them out before you because of the wickedness of these nations. **5**Not for your righteousness or for the uprightness of your heart do you go in to possess their land, but for the wickedness of these nations YHWH your God drives them out from before you, and that he+ may establish the word that YHWH swore to your fathers, to Abraham, to Isaac, and to Jacob.

Faith A political revolution does not establish the justice or legitimacy of the new regime, only the injustice and the conclusion of the old. God's judgment is not in favor of Israel but against the **nations**. Israel must not live presumptuously, as it had at Kadesh-barnea (→1:43–45). Such self-**righteousness** will only precipitate new revolutions in the future. "Being ignorant of the righteousness that comes from God, and seeking to establish their own, they did not submit to God's righteousness" (Rom. 10:3 NRSV).

Hope Yet an ending is still an opportunity for a new beginning. Most of these opportunities are squandered. YHWH may end the reigns of rebels at any time (2:21). When this happens, the typical result is that one wicked reign replaces another (2:22–23)—as when a new majority party in Congress soon embodies the very evils it had campaigned against. The unclean spirit regains its stronghold, and its host is discouraged and disillusioned, and the evil generation is worse off than before (cf. Matt. 12:43–45). However, YHWH chooses to drive out *these* particular nations at this particular time for the extraordinary purpose of **establishing** his+ vow to the patriarchs. This revolutionary moment is not a typical turnover in leadership; it inaugurates a potentially new age. Paul holds such an inaugural in Athens, warning that "while God has overlooked the times of human ignorance, now he+ commands all people everywhere to repent, because he+ has fixed a day on which he+ will have the world judged" (Acts 17:30–31 NRSV).

Love Whether Israel receives a truly new beginning depends on the state of its own **heart**. "Out of the abundance of the heart the mouth speaks" (Matt. 12:34 NRSV)—either to demand a sign of God's unconditional favor and be condemned, or to confess God's grace, obey the Father's will, and be justified (12:36–39). If those who persist in self-righteousness end up living only with more and more demons, those who love God with all their heart and trust God's word live in a fellowship of holy ones with a common Father and the risen Son of Man (12:40) as their common brother and son (12:46–50). As Moses begs Israel to seize its opportunity, so Jesus begs us to seize ours: "Something greater than Solomon is here!" (12:42 NRSV).

> **9:6**Know therefore, that YHWH your God does not give you this good land to possess it for your righteousness; for you are a stiff-necked people. **7**Remember, do not forget, how you provoked YHWH your God to wrath in the wilderness: from the day that you went forth out of the land of Egypt, until you came to this place, you have been rebellious against YHWH. **8**Also in Horeb you provoked YHWH to wrath, and YHWH was angry with you to destroy you.

Faith God calls Israel **stiff-necked** after the sin of the golden calf **in Horeb** (Exod. 32:9; 33:3, 5). Moses accepts God's description in pleading for their life (34:8–9). He is an effective intercessor because he is honest about his people's habitual rebellion but never resigned to it. So he better resists Israel's swings between arrogance and despair. By learning Moses's Torah, Israel gradually gains a measure of his judgment and steadfastness; by fulfilling it with perfect judgment and steadfastness, Jesus "appeared once for all at the end of the age to put away sin by the sacrifice of himself" (Heb. 9:26 RSV).

Love The generation that worshiped the calf perished **in the wilderness**, but its sinful disposition has survived it. All the embarrassing episodes from **Egypt** to the Jordan and beyond (→31:14–18) confirm that Israel has inherited both its ancestors' promises and their depravity. Israel must be as diligent to retain its consciousness of sin as to maintain its **remembrance** of YHWH's grace, or it will lapse into self-**righteousness** in times of success. Likewise, Christians must constantly confess that we "believe . . . in the forgiveness of sins."

Hope The generation at **Horeb** was "unable to enter because of unbelief" (Heb. 3:19 NRSV). Yet the conquests on the east of the Jordan and the crossing to the promised land are gifts to the very same **stiff-necked people** who repeatedly provoked God's **wrath**. God has indeed been destroying his[+] stiff-necked people (→2:34–37), not through annihilation but through the greater work of redemption (→9:4–5). The Messiah extends this pattern of restoration after condemnation: "I begged your disciples to cast it out, but they could not," said the father of a demoniac. "Jesus answered, 'You faithless and perverse generation, how much longer must I be with you and bear with you? Bring your son here.' . . .

Jesus rebuked the unclean spirit, healed the boy, and gave him back to his father. And all were astounded at the greatness of God" (Luke 9:40–43 NRSV).

> 9:9When I was gone up onto the mountain to receive the tables of stone (→5:22), even the tables of the covenant YHWH made with you (→4:11–15), then I stayed on the mountain forty days and forty nights; I neither ate bread nor drank water. 10YHWH delivered to me the two tables of stone written with the finger of God; and on them like all the words YHWH spoke with you on the mountain out of the midst of the fire in the day of the assembly. 11At the end of forty days and forty nights, YHWH gave me the two tables of stone, even the tables of the covenant (Exod. 31:18–32:8).

Faith While hopeless Israel feasts in Moses's absence (Exod. 32:1–5), Moses fasts in hope in God's presence (cf. Deut. 9:18–21). With God's help, Noah, Moses, Elijah, Ezekiel, and Jesus all persevere for **forty days** (and often **forty nights**) of trials, often without **bread** or **water**. When deliverance comes, these emissaries have been readied for the mission that follows. Here the mission is conveyance of the **covenant** to a stubbornly rebellious people who depend upon it for their whole being.

Faith The words that God writes match **the words** that God spoke. They are **alike** rather than identical in that spoken language is not identical to written language. These two forms of communication always operate in different contexts: oral agreements and written agreements carry different weights; oral exchange and written exchange have different tones. Here Moses witnesses to the correspondence of the Spirit's writ to YHWH's word. The spoken word anticipates its hardening in holy writ; holy writ maintains and conveys the life of its spoken origin; both truly mediate the powerful presence of the communicator. YHWH, his+ Word, and his+ Spirit are one, but distinct. Similarly, manifestation, writing, and speech—Martin Luther's and Karl Barth's "threefold form of the Word of God"—are one "indirect identity."

Love The Holy Spirit is **the finger of God** whose power overwhelmed Pharaoh's magicians (Exod. 8:19), cleansed Israel of demons at the advent of the kingdom of God (Luke 11:20), rules and preserves Israel through Torah, and in the coming age dwells in Israel as its new, supreme, life-giving covenantal sign and seal (Rom. 8:2; 2 Cor. 3). The Spirit is not opposed to Torah (Gal. 3:21); the Spirit and his+ Torah are both opposed distinctly to the rebelliousness that Paul calls "the flesh" (5:17). Torah is of and for the sanctifying Spirit who clears away every external and internal obstacle to maturity, freedom, and fellowship for God's people (→9:12–14).

> 9:12YHWH said to me, "Arise, get down quickly from here, for your people whom you have brought forth out of Egypt have corrupted

themselves. They have quickly turned aside (5:32–33) out of the way
I commanded them. They have made themselves a molten image."
¹³Furthermore YHWH spoke to me, saying: "I have seen this people, and
behold, it is a stiff-necked people: ¹⁴let me alone, that I may destroy
them, and blot out their name from under the sky; and I will make
of you a nation mightier and greater than they."

Faith Having associated himself⁺ with Israel's emancipation in the Decalogue
(5:6), here YHWH associates Moses with emancipated Israel in rebellion. Despite
Moses's apparent innocence of an act done while he is away (→31:24–30), he
stands judged with them. Calling Israel **your people** cements Moses's relationship
with Israel and strengthens his courage to intercede for his own.

Faith Moses does not discover the **image** is a calf until he sees it himself
(9:15–17).

Hope In Eden the man had blamed the woman and God for his predicament (Gen.
3:12), thinking only of himself and distancing himself from his own flesh and bone
and from his creator. God's association of Moses with **stiff-necked** Israel exposes
the futility of that temptation. Yet God's command to be left alone to **destroy**
Moses's own people has set that temptation squarely before Moses, putting Moses
in the impossible position of acceding to the destruction of his own people and
legacy. Moses honors God's impossible command by turning it on its head and
putting *God* in the impossible position. He descends from YHWH's presence,
but to reconcile YHWH and Israel rather than witness their destruction. "**Leaving** YHWH **alone**" in this way—defusing his sender's will to destroy sinners by
accepting his mission to remain with them—is how Moses respects YHWH's
will to make of Moses **a nation mightier and greater than** the wretched idolaters
down the mountain. They will be a people not literally descended from Moses
but kindred in the grace for which he has pleaded. The pattern recurs through
Israel's apostasy and exile in →29:16–21 and its surrounding passages. This striking fulfillment of God's will by inverting it is of course just what Jesus does in
accepting his bitter mission to become a curse for us whom the Torah condemns
(→21:22–23) in order to secure the Torah's blessings on Abraham.

Love God responds as **quickly** through his⁺ servant as Israel **turns aside** from its
sanctified end (→9:9–11). God's "holy ones" live in a constant social and personal
battle between the realms of light and darkness—the lordly Spirit versus legions
of unclean spirits. This spiritual warfare is as pitched in our day (Eph. 6:10–20)
as Moses's, and its outcome no less certain (Zech. 4:1–7; Rev. 5:6; 11:4–13).

⁹:¹⁵So I turned and came down from the mountain, and the mountain
was burning with fire: and the two tables of the covenant were in my
two hands. ¹⁶I looked, and behold, you had sinned against YHWH your
God; you had made yourselves a molten calf: you had turned aside
quickly out of the way YHWH had commanded you. ¹⁷I took hold of

the two tables, and cast them out of my two hands, and broke them before your eyes.

Hope In Exod. 32:11–14 Moses intercedes for Israel before **coming down**. Here his intercession is recounted after the story of his discovery, shock, and condemnation. Summarizing the events of Exod. 32–34 out of sequence makes the **molten calf** emblematic of Israel's habitual sinfulness and need of restoration. Israel's grave sin has jeopardized its standing before YHWH. "Those who do such things will not inherit the kingdom of God" (Gal. 5:21 NRSV). **Casting out** the copies of the covenant (→4:11–15) does not annul God's will, but indicates that in the breach the covenant must take the new and radical form (→9:18–21) of propitiation.
Faith Israel preferred a god from fire to the **fire** of God (→5:25–26). With tragic irony sin prefers the creature to the creator (→25:4), foolishness to wisdom, and condemnation to generosity (Rom. 1:22–23, 25, 32). "When you see the desolating sacrilege set up where [he] ought not to be (let the reader understand), then . . . flee" (Mark 13:14 NRSV).
Faith These verses' dramatic details both stress how critical Israel's failure has been and describe its way back. They are something of a prefigural passion narrative. The telling absurdity of the forged calf matches Israel's rejection of "Jesus of Nazareth, a man attested to you by God with mighty works and wonders and signs which God did through him in your midst" (Acts 2:22 RSV). The **molten calf** incident reveals not the agnosticism of an era in which God has long seemed absent, but outright rebellion in spite of God's power: "We have no king but Caesar" (John 19:15 RSV).
Love The **broken tablets** are a eucharistic sign of fellowship with God maintained in fidelity's breach: "The Lord Jesus on the night when he was betrayed took bread, and when he had given thanks, he broke it" (1 Cor. 11:23–24 RSV). Both the tables and Christ's body will be remade on the other side of their sufferings, and their people with them.

> [9:18]I fell down before YHWH, as at the first, forty days and forty nights. I neither ate bread nor drank water, because of all your sin that you sinned, in doing what was evil in the sight of YHWH, to provoke him[+] to anger. [19]For I was afraid of the anger and hot displeasure with which YHWH was angry against you to destroy you. But YHWH listened to me that time also. [20]YHWH was very angry with Aaron to destroy him: and I prayed for Aaron also at the same time. [21]I took your sin, the calf you had made, and burnt it with fire, and stamped it, grinding it very small, until it was as fine as dust; and I cast its dust into the brook that descended out of the mountain.

Faith Moses has obeyed YHWH and left the heights of Sinai to proclaim his[+] judgment; but then he returns **before YHWH** (10:10) and repeats his extended fast, now for renewal. The second forty-day season of Jesus's ministry occurs similarly after his rejection, passion, and vindication: he appears with his disciples preparing to "restore the kingdom to Israel" (Acts 1:6 NRSV) through the power of apostolic witness in the Holy Spirit (1:8). God's forgiveness turns the crime of Jesus's crucifixion into a new beginning for his own people and all others.

Faith The utter failure of the formal priesthood calls for intercession from the one whom the priesthood was ordained to assist. **Aaron** is spared for the time being, and his line for far longer (cf. 10:6–7). However, ultimately a priest of the order of Melchizedek will come to all Israel's aid (Heb. 7:11 on Ps. 110:4). It is from above that Israel's sin is identified, confronted, conquered, put away, and atoned for—from the covenant, the prophet, the fire, and the watery **brook** that all **descend** from **the mountain** of YHWH (→21:1–9).

Hope Moses had not shared Israel's fear of Sinai's fire (→5:4–6), which Israel had descended the mountain to flee. Now that Israel has made a god for itself from fire (→9:15–17), Moses the intercessor assumes Israel's **fear** of God's wrath. Yet he descends from Sinai with **fire** of YHWH's judgment to purge its sin. He represents both the wrath and the mercy of God.

Love In **falling down** on account of Israel's **sin**, Moses assimilates both halves of the Decalogue—fidelity to God and fidelity to neighbors—and provides an intelligible and living form of God's instruction by which Israel can learn and live.

Love In Exod. 32:14 God repents of his[+] promise to destroy Israel (32:10). God's **listening** here is a softer term for God's receptivity to Moses (but →32:26–31). Grace has brought us into the Lord's own triune life, the Spirit interceding for us when we pray according to the will of God (Rom. 8:26–27).

Love Israel had been mastered by the product of its own perversity, "under the power of sin" (Rom. 3:9 NRSV). Seizing, **burning**, and **stamping** the **calf** expose the emptiness of **sin's** power and the real power of prophetic truthfulness to deliver sin's slaves. "He[+] has put all things under his feet and has made him the head over all things for the church" (Eph. 1:22 NRSV).

> **9:22** At Taberah (Num. 11:1–3) and at Massah (Exod. 17:1–7; →6:13–16) and at Kibroth Hattaavah (Num. 11:4–34) you provoked YHWH to wrath. [23] When YHWH sent you from Kadesh-barnea (Deut. 1:20–21), saying: "Go up and possess the land I have given you," then you rebelled against the commandment of YHWH your God (1:26–28), and you did not believe him[+] or listen to his[+] voice. [24] You have been rebellious against YHWH from the day I knew you.

Faith Starting with Horeb, Moses alternates between stories he has already told and stories he has not. The effect substantiates 9:7's claim of unceasing **rebellion**, which 9:24 repeats in conclusion. Israel now has a chance to put aside the record it accumulated under Moses in the wilderness and gain a fresh start in the land under Joshua (→1:37–38; cf. Josh. 24:1–18). By contrast, the Septuagint's "**the** day he+ **knew you**" suggests that Israel will refuse to know its Savior even in Moses's absence (→31:14–18; cf. Josh. 24:19–28)—yet also that its Savior's original love will not be thwarted (→9:25–29). God's servants have since accumulated a much longer record of failures and betrayals, yet "love never fails" (1 Cor. 13:8).

Hope Despite popular impressions, YHWH is not essentially **wrathful**. God's negative qualities emerge only in holy response to ours. The contradictions of sin necessarily arouse divine contradictions of judgment against God's beloved.

> **9:25**So I fell down before YHWH the forty days and forty nights that I fell down, because YHWH had said he+ would destroy you. **26**I prayed to YHWH, and said: "Lord YHWH, do not destroy your people and your inheritance, that you have redeemed through your greatness, that you have brought forth out of Egypt with a mighty hand. **27**Remember your servants, Abraham, Isaac, and Jacob; do not turn to the stubbornness of this people, or to their wickedness, or to their sin, **28**lest they of the land you brought us out from say: 'Because YHWH was not able to bring them into the land he+ promised to them, and because he+ hated them, he+ has brought them out to kill them in the wilderness.' **29**Yet they are your people and your inheritance, which you brought out by your great power and by your outstretched arm (Exod. 32:11–13)."

Faith God has made Israel Moses's responsibility in →9:12–14. Now Moses takes responsibility by reminding God that Israel is also God's responsibility. These two are not passing the buck but negotiating Israel's role in their relationship, to Israel's benefit. Jesus's high priestly prayer works similarly: as the Son's disciples are from the Father (John 17:6), the Son works for their unity (17:12). Since they belong to the Father (17:9–10), he then pleads to the Father for their unity (17:12), that observers will know the Father in the Son (17:25–26). "I do not pray that you should take them out of the world, but that you should keep them from the evil one" (17:15 RSV, adapted).

Faith Israel's failure is complex—habitual obstinacy that reveals a wicked heart. Moses's instruction addresses all three deficiencies: his commandments (6:1–3) embody total love of Israel's one God (6:4–6) habituated in lives of practiced faithfulness (6:7–9). Christ's atonement also operates at multiple levels: its sacrifice takes away **sin** (Rom. 3:21–26); its victory conquers **wickedness** (8:31–39); and its example pours new life into **stubborn** hearts (5:2–8).

Love "Not all Israelites truly belong to Israel. . . . They are beloved for the sake of their forefathers" (Rom. 9:6 NRSV; 11:28 RSV). Moses points out that it would be wrong for the unbelieving generation of Horeb, or any other, to frustrate God's greater work in all Israel for the sake of the patriarchs and God's reputation beyond his+ **people**. "I have guarded them, and none of them is lost but the son of perdition, that the scripture might be fulfilled" (John 17:12 RSV). Moses's brilliant intercession reconnects the patriarchs, his present generation, his own acts of faithfulness, the land's future heirs, and even their Gentile oppressors in God's economy of universal salvation (→1:8; →30:17–20). God can tolerate idolatrous and rejected generations, not for their own sake but to rescue the whole people (Hos. 2 in Rom. 9:25–26), enduring "with much patience the vessels of wrath . . . in order to make known the riches of his⁺ glory for the vessels of mercy . . . not from the Jews only but also from the Gentiles" (9:22–23 RSV).

Love Moses cleverly makes one of Israel's most egregious complaints, that **YHWH hates them** (1:27), an **Egyptian** taunt. To be known in his⁺ true identity as love (Hos. 2:19), God must preserve his⁺ wayward beloved (2:14–17) while Moses pleads with her to be reconciled (2:2). "I will make [your name] known, so that the love with which you have loved me may be in them, and I in them" (John 17:26 NRSV).

DEUTERONOMY 10

^{10:1}At that time YHWH said to me, "Cut two tables of stone like the first, and come up to me onto the mountain, and make an ark of wood. ²I will write on the tables the words that were on the first tables that you broke, and you shall put them in the ark." ³So I made an ark of acacia wood, and cut two tables of stone like the first, and went up onto the mountain, having the two tables in my hand. ⁴He⁺ wrote on the tables, according to the first writing, the ten commandments, which YHWH spoke to you on the mountain out of the midst of the fire in the day of the assembly, and YHWH gave them to me. ⁵I turned and came down from the mountain, and put the tables in the ark I had made, and there they are as YHWH commanded me.

Faith Israel receives its new beginning, not for its merit (→9:4–5) but for the sake of God's legacies (→9:25–29). "They are justified by his grace as a gift . . . to show [God's] righteousness" (Rom. 3:24–25 NRSV).

Faith The **ark** makes **the words** portable. Israel will follow the Decalogue on the move through the wilderness, across the Jordan, and into the land. In the Messiah the Word will be on the move again: as the Baptist "watched Jesus walk by, he exclaimed, 'Look, here is the Lamb of God!' The two disciples heard him say this, and they followed Jesus" (John 1:36–37 NRSV).

Faith The Decalogue is now to be written on **stone** from below, hidden in an **ark** of Israel's making, and held indirectly rather than in Moses's hands. While their **words** are still from YHWH, the responsibility for bearing them along the way belongs to Israel, delegated to the Levites (10:6–9; →31:9–13). This responsibility is necessarily problematic given Israel's chronic irresponsibility—and the ark will someday be lost through that irresponsibility. Yet the word of YHWH endures despite all faithlessness (John 1:17).

Faith In this account gold is not mentioned. Whereas in Exod. 37:1–9 the **ark's** gold plating contrasts with the golden calf, here its absence yields an even starker contrast between ornate idolatry and practical obedience. "It is time for [YHWH] to act, for your law has been broken. Truly I love your commandments more than gold" (Ps. 119:126–27 NRSV).

Love In response to the golden calf incident, the ten words of Exod. 34:14–26 are dramatically different from those of Exod. 20. They liturgically remediate Israel in the face of its abject liturgical failure below Sinai. If Moses had written 34:11–26 on the other side of the same tablets, as some Jewish traditions claim, it would have been an appropriate illustration that, in the words of Protestant Reformers, "the word of God preached is the Word of God." However, here there is no indication of different words on the tablets themselves. Instead, Moses's words in Deut. 12–26 are expansions and applications of the tables' original words in Deut. 5, proper to Israel's new theological and social context. They do work like that of God's further directions in Exod. 34, moving Israel away from its embarrassing past and toward its hope (→31:24–30).

Hope Moses has worked for YHWH on sinful Israel's behalf. In contrast to Exodus, *he* has made the tables and crafted the ark, not Bezalel (Exod. 37:1–9) with others' assistance (35:10–12). His final task—the occasion for the whole of Deuteronomy—is to show all these to Israel and persuade his people to take them up in faith. Likewise, the task of showing God's kingdom and righteousness to all who will listen and enter belongs solely to Moses's antitype: "Everyone then who hears these words of mine and does them will be like a wise man who built his house on rock" (Matt. 7:24 NRSV).

> **10:6**(The sons+ of Israel traveled from Beeroth Bene Jaakan to Moserah. There Aaron died, and there he was buried; and Eleazar his son ministered in the priest's office in his place [→9:18–21; →32:48–52]. **7**From there they traveled to Gudgodah; and from Gudgodah to Jotbathah, a land of brooks of water.) **8**At that time YHWH set apart the tribe of Levi to bear the ark (→10:1–5; →31:9–13) of the covenant of YHWH, to stand before YHWH to minister to him+, and to bless in his+ name, to this day. **9**Therefore Levi has no portion or inheritance with his brothers; YHWH is his inheritance, as YHWH your God spoke to him. **10**I stayed on the mountain, as at the first time, forty days and forty nights, and YHWH listened to me that time also; YHWH would not destroy you. **11**YHWH said to me, "Arise, take your journey before the people; and they shall go in and possess the land I swore to their fathers to give them."

Faith In Deuteronomy the **Levites'** major role elsewhere in the Pentateuch (Num. 1:47–54; 3:4–39) recedes into the background, with instruction to all Israel (→1:1a) taking precedence. Like Aaron and especially Moses, the Levites' role is not to be a conventional clan but to be associated with YHWH on the one hand

and all Israel on the other, and in each capacity to face each one on the other's behalf (1 Tim. 2:1–6).

Hope The awkward parenthetical travel narrative in 10:6–7, featuring obscure place-names and chronicling a death and succession that lie in the future, anticipates YHWH's merciful command for Moses to move on from Sinai. (Some translations parenthesize 10:6–9, but 10:8–9 fit in the immediate context of 10:5 and return to referring to Israel as **you**.) God's words to Moses reflect the preceding verses' remarkable intercession by honoring both YHWH's will to start again with Moses and Moses's will to preserve his people. They return us to the scene of the opening narrative of Deuteronomy (→1:6–7a), now having supplied the necessary background for Israel's vital need to obey.

Hope Brook (*nachal*) and **inheritance** (*nachalah*) are near homonyms. Inheritance streams to the heir who **possesses** (*nachal*). The relationship between 10:6–7 and 10:8–9 is still unclear, but the wordplay might explain the juxtaposition. The verdant lands beyond the wilderness compare with God streaming to the priestly Levites as their portion. We might even imagine the living **water** of the Spirit of YHWH streaming to and through the rock and heir to his body the church as its guarantee of deliverance rather than destruction. They are analogous blessings, whether the juxtaposition here is coincidental.

> ¹⁰:¹²Now, Israel, what does YHWH your God require of you, but to fear YHWH your God, to walk in all his⁺ ways, and to love him⁺, and to serve YHWH your God with all your heart and with all your self, ¹³to keep the commandments of YHWH and his⁺ statutes I command you this day for your good? ¹⁴Behold, to YHWH your God belongs heaven and the heaven of heavens, the earth, with all that is therein. ¹⁵Only YHWH had a delight in your fathers to love them, and he⁺ chose their seed after them, even you above all peoples, as at this day. ¹⁶Circumcise therefore the foreskin of your heart, and be no more stiff-necked.

Hope "See that you do not refuse him who is speaking" (Heb. 12:25a RSV). Moses returns to his argument, now intensified by historical recollection: since **only YHWH** was behind these events, not reciprocating in **fear** of his⁺ grace (Heb. 10:17) but remaining **stiff-necked** is even greater failure. As exposure to God lengthens, God's people become more and more accountable for responding to YHWH in faith—until both the threat of judgment and the extent of deliverance are revealed as cosmic and apocalyptic, involving **heaven and the heaven of heavens, the earth, and all that is therein**. The apocalyptic scope of its dawning era pervades the New Testament as the Messiah's disciples reflect on the epochal events of their witness. "If they did not escape when they refused the one who warned them on earth, how much less will we escape if we reject the one who warns from heaven! At that time his⁺ voice shook the earth; but now he⁺

has promised, 'Yet once more I will shake not only the earth but also the heaven'" (Heb. 12:25b–26 NRSV).

Love If God acted for Israel's good when Israel was disobedient, how much more will God act **for** Israel's **good** when it **keeps the commandments**. The good news of God's grace orients its recipients toward a new and living future in lives of righteousness, for "we are receiving a kingdom that cannot be shaken" (Heb. 12:28 NRSV). If literal circumcision formally entrusts the seed of Israel's future to the God of Abraham (→30:6–10), **circumcision** of the **heart walks** in the Spirit's infilling hope (Rom. 2:29) to live (Deut. 30:6) toward God's eternal future by the power of baptism (Col. 2:11–12; →5:16).

Love Love and **service** promise blessings that correspond to the coming foreshadowing of curses (→11:1–7). God's extraordinary forgiveness is one more sign that Israel is beloved of God (7:7–8). Since God set aside the estrangement that Israel brought upon itself, Israel ought to **love** God in return (6:5) and love strangers as well as neighbors (10:19). "Her sins, which were many, have been forgiven; hence she has shown great love" (Luke 7:47 NRSV). God's love of strangers drives atonement, which funds our mission to renew and enlarge divine fellowship down the generations and across the globe. "Let mutual love continue. Do not neglect to show hospitality to strangers" (Heb. 13:1–2 NRSV).

> ^{10:17}For YHWH your God, he[+] is God of gods, and Lord of lords, the great God, the mighty, and the awesome, who does not respect persons, or take reward. ¹⁸He[+] executes justice for the fatherless and widow, and loves the foreigner, in giving him[+] food and clothing. ¹⁹Therefore love the foreigner; for you were foreigners (→10:12–16) in the land of Egypt. ²⁰You shall fear YHWH your God; you shall serve him[+], and you shall cling to him[+], and you shall swear by his[+] name. ²¹He[+] is your praise, and he[+] is your God, who has done for you these great and awesome things your eyes have seen. ²²Your fathers went down into Egypt with seventy persons; and now YHWH your God has made you as the stars of the sky for multitude.

Faith The apparently odd claim that God **does not respect persons** in fact follows from Moses's account of Israel's election. Israel will not receive blessings as a **reward** for its own righteousness; having tasted of the same destruction that all wicked nations bring on themselves, it knows its own depraved heart. As a beneficiary of the extensive mercy of a merciful God, it must turn and exercise the hospitality originally shown it when its **fathers went down into Egypt**. At that time their humiliated clan was saved from famine to become a great nation (Gen. 46:3–7; →26:1–11). Through God's mercy (→32:26–31) the world's many other outcasts can find refuge and someday become the greatest peoples in his[+] kingdom (Matt. 18:1–4). "I looked, and there was a great **multitude** that no one could count, from every nation" (Rev. 7:9 NRSV).

Hope How can a God condemning whole peoples have compassion on the **fatherless**, **widow**, and **foreigner**? Yet in these chapters both qualities reflect one consistent character. God is no mere patron of one tribe over others. As **God of gods and Lord of lords**, YHWH tolerates no petty spiritual or social tyranny as all lesser powers must (cf. 1 Cor. 8:4–6; Rev. 19:15–16). Rather, **the great God** steadfastly pursues a mysterious campaign to end all sin among all peoples through this particular people (→29:16–21). That entails withholding punishment at some times and exacting it at others, not in a pattern that shows petty favoritism or procures some earthly **reward**, but in ways consistent with the divine purpose of favor on all (Rom. 11:30–32), starting with Israel (→23:19–25).

Love The nations could read God's destruction of errant Israel as a sign of his⁺ hatred even of his⁺ own people or of their own supremacy (→32:26–31), but the implications of any divine response to sin are universal (Rom. 2:9). God's mercy on estranged Israel is conversely a sign to the nations not just that God **loves** Israel but that God loves the stranger and the **foreigner** through Israel (→9:25–28; →23:1–8; Rom. 2:10). So election of and through the patriarchs is to the service of mercy on all **persons** (Rom. 2:11) and eternal **praise**.

DEUTERONOMY 11

11:1 Therefore you shall love YHWH your God, and keep his⁺ instructions, and his⁺ statutes, and his⁺ ordinances, and his⁺ commandments, always. **2**Know this day: for I do not speak with your children who have not known, and who have not seen the chastisement of YHWH your God, his⁺ greatness, his⁺ mighty hand, and his⁺ outstretched arm, **3**and his⁺ signs, and his⁺ works, which he⁺ did in the midst of Egypt (Exod. 14:27–15:21) to Pharaoh the king of Egypt and to all his land; **4**and what he⁺ did to the army of Egypt, to their horses, and to their chariots; how he⁺ made the water of the Sea of Reeds overflow them as they pursued after you, and how YHWH has destroyed them to this day; **5**and what he⁺ did to you in the wilderness, until you came to this place; **6**and what he⁺ did to Dathan and Abiram, the sons of Eliab, the son of Reuben; how the earth opened its mouth, and swallowed them up, and their households and their tents and every living thing that followed them, in the midst of all Israel: **7**but your eyes have seen all the great work of YHWH that he⁺ did.

Plain Moses shifts from past blessings (→10:12–16) to past curses. Both rabbinic and critical commentaries note the absence of Korah alongside **Dathan and Abiram** (cf. Num. 16; Sir. 45:18). There is no need for rabbinic speculation of deference to Moses's family or for source-critical speculation on Numbers to solve the puzzle. Dathan and Abiram resisted because Moses and Aaron had led them out of **Egypt**, "a land flowing with milk and honey," and failed to bring them into another (Num. 16:13–14). Korah's complaint, that Moses and Aaron were hoarding power (16:3), does not fit the theme of God's steadfastness to liberate, sustain, and settle obstinate Israel.

Faith Moses's contemporaries bear unique responsibilities. He has already distinguished the past two generations, whose **eyes have seen all the great work of YHWH** in **Egypt** and the **wilderness**, from the patriarchs (→5:1–3). Now he distinguishes them from the **children** of the land (including Deuteronomy's readers) "who have not seen and yet believe" (John 20:29 RSV). Each link in the chain plays its distinct role in the one work of glorification. Jesus's contemporaries bear witness to his signs and wonders and mighty works of deliverance (Acts 2:22, 32; 1 Cor. 15:1–11; 1 John 1:1–4), and future generations preserve that witness in its integrity (→6:7–9) and remain alert to fresh signs of the kingdom.

Faith YHWH's judgments make known YHWH's name **within Egypt** as well as **within Israel**, "in all the earth" (Exod. 9:16, my translation). God is not merely an experience that some religiously sensitive people share or an idea hosted by a compatible worldview, but an active agent shaping a concrete cosmic history. Israelites are the primary witnesses, but Israel's enemies will **see** and **know** YHWH too (→32:40–43). "When the centurion saw what had taken place, he praised God and said: 'Truly this one was just'" (Luke 23:47, my translation).

Hope YHWH has overcome every obstacle that has threatened Israel's inheritance: **Pharaoh**, his **armies**, the **wilderness's** aridity, Israel's stubbornness, and Canaanite opponents. "The one who calls you is faithful, and he[+] will do it" (1 Thess. 5:24 RSV).

Love The living legacy of YHWH's past deliverances confirms the eternal and thus present force of the covenant. By the same logic the Spirit's continuing leadership of the church confirms to Paul the eternity and present power of "the law of Christ" (Gal. 6:2b). "The whole [Torah] is fulfilled in one word, 'You shall love your neighbor as yourself.' . . . If you are led by the Spirit you are not under the [Torah]. . . . The fruit of the Spirit is love . . . ; [not against such is the Torah]. . . . If we live by the Spirit, let us also walk by the Spirit. . . . Bear one another's burdens" (Gal. 5:14, 18, 22, 23, 25; 6:2a RSV adapted).

> **11:8**Therefore you shall keep all the commandment I command you this day, that you may be strong, and go in and possess the land you go over to possess; **9**and that you may prolong your days in the land, which YHWH swore to your fathers to give to them and to their seed, a land flowing with milk and honey. **10**For the land you go in to possess is not as the land of Egypt, that you came out from, where you sowed your seed and watered it by your foot as a garden of herbs; **11**but the land you go over to possess is a land of hills and valleys and drinks water of the rain of the sky, **12**a land YHWH your God cares for: the eyes of YHWH your God are always on it, from the beginning of the year even to the end of the year. **13**If you shall listen diligently to my commandments I command you this day, to love YHWH your God, and to serve him[+] with all your heart and with all your self, **14**"I will give the rain of your land in its season, the former rain and the latter rain, that you may gather in your grain, and your new wine,

and your oil. ¹⁵I will give grass in your fields for your livestock, and you shall eat and be full."

Plain Moses shifts from speaking of YHWH in the third to the first person. Is he claiming prophetic power to rule the skies from beyond the grave? Has YHWH been assimilated into Moses's character? Was the Deuteronomist careless? Or is the veil temporarily lifted for us to see that Moses has been constructing YHWH all along by putting words in his⁺ mouth? Adding quotation marks to 11:14–15 suggests the most natural reading: Moses is directly repeating a promise from YHWH rather than paraphrasing. This might then be akin to a "word of knowledge."

Faith Canaan's unpredictable **water** supply and vulnerable place along the trade routes among regional powers make it seem an insecure and inhospitable place for God's people. In fact, these very qualities suit a people whose God alone is their sentinel who has the water of life and has sent **them and their seed** to bless all the earth's families (→5:16). "Go . . . teaching them to obey all I have commanded you. And behold, I am with you always, to the end of the age" (Matt. 28:19–20, my translation).

Hope Evangelical interpretation of Joel 2:23 saw in Canaan's agricultural seasons the first and second comings of Jesus Christ or the establishment and restoration of the church, perhaps through the first-century and twentieth-century Pentecostal outpourings of the Holy Spirit. Joel 2:28's "after this" suggests otherwise: all the preceding blessings anticipate the apostles' Pentecost. Yet the **rain**, **grain**, **new wine**, **oil**, **grass**, and **being full** in this passage do carry eschatological significance. Ordinary blessings of Israel in the **land** (along with others such as Sabbath rest, children, and peace) become stock images of extraordinary restoration in the fullness of time, and the absence of the **former** drives sufferers to hope in the **latter**. Every day, every week, every season, and every annual cycle foreshadow the age to come, not just before the first advent but also now as we prepare for the last.

Love The old covenant included **land**. Where is it in the new? Canaan is the church. Forty years in the dry wilderness have been retraining Israel to know that **water** from God is not assumed and manipulated like magic or water carried **by foot**, but provided and received from **the sky** in love. We are to reap Canaan's renewal (→32:40–43) by having Canaan's climate, drinking in the Spirit and becoming gushing springs (John 4:14) that sustain fruit harvested for eternal life (4:34–36).

Love Moses's rhetoric for **Egypt's** environment is a confined garden, but for Canaan's expansive fields. Egypt's crops were predictable, dull, and limited; Canaan's coming harvests are surprising, adventurous, and plentiful.

> ¹¹:¹⁶Take heed to yourselves, lest your heart be deceived, and you turn aside, and serve other gods, and worship them; ¹⁷and the anger of YHWH be kindled against you, and he⁺ shut up the sky, so that there shall be no rain, and the land shall not yield its fruit; and you

perish quickly from off the good land YHWH gives you. [18]Therefore you shall lay up these my words in your heart and in yourself; and you shall bind them for a sign on your hand, and they shall be for symbols between your eyes. [19]You shall teach them to your children, talking of them, when you sit in your house, and when you walk by the way, and when you lie down, and when you rise up. [20]You shall write them on the doorposts of your house, and on your gates (6:7–9); [21]that your days may be multiplied, and the days of your children, in the land YHWH swore to your fathers to give them, as the days of the heavens above the earth.

Hope The God of the heavens is supplying Israel with eternal **words** as well as seasonal rain (cf. 8:3). To spurn one is to forego the other and refuse the common point of both. "**Store up** for yourselves treasures in heaven. . . . For where your treasure is, there **your heart** will be also" (Matt. 6:20–21 NRSV).

Love Surprisingly, God is as active in **shutting up the sky** as in regularly giving rain and grass (11:14–15). Modern naturalism denies both, while conventional Western supernaturalism reckons one a plausible intervention against the normal operation of the other. Moses does not interpret either the weather or the times through a dichotomy between the physical and the spiritual. For him, both Canaan's typical seasons and its occasional droughts, as well as wars of human doing and wonders of no natural explanation, serve God's purposes. To cultures used to reducing analysis to efficient causes, this could seem primitive and unscientific. But that would misunderstand the Mosaic paradigm. Throughout the Pentateuch God has shaped Israel by situating it in a variety of environments (e.g., 8:2–6). Israel in the land and later in exile will be shaped by further divine warnings and judgments, through natural means as well as supernatural. Moses's theological meteorology reflects the covenantal quality of Israel's life, in which both the ordinary and the extraordinary are charged with purpose and accountability. No conditions, fair or foul, relieve God's people of the responsibility of discerning the times and responding faithfully. Israel and then the church maintain this sensibility across their many cultural shifts through the Old Testament, intertestamental, and New Testament periods. Modernity's inability to accommodate it is a sign of its own limits, not the limits of Israel's prescientific mindset.

[11:22]For if you shall diligently keep all this commandment that I command you, to do it, to love YHWH your God, to walk in all his[+] ways, and to cling to him[+]; [23]then YHWH will drive out all these nations from before you, and you shall dispossess nations greater and mightier (→7:1) than yourselves. [24]Every place your foot shall tread on shall be yours: from the wilderness, and Lebanon, from the river, the river Euphrates, even to the hinder sea shall be your border. [25]No man shall be able to stand before you: YHWH your God shall lay the fear of you and the dread of you on all the land you shall tread on, as he⁺ has spoken to you.

Faith Moses's assurances (→9:1–3) are repeatedly combined with warnings of the consequences of arrogance (9:4–7), disobedience (9:8–10:11), and forgetfulness (10:12–11:9). The Torah is not out of reach (→30:11–16), but only a truly faithful Israel will gain and hold the land of promise. One day "the cornerstone of Judah" will forever restore the land (Zech. 9–10).

Hope Moses uses an inspiring image: as Israel **walks** in faith YHWH's promise will unfold, all the way to its full extent (→1:7b). Yet "the earth is [YHWH's] and all that is in it" (Ps. 24:1 NRSV), so Canaan's borders are not his⁺ people's final boundaries. Jesus repeatedly crosses over into Gentile country, then assures his disciples that "you will receive power when the Holy Spirit has come upon you; and you will be my witnesses in Jerusalem, in all Judea and Samaria, and to the ends of the earth" (Acts 1:8 NRSV). Despite every opposition, they indeed bear the good news unhindered even to Rome (28:30–31).

Hope Moses's term **the hinder sea** for the Mediterranean implies that he is facing east with his back to the land, facing the Israelites who will conquer the land he cannot enter. Just as aptly, traditional Christian architecture placed pulpits to the side, as preacher and audience all stand in the same position with respect to God's promises. So our words "encourage one another" and we "build one another up" (1 Thess. 4:18; 5:11 RSV).

Love Like Pharaoh, many work all their lives to inspire **dread** in others. God grants fearsomeness to unlikely Israel, not through strategic or numerical superiority but simply because they **cling to** God (→4:3–4). Holiness terrifies us because we are unable to frustrate it, corrupt it, co-opt it, compromise with it, **stand before** it, or even comprehend it. "Who will accuse the elect of God?" (Rom. 8:33, my translation). One can, however, submit to it and enter into its strength. Peter originally trembles before Jesus and begs him to depart from him (Luke 5:7–9), but following the Lord turns him into a personification of Moses's fulfilled word: a witness whose boldness inspires fear among authorities, crowds, and even colleagues (Acts 4–5).

> ¹¹:²⁶Behold, I set before you this day a blessing and a curse (Deut. 27–28): ²⁷the blessing, if you shall listen to the commandments of YHWH your God I command you this day; ²⁸and the curse, if you shall not listen to the commandments of YHWH your God, but turn aside out of the way I command you this day, to go after other gods, which you have not known. ²⁹When YHWH your God shall bring you into the land you go to possess, you shall set the blessing on Mount Gerizim, and the curse on Mount Ebal. ³⁰Are they not beyond the Jordan, behind the way of the going down of the sun, in the land of

the Canaanites who dwell in the Arabah, over against Gilgal, beside the oaks of Moreh? [31]For you are to pass over the Jordan to go in to possess the land YHWH your God gives you, and you shall possess it, and dwell therein. [32]You shall do all the statutes and the ordinances I set before you this day.

Plain It is hard to reconcile the scene at **Gilgal** in Josh. 4:24–5:12 with the geographical details here and in Deut. 27. Still, both locations are associated with restoration, witness, and judgment (2 Kgs. 2:1–2; Hos. 9:15; Amos 4:4).

Faith What Scholastic theology calls "operative grace" from God's sheer initiative implies "cooperative grace" as Israel bears what it had received into its new context. **Listening** and **turning aside** are both aural and spatial: people turn toward speakers to follow what they are saying and away from those they wish to ignore (cf. Luke 5:1). Willingness to turn is what it means to "have ears to hear" God's promises and warnings (8:8; 14:35). And **setting** down the **blessing** that has been **set before** us is the core task of apostleship (Acts 1:2, 21–25; 2:42).

Hope On the day of the Son of Man "there will be two in one bed; one will be taken and the other left. There will be two women grinding meal together; one will be taken and the other left" (Luke 17:34–35 NRSV). **Gerizim** and **Ebal** are two small mountains in the center of Canaan only two miles apart, between which its western road (**the way of the going down of the sun**) may have run. As the setting of Deut. 27's covenant inaugural, they symbolize the immanence of the consequences of obedience and disobedience on Israel in the land. Like the kingdom of God, these judgments of **blessing** and **curse** are in Israel's very midst (Luke 17:20–21). **To pass over the Jordan** is like entering the kingdom: it draws nearer to God's eschatological goal to **dwell therein**, approaching and so inviting God's judgment for restoration and purification.

Love Abraham traveled to **the oaks of Moreh**, where YHWH promised the land to his seed, and he subsequently built an altar there (Gen. 12:6). **Blessing** and **curse** is the legacy of his whole saga: "Go from your country and your kindred and your father's house to the land that I will show you. I will make of you a great nation, and I will bless you, and make your name great, so that you will be a blessing. I will bless those who bless you, and the one who curses you I will curse; and in you all the families of the earth shall be blessed" (12:1–3 NRSV). Combining that scene with the present one sets the Torah's commandments in that ultimately ecclesial framework, as a means by which Israel will become a blessing and curse to itself and then to all others.

DEUTERONOMY 12

12:1 These are the statutes and the ordinances you shall do in the land YHWH, the God of your fathers, has given you to possess all the days you live on the earth.

Hope Is this Torah only for life **in the land**, or is it for **all** time? Jewish and other traditions, including the Christian faith, have taken various complex stances in the long argument over that question. Moses's last introduction here to **the statutes and ordinances** makes the land a lifelong gift to Israel and makes the Torah life in and for that land. Torah observance concerns possession of the land of God's promises, and many provisions specifically have Canaan as their context. Yet as a contextualization and amplification of the Decalogue, the Torah applies in some sense beyond Canaan (Isa. 2:3) and even into the apostolic age in which God's people wait for Messiah's return (Jas. 2:8; 1 Cor. 9:8–10).

12:2 You shall surely destroy all the places in which the nations you shall dispossess served their gods, on the high mountains, and on the hills, and under every green tree: **3**and you shall break down their altars, and dash in pieces their pillars, and burn their Asherim with fire; and you shall cut down the engraved images of their gods; and you shall destroy their name out of that place.

Faith As this is the first of Moses's ordinances and corresponds to the beginning of the Decalogue, one suspects that it is also the real reason behind the wiping out of the nations. The Torah punishes Israelite idolatry just as vociferously (→13:12–18). Israel's downfall will in fact be its failure to **destroy** or refuse the temptations of foreign and Canaanite idolatry (e.g., 1 Kgs. 11:1–10; 12:25–33; 15:14; 16:25–26, 31–33), and the idols of its captors will be a snare all the way to the end of the age (Rev. 2:20–23). Its restoration will be as a body that bears "the marks of Jesus" (Gal. 6:17) and so bears no other **name** and no other gospel.

Hope Both cosmic and personal sanctification move from the obvious and grand (**on mountains**) to the hidden and miniscule (**under trees**), but not from the important to the trivial. The depths that lie beyond our powers of vision are not negligible, but matters for the Holy Spirit (Eph. 5:11–14), who alone can discern all things (1 Cor. 2:14–15).

Love If in the messianic age the land is now the church (→11:8–15), the land's cleansing is now the church's purification. Moses's orders are then that we "no longer live as the Gentiles live, in the futility of their minds" (Eph. 4:17 NRSV) but put away our old corporate self and take on the new (4:22–23). Abolishing every evil **name** that has no **place** in Christ's baptismal—sacrificed and restored—body (5:1–5) is taking up residence in Christ (4:24) as the Spirit takes up residence in us (5:15–19) and the Lord Jesus Christ is named (5:20; →12:4–7).

> ^{12:4}You shall not do so to YHWH your God. ⁵But to the place YHWH your God shall choose out of all your tribes, to put his⁺ name there, even to his⁺ habitation you shall seek, and there you shall come; ⁶and there you shall bring your burnt offerings, and your sacrifices, and your tithes, and the wave offering of your hand, and your vows, and your freewill offerings, and the firstborn of your herd and of your flock: ⁷and there you shall eat before YHWH your God, and you shall rejoice in all you put your hand to, you and your households, in which YHWH your God has blessed you.

Faith **You shall not do** what? Destroy YHWH's name from Canaan (cf. 12:3b)? Worship according to sheer personal preference (12:8)? Or worship with images on mountains, at altars, and under pillars and trees (12:2–3a)? The lack of an obvious antecedent is puzzling. A popular but grammatically unlikely answer is that Moses is forbidding decentralized worship (12:5). All these answers are acceptable theologically, and they work together plausibly, but the first is the starkest and most interesting. Moses has already warned Israel not to forget YHWH after it settles (→6:10–12). Ancient and contemporary pagan "faith"—its habits of projection, superstition, magical thinking, fealty to power, and debilitating fear of the unknown, whether directed at one high god, a whole pantheon, or social principalities and powers—is a shallow substitute for trust in YHWH, but a substitute nonetheless. One will inevitably expel the other from a place, for "you cannot serve two masters" (Luke 16:13, my translation). Neglecting the Holy Spirit will invite armies of unclean spirits back into a land—even the new land that is the church—and leave it worse than before (11:24–26).

Love **Tribes** is literally metonymic, meaning the lands belonging to the tribes (12:14), yet the word's significance is ultimately greater. YHWH's **name** dwells in the tabernacle (12:21; 26:2) and then the Jerusalem temple (1 Kgs. 9:3; 14:21). Yet through their Levitical priests God also puts his⁺ name on all Israel (Num. 6:22–27; →28:7–14). These two chosen places, the temple and the tribes of Israel, converge in the lion of the tribe of Judah (Rev. 5:5) whose body is the destroyed and risen temple (John 2:21; Rev. 21:3, 22). Upon him God has put the name above every name (Phil. 2:5–11). In the fullness of time, then, the Israel of God comes to the Lord's table with **offerings** of ministry and its support (2:17; 4:18), **sacrifices** of worship (Rom. 12:1), **tithes** to the living one (Heb. 7:8), apostolic **vows** (Acts 18:18), and heaven's very **firstborn** (Heb. 12:23) to **eat before YHWH** in remembrance (1 Cor. 11:25) and to **rejoice** in the lamb's blessings (1 Thess. 5:16). These gatherings are not decentralized or idiosyncratic worship; indeed, because the Lord's body is one (Eph. 4:4–6), the church's devotion in the Spirit centralizes worship across the ages and among all nations and **households** in ways the old rites never could.

> [12:8]You shall not do as all we do here this day, a man[+] whatever is right in his[+] own eyes; [9]for you have not yet come to the rest and to the inheritance YHWH your God gives you. [10]But when you go over the Jordan and dwell in the land YHWH your God causes you to inherit, and he[+] gives you rest from all your enemies around you, so that you dwell in safety; [11]then to the place YHWH your God shall choose, to cause his[+] name to dwell there, you shall bring all I command you: your burnt offerings, and your sacrifices, your tithes, and the wave offering of your hand, and all your choice vows that you vow to YHWH. [12]You shall rejoice before YHWH your God, you, and your sons, and your daughters, and your male servants, and your female servants, and the Levite who is within your gates (→12:15–19), because he[+] has no portion or inheritance with you. [13]Take heed to yourself that you do not offer your burnt offerings in every place you see; [14]but in the place YHWH shall choose in one of your tribes, there you shall offer your burnt offerings, and there you shall do all I command you.

Faith The phrase **right in his[+] own eyes**, buttressed by **every place you see**, soon gains a tragic overtone (Judg. 21:25) as idiosyncratic worship, syncretism, and tribalism cloud Israel's judgment. While here it refers only to worship, worship is a leading indicator of all of life. "We walk by faith, not by sight" (2 Cor. 5:7 NRSV). As Israel is to make and harbor no sacred images (Deut. 4:15–20; 5:8–10; 12:2–3), so Israel is to worship not as it sees but as YHWH has chosen. Israel saw no form at Horeb or even in Egypt as the Holy Spirit worked deliverance. Unless it remembers what it saw of its invisible God (→4:9–10), Israel will lose its sense of reality. It will misinterpret Canaan's phenomena in all the ways that lead naturally to paganism. It will try to harness their power sinfully by turning them into sacred spaces disconnected from that story. So it is in the messianic age, where rumors of Christ's appearance are self-discrediting (Mark 13:21–23) and where "blessed are those who have not seen and yet believe" (John 20:29 RSV).

Hope Shifting from promise to fulfillment changes the rules for worship by altering its character from expectation to remembrance. The unashamedly celebratory character of Israel's worship in the land intensifies in the messianic age. As Israel's worship shifts from penitence in the wilderness to celebration in Canaan, so John the Baptist fasts in the desert while the Son of Man eats and drinks with friends (Matt. 11:18–19). The master's faithful waiters enter into his joy (25:21, 23). This is already true in the persecuted church, because its safety is already sure. "Even if I am to be poured as a libation . . . I am glad and **rejoice** with you all" (Phil. 2:17 RSV). Yet Christian worship at the ends of the ages naturally features both kinds of devotion. Jesus's church, already celebrating the breaking in of the new in the midst of the old, must nevertheless wait and prepare for the final shift and the joyful banquet that will follow (Matt. 25:1–13).

Hope Theophanies and tabernacle can focus Israel's worship in the wilderness, but no one **place** can, for while God is in its midst Israel's goal still lies ahead and in the future. Only once Israel inherits its **rest** can it focus on God in God's established holy place. Deuteronomy's life in and for the land is the church's life in and for the kingdom of heaven. Heaven is God's chosen place for his+ chosen and exalted one, and Christ's session is the rest his disciples strive to enter (Heb. 4:1–11 on Ps. 95) as we draw near his throne (Heb. 4:14–16). Christ's ascension orients his church to "seek the things that are above, where Christ is, seated at the right hand of God," and toward the glory that will come with him (Col. 3:1–4 NRSV).

> 12:15Notwithstanding, you may kill and eat flesh within all your gates (→28:49–52), after all the desire of your soul, according to the blessing of YHWH your God that he+ has given you: the unclean and the clean may eat of it, as of the gazelle and the hart. 16Only you shall not eat the blood (→12:20–28); you shall pour it out on the earth as water. 17You may not eat within your gates the tithe of your grain, or of your new wine, or of your oil (→24:17–22), or the firstborn of your herd or of your flock, or any of your vows that you vow, or your freewill offerings, or the wave offering of your hand; 18but you shall eat them before YHWH your God in the place YHWH your God shall choose, you, and your son, and your daughter, and your male servant, and your female servant, and the Levite who is within your gates: and you shall rejoice before YHWH your God in all you put your hand to. 19Take heed to yourself that you do not forsake the Levite as long as you live in your land.

Faith Not all **eating** is explicit worship. Turning all of life into formal liturgy is not only impractical but ignores humanity's mission to represent God through its focus on creation (Gen. 2:15). Israel's faith necessarily includes the profane along with the sacred (→15:19–23). Jesus's respect for the profane disturbs the Pharisees who pursue Israel's redemption through its thorough sacralization.

Hope Israel's complex life of sacred and profane does not imply the static two-level universe of many paganisms, but points forward to new creation in the fullness of time.

Hope God directs Peter to **kill and eat** the things he[+] has made clean (Acts 10:9–16). This is not to diversify Israel's diet but to include **the unclean** with **the clean** at the Lord's table (10:34–35), as God has shown that no one should anymore be called profane or unclean (10:28). The apostles celebrate this **blessing** by feasting for days within the gates of Cornelius's newly baptized household (10:48).

Hope Omnivorism is sometimes described as a divine concession to human depravity, but in Genesis it is a blessing. Following God's judgment and Noah's sacrifice (Gen. 8:20–22), God grants humanity new and greater dominion by allowing the eating of flesh (9:1–4). The human **desire** for meat, then, carries eschatological resonance. Significantly, the risen Jesus eats "the fish of the sea" (9:2) with his companions (Luke 24:42–43), and his Spirit-filled church situates the Noachic covenant within God's eschatological purpose of unifying all nations in Christ (Acts 15:13–21).

Love Children, **servants**, and **Levites** might not seem to be heirs. Their deliberate inclusion here shows that the church is not a class society in which only some inherit. We "are all one in Christ Jesus . . . heirs according to promise" (Gal. 3:28–29 RSV). Christians must be vigilant to identify in our own midst the heirs whom our culture and even our faith train us to overlook (→23:1–8).

Love Supporting the priestly tribe taxes the rest of Israel while offering no corresponding material benefits. In such an arrangement cynicism is a constant danger on all sides: the priesthood will be tempted to corruption, while the other tribes will be tempted to neglect it and seek a less onerous arrangement. Sure enough, Israel rejects Samuel's sons and calls for civil order through a king styled after the nations' rulers (1 Sam. 8). Paid clergy today face the same temptations and resentments. Indeed, Reformation-era Europe's ecclesiastical rot, theological revolution, and decline into modernity are a kind of replay of the rise of the Israelite monarchy in the Christian era from which the church has not yet recovered. Deuteronomy addresses our problem by reversing Israel's imaginative spiritual hierarchy: it is not the priests who are responsible for the people but the converse. Israel must "take ownership" of its **Levites** and **rejoice** with them over the God-given fruit of its labor. The Levites are not an income tax for civil service but a **tithe**, a living sign that Israel's sacrifices are received with the free and abundant **blessing of YHWH**. In a secular arrangement like the modern welfare state, supporting an inefficient clergy can be a prophetic sign against the absolutism of civil authority. Under pressure to satisfy worldly powers, disciples of Jesus "render to Caesar the things that are Caesar's" but also "to God the things that are God's" (Luke 20:20–26 RSV).

> **12:20**When YHWH your God shall enlarge your border, as he[+] has promised you, and you shall say: "I want to eat meat," because your soul

desires to eat meat; you may eat meat, after all the desire of your soul. [21]If the place that YHWH your God shall choose, to put his[+] name there, is too far from you, then you shall kill of your herd and of your flock, which YHWH has given you, as I have commanded you; and you may eat within your gates, after all the desire of your soul. [22]Even as the gazelle and as the hart is eaten, so you shall eat of it: the unclean and the clean may eat of it alike. [23]Only be sure that you do not eat the blood: for the blood is the life; and you shall not eat the life with the flesh. [24]You shall not eat it; you shall pour it out on the earth as water. [25]You shall not eat it; that it may go well with you, and with your children after you, when you shall do what is right in the eyes of YHWH. [26]Only your holy things that you have, and your vows, you shall take, and go to the place YHWH shall choose: [27]and you shall offer your burnt offerings, the flesh and the blood, on the altar of YHWH your God; and the blood of your sacrifices shall be poured out on the altar of YHWH your God; and you shall eat the flesh. [28]Observe and hear all these words I command you, that it may go well with you, and with your children after you forever, when you do what is good and right in the eyes of YHWH your God.

Plain **Eating** to appropriate another's qualities or life force, as some cultures have done, supposes life to be transferable and independent of the creator: the *nephesh* (here **soul**; "self" in 6:5, translatable elsewhere also as "life, person, inner being") would consume another *nephesh* from which to draw strength to live. To **pour out** the **blood**, on either the **earth** or the **altar**, makes the proper distinction between the gift of life and its giver. What is eaten is no longer living or life-giving, merely food. Scientific cultures no longer regard blood as **life**, so this imagery has lost much of its force (→30:6–10). Nevertheless, eating food rather than life trains us to place trust in YHWH as life-giver.

Hope These are practices for Israel's near age of fulfillment: they imply rest from enemies and an Israel so spread out that the tabernacle is inconveniently far. Their dietary regulations concern only that former era, for Christians "have an altar from which those who officiate in the tent have no right to eat" (Heb. 13:10 NRSV). Still, this passage guides us who sacrifice with praise at Christ's **altar** (13:15–16). As the new "land" that spans nations and kingdoms (Acts 15:23–29), the church has as its only **border** the boundary between futility and hope that its people cross in baptism, and its rest is the confidence of life from the dead that its people remember through communion. Since God has **put his[+] name** on the gathered earthly body and its heavenly head (→12:4–14), the limiting factor is no longer a family's distance from the tabernacle or temple but the availability of the gathering itself. So the eschatological context of this passage's two sets of rules is what the Orthodox Church calls "the liturgy" and "the liturgy after the liturgy." Our **holy things** and **vows** are for when we are in the Lord Jesus Christ's presence (Matt. 18:20; 1 Cor. 5:4–5). When Christians are not in church, **the clean** enjoy YHWH's blessings even with **the unclean** in joyful and evangelistic hospitality with outsiders.

Love We honor, confuse, or oppose our ecclesial and our mundane lives in how we treat **the life with the flesh**. If the giver of life is the Spirit of YHWH (Ps. 104:30), then drinking **blood** would grasp after the Spirit, and offering it to any presence besides YHWH would offer the Spirit to other powers. This is absurd. The Spirit can be received only as given. So worship offers life on an **altar** to YHWH from whom it came, and profane life returns it to the **earth** YHWH first enlivened (Gen. 1:24–25).

> **12:29**When YHWH your God shall cut off the nations from before you where you go in to dispossess them, and you dispossess them and dwell in their land, **30**take heed to yourself that you not be ensnared to follow them, after they are destroyed from before you; and that you not inquire after their gods, saying: "How do these nations serve their gods? I will do likewise." **31**You shall not do likewise to YHWH your God: for every abomination to YHWH, which he⁺ hates, have they done to their gods; for even their sons and their daughters do they burn in the fire to their gods. **32**Whatever thing I command you, that you shall do: you shall not add thereto, or reduce it (→4:1–2).

Faith "To the rest of you in Thyatira . . . I say, I do not lay on you any other burden; only hold fast to what you have until I come" (Rev. 2:23–25 NRSV).

Love The line between idolatry and syncretism is often imaginary. Aaron fashions **gods** to lead Israel (Exod. 32:1) as (or upon?) a golden calf (32:4), then calls their frenzy a festival to YHWH (32:5–6). In folk religion, overactive curiosity and undisciplined reason enslave people in occult superstition that is commonly folded into the Christian faith. Among the learned the same combination drives successions of intellectual fads and frivolities that disfigure the societies they are intended to save. Many of these ideologies spread for generations after their folly has become obvious, so that believers in effect sacrifice **their sons and their daughters** to their lusts and illusions. Both neocolonialism's romantic nostalgia for great civilizations and postcolonialism's romantic nostalgia toward the cultures of conquered peoples make their adherents particularly vulnerable to the temptation to **inquire after** the lost ways of their own or others' ancestors and **do likewise** toward a new end. The gnostic Christian pluralism now fashionable among some scholars of antiquity, the trendy, selective, and shallow revivalism of pre-Columbian religions in the Americas, and the constant readaptation of Marxism in social studies and even theology after a century of spectacular failures are only several of many contemporary examples. The call to baptism confronts us with a definitive end to futility (Eph. 4:17). The baptismal church accepts God's righteous rejection of our "former way of life" (4:22) and lives through sharing in Jesus's resurrection. Minds that are so renewed (4:23–24) heed the Spirit's warnings against subsequent idolatry: "You have already spent enough time in doing what the Gentiles like to do. . . . They will have to give an accounting to him who stands ready to judge the living and the dead" (1 Pet. 4:3–5 NRSV).

DEUTERONOMY 13

13:1 If there arise in your midst a prophet or a dreamer of dreams, and he⁺ give you a sign or a wonder, **²**and the sign or the wonder come to pass of which he⁺ told you, "Let us go after other gods" (which you have not known) "and let us serve them," **³**you shall not listen to the words of that prophet or to that dreamer of dreams. For YHWH your God proves you, to know whether you love YHWH your God with all your heart and with all your self. **⁴**You shall walk after YHWH your God, and fear him⁺, and keep his⁺ commandments, and obey his⁺ voice, and you shall serve him⁺, and cling to him⁺. **⁵**That prophet or that dreamer of dreams shall be put to death, because he⁺ has spoken falsehood toward YHWH your God, who brought you out of the land of Egypt, and redeemed you out of the house of bondage, to draw you aside out of the way YHWH your God commanded you to walk in. So you shall put away the evil from your midst.

Faith "Beware that no one leads you astray. Many will come in my name and say: 'I am he!'" (Mark 13:5–6) or "'There he is!'" (13:21–22). Works of power bring amazement, and amazement without discernment yields uncritical submission (→18:20–22). The **other gods** who are most powerful today are "secular" principalities that command millions with promises of peace and prosperity. "In amazement the whole earth followed the beast. They worshiped the dragon . . . and they worshiped the beast, saying, 'Who is like the beast, and who can fight against it?'" (Rev. 13:3–4 NRSV). YHWH's **signs** and **wonders** are like these miracles in amazing many, but unlike them in that they **redeem** the dragon's captives. Those who **have known** God's son and heir (Mark 12:6–7) will not be deceived. Our obedience is unlike the compliance of the nations, reflecting the trust of a free people (Rev. 13:8).

Love "He said to them, 'Why are you afraid? Have you still no faith?' And they were filled with great awe and said to one another, 'Who then is this?'" (Mark

4:40–41 NRSV). Awe takes time to develop into trust, let alone **love**. Immature disciples are susceptible to being drawn **aside** to **falsehood**. While Jesus discounts the fickle support of crowds whose awe and obedience fade when he withholds his wonders, the Spirit is vigilant in the **midst** of God's people to **prove** its holy ones. The church that Augustine called a *corpus mixtum* is not a passive mixture of faith and unfaith but a continuing struggle to be itself. It no longer excises **evil** by execution, but by discernment of spirits (1 John 4:1–6), self-discipline (5:21), and perseverance. "Here is ... the endurance of the saints, those who keep the commandments of God and the faith of Jesus" (Rev. 14:12 RSV).

Hope In the interval between the kingdom's two advents, the time for actively punishing false prophets has passed. The church casts not stones at them but woes (e.g., Luke 6:26), not least because people have so often rendered the wrong verdicts. Warnings are sufficient because in rejecting God's powerful grace, deceivers flee to so-called strongholds that are really at the doomed margins of the old creation, making themselves finally irrelevant. "You who forsake [YHWH], who forget my holy mountain, who set a table for Fortune and fill cups of mixed wine for Destiny; I will destine you to the sword, and all of you shall bow down to the slaughter; because, when I called, you did not answer, when I spoke, you did not listen, but you did what was evil in my sight, and chose what I did not delight in. Therefore thus says [YHWH] God: My servants shall eat, but you shall be hungry; my servants shall drink, but you shall be thirsty; my servants shall rejoice, but you shall be **put to** shame" (Isa. 65:11–13 NRSV; cf. Luke 6:25).

> **13:6**If your brother, the son of your mother, or your son, or your daughter, or the wife of your bosom, or your friend, who is as your own self, entice you secretly, saying: "Let us go and serve other gods," which you have not known, you or your fathers; **7**of the gods of the peoples who are around you, near to you, or far off from you, from the one end of the earth even to the other end of the earth; **8**you shall not consent to him or her or listen to him⁺; neither shall your eye pity him⁺, neither shall you spare, neither shall you conceal him⁺: **9**but you shall surely kill him⁺; your hand shall be first on him⁺ to put him⁺ to death, and afterward the hand of all the people. **10**You shall stone him⁺ to death with stones, because he⁺ has sought to draw you away from YHWH your God, who brought you out of the land of Egypt, out of the house of bondage. **11**All Israel shall hear, and fear, and shall not do any more such wickedness as this is in your midst.

Faith Loyalty is a power even stronger than awe (→13:1–5). Human family and social ties are necessary and good, but sin exploits them for destructive purposes. Corruption twists them into rivalries of God by pressuring the loyal to compromise while maintaining the appearance of integrity: "You will say, 'Do here also in your hometown the things that we have heard you did at Capernaum'" (Luke 4:23 NRSV). Such manipulation is a heinous distortion of the very relationships that make us human (Gen. 2:24).

Faith God's justice inevitably contradicts and exposes these quietly imperious loyalties (Luke 12:2–3; →13:12–18). But whereas the Torah commends this by public disclosure, the gospel accomplishes it by inversion—by provoking a reaction to God's publicly offered grace. The results turn the scene in Deuteronomy on its head: "They . . . led him to the brow of the hill on which their town was built, so that they might hurl him off the cliff" (Luke 4:29 NRSV). "You will be betrayed even by parents and brothers[+], by relatives and friends; and they will put some of you to death. You will be hated by all because of my name" (21:16–17 NRSV).

Hope Loyalty to God overrides corrupted loyalties to family and friends: "Whoever comes to me and does not hate father and mother, wife and children, brothers and sisters, yes, and even life itself, cannot be my disciple" (Luke 14:26 NRSV). Yet Deuteronomy's judicial procedure is impractical. A traitor might frame someone by alleging a private conspiracy. Protecting the innocent requires safeguards such as multiple witnesses (→17:2–7; →19:15–21), which can weaken the provision to the point of unenforceability; and the social cost of disloyalty to allies tempts groups to ignore the rule until whole societies are compromised (→12:8–14). By contrast, confrontation with the aim of reconciliation, publicized only as necessary and without criminal sanction (Matt. 18:14–20), advances the same goals without the liability to the same abuse—and with the possibility of restoration, for "if he[+] listens . . . , you have gained your **brother**[+]" (18:15 RSV).

Love The irony of ones so close betrayed for the sake of **gods** from **afar** reveals the act's sheer perversity. As in Eden, so in Canaan: apostasy sacrifices fellowship in the pursuit of alienation.

Love Consent, **listening**, **pity**, **sparing**, and **concealment** are the temptations of those who love. To give in to them is **more wickedness**, whose pact to overlook the betrayal betrays the Savior's loyalty all over again. It forsakes YHWH's exodus from **Egypt** in order to build a new **house of bondage**. For forgiven sinners to judge their loved ones is wrenching, but the alternative is worse for everyone: "Whoever denies me before others, I also will deny before my Father in heaven. . . . Whoever loves father or mother more than me is not worthy of me; and whoever loves son or daughter more than me is not worthy of me" (Matt. 10:33–37 NRSV). Yet whoever "loses his or her **self** for my sake will find it" (10:39, my translation).

> **13:12**If you shall hear in one of your cities that YHWH your God gives you to dwell there, **13**"Worthless men are gone out from your midst and have drawn away the inhabitants of their city, saying: 'Let us go and serve other gods,'" which you have not known; **14**then you shall inquire, and search, and ask diligently; and, behold, if it be truth, and the thing certain, that such abomination is done in your midst, **15**you

shall surely strike the inhabitants of that city with the edge of the sword, destroying it utterly, and all that is therein and its livestock with the edge of the sword. **¹⁶**You shall gather all its spoil into the midst of its street, and shall burn with fire the city, and all its spoil every whit, to YHWH your God. It shall be a heap forever, it shall not be built again. **¹⁷**Nothing of the offered thing shall cling to your hand; that YHWH may turn from the fierceness of his⁺ anger, and show you mercy and show you love (30:3), and multiply you, as he⁺ has sworn to your fathers; **¹⁸**when you shall listen to the voice of YHWH your God, to keep all his⁺ commandments I command you this day, to do what is right in the eyes of YHWH your God.

Faith The corruption of a few eventually corrupts the many. But "nothing is covered up that will not be uncovered, and nothing secret that will not become known" (Matt. 10:26 NRSV). A whole **city's** sin cannot remain concealed like a family secret (→13:6–11), at least not for long. The report of apostasy in 13:13 is worded confusingly, but clearly has the quality of hearsay. A process of careful investigation is thus in order, which yields truly public findings—a judgment vindicating or condemning a whole civil society. Due process comes differently in the new covenant: from Christ's given Paraclete, who convicts the world of sin and justice and judgment, for "the ruler of this world has been condemned" (John 16:8–11 NRSV) and the Son vindicated in glory (16:14).

Hope A lost town is no different than Canaanite *cherem* (→2:34–37). Having forfeited its covenantal standing, its name shall be wiped out (→7:2–5; →12:2–3). Yet the last days offer an extraordinary last chance for the towns of Israel to repent before the last judgment (Matt. 10:5–15; cf. Jonah 3–4). Afterward "it will be more tolerable for the land of Sodom" than for the cities who spurn their wonders (Matt. 10:15 NRSV; 11:24).

Love Moderns think primarily in the categories of the individual and the nation-state, but the Torah has a fuller appreciation of human life. The last two passages concern discipline of leaders and intimate relationships; this one concerns discipline at the next level of organization along the scale from one person to a whole people. As another fundamental social unit, the **city** is another fundamental ecclesial category. The prophets address cities (Isa. 3:8; 13:1; 17:1; 21:11; 23:1). Jesus addresses cities in the Gospels (Matt. 11:21; 23:37). New Testament letters (some from Jesus; Rev. 2–3) are often to churches in cities. A holy gathering in a city is the key to that city's life (Gen. 18:22–33) and peace (Jer. 29:7). As a few corrupt the many, so a few may now sanctify many. Even a foreign city is a gift to the faithful who dwell there, and a primary goal of their mission. The church in a city is an essential means of reminding that city of the Spirit's discipline, through the patient and honorable witness of its own good conduct (1 Pet. 2:11–12).

Love Meanwhile, the Spirit warns churches that have abandoned the love of Christ that he will come and remove them from their place (Rev. 2:4–7) in Christ's kingdom. Schism is one earthly sign of this; another is lenience. The book of Judges shows God's people tolerating cities' apostasies against God (Judg. 17–18) and zealously punishing only cities that offend its tribes' honor (Judg. 19–20).

Love If pity is the temptation of those who love, conservation is the temptation of those who amass. Israel is not to withhold **cities** or fortunes from God's judgment out of insecurity, for God has **multiplied** it rather than chosen it for its strength (→7:6–8). By setting conventional power above self-discipline, Israel becomes a paganized and fallen empire. It is reconstituted in exile through the word of its prophets and later restored "by God the Father and sanctified by the Spirit to be obedient to Jesus Christ and to be sprinkled with his blood" (1 Pet. 1:1–2 NRSV).

DEUTERONOMY 14

14:1 You are the children of YHWH your God: you shall not cut yourselves or make any baldness between your eyes for the dead. **2**For you are a holy people to YHWH your God, and YHWH has chosen you to be a people for his⁺ own possession, above all peoples who are on the face of the earth.

Faith By the end of the monarchy these were recognized grieving practices in Israel (cf. Jer. 16:6; 41:5; 47:5), evidently shared with pagan neighbors. So Israel mourns the catastrophes of Jeremiah's day with habits that show it has lost its sense of being YHWH's chosen **children**.

Hope God's **children** should "not grieve as others do who have no hope" (1 Thess. 4:13 NRSV). YHWH has **chosen** Israel as the beneficiary of God's everlasting faithfulness to the patriarchs. This is a sign that God "is God not of **the dead**, but of the living; for to him⁺ all of them are alive" (Luke 20:38 NRSV). Even before the first Easter, the life of Israel is already sufficient evidence of the resurrection of the dead (Ezek. 37:1–14).

Love God's heirs are thus to encourage one another even as we mourn our dead, for "the dead in Christ will rise first" (1 Thess. 4:16 NRSV). Christian practices such as burial in churchyards, facing east, with hopeful liturgies all respect that the risen Christ holds all things, even the dead, as his **possession**.

14:3 You shall not eat any abominable thing (→14:21). **4**These are the animals you may eat: the ox, the sheep, and the goat, **5**the hart, and the gazelle, and the roebuck, and the wild goat, and the ibex, and the antelope, and the chamois. **6**Every animal that parts the hoof, and has the hoof cloven in two and chews the cud, among the animals, that may you eat. **7**Nevertheless these you shall not eat of them that chew the cud, or of those who have the hoof cloven: the camel, and the hare, and the rabbit; because they chew the cud but do not part the hoof, they are unclean to you. ⁸The pig, because it has a split hoof but does not chew the cud, is unclean to you. Of their flesh you shall not eat, and their carcasses you shall not touch.

Plain The debate over the reasons and underlying logic of the Torah's distinctions among foods is inconclusive. Hygiene, health, and taxonomy are often proposed, but the first two are neither consistent with the distinctions nor mentioned in the text, and the third is tautologous. Because Deuteronomy uses **abomination** for engraved images (→7:25–26), some suggest that this forbidden diet may have special religious significance for Israel's neighbors. Yet whole categories of animals are forbidden, not just specific ones. Others posit a source of Lev. 11's rules and thus Deuteronomy's in the arbitrary conventions of Jerusalem's priesthood; however, multiple Torah traditions unanimously claim that God is the source of Israel's dietary rules (e.g., Exod. 22:30; 34:26b), so Israel itself understands the matter differently. It may well be that here, as in so many places (e.g., 1 Cor. 11:2–16 on head coverings), the logic was obvious in an original cultural context that is obscure to us. It may also be that, as with so many cultural conventions (e.g., the pronunciation of "shibboleth" in Judg. 12:5–6), the rules themselves become the point, differentiating a group's insiders from outsiders. These are especially common in eating and clothing.

Hope Categorizing the Torah's rules as ceremonial, ritual, and ethical in order to pronounce some obsolete is artificial and problematic. Nevertheless, among its rules are "regulations for the body imposed until the time comes to set things right" (Heb. 9:10 NRSV). "I know and am persuaded in the Lord Jesus that nothing is unclean in itself; but it is unclean for anyone who thinks it unclean" (Rom. 14:14 NRSV). If God declared certain foods **unclean to** Israel through Moses and its priesthood, God may declare them clean to all peoples through Jesus the high priest (Mark 7:23) and his angelic and apostolic heralds (Acts 10:15; 11:9) once that time has arrived. Since both the old declaration identifying Israel as a nation and the new declaration identifying the Israel of God serve the same ultimate purpose in two different moments of its accomplishment, there is no more contradiction than among the covenants announced in Noah's (Gen. 9:3–4), Moses's, and Jeremiah's (Jer. 31:31–34) day.

Love Deuteronomy applies to all Israel the categories of Lev. 11's *kashrut* in a simpler and more memorable arrangement—as one would expect from its homiletical form. These distinguish Israel from its neighbors (Lev. 11:45–47; cf. Deut. 14:2), making cultural space for Israel to manifest its holiness, and through it God's holiness (Lev. 11:44). This is essential to its mission to be and bear God's alternative to the world. Yet Israel's divine holiness is definitively manifested not in these Torah customs but in the offering of Jesus on behalf of all. Thus "no distinction" (Rom. 3:22–25) between Jew and Gentile distinguishes the holy from the common, but only the shared body of the "one new human being" of all nations in whose holy temple God dwells (Eph. 2:15–22).

Love **Hares** and **rabbits** only appear to **chew cud**. As with other phenomena (such as the "setting" and "rising" sun), God speaks in scripture from within the perceptual worlds of its original audiences rather than those of our more scientific cultures. This is not a problem for biblical inspiration but an essential ecclesial quality of it.

> 14:9These you may eat of all that are in the waters: whatever has fins and scales may you eat; 10and whatever does not have fins and scales you shall not eat; it is unclean to you. 11Of all clean birds you may eat. 12But these are they of which you shall not eat: the eagle, and the vulture, and the osprey, 13and the red kite, and the falcon, and the kite after its kind, 14and every raven after its kind, 15and the ostrich, and the owl, and the seagull, and the hawk after its kind, 16the little owl, and the great owl, and the horned owl, 17and the pelican, and the vulture, and the cormorant, 18and the stork, and the heron after its kind, and the hoopoe, and the bat. 19All winged creeping things are unclean to you: they shall not be eaten. 20Of all clean birds you may eat.

Plain Only a general rule is given in the case of **water** creatures, while only specifics are given for **birds** (though the specifically forbidden birds are generally either predators or scavengers). The **bat** is of course a rodent, and **creeping things** are insects (→14:3–8).

> 14:21You shall not eat of anything that dies of itself: you may give it to the foreigner living among you who is within your gates, that he+ may eat it; or you may sell it to a foreigner: for you are a holy people to YHWH your God. You shall not boil a young goat in its mother's milk.

Love People from other lands would often be traders, whereas Israel's resident aliens would often be poor and so objects of charity.

Love To eat carrion is not kosher, but it is not wickedness. Whereas the Canaanites' wickedness was responsible for their expulsion from the land (9:4–5), it is acceptable for both resident aliens and **foreigners** to eat food forbidden to Israel. This is another sign that at least some of these laws do not (as some now claim) signify a divine aversion to confusing the orderly categories of creation. Why should Israel hand its property over so that resident aliens can confuse those same categories in the land? This kind of rule is not a moral standard for all peoples (→14:3–8), let alone a moral standard for an ethically elitist Israel, but a cultural relativity that concerns ancient Israel's distinct identity over against other peoples as **a holy people to YHWH**. This is how the rules have actually functioned: not to teach ethical principles (centuries of rabbis and scholars have not been able to deduce such principles consistently or persuasively anyway), but to conserve Israel's character as a people of YHWH's possession (14:2) and resist pressure for cultural assimilation, which they have done with remarkable success. Whatever other purposes they might have originally served, this is how God has used them.

Love Some understand Acts 15:28–29's dietary rules for Gentile believers to be those pertaining to **foreigners** living in the land; on the contrary, that would maintain the exclusivity of ethnic Israel's holiness within the kingdom's **gates**, which contradicts the Jerusalem assembly's new appreciation of "the Gentiles over whom my name has been called" (Amos 9:11–12 Septuagint in Acts 15:15–17). Every strand of New Testament tradition betrays the apostolic sense that, in reconciling Jew and Gentile, Christ's work has forever set aside the commandments and ordinances that purposefully separated them.

Faith In the Gospels Jesus violates some of the purification rites (Mark 7:1–23) and Sabbath customs (Matt. 12:1–14; Luke 13:10–17; 14:1–6; John 5:1–24; 9:13–17; →5:12–15) of his day. There is no evidence that he violates this chapter's laws of *kashrut*. However, he disputes his people's theology of purity. He makes defilement a matter of evil hearts, not stomach contents (Mark 7:14–23). This both corrects popular misunderstandings of Torah (cf. 7:1–13) and transforms the Torah itself (7:19b). Holiness had indeed been associated with *kashrut*, but not a function of diet; and from now on, holiness will be the gift of a new, penitent heart and of deliverance from all uncleanness (Ezek. 36:26–31; 2 Cor. 3).

Hope The last rule is much narrower than rabbinic Judaism's laws of *kashrut*: it refers only to the **milk** of a kid's own **mother**. (Some see a Canaanite fertility rite, but that is baseless.) It is Israel's most poignant dietary rule (→22:6–7), so especially suggestive of symbolic interpretation. While in Exodus the rule is associated with a number of distinctions of worship, time, and food (Exod. 23:10–19; 34:18–26), here it pertains to Israel's holiness. These overlap in respect to the season of livestock maternity (cf. 34:19–20) alongside the times of agricultural Sabbath, annual pilgrimage, and firstfruits (e.g., Deut. 14:22–26). All remember God's faithfulness and anticipate God's further blessing through sacrifice. By contrast, **boiling** a kid in its mother's milk simultaneously perverts both childhood and motherhood, evoking similar perversions in times of distress and even famine (→28:53–57). This practice seems closer to the curses for covenant unfaithfulness than to the life of blessing that God intends for Israel.

> **14:22**You shall surely tithe all the increase (cf. Lev. 27:30–33; Num. 18:21–32) of your seed that comes forth from the field year by year. **23**You shall eat before YHWH your God, in the place he[+] shall choose to cause his[+] name to dwell, the tithe of your grain, of your new wine, and of your oil, and the firstborn of your herd and of your flock, that you may learn to fear YHWH your God always. **24**If the way is too long for you, so that you are not able to carry it, because the place is too far from you where YHWH your God shall choose to set his[+]

name, when YHWH your God shall bless you, ²⁵then you shall turn it into money, and bind up the money in your hand, and shall go to the place YHWH your God shall choose: ²⁶and you shall bestow the money for whatever your soul desires, for cattle, or for sheep, or for wine, or for strong drink, or for whatever your soul asks of you; and you shall eat there before YHWH your God, and you shall rejoice, you and your household.

Faith "Do not be like a horse or a mule, without understanding, whose temper must be curbed with bit and bridle.... Be glad in [YHWH] and rejoice, O righteous, and shout for joy" (Ps. 32:9–11 NRSV). "**Rejoice!**" (Phil. 4:4). The Holy Spirit grows joy through the power of God's word in cooperation with those it reaches. The Thessalonians "received the word with joy inspired by the Holy Spirit" (1 Thess. 1:6 NRSV).

Faith How can **rejoicing** in God produce **fear** of God? The two seem mutually exclusive, for our modern culture of emotivism considers joy authentic only when it originates freely in supposedly autonomous human wills. A better name for such "joy" is pleasure. A culture of pleasure fears not God but pleasure's absence. Instead, this Torah trains Israel to use its **desires** to remember its prosperity as covenantal blessing (→15:19–23). "The boundary lines have fallen for me in pleasant places; I have a goodly heritage" (Ps. 16:6 NRSV). A culture formed by vigilant remembrance does not merely satisfy desires or experience fleeting pleasures but receives the gift of steady, sober joy. The church receives such training when it meets on the first day of the week with sacrifices of praise and **increase** (1 Cor. 16:1–4) to remember Christ's beginning of its new life. "They left the tomb quickly with fear and great joy, and ran to tell his disciples" (Matt. 28:8 NRSV).

Hope The promise of this command eventually extends to the ends of the earth (→12:4–7). In desolate Jerusalem "there shall once more be heard the voice of mirth and the voice of gladness ... as they bring thank offerings to the house of [YHWH]" (Jer. 33:10–11 NRSV). Rather than the perversity of the previous verse in which the milk of life seasons the young flesh for which it was intended (→14:21), God's restorative justice bears Jerusalem anew from above and calls "all nations and tongues" to come to that **place** and celebrate YHWH's glory: "Shall I open the womb and not deliver? ... Rejoice with Jerusalem ... that you may nurse and be satisfied from her consoling breast.... You shall be comforted in Jerusalem" (Isa. 66:9–11, 13 NRSV). This word is fulfilled at a particular Pentecost festival (Acts 2:37–42).

Love Here the **tithe** is a pilgrimage, vacation, and fiesta all in one, presumably at the Festivals of Weeks and Booths (16:1–15). Yet those occasions are too brief to consume a whole tithe, unless the feast is truly lavish or much is left with the priests. Tithing today is basically support for clergy and facilities. This is a legitimate use (→14:27–29), perhaps explaining the discrepancy; yet tithing's quality of celebration has receded. The church's first task and sacrifice is to **rejoice** together in the

Lord Jesus. The spirit of the joyful pilgrimage survives in Paul's far-flung churches, in which believers relay their **monetized** joy to their brothers and sisters in Zion (1 Cor. 16:2–3). Such offerings allow today's worldwide church of billions to celebrate as one, for God's **household** includes all of Christ's coheirs "by the generosity of your sharing with them and with all others" (2 Cor. 9:13 NRSV).

> **14:27**The Levite who is within your gates you shall not forsake, for he has no portion or inheritance with you. **28**At the end of every three years you shall bring forth all the tithe of your increase in that year, and shall lay it up (→26:12–15) within your gates: **29**and the Levite, because he has no portion or inheritance with you, and the foreigner living among you, and the fatherless, and the widow who are within your gates, shall come, and shall eat and be satisfied; that YHWH your God may bless you in all the work of your hand that you do.

Faith The implementation of the **tithe** for the **Levites** and the poor shifts to account for social changes in Israel, from the eras of the centralized Jerusalem priesthood (Neh. 10:38–39; 13:10–12) to the age of Israel's exiled and royal priesthood (1 Pet. 2:9). All these sacrifices serve the Son of Man, the judge and intercessor without a place to lay his head (Luke 9:57–58).

Hope Would the poor **tithe** of a society much poorer than ours last through all **three years**? If so, it would be a marginal benefit to help the poor "catch up" rather than relief on the level expected in modern welfare states. Israel's poor would either be few or have other means of support (→24:17–22) in order to **be satisfied** on one-thirtieth of others' agricultural incomes. If not, the relief would be momentary. Christ's advent overcomes this dilemma: the multitude that Jesus feeds with five loaves and two fish are satisfied (Luke 9:17a), at events that do not merely preserve a social status quo but signify Israel's covenant restoration (Isa. 61:1–2 in Luke 4:16–21; →30:6–10).

Hope YHWH **blesses** not merely with social peace, freedom from fear of misfortune, and the **tithe's** other immediate benefits, but also with the extraordinary blessing of **all the work of** Israel's **hand**. All productivity, not just charity, is providential as long as Israel does God's work of looking after the vulnerable (10:18). In feeding the multitude the apostles' act of faithful generosity even yielded twelve baskets of leftovers (Luke 9:17b).

Love Israel's heirs include those who through identity or circumstances have **no portion or inheritance with** them: the **Levite** and the **foreigner** on the one hand, and the **fatherless** and the **widow** on the other (→26:12–15). In return, these dispossessed share their inheritances. The Levites' inheritance is YHWH (→18:1–8); the nations' inheritance comes to Israel through the power of his⁺ works (Ps. 111:5–6); widows and orphans receive the justice of the God who freed the Hebrews (→24:17–22). Their interaction resembles the workings of the apostolic body in which teachers are honored and supported, widows and orphans become protected servants, none are resented, and all are blessed (1 Tim. 5:1–22). To forsake any of these, even the foreigner, is to compromise the fellowship of saints. "Do not trust in these deceptive words: 'This is the temple of [YHWH]. . . .' For if you truly amend your ways and your doings, . . . if you do not oppress the alien, the orphan, and the widow, . . . then I will dwell with you in this place, in the land that I gave of old to your ancestors forever and ever" (Jer. 7:4–7 NRSV).

DEUTERONOMY 15

^{15:1}At the end of every seven years you shall make a release. ²This is the way of the release: every creditor shall release what he⁺ has lent to his⁺ neighbor; he⁺ shall not exact it of his⁺ neighbor and his⁺ brother⁺; because YHWH's release has been proclaimed. ³Of a foreigner you may exact it: but whatever of yours is with your brother⁺ your hand shall release. ⁴However there shall be no poor with you, for YHWH will surely bless you in the land YHWH your God gives you for an inheritance to possess, ⁵if only you diligently listen to the voice of YHWH your God, to do all this commandment I command you this day. ⁶For YHWH your God will bless you, as he⁺ promised you: and you shall lend to many nations, but you shall not borrow; and you shall rule over many nations, but they shall not rule over you.

Plain Deuteronomy 15's rules are easier to reconcile with Exod. 21–23 on fallow years and family release than with the Jubilee provisions of Lev. 25, which seem to be independent traditions with similar concerns.

Faith Isaac's blessing of Jacob promised, "Let **nations** serve you, and nations bow down to you" (Gen. 27:29, my translation). Socialist and liberationist readings of biblical release and Jubilee passages often treat this command as radical and egalitarian. Actually it is conservative and ethnocentric, even mercantilist. It protects individual Israelites from becoming slaves and lords of a landed aristocracy—from acquiring Gentile economic structures. Like other commands in Deuteronomy, it conserves Israel's distinctiveness and international preeminence (→31:9–13). Isaac's word is fulfilled in the master who only lends but never borrows, for whom five talents are "little" (Matt. 25:21)—the Son who receives all things from the Father (11:27) and gives rest to the heavy laden (11:28).

Hope Jacob bought Esau's birthright and obtained his blessing, and this exchange is irrevocable (Gen. 27:32–37; Rom. 11:29). The seventh-year release restores Jacob's inheritance, for it is a security even this people's own debts cannot squander. "'From whom do kings of the earth take toll or tribute? From their children or from others?' When Peter said, 'From others,' Jesus said to him, 'Then the children are free'" (Matt. 17:25–26 NRSV).

Hope "He has sent me to **proclaim** good news to the **poor** . . . **release** to the captives" (Isa. 61:1–2 in Luke 4:16–21, my translation).

Love Israel's distinctiveness is the church's distinctiveness (Acts 2:44–47; 4:32–37). If the master is rich and generous, it is unrighteous for his servants to leave each other bound in destitution. Yet creditors maintain this righteousness at great personal cost. **Release** effectively binds lenders rather than borrowers. It exposes them to repeated loss, fraud, and folly. They are compensated (→15:7–11) in knowing that theirs is the Father's generosity (Matt. 20:15–16) and that they are forgiven much more (18:33) and destined to an even more prosperous heavenly future (6:19–21; 19:21).

> **15:7**If a poor man⁺, one of your brothers⁺, is with you within any of your gates in your land that YHWH your God gives you, you shall not harden your heart or shut your hand from your poor brother⁺; **8**but you shall surely open your hand to him⁺, and shall surely lend him⁺ sufficient for his⁺ need, which he⁺ lacks. **9**Beware that there not be a base thought in your heart, saying: "The seventh year, the year of release, is at hand," and your eye be evil against your poor brother⁺, and you give him⁺ nothing; and he⁺ cry to YHWH against you, and it be sin to you. **10**You shall surely give him⁺, and your heart shall not be grieved when you give to him⁺; because for this thing YHWH your God will bless you in all your work, and in all you put your hand to. **11**For the poor will not cease out of the land: therefore I command you, saying: "You shall surely open your hand to your brother⁺, to your needy, and to your poor, in your land."

Faith Poverty will **not cease** on its own. "For always the poor you have with you, and whenever you wish you can do them good, but me you do not always have" (Mark 14:7, my translation). The woman who anoints Jesus for burial appreciates that **the year of release is at hand** and that he is the Father's ransom for many (10:45). The very ones who fail to see this and scold her for wasting the perfume can open their own hands to the poor if they think they live in ordinary times. That they **harden** their **hearts** when she gives to him reveals not just eschatological ignorance but the **sin** of unforgiving greed.

Faith The previous passage promises that Israel will have no poor, if they diligently listen to YHWH and obey all his⁺ Torah. Those poor are being saved from hopeless debt accumulating from the borrowing described in this passage, so the two passages do not contradict. Nevertheless, this passage's warning suggests that Israel will not listen or do all the Torah. To inherit its extraordinary blessings, its faithful will face the extraordinary burden of meeting the needs of the **poor** in a context of injustice. So the Son became poor to enrich his brothers and sisters (2 Cor. 8:9). Those who remember his generosity and forgiveness by **opening** their **own hands** are his prophets and apostles (6:10).

Hope The nearness of the **year of release**, whether in the Torah's seven-year cycle or in the age of the risen Messiah, raises both reasonable suspicions that borrowers might defraud their lenders and unfair resentment of the truly needy who will not be able to repay. This commandment does not allow lenders to judge the hearts and intentions of the **poor**. Instead it commands generosity regardless of the borrower's motives and promises to bless the faithful lender. This prevents **grievances** on both sides from driving apart the prosperous from the **needy**—for each is the other's **brother**+.

Love While we are not to judge one another's intentions, we are to discern one another's **needs**. Even in the fellowship of sharing in Acts (→15:1–6), some remain hungry (Acts 6:1–6). The prosperous are not at the mercy of the desires of the needy. The commandment makes sufficiency a criterion for just lending that both parties negotiate. "Admonish the idlers, encourage the fainthearted, help the weak, be patient with all of them" (1 Thess. 5:14 NRSV; cf. 2 Thess. 3:6–13). This task easily turns brothers and sisters into opponents if they consider only their own interests, so the church that shares needs constant reminding of its mission. "May the Lord direct your hearts to the love of God and to the steadfastness of Christ" (3:5 NRSV; cf. 1 Thess. 5:15–18).

Love Poverty is not romanticized here, nor is wealth demonized. It is not the wealthy who are wicked, for they are sources of blessing for the needy, but only the merciless (Matt. 18:23–35).

> [15:12]If your brother+, a Hebrew man or a Hebrew woman, is sold to you, and serves you six years; then in the seventh year you shall let him+ go free from you. [13]When you let him+ go free from you, you shall not let him+ go empty: [14]you shall furnish him+ liberally out of your flock, and out of your threshing floor, and out of your winepress; as YHWH your God has blessed you, you shall give to him+. [15]You shall remember that you were a bondservant in the land of Egypt, and YHWH your God redeemed you: therefore I command you this thing today. [16]If he+ tells you, "I will not go out from you," because he+ loves you and your house, because he+ is well with you, [17]then you shall take an awl and thrust it through his+ ear to the door, and he+ shall be your servant forever. Also to your female servant you shall do likewise. [18]It shall not seem hard to you, when you let him+ go free from you; for

to the double of the hire of a hireling he⁺ has served you six years:
and YHWH your God will bless you in all you do.

Faith "We are children, not of the slave but of the free woman. For freedom Christ
has set us **free**" (Gal. 4:31–5:1 NRSV). Like the Decalogue, this Torah command
is an "exodus ethic": freedom is the right life for a freed people. The temporal
circumstances that lead to slavery may persist even in the land of promise, even in
the church, but they may not characterize its society. The prophets discern Israel's
failure to honor the Torah here, lament its conformity to **Egyptian** standards
of power before **brotherhood**⁺, and foretell its children's return to their true
inheritance of freedom (Isa. 54 in Gal. 4:26–30).

Faith We rejoice in freeing worthy **servants**, but our extraordinary Father rejoices
in freeing even unworthy ones for the sake of **brotherhood**⁺ (Luke 15:17–32).

Hope Liberation theology draws on the progressive category of political revolution. The aristocratic and capitalistic order it opposes draws on the ideology of
individual rights. Both miss the teleology of this commandment. The emigrat-
ing **Hebrews** had recovered some of the **Egyptian** wealth they were due, but
only because of the fear of their former owners (Exod. 12:33–36). In Israel, by
contrast, the emancipation of a slave is joyful for all concerned. All share in the
Sabbath blessing of the slave's labor, not least the slave. Thus slavery is released
from resentment and exploitation to become an arrangement that is unequal yet
beneficial to all parties. This is confirmed and radicalized in the further provision
for entering into servanthood **forever**, not by necessity (since the slave would have
received **liberally** upon leaving the master's service) but by **love**. Free obedience
characterizes Christian covenanting, as it looks forward to no other arrangement
than itself. As the time of the ultimate Passover drew near, the Lord "loved his own
. . . to the end" (John 13:1 NRSV), enrolling his disciples into his own perpetual
commandment of freely rendered service in love for one another (13:15–16,
34–35). We are free to leave (6:66–67) Christ's service of friendship (15:14–15),
but we are freer if we remain (8:31–32).

Love Human sociality means structure, and structure means power relationships. The exodus did not end **Hebrew** slavery, but it ended its hopelessness. The
kingdom of God has come to our world of power relationships not to abolish
them but to end their injustice, transforming them within its new and **redeemed**
peoplehood. In economies where employees' indebtedness, poverty, or political
powerlessness make them practically serfs, bosses are not to abuse the powerless
or treat their servitude as a permanent relationship—for **brotherhood** and sis-
terhood, not slavery, is their permanent relationship (Eph. 6:5–9). The rules of
Israel thus point to a new humanity (2:14–16), still socially structured but now
peacefully and fraternally restructured.

¹⁵:¹⁹All the firstborn males that are born of your herd and of your flock
you shall sanctify to YHWH your God: you shall do no work with the

firstborn of your herd or shear the firstborn of your flock. [20]You shall
eat it before YHWH your God year by year in the place YHWH shall
choose, you and your household. [21]If it has any blemish, is lame or
blind, or has any defect whatever, you shall not sacrifice it to YHWH
your God. [22]You shall eat it within your gates: the unclean and the
clean shall eat it alike, as the gazelle, and as the hart. [23]Only you shall
not eat its blood (→12:20–28); you shall pour it out on the ground
as water.

Faith Liturgical discipline is as important to the justice of Israel as any other
social practice, because it maintains the memory of Israel's hard-won identity.
The occasion for setting apart male **firstlings** is one of the pilgrimage festivals
(16:1–17) that remember the turning points in Israel's redeemed life. In these
festivals Israel eats in God's presence so that it may learn to fear God (→14:22–26)
and understand itself. Using a **defective** animal or one that has already been
worked or **shorn** betrays the wholeness of the redemption story—and obscures
the celebration's typological symbolism with the flawless sacrifice of the only Son,
whose only work was the work of his Father (John 5:17–20), and the purity of
his bride who is clothed with her deeds (Rev. 19:7–8).

Love Demanding perfection in its proper place is not the same as practicing per-
fectionism. A flawed **firstling** is still good, but it is suitable only for ordinary
use. Yet that ordinary use still serves to strengthen the fellowship of Israel. Both
perfect gifts and imperfect gifts, and both holy and common things, build up the
body—which is itself perfect and imperfect, holy and common—according to
the purpose of their divine giver.

DEUTERONOMY 16

16:1 Observe the month of Abib, and keep the Passover (Exod. 12:1–20) to YHWH your God; for in the month of Abib YHWH your God brought you forth out of Egypt by night. **²**You shall sacrifice the Passover to YHWH your God, of the flock and the herd, in the place YHWH shall choose, to cause his⁺ name to dwell there. **³**You shall eat no leavened bread with it. You shall eat unleavened bread with it seven days, even the bread of affliction; for you came forth out of the land of Egypt in haste: that you may remember the day you came forth out of the land of Egypt all the days of your life. **⁴**No yeast shall be seen with you in all your borders seven days; neither shall any of the flesh, which you sacrifice the first day at evening, remain all night until the morning. **⁵**You may not sacrifice the Passover within any of your gates that YHWH your God gives you; **⁶**but at the place YHWH your God shall choose, to cause his⁺ name to dwell in, you shall sacrifice the Passover at evening, at the going down of the sun, at the season that you came forth out of Egypt. **⁷**You shall boil (cf. Exod. 12:9) and eat it in the place YHWH your God shall choose: and you shall turn in the morning, and go to your tents. **⁸**Six days you shall eat unleavened bread. On the seventh day shall be a solemn assembly to YHWH your God; you shall do no work.

Faith Pesach connotes protection, not passing over. YHWH's judgment on Pharaoh's domain freed the Hebrews, whose firstborn the **sacrifice** spared. They were delivered from *both* Pharaoh and the angel of death. Moreover, at Israel's restoration its prince is to supply a paschal sin offering as well (Ezek. 45:21–22). All these sacrifices converge on the cross.

Faith No event in the Tanakh compares to the exodus (→34:10–12); no other night is like that **night**. Yet the church remembers a night that is like it: the night the Lord was betrayed (1 Cor. 11:26). **Keeping the Passover** enables Israel and thus all nations to appreciate the unique significance of Jesus's covenanting blood, offered body, and resurrection peace as a new liberation from every captivity.

Faith None of the lamb is to **remain** because salvation is not a standing that licenses further "pollutions of the nations of the land" (Ezra 6:19–21 NRSV) but a sudden emancipation that begins a permanently changed life (cf. 6:1–18).

Hope "Hurry, my beloved" (Song 8:14 NJPSV, read at Pesach). Deuteronomy's liturgical year incorporates Israel's hope ("next year in Jerusalem!") into what is fundamentally a review of deliverance now long past. The Christian year from Advent to Advent has poles of both loving remembrance and eager anticipation ("he died . . . was raised . . . sits . . . shall return").

Hope **Passover's** seven days suggest a pilgrim Israel that must remain on the move from the **night** of its freedom to its appointed day of rest. **Yeast** during the festival then connotes complacency with imperfection. The church celebrates a more radical, perpetual Passover (1 Cor. 5:6–8), eating **bread of affliction** as it awaits the day of the Lord (5:5). "Sincerity and truth" rid it of the yeast of "malice and evil" that still characterize life outside its **borders** (5:8–13). (This vigilance supports the Western tradition of the unleavened eucharistic host.)

Love **Egypt** denied the Hebrews a **place** to worship together, so they sacrificed in their homes. Making the feast a pilgrimage includes an element of realization in the remembrance: the exodus is also out of isolation into universal fellowship. Similarly, Christians eat in our homes before celebrating Christ's Pascha in church (1 Cor. 11:33–34) on **the first day** (16:2).

> **16:9**You shall count for yourselves seven weeks: from the time you begin to put the sickle to the standing grain you shall begin to number seven weeks. **10**You shall keep the Feast of Weeks to YHWH your God with a tribute of a freewill offering of your hand, which you shall give as YHWH your God blesses you: **11**and you shall rejoice before YHWH your God, you, and your son, and your daughter, and your male servant, and your female servant, and the Levite who is within your gates, and the foreigner, and the fatherless, and the widow, who are in your midst, in the place YHWH your God shall choose, to cause his[+] name to dwell there. **12**You shall remember that you were a bondservant in Egypt: and you shall observe and do these statutes.

Plain The Feast of Weeks (Shavuot) is the conclusion of Israel's **grain** harvest, begun at Passover. Those **seven weeks** of reaping tell Israel whether its precarious growing season (→11:8–15) has been a success.

Faith While seasonal regularities drive many pagan sagas of historical cyclicality, here they serve Israel's sense of discontinuous yet eternal time. Every new harvest extends God's blessing (→8:6–10) to the patriarchs (→26:1–11). The dividends culminate with Jesus's final pilgrimage to Jerusalem as the Feast of Unleavened

Bread looms (Luke 22:1). Jesus assures his bewildered disciples that following the Passover they will be strengthened (22:32). His appearance to Simon does indeed inaugurate a harvest of faith (24:33–34). Following his victory his disciples keep the Feast of Weeks, heading joyfully for the temple to praise God (24:52–53) and staying in the city while they wait to be clothed with power (24:49).

Love "You left your father and mother and the land of your birth and came to a people you had not known before. . . . May you have a full recompense from [YHWH], the God of Israel, under whose wings you have sought refuge!" (Ruth 2:11–12 NJPSV, read at Shavuot). Following the messianic Pentecost, **widows** (Acts 6:1), **fatherless** (cf. 4:35), Gentiles (10:44–45), priests (6:7), **male and female servants** (2:18), and Israel's family at home and abroad (2:5–11) are all "harvested" together (Luke 10:2) through the promise "to you and to your children and to all that are far off, every one whom the Lord our God calls to him" (Acts 2:39 RSV).

> **16:13**You shall keep the Feast of Tents seven days, after that you have gathered in from your threshing floor and from your winepress: **14**and you shall rejoice in your feast, you, and your son, and your daughter, and your male servant, and your female servant, and the Levite, and the foreigner, and the fatherless, and the widow, who are within your gates. **15**You shall keep a feast to YHWH your God seven days in the place YHWH shall choose; because YHWH your God will bless you in all your increase, and in all the work of your hands, and you shall be altogether joyful.

Faith Recalling the wilderness at harvest time highlights both God's steadfast providence in sustaining Israel at every stage of its new life and the radically conditional character of its prosperity. The one crying in the wilderness announces that the Messiah's "winnowing fork is in his hand, and he will clear his threshing floor and will gather his wheat into the granary" (Matt. 3:12 NRSV). **Rejoicing** at God's **ingathering** begins early when the Son of Man comes eating and drinking with the outcasts within Israel's **gates** (11:19), but it is interrupted when his own heralds take offense at him (11:4–6). The kingdom suffers violence (11:12–17) because it celebrates a future the world dreads (→16:16–17). The Fourth Gospel captures this dynamic when Jesus refuses to attend his unbelieving brothers' **Feast of Tents**, for "my time has not yet come, but your time is always here" (John 7:6 NRSV), yet still comes to Jerusalem secretly to teach his Father's teaching (→31:9–13), as if at a festival of his own (John 7:1–13), amid his opponents' complaints and plots against him (7:14–31).

Hope The feasting of those who look back but not ahead is futility, for "I considered all that my **hands** had done and the toil I had spent in doing it, and again, all was vanity and a chasing after wind" (Eccl. 2:11 NRSV, read at Sukkot; →28:20–26). As the Feast of Unleavened Bread looks back on exodus and forward to the cross

(→16:1–8), and the Feast of Weeks back to Sinai and forward to Pentecost (→16:9–12), so the Feast of Tents at the end of Israel's year looks back on the wilderness (cf. Lev. 23:39–43) and the **increase** of the land and forward to the good news of the coming global harvest. "[YHWH] will become king over all the earth; on that day [YHWH] will be one and his⁺ name one. . . . Then all who survive of the nations that have come against Jerusalem shall go up year after year to worship the King, [YHWH] of hosts, and to keep the Festival of Booths. If any of the families of the earth do not go up to Jerusalem to worship the King, [YHWH] of hosts, there will be no rain upon them" (Zech. 14:9, 16–17 NRSV; cf. Rev. 21:22–27).

Love In the Western text tradition of Acts 18:21, God's apostle to the nations goes to Jerusalem to **keep** this **feast**. "There is nothing better for one than to eat and drink, and find enjoyment in one's toil. This also, I saw, is from the hand of God" (Eccl. 2:24, my translation, read at Sukkot). **Rejoicing** in Jesus Christ by feasting together is basic to life in the church (→32:10–14). Yet so is fasting. God used both in the wilderness and in the land to train Israel to respond to his⁺ grace with faith. Healthy Christian communities order both feasts and fasts to their good news and Christ's call to vigilance until his return. "Happy are you, O land, when your king is a nobleman, and your princes feast at the proper time—for strength, and not for drunkenness!" (Eccl. 10:17, my translation).

> **16:16**Three times in a year shall all your males appear before YHWH your God in the place he⁺ shall choose: in the Feast of Unleavened Bread, and in the Feast of Weeks, and in the Feast of Tents; and they shall not appear before YHWH empty: **17**every man shall give as he is able, according to the blessing of YHWH your God that he⁺ has given you.

Faith Moses's command is realized in the Son who appears as a **male** of Israel—his gender is not significant in all respects, but here it is—before his Father at Passover, offering his own life (Luke 22:15–22; 1 Cor. 5:7; Rom. 5:6–8), at Pentecost offering his Holy Spirit (Acts 2:33; Rom. 5:5), and at his coming offering himself and all that belongs to him (Acts 15:14–18; 1 Cor. 15:27–28). In the power of the Spirit he is able to gain, save, and **give** all things, even impossible gifts, with which he has been **blessed** (Luke 18:24–27).

Hope "No one after drinking old wine desires new" (Luke 5:33–39 RSV). The kingdom's approach exposes a relationship of past to future in these festivals that some find incomprehensible and intolerable. Jesus's Jewish opponents arrest him at his Passover, scoff at his Pentecostal outpouring of the Spirit, and hand him over when he warns of his coming as Son of Man. Anti-Jewish Gentiles try to strip the kingdom's future of its past by denying the gospel's continuities with the old and by persecuting Jews who worship as Jesus and his first disciples did. Both reactions show contempt for Mary's joy that in Jesus God "has helped his⁺ servant Israel, in remembrance of his[+] mercy, as he[+] spoke to our fathers, to Abraham and to his posterity for ever" (Luke 1:54–55 RSV; cf. Acts 15:18). These reactions must be liturgically as well as literally violent because we worship in the ways we hope. **Love** Pascha (or Easter), Pentecost, and Advent mark the fulfillment and renewal of each of these feasts. In the baptismal, missional, eucharistic life of God's blessed ones, all (not just **males**) are "sons" and heirs, and their gatherings in every place and age (not just Jerusalem or any other locality) are his[+] chosen dwelling **place**.

> [16:18]You shall make judges and officers in all your gates, which YHWH your God gives you, according to your tribes; and they shall judge the people with righteous judgment (→1:15–17). [19]You shall not wrest justice: you shall not respect persons. Neither shall you take a bribe, for a bribe blinds the eyes of the wise, and perverts the words of the righteous. [20]You shall follow what is altogether just, that you may live, and inherit the land YHWH your God gives you. [21]You shall not plant for yourselves an Asherah of any kind of tree beside the altar of YHWH your God, which you shall make for yourselves. [22]Neither shall you set yourself up a pillar, which YHWH your God hates. [17:1]You shall not sacrifice to YHWH your God an ox or a sheep in which is a blemish or anything evil, for that is an abomination to YHWH your God.

Faith Human history is replete with favoritism, tribal preferentiality, prejudice, and idolatry (Rev. 9:20–21), but "God shows no partiality" (Acts 10:34 NRSV; →1:15–17a; →10:17–22). God's steadfast will is the only stable basis for fairness toward persons. Jesus's worshipful service to the Father (Matt. 7:21–23), his complete refusal to bow down to opposing principalities (4:8–10), and his love of others as himself (22:34–40) recapitulate Israel's ordered worship, politics, and love as an **unblemished** offering to God through the eternal Spirit on a Roman cross (Heb. 9:14–15). Christ rules not two kingdoms but one: "The government is on his shoulders" (Isa. 9:6, my translation).

Love Following requirements for annual gathered liturgies (16:1–17), this passage begins a section on polity in the **land**, in which civil justice frames standards regarding idolatry and sacrifice. To American eyes this can seem a random, even perverse juxtaposition; but polity is an aspect of Israel's holy life just as worship determines its politics. Acts of worship arise from within Israel's own inheritance of freedom (5:6). Proper worship does justice to the God of Israel, and only a properly worshipful spirit truly does justice to God's people.

Love Because "an idol is nothing" (1 Cor. 8:4, my translation) but a human projection, idolatry and partiality are inextricably connected. Disillusioned with his Lord, Judas Iscariot was **bribed** to betray him and follow his own course (Acts 1:25). A multicultural civil order that celebrates idols and false messiahs alongside YHWH is divided against itself, unable to resolve the dilemma between particularity and universality it has itself introduced. Meanwhile, the betrayed one who put the Father's will before his own was raised as the head of a universal church (Col. 1:17–20), able to **live** in common (Acts 2:44–47) with hearts knit together in love (Col. 2:2) and partial to none (3:11–17, 25). "I will leave in the midst of you a people humble and lowly. They shall seek refuge in the name of [YHWH], those who are left in Israel" (Zeph. 3:12 RSV).

Hope "If you show partiality, you commit sin, and are convicted by the law as transgressors. For whoever keeps the whole law but fails in one point has become guilty of all of it" (Jas. 2:9–10 RSV). The modern West cherishes the ideals of equality and community, but its structures depend on distinctions between sacred and secular, and justice in its ordinary sense is bound to the latter. It construes societal hope as political, consensual, and coercive, but eternal hope as spiritual, subjective, and voluntary. Sundering the concerns of the Torah in this way frees modern societies from many religious forms of tyranny, but it condemns them to interminable conflicts and wars over the nature of justice, the terms and bounds of equality, and the relevance of God. As a community that is neither coercive nor voluntary but responsive to "the word of truth," the church dwells peaceably but problematically alongside this and every other unstable temporal arrangement. A social reality brought forth by the Father rather than human wills, it is privileged to bear witness to his⁺ future as "a kind of first fruits of his⁺ creatures" (Jas. 1:17–18 NRSV) set to inherit the new earth God has promised.

DEUTERONOMY 17

17:2 If there be found in your midst, within any of your gates that YHWH your God gives you, man or woman (→29:16–21), who does what is evil in the sight of YHWH your God, in transgressing his[+] covenant, [3]and has gone and served other gods (5:7) and worshiped them, or the sun, or the moon, or any of the army of the sky, which I have not commanded (13:1–18); [4]and it be told you, and you have heard of it, then you shall inquire diligently; and behold, if it be true, and the thing certain, that such abomination is done in Israel, [5]then you shall bring forth that man or that woman who has done this evil thing to your gates, the man or the woman, and you shall stone them to death with stones. [6]At the mouth of two witnesses, or three witnesses, shall he[+] who is to die be put to death; at the mouth of one witness he[+] shall not be put to death. [7]The hand of the witnesses shall be first on him[+] to put him[+] to death, and afterward the hand of all the people. So you shall put away the evil from your midst.

Faith This commandment is fulfilled more in its breach than its observance. As Israel drifted into idolatry and hypocrisy, its prophets "were stoned to death" (Heb. 11:37 NRSV)—and "Jesus the pioneer and perfecter of our faith . . . endured the cross" (12:2 NRSV). Every stage in Jesus's passion is an abuse of the Torah's procedure. Betrayed on a pretext (Mark 14:10), Jesus is arrested on false pretenses (14:43–49); his true witnesses desert and deny him (14:50, 66–72); false witnesses cannot agree about Jesus's crimes (14:55–59; →19:15–21); the Sanhedrin hands him over to lawless magistrates on his testimony to the truth (Mark 14:60–65; 15:1); crowds and leaders call for his crucifixion despite Pilate's protests (15:6–14); and Rome has him killed without sufficient evidence (15:2–5, 12, 15). Yet all this abuse *does* **put away the evil from** Israel's **midst**, not because these actions are just but because the bloodied judge who condemns the world's injustice secures its forgiveness. His punishment exposes the injustice of our depravity and releases us from it.

Hope Church discipline honors both the Torah's logic and the kingdom's coming. On the day of the Lord Jesus "the saints will judge the world" (1 Cor. 6:2 NRSV). Until then we are to judge only those within the **gates** of our fellowship (5:12) and drive out **the evil** from among us (Deut. 17:7 in 1 Cor. 5:13). We do this not with **stones** but with dissociation (5:9–11) in hope of restoration on that final day (5:5). Thus the church both trains for that future task of judgment and begins its accomplishment.

Love It remains the responsibility not just of Israel's formal judiciary but of **all** God's **people** to act justly, to **witness** to injustice, and following due process to execute justice. The church's leaders and its led all play vital roles in the procedure Jesus outlines in Matt. 18:15–20—as accusers, witnesses, judges, and collective jury. His process works only when all his disciples are able to discern justice and injustice; the just discipline of a church requires a disciplined church. Bearing the multiple testimonies of the Spirit that vindicate worship of the risen Son, Jesus's servants are sometimes mistreated as he was, even by fellow servants; and their gracious discipline is refined through that suffering (Acts 6:8–8:3) "so that it may be made clear that this extraordinary power belongs to God and does not come from us" (2 Cor. 4:7–12 NRSV).

> [17:8]If there arises a matter too hard for you in judgment, between blood and blood, between plea and plea, and between stroke and stroke, being matters of controversy within your gates, then you shall arise, and go up to the place YHWH your God shall choose; [9]and you shall come to the priests the Levites, and to the judge who shall be in those days. You shall inquire, and they shall show you the sentence of judgment. [10]You shall do according to the tenor of the sentence they shall show you from that place YHWH shall choose; and you shall do according to all they shall teach you: [11]according to the tenor of the law they shall teach you, and according to the judgment they shall tell you, you shall do; you shall not turn aside from the sentence that they shall show you, to the right hand or to the left (→5:32–33). [12]The man[+] who does presumptuously, in not listening to the priest who stands to minister there before YHWH your God, or to the judge, even that man[+] shall die: and you shall put away the evil from Israel. [13]All the people shall hear, and fear, and do no more presumptuously.

Plain The Hebrew text could require disputants to bring their case to the **priests** *then* the **judge**, to the priests *or* the judge, or to the priests *and* the judge.

Faith Israel's judges act in light of YHWH's **judgment** (1:17a). In Moses's absence (cf. 1:17b), judgment of difficult cases now falls to the central **priestly** magisterium, which is the wellspring of the nation's knowledge of Torah. Delegating divine power in this way obscures the Torah's truth and authority when Jerusalem's judiciary is corrupt, its prophets false, and its people ignorant—because then Israel's law appears to be a merely human institution acting to advance the interests of the powerful. The crisis can be resolved only as YHWH continues to judge righteously, negating all nations' injustices, purifying their service, and restoring Jerusalem's teaching authority (Zeph. 3:3–13). That prophetic assurance anticipates the Messiah, whose adjudication of perplexing dilemmas amazes crowds and irks the authorities whose hypocrisy it exposes (Mark 12:13–17). Jesus's wise interpretations confirm the Torah's moral authority to Israel and display it to Gentiles. In him, Israel's and God's authoritative teaching are fully united.

Hope "Do not judge, and you will not be judged; do not condemn, and you will not be condemned. Forgive, and you will be forgiven; give, and it will be given to you" (Luke 6:37–38 NRSV). These words are commonly misunderstood as a license for Christian inaction toward injustice. But such passivity is even more disobedient and foolish than ignoring the **Levites'** judgments, for "the one who hears and does not act [on Jesus's words] is like a man⁺ who built a house on the ground without a foundation" (6:49 NRSV). The returning king in the parable of the pounds tells his servants to "bring those enemies of mine who did not want me to reign over them here, and kill before me" (19:27, my translation). A people that accepts injustice is useless and doomed. Yet Israel's ruling **judge** is also its interceding **priest**; Jesus's call not to judge is in reality a warning to accept his forgiveness at once (along with the judgment it implies), address conflict mercifully, and confront injustice with his wisdom and hope. Such faithfulness qualifies disciples to share in Jesus's eschatological office as supreme judge: "The measure you give will be the measure you get back. . . . Everyone who is fully qualified will be like the teacher" (6:38, 40 NRSV).

Love "First take the log out of your own eye, and then you will see clearly to take the speck out of your neighbor's eye" (Luke 6:42 NRSV). Jesus does not want to have to intervene in every dispute among his people, but to raise up reliable disciples who **judge** and intercede as he would—at home, in the assembly, and in all their neighborhoods. In this way he changes his people's "shame into praise and renown in all the earth" (Zeph. 3:19 NRSV). The authority to judge between believers falls on those with wisdom and good standing in the church (1 Cor. 6:4–6a). Difficult cases are not just matters for prayer, supernatural consultation (cf. Exod. 28:30), or deference. The church faces them squarely, confident that its Spirit "of wisdom and understanding . . . of counsel and might . . . of knowledge and the fear of [YHWH]" (Isa. 11:2 NRSV) equips it for the task of judging its own "ordinary matters" (1 Cor. 6:3). Much of the New Testament and subapostolic literature is material for training churches and their leaders in just these skills.

> ¹⁷:¹⁴When you have come to the land YHWH your God gives you, and shall possess it, and shall dwell therein, and shall say: "I will set a king

over me, like all the nations that are around me"; ¹⁵you shall surely set him king over yourselves whom YHWH your God shall choose: one from among your brothers you shall set king over you; you may not put a foreigner over you, who is not your brother. ¹⁶Only he shall not multiply horses to himself or cause the people to return to Egypt, to the end that he may multiply horses; because YHWH has said to you, "You shall not go back that way again." ¹⁷Neither shall he multiply wives to himself, that his heart not turn away: neither shall he greatly multiply to himself silver and gold (→7:25–26). ¹⁸When he sits on the throne of his kingdom, he shall write him a copy of this law in a book, out of that which is before the priests the Levites: ¹⁹and it shall be with him, and he shall read therein all the days of his life; that he may learn to fear YHWH his God, to keep all the words of this law and these statutes, to do them; ²⁰that his heart not be lifted up above his brothers, and that he not turn aside from the commandment, to the right hand or to the left (→5:32–33), so that he may prolong his days in his kingdom, he and his sons⁺, in the midst of Israel.

Plain This passage does not recommend a **king** (cf. 1 Sam. 8). Instead, accepting that a jealous Israel will appropriate its neighbors' monarchy (→28:35–44), it demands to choose the leader from among Israel's own people and for the Torah—not Gentile ways—to be his constitution. This implies divine tolerance for a range of culturally sensitive institutional polities under the rule of law.

Faith How can YHWH keep choosing **kings** when a monarchy is lifelong and succession is hereditary? In Israel's history God transcends the limits of royal lineage with two extraordinary actions that are typologically related: first, by rejecting Saul and choosing David (1 Sam. 13:13–14; 15:23), whose line endures forever (2 Sam. 7:4–16); second, by sending a Son who is born king (Matt. 2:1–2) in David's legal line (1:1–17), displacing his Herodian rivals (2:3–23) and ending royal genealogies forever (1:17; 1 Tim. 1:4). Jesus radically fulfills the Torah's command (Matt. 5:17–20) not to rule with armies, treaties, and appropriated wealth as Pharaoh had or to **lift** himself **above his brothers**, but to serve and prefer the least, and only thus to inherit his kingdom and judgment over Israel (Luke 22:24–30).

Hope Many take these strange provisions for a monarchy as a sign of its later composition. Whether it is or not, this passage is one of many important signs of Deuteronomy's orientation toward Israel's future. God has added the Torah to Israel because of the transgressions (Gal. 3:19) of a young and undisciplined but beloved people, not to preserve youthful innocence but bring maturity (3:22–26). The covenant's terms address Israel's urgent needs and incapacities—for memory, structure, justice, remediation for wrongs, holiness, worship, peculiarity, and now protection. Surrounded by empires, Israel knows its strategic vulnerability and will be unable to resist the pressure to compensate. The word of God meets Israel at its point of need and sees it through, regulating its future monarchy and providing a worthy heir, to move the **sons**[+] of Israel forward to prosperity under his cosmic dynasty rather than behind to defeat or **back** to the **way** of slavery, cultural assimilation, and dissolution (→28:63b–68).

Hope "May **gold** of Sheba be given to him" (Ps. 72:15 NRSV). While power through earned or extorted wealth is inappropriate for the **king** of God's choosing, wealth through voluntary tribute in gratitude for his mercy and salvation is entirely fitting. "May all kings fall down before him, all nations give him service. For he delivers the needy when they call" (72:11–12 NRSV).

Love The church remains a constitutional monarchy, not because the Torah is superior to Jesus but because "not one jot or tittle will pass from the law until all is accomplished" (Matt. 5:18, my translation). If the immortal Jesus remains bound to keep the Torah's wisdom as he rules, so do his servants (John 13:16). Knowing and obeying the **book** of God's rule (→28:45–48) is essential to fruitful leadership in the church. Having inherited both his new covenant and his everlasting throne, his bride and queen inherits also the gifts and the call by which he rules: his Spirit, his mission, his commandments, and the Torah that his passion has reforged as Old Testament.

DEUTERONOMY 18

^{18:1}The priests the Levites, all the tribe of Levi, shall have no portion or inheritance with Israel: they shall eat the offerings of YHWH made by fire, and his⁺ inheritance. ²They shall have no inheritance among their brothers: YHWH is their inheritance, as he⁺ has spoken to them. ³This shall be the priests' due from the people, from those who offer a sacrifice, whether it be ox or sheep, that they shall give to the priest the shoulder, and the two cheeks, and the maw. ⁴The firstfruits of your grain, of your new wine, and of your oil (→24:17–22), and the first of the fleece of your sheep, you shall give him. ⁵For YHWH your God has chosen him out of all your tribes, to stand to minister in the name of YHWH, him and his sons forever. ⁶If a Levite comes from any of your gates out of all Israel, where he lives as a foreigner, and comes with all the desire of his soul to the place YHWH shall choose; ⁷then he shall minister in the name of YHWH his God, as all his brothers the Levites do, who stand there before YHWH. ⁸They shall have like portions to eat, besides that which comes of the sale of his patrimony.

Hope The Levites (who in Deuteronomy seem synonymous with Israel's priesthood) have cities and may still own and inherit property (**patrimony**); what they lack is specific tribal territory (12:12). **Standing** to serve in YHWH's house (Heb. 10:11), YHWH is their only homeland, a house of many dwellings (John 14:2), a city to come for which they sacrifice praises on all Israel's behalf (Heb. 13:14–15), and food that endures (John 6:27). This is not an otherworldly let alone a gnostic legacy, but an eternal one on God's new earth. Gifts of **dues**, honor, and **firstfruits** (→12:15–19) are fitting to a people whose very ancestry looks forward.

Love Constituting Israel under Torah has kept classes of people on the margins of its familial structures. These need the protection that the following chapters offer. "Clergy" are among those classes. The **Levites** are a living **sacrifice** (Num. 8:5–26)—an apparent economic drag on fellow Israelites whose welfare is actually necessary to the health of the whole. As YHWH's representatives, this tribe already lives like **foreigners** in the midst of its landed kin, embodying in itself both YHWH's identity with Israel and his[+] otherness. Because of the centralization of worship at **God's chosen place** and because sacrificial worship can easily be neglected, the Levitical priests who are commissioned to teach Torah, receive sacrifices for God, and guard Israel's public health are politically and economically vulnerable (→12:15–19). They must be protected even from the possibility of a few in their own **tribe** forming a cartel to control Israel's liturgical resources. A corrupt priesthood would support too few Levites, neglect less lucrative responsibilities such as teaching, and abuse its judicial power. The Levites' vulnerability thus threatens to impoverish all Israel. Indeed, priestly corruption is one of the causes of Israel's ruin (1 Sam. 8:1–5). Concentrated Christian magisterial power, sacerdotal corruption, and widespread popular ignorance confirm that the church is susceptible to the same distortions, and uneven results of reform confirm that remedies can be as distortive as Israel's monarchy. Disciples in Jesus's fellowship who are called to be missionaries, teachers, and worship leaders need similar structural protections. "Let the elders who rule well be considered worthy of double honor, especially those who labor in preaching and teaching; for . . . 'The laborer deserves his[+] wages'" (Luke 10:7 in 1 Tim. 5:17–18 RSV; →25:4).

Faith "Do not neglect to show hospitality to strangers, for thereby some have entertained messengers" (Heb. 13:1, my translation). **Levites** have a right to serve and be supported at **God's chosen place**. But Jesus *brings* God's chosen place: the kingdom of God. So his representatives are missionaries who travel in his way (Luke 10:1). His seventy servants, like YHWH's Levites, deserve material support for heralding his coming (10:7). They find it not at the temple but at Jesus's destinations. A family that receives them becomes a "son of peace" (10:6 RSV) that feeds and shelters them in holy fellowship, while one that refuses them invites eschatological judgment (10:12), for the one "who rejects you rejects me, and . . . him[+] who sent me" (10:16 RSV).

Love "The one who proclaims the gospel should live by the gospel" (1 Cor. 9:14, my translation). Paul appeals to both Deuteronomy's rules on priestly compensation (→25:4) and on menial service. As Deuteronomy commands compensation even for **Levites** of independent means, so Paul insists even on rights he does not use (1 Cor. 9:3–18). Because God's servants in Christ, like the Levites, belong to YHWH, their rights are YHWH's.

> **18:9**When you have come into the land YHWH your God gives you, you shall not learn to imitate the abominations of those nations. **10**There shall not be found with you anyone who makes his[+] son or his[+] daughter pass through the fire, one who uses divination, one who practices sorcery, or an enchanter, or a sorcerer, **11**or a charmer, or a consulter with a familiar spirit, or a wizard, or a necromancer.

¹²For whoever does these things is an abomination to YHWH, and because of these abominations (→7:25–26) YHWH your God drives them out from before you. ¹³You shall be unblemished with YHWH your God. ¹⁴For these nations that you shall dispossess listen to those who practice sorcery and to diviners; but as for you, YHWH your God has not allowed you to do so.

Faith While some of these forbidden practices are obscure (and their translations conjectural), they reflect a common goal: to learn, manipulate, or prevent the future by spiritual technique. These powers try to "obtain the gift of God" (Acts 8:20 NRSV) or evade it (→23:3–5). They are "works of the flesh" (Gal. 5:19–21; cf. Acts 8:23) that futilely oppose the Spirit (Gal. 5:17). None honor the reality-making power of the word of God, to whom alone Israel is to listen (→18:15–19). And none can withstand it: the demons submit to the Son of the Most High God (Luke 8:26–39) and to his disciples in his name (9:1; 10:17–19).

Hope **Divination**, **sorcery**, and other such forbidden practices appeal to the self-centered "common sense" of much folk religion worldwide and are exceedingly difficult to abolish. Yet the Torah, prophets, and New Testament (e.g., Acts 19:11–20) agree that they are incompatible with faith. Protestant Reformers were intolerant of them but were less successful than the Enlightenment in marginalizing them. This is not because the Enlightenment strengthened faith but because it yielded more reliable and effective techniques for getting what people want. Given sorcery's association with anger, greed, and lust in biblical vice lists, it is not clear that its modern counterparts are any less abominable to God. As their use in Israel invites slaughter and exile similar to the Canaanites' (Jer. 19), so their continuation on earth until the end of days will bring apocalyptic plagues (Rev. 9:21) and an eternal end (10:1–7).

Love "What fellowship has light with darkness?" (2 Cor. 6:14, my translation). Superstition is a constant enemy of faith. It is incredible in an Israel that trusts in the God who outdid Pharaoh's magicians and freed it from Egypt and who spoke Torah out of Sinai's fire. It is even more **abominable** for a church exorcised through Jesus's name, gifted with the Spirit for warfare against principalities and powers in the heavenly places (Eph. 6:10–17), and tasked to proclaim his kingdom (Luke 9:2). The same unbelief that causes people to cling to social status, money, worldly power, and rights for deliverance causes us to seek other forbidden powers that will only frustrate, divide, and enslave. Christ's holy fellowship has his Holy Spirit, who is the eyes of the Lamb (Isa. 11:1–4 in Rev. 5:6) who knows even the deepest things of all (1 Cor. 2:9–16). The Spirit discloses these things to us both in generalities, in the "plan of the mystery" of the good news itself (Eph. 3:1–12), and in specifics, in words of knowledge given as God chooses to inform (1 Cor. 12:8). Lest superstition blind us and rob us of that costly insight, we are to be vigilant against any **blemish** that would hinder our perfection in Christ's holiness (2 Cor. 6:14–7:1) and cost us our royal inheritance (Gal. 5:21).

18:15YHWH your God will raise up to you a prophet from your midst, of your brothers⁺, like me. You shall listen to him. **16**This is according to all you desired of YHWH your God in Horeb in the day of the assembly, saying: "Let me not hear again the voice of YHWH my God or see this great fire any more, that I not die." **17**YHWH said to me, "They have well said what they have spoken. **18**I will raise them up a prophet from among their brothers⁺, like you; and I will put my words in his mouth, and he shall speak to them all I shall command him. **19**Whoever will not listen to my words that he shall speak in my name, I will call him⁺ to account.

Faith For obvious theological reasons, Christians and Muslims read this promise as fulfilled in a single messenger typologically similar to Moses, whereas Jews read it as fulfilled in a succession of **prophets** compared with whom Moses is in a class by himself.

Faith "What God foretold by the mouth of all the prophets, that his⁺ Christ should suffer, he⁺ thus fulfilled" (Acts 3:18 RSV). Moses has long been indispensable to Israel. Now his tenure is ending. If he is anxious about how Israel will fare without him (→3:23–25; →31:1–8), the people must be terrified (→31:24–30). So Moses reassures Israel that his office will not cease with him. YHWH appointed Moses to mediate the Torah that Israel could not yet stand to hear (5:30–31), and God has promised so to act again. Yet of all the Old Testament prophets God sends Israel, none has a comparable legacy (Luke 20:10–12), and this promise stands unfulfilled at the time of Deuteronomy's finalization (→34:10–12). Moses's legacy is fully refreshed only with the sending of "the Christ appointed for you [Jews], Jesus" (18:15–20 in Acts 3:20 RSV), whose signs and wonders accomplish what Moses's turned out only to anticipate. God's **words** in the prophets' **mouths** (Jer. 1:9) turn out to herald his coming: "All the prophets who have spoken, from Samuel and those who came afterwards, also proclaimed these days" (Acts 3:24 RSV).

Hope The emphatic pronoun **I** in 18:19 stresses that only YHWH disciplines his⁺ people who reject his⁺ prophet (cf. 1 Sam. 28:15–19; 1 Kgs. 20:35–36). They are not to be punished immediately, like false prophets (→18:20–22) and even those who stand in contempt of judges (→17:8–13). Usually their reckoning is eschatological, for heaven has received the prophet like Moses "until the time for establishing all that God spoke" (Acts 3:21 RSV). As the interval between Moses's return and the exodus was a time of signs and wonders of judgment during which God overlooked the Hebrews' grumbling (Exod. 5:19–6:1), the interval between Messiah's ascension and his return is one of gracious signs of mercy that invite everyone to enter his kingdom and gain its blessings (Acts 3:25–26).

Love Israel's duty is to **listen** (→5:27), and many Israelites do (Acts 4:4). Yet many others do not (4:1–3), eventually turning the good news of Jesus toward the nations (18:6; 28:25–28). This suggests a pattern for church discipline against unbelief: not to punish or even excommunicate those who hear but do not heed the Lord

(Luke 6:46–49), but simply to warn them of the consequences (13:24–30) and focus preaching on outsiders who will (7:1; 14:15–24).

Love As God acted to give Israel the truth it could not then bear through Moses, and will act again to send **a prophet like** him, so in that later time God will act yet *again* in the Spirit of truth to lead his[+] people into all the truth of the Father and the Son (John 16:12–15). As Israel could be better off in Moses's absence, so we can be better off in Jesus's absence (16:7–8), with the gift of God himself[+] in the assembly as his[+] own guarantee. This passage is not merely a promise of leadership; it forces humanity's entry into God's triune mutual knowledge.

> **18:20**But the prophet who shall speak a word presumptuously in my name, which I have not commanded him[+] to speak, or who shall speak in the name of other gods, that prophet shall die." **21**If you say in your heart, "How shall we know the word YHWH has not spoken?" **22**when a prophet speaks in the name of YHWH, if the thing does not follow or happen, that is what YHWH has not spoken. The prophet has spoken it presumptuously; you shall not be afraid of him[+].

Faith After-the-fact confirmation seems like a dangerously naïve test that yields false positives (→13:1–5). But this criticism rests on a common misconception: prophecy does not merely predict an already inevitable fate, as many suppose, but brings about a divinely determined future (Jer. 1:10). A failed prophecy has not *worked*; it has not come "in power and in the Holy Spirit and with full conviction" but "only in word" (1 Thess. 1:5 RSV). Its speaker is proffering his or her own lying spirit as the liberating Spirit of YHWH (1 Kgs. 22:23; Isa. 61) and his or her own **presumptions** as the **word** of God (1 Kgs. 22:28; Isa. 55:10–11), a blasphemy that violates the covenant's very heart and calls for punishment (Jer. 28:17). Moses's test of true prophecy simultaneously disconfirms every false Messiah (Mark 13:5–6, 21–22) and confirms the prophetic Spirit of the Word made flesh and of his apostles' preaching.

Hope "False **prophets** also arose among the people, just as there will be false teachers among you" (2 Pet. 2:1 NRSV). If the Constantinian age saw royal and judicial abuse in the church and if high sacramental theology brought priestly abuse, the Protestant focus on doctrine and the Enlightenment focus on knowledge and information have encouraged a flood of prophetic abuse. Contemporary Christians are now used to a pantheon of **other** ideological **gods**, conflicting revisions of apostolic doctrine, and ever-shifting apocalyptic timelines. This passage reassures **fearful hearts** confused by this chaos. We do not even need to wait to disconfirm and disregard false prophecies, for the story of Jesus has already confirmed the prophetic word (1:19–21) and proved that "the Lord knows how to rescue the godly from trial, and to keep the unrighteous under punishment until the day of judgment" (2:9 NRSV).

Love Judging prophetic authenticity is often treated as a propositional, epistemic, and doctrinal challenge, but Christ's suffering reveals that the most profound manifestations of sin and truth are ethical (→13:1–5). False **prophets** are wolves in sheep's clothing, predators pretending to belong in the fold. The church discovers them not so much by weighing their claims—it may be too compromised to be able to do that anyway (cf. Jer. 43:1–3)—as by judging their fruits (Matt. 7:15–16). Prophecy that is of God yields the fruit of love for one another (1 John 4:7–8), testifying to Christ come in the flesh (4:2). False prophecy does evil rather than the Father's will (Matt. 7:21–23) and pursues other "loves" that, as Augustine said, are better called hate (1 John 4:20).

DEUTERONOMY 19

¹⁹:¹When YHWH your God shall cut off the nations whose land YHWH your God gives you, and you succeed them and dwell in their cities and in their houses, ²you shall set apart three cities for you in the midst of your land YHWH your God gives you to possess. ³You shall survey for yourselves the way, and divide the borders of your land that YHWH your God causes you to inherit into three parts, that every manslayer⁺ may flee there. ⁴This is the case of the manslayer⁺ that shall flee there and live: whoever kills his⁺ neighbor unawares, and did not hate him⁺ in time past—⁵as when a man⁺ goes into the forest with his⁺ neighbor to chop wood, and his⁺ hand fetches a stroke with the axe to cut down the tree, and the head slips from the handle and lights on his⁺ neighbor so that he⁺ dies; he⁺ shall flee to one of these cities and live—⁶lest the avenger of blood pursue the manslayer⁺ while his⁺ heart is hot, and overtake him⁺ because the way is long, and strike him⁺ mortally; whereas he⁺ was not worthy of death, inasmuch as he⁺ did not hate him⁺ in time past. ⁷Therefore I command you, saying: You shall set apart three cities for yourselves.

Plain Whereas Deuteronomy's regulations for monarchy (17:14–20) concern a more distant future, they provide right away for effective prevention against abusive punishment. Deuteronomy's contemporary readers should not imagine here a modern nation-state with civil agencies for police, justice, welfare, planning, and the like. Ancient Israel is closer to a modern frontier society whose institutions are familial, tribal, and local. These Levitical (Num. 35:6) **cities** of refuge help counter their inherent biases of familial blood vengeance and protect accidental killers from overly harsh punishment.

Faith The uncharacteristically long **case** in 19:5 is almost parabolic in arousing our sympathy for the slayer. God has foreseen—or perhaps remembered (Gen. 34:25–31)—not only how unchecked tribal justice weakens Israel but how righteous anger causes undue suffering. This twist in the law anticipates a more stable solution to come: rather than rely forever on the Torah's measures against **hot** human **hearts**, God addresses the root cause by giving Israel first a new heart of flesh and then a new spirit (Ezek. 36:26–27) of Christ's outpoured love for enemies and sinners (Rom. 5:5–11). The priestly work of Christ begins to render the priestly **cities** of refuge obsolete (cf. Heb. 8:13).

Hope "If it is possible, so far as it depends on you, live peaceably with all. Beloved, never **avenge** yourselves, but leave room for the wrath of God" (Rom. 12:18–19 NRSV; →32:32–35). The kingdom of God is an eternal city of refuge, not because forgiven sinners are out of the wrathful world's immediate reach but because the coming Son of Man will redeem his persecuted ones from every enemy. Meanwhile the kingdom's ambassadors defuse vengeance when we "rejoice in hope, be patient in suffering, persevere in prayer" (Rom. 12:12 NRSV) and so "overcome evil with good" (12:21 NRSV).

Love Israel is to plan ahead for woe. Life in the promised **land** is a real life involving misfortune, conflict, temptation, and grim duty. A community that does not allow for such contingencies will suffer and fall from its naïveté. As God has already provided places for these **cities** of refuge (6:10), so Christ has prepared the church for just such happenings with a host of ethical guidelines, social structures, and means of grace. These make it a sign to the world of the possibility of impossible blessing in the present and of eternal life to come (Matt. 19:16–30).

> **19:8**If YHWH your God enlarges your border, as he⁺ has sworn to your fathers, and gives you all the land he⁺ promised to give to your fathers; **9**if you keep all this commandment to do it, which I command you this day, to love YHWH your God, and to walk ever in his⁺ ways; then you shall add three cities more for yourselves besides these three: **10**that innocent blood not be shed in the midst of your land, which YHWH your God gives you for an inheritance, and so blood be on you. **11**But if any man⁺ hates his⁺ neighbor, and lies in wait for him⁺ and rises up against him⁺ and strikes him⁺ mortally so that he⁺ dies, and he⁺ flees into one of these cities, **12**then the elders of his⁺ city shall send and bring him⁺ there, and deliver him⁺ into the hand of the avenger of blood, that he⁺ may die. **13**Your eye shall not pity him⁺, but you shall put away the innocent blood from Israel, that it may go well with you.

Faith In his⁺ mission to convict the world of sin and justice and judgment, the Spirit testifies to every audience the definitive playing out of this passage's dual scenario—with Jesus crucified by unbelief and ascended in **innocence**, and the ruler of this world (who **lies in wait** like a predator; 1 Pet. 5:8) condemned and unspared (John 16:8–11). This story is the good news of the Son who is eternally in the Father (14:11), his refuge and ours (20:17).

Hope Everywhere God's kingdom goes, God's justice goes. YHWH *does* **enlarge** Israel's **border**, not just to the Euphrates (11:24) or even the ends of the earth (Ps. 2:8) but into the deepest recesses of the human heart (e.g., Joel 3:18; Isa. 43:19–21; and Ezek. 47:1–12 in John 7:38–39) and outward to the borderless expanse of all things (16:15). Deuteronomy's **cities** of refuge reflect the local cultural institution of **blood vengeance**; the broader need that Israel shares with all nations is restraint of passions—whether retaliation, **hatred**, or **pity**. So this provision's scope goes far beyond just **three cities more** to every gift of grace that sanctifies in the truth (17:17).

Love YHWH holds Israel collectively responsible both for unpunished guilt and for punished innocence. Popular Protestant theology so emphasizes justification by grace through faith in Christ's atonement that it can appear that God's only provision for maintaining Israel's guiltlessness in the face of total depravity is atoning sacrifice. Yet the Reformers themselves stressed that God also commands community practices that restrain sin and acknowledge **innocent blood**. The people *as* a people steward resources of place, leadership, and character for their own justice and health. "Seek first [God's] kingdom and his⁺ righteousness" (Matt. 6:33 RSV): Jesus's atonement and his rule together create the possibility of fulfilling God's promise of a free and just Israel that walks **forever in his⁺ ways**.

Love "Let what you heard from the beginning abide in you" (1 John 2:24a NRSV). These refuges function only if they are accessible and if their **elders** are dutiful. Despite its founding story and all God's gifts, the church has abused the innocent and favored the guilty. "We have sinned against you in thought, word, and deed," it confesses, "by what we have done, and by what we have left undone." We are jointly accountable not only for historic persecutions, crusades, genocides, and clerical corruption, but also for similar sins in the present: we single out particular categories of sins (such as homosexuality or racism) for special and even unique intolerance and vilify Christians of other traditions (such as Protestant fundamentalism or Roman Catholicism) who do not share our sensibilities. We put up with heretical leaders and ignorant parishioners, fall for scammers and abusers in our ranks who prey upon the innocent, and **pity** immoral clergy who have abused the power in their positions. It does not **go well with** those who do not walk as Christ walked (2:6): our moral failure causes suffering, betrays our witness, confuses everyone, and grieves the Holy Spirit. The church's preeminent weapon against these evils is confession of sin, as some liturgies put it, "that we may delight in your will, and **walk in** your **ways**, to the glory of your name." Restoration renews obedience to our evangelical duty to serve in the Father's refuge freeing the innocent and justifying the guilty (1:9; 2:1–5). "If what you heard from the beginning abides in you, then you will abide in the Son and in the Father. And this is what he has promised us, eternal life" (2:24b–25 NRSV).

19:14 You shall not remove your neighbor's landmark, which they of old time have set, in your inheritance that you shall inherit in the land YHWH your God gives you to possess.

Plain Moving an ancestral boundary **marker** not only steals (→5:19) and defrauds one's **neighbor** (→5:20), but robs a family of the past, present, and future that YHWH has promised and secured. It is an act of subtle dispossession against God's will—a silent naming of YHWH in vain (→5:11).

Faith Christ suffered the world's attempt to dispossess him. "Those tenants said to one another, 'This is the heir; come, let us kill him, and the **inheritance** will be ours'" (Mark 12:7 NRSV). Today he suffers identity theft (13:6, 22) that grasps for power over what only he **possesses**.

Hope Israel's return from exile as spoken by the prophets shows that "the gifts and the call are irrevocable" (Isa. 59:20–21 and 27:9 in Rom. 11:26–29 RSV). Christian supersessionism or "replacement theology" honors the newness of God's offer of grace to the whole world, but by wrongfully dispossessing the Israel of **old**. The risen Jesus refused to dispossess his faithless disciples, but offered them the same peace (Luke 24:36) he offers all the towns of Israel (10:5; Matt. 10:13) until his return (10:23). Dispossession is the prerogative of the master alone (Mark 12:9–11), who has chosen to replace not the tribes of Israel themselves but only their incompetent leaders (11:27; 12:12). His offer of peace stands to this day for his kin and Paul's to accept. "They have now been disobedient in order that, by the mercy shown to [Gentiles], they too may now receive mercy" (Rom. 11:31 NRSV).

Love The world's conspiracy to dispossess the heir of all things reveals our dispossessive hearts toward one another. But "God has so arranged the body, giving the greater honor to the inferior member, that there may be no dissension within the body, but the members may have the same care for one another" (1 Cor. 12:24–25). A radical form of dispossession in the church is the wrongful schismatic excommunication of brothers and sisters; lesser counterparts are elitism and populism. Excluding and subordinating rightful members of Christ's body tries to assert control over the Son's freely shared inheritance and causes all to suffer (3:4; 12:26a). Honoring one another confesses Christ's lordship together in our common Spirit, bringing ecumenical joy and health to all (12:3, 26b).

19:15 One witness shall not rise up against a man⁺ for any iniquity, or for any sin, in any sin that he⁺ sins: at the mouth of two witnesses, or at the mouth of three witnesses, shall a matter be established (→13:6–11; →17:2–7). **16**If an unrighteous witness rises up against any man⁺ to testify against him⁺ of wrongdoing, **17**then both the men⁺ between whom the controversy is shall stand before YHWH, before the priests and the judges who shall be in those days; **18**and the judges shall make diligent inquisition. And behold, if the witness is a false witness, and has testified falsely against his⁺ brother⁺, ¹⁹then you shall do to him⁺ as he⁺ had thought to do to his⁺ brother⁺. So you shall put away the evil from your midst. ²⁰Those who remain shall hear, and fear, and shall henceforth commit no more any such evil in your midst. ²¹Your eyes shall not pity: life for life, eye for eye, tooth for tooth, hand for hand, foot for foot.

Plain The retaliatory limit of **eye for eye** is more directly relevant to Exod. 21:24–25 and Lev. 24:20 (cf. Heb. 10:28; Matt. 5:38–39; but →25:17–19). Here the focus is on arriving at a verdict that warrants it.

Faith Justice means telling our stories right, **sin** notwithstanding. However, sin turns our social constructions of reality into social distortions, justice notwithstanding. Conventional remedies, familiar to civil law as well as responsible historiography and journalism, include the tactics alluded to here: corroboration, reliability of character, cross-examination, strict rules of evidence, and punishment of misrepresentation and perjury. These are of great value under normal circumstances. Yet they can be frustrated—by conspiracy, mass deception, intimidation, tampering, and corruption, all of which sinfully manipulate methods of **inquisition**. **Unrighteous witness** has been endemic in Israel's experience, from Joseph's brothers and Potiphar's wife to Daniel's rival prophets to Haman's plot—and of course to the Messiah's enemies (→17:2–7). Once perjury becomes normalized, injustice becomes a power that demands servility.

Hope These cases also attest to the ultimate confuting of **unrighteous** testimony by divine testimony—the only truly reliable kind (John 5:31–47; 8:13–19; 1 John 5:6–12). "You are justified in your sentence and blameless when you pass judgment" (Ps. 51:4 NRSV). It redirects our **fear** away from the power of injustice toward the power of the living God (Heb. 10:31). "You plotted **evil** for me," Joseph tells his brothers, "but God planned it for good" (Gen. 50:20, my translation; cf. Heb. 11:22). The assurance that YHWH has consistently vindicated his⁺ cloud of truthful witnesses (12:1) turns what would be an intolerable reign of lies into a hopeful, even productive, life in the Father's loving discipline (12:2–9). It even yields the patience, holiness, and righteousness (12:10–11) that we need to be the truthful **witnesses** that Deuteronomy aims for and that the peaceful rule of law depends on (12:11). Perseverance in light of the good news is God's way out of the world's captivity to judicial injustice.

Love The slandered neighbor (→5:20) is repeatedly called **brother⁺**, adding to the sense of betrayal and to the urgency of an equitable response. These relationships include those within the people of God, and wrenching fairness must characterize them all (e.g., Matt. 18:15–20). Christians are not to resist **evildoers** who mistreat us (Deut. 19:21 in Matt. 5:38–39; Heb. 12:14–15); but such personally costly grace is the antithesis of comfortable leniency. Showing forbidden **pity** on **false witnesses** would not only harm the accused but violate the truth itself and endanger all who rely on it for protection against unobstructed injustice.

DEUTERONOMY 20

20:1 When you go forth to battle against your enemies, and see horses, chariots, and a people more than you, you shall not be afraid of them; for YHWH your God is with you, who brought you up out of the land of Egypt. **2**When you draw near to the battle, the priest shall approach and speak to the people **3**and shall tell them, "Hear, Israel, you draw near this day to battle against your enemies. Do not let your heart faint; do not be afraid, or tremble, or be scared of them; **4**for YHWH your God is he[+] who goes with you, to fight for you against your enemies, to save you."

Hope Military policy follows naturally from civil policy; both call for disciplined governance in order to avoid disaster. These war scenarios reflect conditions under the monarchy, with wars of empire (20:10–15a) and sieges (20:19–20) as well as continued conquest in the land (20:15b–18), so these rules are permanent. **Horses**, **chariots**, and superior numbers are intimidating sights, but Israel will face far more intimidating military tribulations. Much of Israel's Old Testament and intertestamental history and all of the church's New Testament history reflects social situations so precarious, with such formidable enemies, that the realistic alternatives are perseverance or surrender. Yet the Torah's rules continue to apply: from **Egypt** to the eschaton, **battle** is patient prayer under persecution, victory is perseverance through suffering, salvation is deliverance, YHWH's presence becomes the coming of the Son of Man, and the **priest's** encouragement becomes apocalyptic prophecy when hearts are growing faint (Ezek. 1:3).

Faith Presumably these campaigns are waged not at Israel's initiative but at divine or enemy initiative, demanding of Israel a response of trust. Moses's encouragement echoes Sinai (→5:4–6) and his own words at Kadesh-barnea (1:29–31), calling Israel back on its memories of past deliverance (→7:16–21). The **priest's** encouragement echoes the Shema (6:4), making lopsided **battle** a stark instance of loving YHWH with all Israel's **heart** and might (6:5). Jesus the **Savior** is on both sides of this alliance. Besides being the supreme example of trust in YHWH's deliverance in battle under apocalyptic conditions, he is the divine warrior who conquers every **enemy** of Israel when all other hearts have failed (Rev. 5:5–14; 19:11–16).

Love "Be strong in the Lord and in the strength of his power" (Eph. 6:10 NRSV). The missionary task of the church militant is often portrayed in terms of warfare that echo the Torah and its later apocalyptic framework (6:10–20). The Western pluralistic contemporary context has made the prospect of evangelism more intimidating than physical **battle**. Most enculturated Western Christians have become demoralized and have censored ourselves. Ironically, our misplaced love of peace withholds the very peace that we seek (cf. 6:15). Our seminary-educated Western priesthood often leads the retreat, but Christ's **priests** actually bear the special responsibility of encouraging every discouraged disciple to "stand firm" (6:13) as we struggle "against the cosmic powers of this present darkness" (6:12, my translation) with God's gifts (6:14–16) and God himself[+] (6:17) as our defensive and offensive weaponry. Whether the church envisions its task in military imagery or any other, it can achieve nothing apart from bold apostolic proclamation of the mystery (6:19–20) of Christ's victory.

> **20:5**The officers shall speak to the people, saying: "What man is there who has built a new house and has not dedicated it? Let him go and return to his house, lest he die in the battle and another man dedicate it. **6**What man is there who has planted a vineyard and has not used its fruit? Let him go and return to his house, lest he die in the battle and another man use its fruit. **7**What man is there who has pledged to be married a wife and has not taken her? Let him go and return to his house, lest he die in the battle and another man take her." **8**The officers shall speak further to the people, and they shall say: "What man is there who is fearful and fainthearted? Let him go and return to his house, lest his brother's heart melt as his heart." **9**When the officers have made an end of speaking to the people, they shall appoint captains of armies at the head of the people.

Faith "Many are called, but few are chosen" (Matt. 22:14 NRSV). This passage does not describe a conventional conscripted force or a professional volunteer army. It is simply the people of God mobilized for a particular task. The test for service in any given campaign is not legal obligation, loyalty to the state, support for the cause, or military potential, but only being in the right circumstances and having the courage to act. Gideon's army is the classic example (Judg. 7:2–3), but many others arise, out of a variety of situations: "Who knows whether you reign for such a time as this" (Esth. 4:14, my translation).

Hope Most every **death in battle** is lamentable and unfair. What distinguishes the scenarios in 20:5–7 is the prospect of being killed with one's life in an unconsummated state, so that one's arriving future falls to another. This would be a tragic antisign of God's covenant faithfulness—or even a sign of God's covenantal justice on the unfaithful (28:27–34). Either way, it is inappropriate. The proper warriors for securing God's covenant promises either have no such commitments—such as Jesus himself or Paul—or already experience their fulfillment—such as Peter and other apostles who travel with their spouses (1 Cor. 9:5) or disciples like Lydia who retain their businesses (Acts 16:14). Conversely, both socially and spiritually immature believers—people who have yet to come into their full stature (cf. Eph. 4:13)—are poor candidates for extremely risky ventures. Only those who can bear the cost ought to take them on (Luke 14:28–30).

Love God's powerful presence does not make Israel impervious; rather, "you will stretch out your hands, and another will gird you and carry you where you do not wish to go" (John 21:18 RSV). The **officers'** cuts respect the real risk of casualties and consequences of discouragement. Here is an image of pastoral consideration for believers' differing proportions of faith (Rom. 12:6). Leaders should organize the church (and theological education!) in such a way that the strong do not overwhelm the weak and the weak do not dispirit the strong. It is a sin for a **fainthearted** soldier to fight "because he[+] does not act from faith" (14:23 RSV). Conversely, the strong do not put down the weak, but they do not keep them around to spread the views that set them back in the first place (14:1). In both ways the powerful "bear with the weaknesses of the powerless" (15:1, my translation).

> **20:10**When you draw near to a city to fight against it, then proclaim peace to it. **11**If it makes you an answer of peace, and opens to you, then all the people who are found therein shall become tributary to you, and shall serve you. **12**If it will make no peace with you, but will make war against you, then you shall besiege it; **13**and when YHWH your God delivers it into your hand, you shall strike every male of it with the edge of the sword: **14**but the women, and the little ones, and the livestock, and all that is in the city, even all its spoil, you shall take for a prey to yourself; and you shall eat the spoil of your enemies, which YHWH your God has given you. **15**Thus you shall do to all the cities that are very far off from you, that are not of the cities of these nations. **16**But of the cities of these peoples, that YHWH your God gives you for an inheritance, you shall save alive nothing that breathes; **17**but you shall utterly destroy them: the Hittite, and the Amorite, the Canaanite, and the Perizzite, the Hivite, and the Jebusite; as YHWH your God has commanded you; **18**that they not teach you to imitate

all their abominations (→7:2–5) that they have done to their gods;
so would you sin against YHWH your God.

Plain This is one of the Bible's most appalling passages (→2:34–37): **peace** is an invitation to submit to slavery. **Siege** tactics exploit suffering for military advantage. **Women** and children are lumped in with **livestock** and treasure as war booty. Enemy **males**, the only physical threat, are exterminated. Lives are reckoned according to their utility. The only way not to be horrified by these instructions is not to identify, at all, with Israel's victims—so the plain meaning is also ethnocentric to the point of dehumanization. Sentiments in these and other passages (e.g., Exod. 15:1–21; Josh. 6–12; Judg. 5:24–31) suggest that the original audiences do just that, identifying only with YHWH's anointed conquerors and remaining insensitive (as in Deuteronomy), if not downright sadistic, to victims.

Faith Yet the God who **puts males to the sword** to fulfill his promises to Abraham directed Abraham to sacrifice his only son (Gen. 22:1–19), so that "by your seed shall all the nations of the earth gain blessing for themselves, because you have obeyed my voice" (22:18, my translation). And the Father who spares Isaac refuses to spare either his+ own people (→28:20–26) or his+ own Son but gives him up for all (Rom. 8:32). That Son, like his ambassador to the Gentiles and all others who know him, has freely made himself a curse, an offering, and "a servant to all" to save some and share the gospel's blessings (cf. 1 Cor. 9:19–23)—an event so shocking that his people reject his rule and hand him over to the pagan foreign occupiers. The Father's instructions are not the will of a dehumanizing utilitarian God but an awful mission in his+ still mysterious economy of triumphing *over* nations by advocating *for* them and vice versa.

Hope While the passage in itself does not invite readers to sympathize with victims, its broader context demands it (→5:12–15). Deuteronomy remembers that a **faraway** nation had oppressed the Hebrews only recently (→5:4–6), and it foresees that God's people will one day be plundered, put in subjection to distant empires, and even mass-murdered (32:22–25). God is not fickle, and these disasters are not signs of God's sudden favor on its conquerors (Jer. 10:25). They are further wrenching twists in the saga by which "God has consigned all to disobedience that he+ may have mercy on all" (Rom. 11:32, my translation). Only readers who follow all its shifts will know the heart of a God who longs for both universal justice and universal mercy for his+ depraved, beloved world.

Love For those inclined to sympathize with Israel's victims living and dead, honoring the meaning of this passage is a painful discipline. Some simply cannot bring themselves to do it. It is easier to explain away such "texts of terror" as sheer prejudice, unredeemed cultural perspective, the impenetrable mystery of a hidden God, the mere beginning of a trajectory that leads to a progressive future, or "spiritual" texts with no lasting investment in their literal senses, than it is to face them as Torah—as Israel's canonical instructions for confessing YHWH as Lord in loving obedience. While God may overlook such exegetical corner-cutting among those whose faith seems to depend on it, the word still stands above us demanding that we heed it in all its integrity. No Christian community that refuses to do so will last, for it will eventually give way to new ones that do accept God's challenge. Besides, once we somehow excised the terror from the conquest of Canaan, we would still face primordial and patriarchal catastrophes at God's hand, plagues on Egyptian families with no part in Pharaoh's contest against Moses, covenant laws that exclude and cast out unfairly, God's rough justice in the wilderness, Israel's ruin and exile, the prophesied suffering of innocents, Job's anguish and his family's deaths, cosmic apocalyptic judgments past and future, and above all Jesus's rejection. We would be left with not the biblical story but a mutilation. In that comfortably truncated universe of our own making, we could ironically no longer find ourselves—for the Bible's ugliness is the ugliness of our afflicted world, and God's horrifying judgment on it, and the unbearable grief that the Spirit bears with the saints. Nor could we perceive our Messiah—for the scars by which we recognize him would lose their intelligibility. It is precisely the least comfortable words of God that call for the deepest trust. God's past vindication of those who trust makes our trust warranted at the least comfortable times.

Love Every ecclesial reader of this passage is conquering, rejected, exiled, crucified, restored, and glorified Israel. Each is also the conquered, surviving and un-assimilated, corrupting and dominating and exiling, crucifying and persecuting, forgiven and blessed and happily enslaved nations (Gal. 3:28–29). These terrible instructions force us to see ourselves as justly but not simply condemned and as unconditionally but not arbitrarily graced.

Love The swords, captivity, and horror are literal. But in the fullness of time the **sword** to which we are put is the inspired word of God (Eph. 6:17 in →20:1–4), our captivity is citizenship in the commonwealth of Israel and membership in God's household (Eph. 2:12, 19), our lost possessions are multiplied and made incorruptible (2:7; 3:8), and the horror we face is the abolishing and remaking of all human life (2:15). Receiving Christ's **peace** from nearby or afar (2:17)—giving up our lives (5:25) and so rising from the dead (5:14), being subject to one another (5:21, 24) and so coming to power (3:18)—involves a conquest as real and bloody (2:13) as that of Canaan. Rejecting or discounting the terror in this passage trains us away from appreciating the terror of conversion.

> **20:19**When you shall besiege a city a long time, in making war against it to take it, you shall not destroy its trees by wielding an axe against them; for you may eat of them, and you shall not cut them down; for is the tree of the field a human being that it should be besieged by you? **20**Only the trees of which you know that they are not trees

for food, you shall destroy and cut them down; and you shall build bulwarks against the city that makes war with you, until it fall.

Faith For God to watch out for **trees** after consigning whole cities to the sword seems comical. However, this rule concerns the tactics proper to Israel's military goals. To resort to total war against a stubborn enemy, as Elisha advises Israel to do against Moab (2 Kgs. 3:19), would ruin the land that God's people are inheriting. It would be an act of desperation, not faith, like bowing down to the devil in order to gain the Father's inheritance (Matt. 4:8–10). Israel must guard against becoming so caught up in its immediate tasks that it loses perspective. What seems like odd, even obvious, advice turns out to be a prescient measure for protecting mission integrity under pressure—one that modern military strategists sometimes forget.

Hope The shape of God's providence is not self-evident. Discovery takes experience, inquiry, and discernment. As Joseph did not **know** at first that arousing jealousy through boasting had been God's way of protecting his[+] people, so Israel will have to become acquainted with its new home, learning which **trees** God has provided for its sustenance and which are for its conquest. Otherwise it will needlessly deplete its own resources and frustrate the fulfilling of God's promise (Num. 13:20; Joel 2:21–24). Extensive knowledge of our world, like Solomon's grasp of natural science (1 Kgs. 4:33), can perceive God's providence in greater depth and be an eschatological sign to the world of God's goodness (Deut. 4:29–34 in Matt. 12:42). "The sons[+] went in and possessed the land . . . and took possession of houses filled with all sorts of goods, hewn cisterns, vineyards, olive orchards, and fruit trees in abundance . . . and delighted themselves in your great goodness" (Neh. 9:24–25, my translation). Conversely, as Esau despises his birthright (Gen. 25:29–34) and ungrateful Israel loses its land and trees (→28:35–44), so undiscerning Christians who do not appreciate God's gifts surrender their inheritance when their master returns (Matt. 25:14–30).

Love Moses uses the ridiculous image of laying **siege** to **trees** to warn Israel's commanders to use simple common sense in doing the will of God. God's shepherds, in Moses's day and the apostles' and ours, need to be sensible, competent, and prudent (1 Tim. 3:2, 11–12; Titus 1:8), or we will make catastrophic mistakes that impede God's good plans.

DEUTERONOMY 21

²¹:¹If one be found slain in the land YHWH your God gives you to possess, lying in the field, and it is not known who has struck him⁺; ²then your elders and your judges shall come forth, and they shall measure to the cities that are around the slain one: ³and the city that is nearest to the slain one, the elders of that city shall take a heifer of the herd that has not been worked with and has not drawn in the yoke; ⁴and the elders of that city shall bring down the heifer to a valley with running water, which is neither plowed nor sown, and shall break the heifer's neck there in the valley. ⁵The priests the sons of Levi shall come near; for YHWH your God has chosen them to minister to him⁺, and to bless in the name of YHWH; and according to their word shall every controversy and every stroke be. ⁶All the elders of that city who are nearest to the slain one shall wash their hands over the heifer whose neck was broken in the valley; ⁷and they shall answer and say: "Our hands have not shed this blood, neither have our eyes seen it. ⁸Forgive, YHWH, your people Israel, whom you have redeemed, and do not allow innocent blood in the midst of your people Israel." The blood shall be forgiven them. ⁹So you shall put away the innocent blood from your midst, when you shall do what is right in the eyes of YHWH.

Plain This is a versatile transition from polity to an emerging major theme: protection of the vulnerable. The ritual compensates for the failure of conventional social justice. Theories abound interpreting its ambiguous details according to various cultural parallels, but it clearly provides a needed public response to the crisis. The closest **city** takes the case under its jurisdiction. The parties go to a remote area; its flowing **water** may be purgative (→9:18–21). In the presence of other neighboring leaders and with **priests** as YHWH's witnesses, killing **the**

heifer publicly acknowledges the victim (either by evoking the original murder, the murderer's rightful punishment, or the consequences of leaders' false witness). **Washing** the **elders' hands** over it declares the leaders' innocence and incapacity to address the crime any other way. All this is a backdrop for their prayer, which accepts God's standing offer of grace as the only way to forgive Israel of the crime and prevent its guilt for unanswered murder.

Hope Does all this really resolve the matter? "Righteousness does not reach us" (Isa. 59:9 NRSV). The murderer is not punished; the victim's story is not known or told; the stream takes the impurity to its unknown destination. Oddly, the **priests** only witness rather than intercede, so that the animal is a ritual declaration or perhaps a reenactment rather than an atoning sacrifice. In these ways the scene echoes the open-endedness of the original events, seeking rather than bringing closure. "Sovereign Lord, holy and true, how long will it be before you judge and avenge our **blood**?" (Rev. 6:10 NRSV). Closure is in God's wise hands (Isa. 59:16–21; →32:32–35): "The sea gave up the dead that were in it, Death and Hades gave up the dead that were in them, and each was judged according to what he$^+$ had done" (Rev. 20:13, my translation). Meanwhile, by handing the matter over to God for **forgiveness** and resolution—in that order—Israel's leaders have intercepted a tragedy in the making to plead for God to bring it to a **righteous** conclusion.

Love This ceremony's many puzzling features resemble other ancient Near Eastern practices and probably have pre-Israelite roots. This suggests that such actions span cultures and religions. Like Deuteronomy's other constitutional provisions, this one has civil as well as ecclesial applications. In Deuteronomy the real work of the ritual happens in God's answer to the **elders'** prayer in the **priests'** presence. This places indirect responsibility on both civil and ecclesial authorities for the disappeared, the murdered and covered up, the assassinated, the purged, the aborted, and all who have suffered beyond the reach of temporal justice. As God's sign of his$^+$ coming kingdom and invitation to the world to receive his$^+$ grace, the church can be the only truly intelligible sign, especially in secular and pagan societies, of a solution to these otherwise permanent injustices. The church can remind mayors and governors of their obligation to rule with a view toward God's justice, and it can publicly attest to how faithfully they do it. Church leaders must also acknowledge that Christians are among societies' unidentified criminals, condemn their sins, and publicly beg for God to make **right** what we have not. Overlooking the possible crimes of Christians insults victims, impugns the Lord by association, and takes on the victims' bloodguilt (cf. Isa. 59:7).

Faith "If you are angry with a brother$^+$ you will be answerable to judgment" (Matt. 5:21–22, my translation, on →5:17). Eventually all of us are perpetrators of imaginative anonymous murder, and all of us are victims. The world constantly amasses bloodguilt of the heart. It corrodes societies into masses of alienation, resentment, depression, and aggression. Christ's way of investigating our crimes is his order to confess our sins to God and one another (Matt. 5:23–25; 6:12;

Jas. 5:16) and to intercede for all who would kill us, as the Father did in sending his⁺ Son (Matt. 5:43–48). Indeed, the kingdom has rich resources for rooting out anonymous bloodguilt of the heart. The broken one over which we receive our innocence is the flesh and **blood** we share at his table. The untamed stream running under it is the living **water** of the Spirit. The **priests** who judge every conflict are the ascended high priest who forgives and cleanses. The **elders** are pastors who take jurisdiction over our secrets and lead us to **do what is right** in God's **eyes**. Their assurances are the good news that we victims have been acknowledged by our Messiah and freed from the evil eyes of others. Sadly, more and more we neglect these resources. As Catholics have abandoned auricular confession and Protestants have abandoned liturgical confession, our sins have gone unacknowledged and increasingly undiscerned. "Your iniquities have been barriers between you and your God, and your sins have hidden his⁺ face from you so that he⁺ does not hear" (Isa. 59:2 NRSV).

> **21:10**When you go forth to battle against your enemies, and YHWH your God delivers them into your hands, and you carry them away captive, **11**and see among the captives a beautiful woman, and you desire her, and would take her to you as wife; **12**then you shall bring her home to your house; and she shall shave her head, and pare her nails; **13**and she shall put the clothing of her captivity from off her, and shall remain in your house, and bewail her father and her mother a full month: and after that you shall go in to her, and be her husband, and she shall be your wife. **14**If you have no delight in her, then you shall let her go where she will; but you shall not sell her at all for money, you shall not deal with her as a slave, because you have humbled her.

Plain In a context of cultural marriage conventions dominated by Israelite males' interests (→22:22–30), Moses grants foreign **women** captives *some* rights. Many traditional and contemporary commentators, sounding defensive, stress the consideration this passage shows for an unmarried captive woman's rights, social obligations, and feelings. Yet few contemporary women would rejoice to enter this arrangement! Nevertheless, this rule does concern a profoundly vulnerable group: sexual captives of war who attract their captors. These receive Israel's covenant protection and freedom rather than being consigned to perpetual exploitation.

Faith "It was because you were so hard-hearted that Moses allowed you to divorce your wives, but from the beginning it was not so" (Matt. 19:8 NRSV). Like →24:1–4 and many others, this passage (especially in its treatment of an unloved **wife**) seems a concession to the fallenness of Moses's present age—a measure aimed at restraining sin (1 Tim. 1:8–11) rather than preventing evil. These rules are necessary in a world that awaits and resists redemption. Yet they are ethics only for a season in the harsh interim between humanity's promising beginning and the kingdom's coming. To take them as more is to confuse God's good gifts with God's best.

Love Christ's bride is such a prize—desired before her own desiring, liberated from **captivity** and brought into her suitor's **household, humbled** in powerlessness yet **clothed** in the garments of a free woman, treated with patience while mourning her old life, and then bequeathed full membership in the people of God. Yet, like a last Eve to Christ's last Adam, she also gains qualities intended "from the beginning": identification with her head, inheritance of his life-giving Spirit, and assurance that what God has joined together will not be sundered (Matt. 19:6). The sad and unjust ring of this passage applies only where a woman's life before conquest was good or her suitor is a poor match or an opportunist. When her "life" was a kind of death and her suitor is the Son of God, her conversion is an occasion for joy.

> ²¹:¹⁵If a man have two wives, the one beloved, and the other hated, and they have borne him children, both the beloved and the hated; and if the firstborn son be hers who was hated; ¹⁶then in the day that he causes his sons to inherit that which he has, he may not make the son of the beloved the firstborn before the son of the hated, who is the firstborn: ¹⁷but he shall acknowledge the firstborn, the son of the hated, by giving him a double portion of all that he has; for he is the beginning of his strength; the right of the firstborn is his. ¹⁸If a man have a stubborn and rebellious son, who will not obey the voice of his father, or the voice of his mother, and, though they chasten him, will not listen to them; ¹⁹then his father and his mother (17:7) shall lay hold on him, and bring him out to the elders of his city, and to the gate of his place; ²⁰and they shall tell the elders of his city, "This our son is stubborn and rebellious, he will not obey our voice; he is a glutton, and a drunkard." ²¹All the men of his city shall stone him to death with stones. So you shall put away the evil from your midst; and all Israel shall hear, and fear.

Plain The scenarios here are illustrative rather than normative instances of misplaced paternal and filial affection. A monogamous **father** whose will favored a junior **son** over his **firstborn** would still break the commandment, as would a son who was a teetotaling fool (Prov. 23:20–21).

Faith Elders and neighbors accuse Jesus of being a **rebellious son** (Luke 7:34). Even his family relationships are strained (8:19–20). But his antagonists are the true transgressors, setting the stubborn and rebellious powers of their age (Col. 1:16a) above the **firstborn** of all creation (1:15) in handing him over to a cursed death (→21:22–23). However, "wisdom is vindicated by all her children" (Luke 7:35 NRSV). In raising him (Col. 1:18) the Father honors the preeminent Son as **the beginning** and heir of all things (1:16b–18), **putting away the evil** of misbegotten justice not with the stopgap measure of death but the eternal remedy of peace (1:20). God's grace in Jesus Christ is good news for all to **hear** (1:5–6, 23), as well as a warning to **fear** (3:6).

Hope "You have been raised with Christ" (Col. 3:1 NRSV). The Torah prescribes rules for political and financial inheritance. Yet in Israel's story both sin and grace repeatedly seem to violate them. Through the intrigue and the surprises of Genesis's patriarchal narratives, YHWH makes promises to latter-born sons. Further intrigue and surprises shape the line of succession from the patriarchs to Judah, Solomon, and finally Jesus the unlikely son of David (Matt. 1:1–17; Rom. 1:3). However, the Father's faithfulness to the Son respects rather than overrides the Torah's pattern, and only there does God embrace rebellious creation (Col. 2:11–14). As grace does not violate the natural relations of human life but perfects them, so the Torah does not contradict the realization of God's mystery (1:26–27; 2:2–3) but is "a shadow of things to come" (2:16–17, my translation).

Hope The ancient Near Eastern custom of double partiture obliges a **father** to give **a double portion** to his **first son**, establishing a clear line of succession of patriarchal authority. But Christ is the end of every lineage and genealogy (→5:16; →17:14–20), holding total preeminence (Col. 1:18). Though some Christians (notably Puritans) practiced it, double partiture no longer applies in the family of God, in which all share his[+] inheritance in common (1:12; 3:24).

Love Some believe the law is frivolous, or evil, or useful only for measuring human failure; but the gospel is the *whole* Torah. Israel's truly disobedient **sons** have not just been purged (→32:22–25) but also given their **father's** amnesty (Luke 15:11–20; →32:40–43) and accepted as back from the dead (Luke 15:21–24; →32:36–39). In his sins the prodigal son *was* dead; and his obedient **brother** remains a living, if jealous, heir (Luke 15:31). Though in Christ all are heirs, paternal and filial obligations still characterize the new creation (Col. 3:20–21). Indeed, even as reconciled sons the forgiven remain unworthy servants of their Lord (Luke 17:7–10). Restitution cannot be a license to antinomianism, because the kingdom restores rather than annuls human relationship (Col. 3:10). It invites both the world's **loved and hated**, both its obedient and **rebellious**, to enter into human structures as they should be.

Love Obligations—not personal affections—justify actions. Greater affection for a younger child, perhaps because of favoritism for the mother (a growing phenomenon today because of divorce and remarriage), does not override either the old covenantal sign that patrilineal descendants are God's blessing for the sake of Israel's patriarchs or the new sign that all are heirs of a God who shows no partiality (Col. 3:24–25; →1:15–17a; →10:17–22; →16:18–17:1). Likewise, persistent disdain for one's parents (now practically a cultural expectation of adolescents) does not override the commandment to honor one's **father** and **mother** (→5:16), and sympathy for troubled children (also widespread today, along with unprecedented lenience) cannot compromise the bitter parental and ecclesial responsibility to discipline (→8:1–5). In concupiscent hearts, disordering passions reign, exalting selves over neighbors and God and tearing families and communities apart (Col. 1:21), whereas paternal, filial, and pastoral relationships of substantial, mutually deferential, disciplining love image the relations of the triune God (1:15, 19).

> **21:22**If a man⁺ commit a sin worthy of death, and be put to death, and you hang him⁺ on a tree, **23**his⁺ body shall not remain all night on the tree, but you shall surely bury him⁺ the same day; for one hanged is accursed of God; that you do not defile your land that YHWH your God gives you for an inheritance.

Plain Though decaying corpses defile the land and burying cleanses it (cf. 2 Sam. 21:13–14; Ezek. 39:11–16), it is not clear that decay is what causes **defilement** in this passage. Ancient Jews thought decay set in on the fourth day of death, not the second (cf. John 11:39; Ps. 16:10 in Acts 2:31; Mark 16:1). Besides, any unburied corpse would be a concern, not just **hanged** ones. Moreover, hanging is not just an illustrative scenario but a curse linked to defilement. This rule, like many others in Deuteronomy (e.g., →21:10–14 and →24:1–4), limits a practice liable to abuse. As stoning is Deuteronomy's typical form of punishment, the sequence here suggests that a corpse is being hung or impaled in public view as a spectacle (cf., e.g., Gen. 40:19; Esth. 5:14; 6:4). Here hanging signifies a person's definitive, humiliating, divinely authorized end—as for the five kings who hid from Joshua at Makkedah (Josh. 10:22–26) and for Saul and Jonathan at the Philistines' hands (2 Sam. 21:10–14). Burial confines that curse to the transgressor so it does not spread to others in the **land** (Josh. 10:27).

Faith The Messiah foresees his definitive end for many (Mark 10:45; 12:9) at the hands of tyrannical sinners (10:42; 12:3–8; 14:41). Those authorities hold him **worthy of death** for proclaiming himself not only Messiah but also the coming Son of Man (14:61–64). But Joseph of Arimathea, a dissenter in the Sanhedrin, "waiting expectantly for the kingdom of God," keeps the commandment to **bury** Jesus on the evening of his execution (15:43–46 NRSV). This act of faith keeps the curse focused on Christ alone, bringing it to an end when he is risen (8:31; 14:25) and the kingdom come with power (16:6; 9:1).

Faith Torah is not a curse. But it becomes a curse to those who disobey (→28:15–19), impeding God's blessing of all peoples (→27:26 in Gal. 3:1–12). "Christ redeemed us from the curse of the law by becoming a curse for us—for it is written, 'Cursed is everyone hanging on a tree'" (3:13 NRSV). Christ, the heir of God's promises to Abraham (3:15–16 on Gen. 12:1–3), is a **hanged** man who has *not* **committed a sin worthy of death**; the Torah proclaims him **cursed** but innocent. As the recipient of the patriarchal promise and the Torah's curse, he purchases "all who rely on the works of the law" (Gal. 3:10 NRSV) from service to sin (3:22–24) into his freedom, his Spirit, and his Abrahamic blessing for all peoples (3:14). Jesus is a victorious heir, a vicarious sufferer of sin's curse, and a gracious benefactor of his whole **inheritance**. (Paul is not an idiosyncratic interpreter of this passage. The cross of Jesus is repeatedly called **a tree** elsewhere in the New Testament and interpreted in similar ways—1 Pet. 2:24; Acts 5:30; 10:39; 13:29—suggesting that the New Testament church has widely considered the passage an interpretative key to atonement.)

Love The liturgical practice of anathematizing heretics and apostates from centuries past, while ecumenical from Nicea onward, still has an air of overkill. Casting out a brother or a sister from the fellowship is not a sign of eternal condemnation but a cleansing of the church and a warning that we hope will help save the condemned (1 Cor. 5:5). The combination of punishment, example, cessation, and preservation in this passage indicates that a more suitable (and perhaps less ecclesially **defiling**) way would be for the church to condemn and to publicize its disciplinary actions, but refrain from condemning those who are already dead and no longer in a position to hear and repent before the last day. This would effectively consign the condemned to the burial in Jesus that they have assumed in baptism, in patient faith as well as fear.

DEUTERONOMY 22

22:1 You shall not see your brother's[+] ox or his[+] sheep go astray, and hide yourself from them: you shall surely bring them again to your brother[+]. **²**If your brother[+] is not near to you, or if you do not know him[+], then you shall bring it home to your house, and it shall be with you until your brother[+] seek after it, and you shall restore it to him[+]. **³**So you shall do with his[+] donkey; and so you shall do with his[+] garment; and so you shall do with every lost thing of your brother's[+] he[+] has lost, and you have found: you may not hide yourself. **⁴**You shall not see your brother's[+] donkey or his[+] ox fallen down by the way, and hide yourself from them: you shall surely help him[+] lift them up again.

Plain Critical proposals abound for finding a pattern in the collection of rules in 22:1–26:15. This analysis treats them on their own, cross-referencing only as commonality of topic warrants.

Faith If it is "lawful to do good on the sabbath" (Matt. 12:12b NRSV), for instance in pulling one's child or ox out of a well (Luke 14:5; cf. Matt. 12:11), then helping another do that Sabbath work of righting a **fallen** beast is not only lawful but here commanded. The fraternal life of justice, mercy, and faith in Israel is not merely common courtesy or a light matter (23:23). The Lord of the Sabbath (→5:12–15) finds it, as if lost by his siblings, in the heart of the covenant and returns it to them.

Love The reticent sinner's motive is opaque. Preoccupation with a busy life? Inwardly guilty shyness? Or perhaps envy of a neighbor's property (→5:21)? At any rate, the found **garment** is as good as stolen (→5:19) if its discovery goes unreported. Once the person's lost property or **fallen** animal is seen, it is too late not to get involved. The finder is already involved and must either fulfill fraternal obligations or **hide**. In rural settings, small towns, and quiet suburban neighborhoods, hiding means retreating before being noticed, but in the public anonymity of everyday urban life one can hide in full view. Either strategy would be unconscionable among siblings. By repeating the word **brother**⁺ throughout, Moses drives home the point that the covenant creates just that: a brotherhood⁺ in which callousness, indifference, and envy have no rightful place in our life together (cf. Isa. 58:7). In Christ's fellowship indifference to a brother or sister is indifference to him (Matt. 25:40; 1 Cor. 11:29).

Hope "Why do you **hide yourself** in times of trouble?" (Ps. 10:1 NRSV). The psalmist accuses YHWH of the very indifference that God has forbidden—rightly so, in view of →31:14–18. The messianic age is God's superabundant response, but the very ones who prayed for it hide themselves when it approaches (Luke 14:15–24). Help must be received as fraternally as it is offered. Jesus was not ashamed to associate with the shameful: "The one ashamed of me and of my words . . . of this one the Son of Man will also be ashamed when he comes" (9:26, my translation), for "I do not sit with the worthless, nor do I consort with those who hide themselves" (Ps. 26:4, my translation).

> **22:5** A woman shall not wear an article for a man, neither shall a man put on a woman's clothing; for whoever does these things is an abomination to YHWH your God.

Hope The social construction of gender is grounded in the divine construction of both sex and gender. Sexual differentiation is a gift bestowed at our creation (Gen. 1:27; 2:18–25). Humanity uniquely images God (1:26) in unique human relations with God, one another, oneself, and the rest of creation (1:26–4:1). Both of Genesis's creation stories stress that gender informs the relations that constitute humanity in God's image, and vice versa. **Clothing**, however, is a covering for human shame (3:7)—an attempt to confer unearned social status on ourselves, which God transforms into a sign of human indecency (3:21; 1 Cor. 12:23). Cross-dressing (whether for ritual, political, familial, or sexual reasons) is one of several distorted gender relations that Deuteronomy finds incompatible with covenantal life (→22:22–30). It both assumes an unreal natural and social status and denies the specific shape of each sex's beauty and need to recover decency (Gen. 3:16–20). Late modernity shares this self-deception in making family, sex, gender, and marriage separable from one another and negotiable by personal circumstance and preference—as if fashion statements. Deuteronomy considers these institutions inextricable and all covenantally blessed (→7:12–15) and disciplined. Late modern interpreters tend first to notice the imperfections of the Torah's norms and the outcasts they create (such as transvestites). The Torah already acknowledges these legal imperfections, but addresses them by commanding special consideration for the excluded and the marginal (→14:27–29) rather than making the marginalized the basis for some other (pagan, folkloric, libertarian, or progressive) social norm. These political visions represent different, rival, eschatologies. Both the skins that God made in Eden and Deuteronomy's provisions for covenanting sufferers point forward to the mission of the Son "to seek and to save the lost" (Luke 19:10 NRSV)—those cut off not only by sin but also by social status, illness, ethnic difference, captivity, and death—in the year of YHWH's favor (Isa. 61:1–2 in Luke 4:18–19; →15:1–6).

Faith "He was transfigured before them, and his face shone like the sun, and his **clothes** became dazzling white" (Matt. 17:2; cf. 17:9–12). The only true and lasting sexual revolution is through the perfecting cross. Jesus subverts his culture's gender roles without annulling gender distinctions, restoring Israel's structures to their rightful places in God's kingdom and clothing every kind of disciple with himself (Gal. 3:27–28). This is but the beginning of his reconstructive work: social structures are radically changed in the resurrection (Matt. 22:29–30) in mysterious ways that (judging from the glorified Jesus) do not abolish gender; indeed, they reveal its deepest significance (Eph. 5:22–33; Col. 3:18–19).

Love While eschatological Israel waits for that final transformation, it is to respect local constructions of gender that are compatible with covenantal decency (1 Tim. 2:8–10). Culturally conservative clothing, like the ordered and patient life it connotes, signifies the decency of the new selves (Col. 3:10; 1 Pet. 3:3) and the Spirit's virtues (Col. 3:12–14; 1 Pet. 3:4) that eternally clothe every nation, social class, and gender (Rev. 19:7–8).

> **22:6**If a bird's nest chance to be before you in the way, in any tree or on the ground, with young ones or eggs, and the hen sitting on the young, or on the eggs, you shall not take the hen with the young: **7**you shall surely let the hen go, but the young you may take to yourself; that it may be well with you, and that you may prolong your days.

Hope "Be on your guard against all kinds of greed; for one's life does not consist in the abundance of possessions" (Luke 12:15). The rich fool in Jesus's parable is a resident in the land who thinks only of enjoying all that he can gather, ignoring all others and even his own future. Death strips his holdings from him (Luke 12:16–21). Israel's kings begin to consume Israel's inheritance and cut short its **days** in the land when they grasp at worldly power (1 Kgs. 11:1–13) and tax their people onerously (12:1–19). Simon the Magician treats the Holy Spirit as a means to fame rather than God graciously given, jeopardizing his hope and his very life (Acts 8:18–24).

Hope While the reader might hear an empathetic quality in a few of Deuteronomy's laws concerning animals (→14:21; →25:4; also Lev. 22:26–28), the linguistic differences here suggest that a more probable concern is the sustainability of a resource in the land (→20:19–20). This rule condemns as eschatological heterodoxy every utilitarianism that reduces things to their present usefulness—consumerism, welfare statism, environmental plunder, the political theories of pluralism and corporatism, and the like. In their greed these fail to appreciate the nature or purpose of prosperity (→8:17–18), consume the mother with her **young**, and so ultimately yield poverty (→8:19–20).

Love The church must be diligent not to exploit its material and spiritual gifts and not even merely to enjoy them, but to cultivate them, for the growth of Christ's fellowship signifies God's future (Eph. 4:11–15).

> 22:8When you build a new house, you shall make a parapet for your roof, that you do not bring blood on your house if one fall from there. 9You shall not sow your vineyard with two kinds of seed, lest the whole fruit be forfeited, the seed you have sown, and the increase of the vineyard. 10You shall not plow with an ox and a donkey together. 11You shall not wear wool and linen blended. 12You shall make yourselves fringes on the four borders of your cloak, with which you cover yourself.

Faith Critical commentators often try to discern the underlying commonalities or tradition histories that have brought these verses together (cf. the similar combination in Lev. 19:19). A more promising but often overlooked topic is the effect or thesis of the jumble itself. The juxtaposition of rules here and elsewhere in Deuteronomy reflects the amalgamation of liturgical, legal, and practical ethics in Israel's life. The **building** code assigns liability for negligence, a civil concept with wide-ranging social consequences (cf. Exod. 21:33–34). The planting, **plowing**, and weaving prohibitions are practices (some economically advantageous, some not) overlaid with theological significance exposed in the prophets' scenes (e.g., Isa. 28:23–29; 37:30–32) and Jesus's agricultural parables (e.g., Matt. 13:24–30). Tassels (or **fringes**) reinforce this people's religious, ethnic, and thus social identity (Num. 15:37–41), constructing their own practicality and prophetic trajectory. A culture is just such a bewildering amalgam of rules. Its coherence cannot lie in any abstract framework; it can consist only in the life of its people. The Torah's framework is an obedient, wholehearted love for God and neighbor (Matt. 22:34–40) that the Messiah comes to fulfill (5:17–18). The Torah converges in Jesus's life both in its literal senses—he wears a prayer shawl, for instance (14:36), and linen clothes his buried and risen body (John 19:40; cf. Rev. 1:13; 15:6)—and in its deeper significances—he protects his householders from harm (Luke 21:12–19; Matt. 24:9–13). He spreads the unmixed word of God and reaps a great harvest (13:1–23). The deeds with which he clothes the naked and impure are his own righteousness (Rev. 3:18). He sets his disciples apart and alongside one another (Mark 6:7; cf. Matt. 10:5), with common gifts for their common mission (11:28–30).

Hope Even these odd details of Israel's life point forward as one to their realization in God's eschatological kingdom. Crowds seek Jesus "that they might touch even the **fringe** of his garment" (Mark 6:56 RSV; Matt. 14:36). Jesus of course wears *tefillin* (→6:7–9) and his shawl when he prays the Shema (→6:4). But his clothing identifies him as more than a son of Jacob, for "in those days ten men from the nations of every tongue shall take hold of the **cloak** of a Jew, saying: 'Let us go with you, for we have heard that God is with you'" (Zech. 8:23 Septuagint).

Likewise, YHWH's protection of the persecuted from **falling** spares disciples from the world's last wars (Luke 21:9–19; Matt. 24:14); YHWH's harvest (13:24–28) and sorting and treading of the crop gather a healed people (9:38; Rev. 19:15); his[+] garb glorifies (1:13; cf. 15:6; note the gold sashes rather than the priests' **blended** sashes in Exod. 39:29); his paired disciples' evangelism portends final judgment (Mark 6:11; cf. Matt. 10:7, 15); and the prayer he teaches his disciples to pray begs for the kingdom's coming (6:9–13).

Love The Torah's detailed rules and guidelines apply, but differently, as life shifts for monarchical, exilic, Second Temple, Diaspora, and now messianic and pentecostal (as well as rabbinic) Israel. Some rules recede while others gain new prominence. Added significance attaches to some, while others are obscured. Because Torah arises out of YHWH's regard for Israel's life, this is as it must be. Halakic interpretation negotiates Torah's changing applicability in Israel's new life situations to ensure that Israel remains faithful to its life-giving covenant (→30:11–16). It is to reinterpret God's word not by whim, nor to change its terms (→4:1–2), but only by faithfulness to that word in the life into which the Spirit has now led it (2 Chr. 31:20–21). The process is both unpredictable in advance and consistent in hindsight because it involves the chaotic intermingling (and even interference) of the consistent divine covenant and its ever new settings. Since the fundamental shift in Israel's situation is from the old age to the new in the coming of the messianic kingdom, halakah's decisive reshaping concerns the missional life of Christ's apostles. Criminal negligence is a matter for the teaching office (Matt. 18:6–7; Jas. 3:1), and rules about beasts inform the treatment of fellow workers (1 Cor. 9:9–12; 1 Tim. 5:17–18) and guidelines for marriage in the church (2 Cor. 6:14–7:1). Prayer shawls are not carried over into the church's life, while pure **linen** becomes the saints' deeds that clothe the church (Rev. 19:8). Apocalyptic sashes of gold (1:13; 15:6), designating authority to act on YHWH's behalf, surpass the priestly sashes of the mixed fabric (Exod. 39:29) that Deuteronomy forbids laity to wear. These shifts are not facile spiritualizing, but reorientations determined by progress in the accomplishing of God's eternal agenda. They do not change, annul, or abolish the Torah, because they formed and guided Jesus Christ, and they still stand ready for providential use wherever the Spirit identifies a place for them in lighting the paths of disciples in other missional contexts. God has already prepared Torah for those who love him[+], in ways no eye had seen or ear heard or heart conceived, yet the Spirit has now revealed (1 Cor. 2:9–10; cf. Isa. 64:4).

> [22:13]If any man takes a wife, and goes in to her, and hates her (→24:1–4), [14]and accuses her of shameful things, and brings up an evil name on her, and says: "I took this woman, and when I came near to her, I did not find in her the tokens of virginity," [15]then shall the father of the young lady and her mother take and bring forth the tokens of the young lady's

virginity to the elders of the city in the gate; [16]and the young lady's father shall tell the elders, "I gave my daughter to this man to wife, and he hates her; [17]and behold, he has accused her of shameful things, saying: 'I did not find in your daughter the tokens of virginity,' and yet these are the tokens of my daughter's virginity." They shall spread the cloth before the elders of the city. [18]The elders of that city shall take the man and chastise (→25:1–3) him; [19]and they shall fine him one hundred shekels of silver, and give them to the father of the young lady, because he has brought up an evil name on a virgin of Israel: and she shall be his wife; he may not put her away all his days. [20]But if this thing be true, that the tokens of virginity were not found in the young lady, [21]then they shall bring out the young lady to the door of her father's house, and the men of her city shall stone her to death with stones, because she has done folly in Israel, to prostitute herself in her father's house: so you shall put away the evil from your midst.

Faith The same Hebrew verb describes **prostitution** and all fornication. Both trivialize an act at the heart of human life and hope (Gen. 4:1) and the core of Israel's social structure. Ironically, as concerned as Israel is about her daughters' virginity, she herself is neither virginal nor faithful when it comes to God (Deut. 31:16; Hos. 1–3). And though YHWH exposes her transgressions, he[+] neither **hates her** nor leaves her unpunished. Rather, he[+] kills her through his baptismal word (6:5) to restore her (6:11b–7:1a). This death and resurrection repristinate not just Israel but all nations (Hos. 1:6 in 1 Pet. 2:7–10; Hos. 2 in Rom. 9:25–27; →22:22–30).

Hope "Shun fornication!" (1 Cor. 6:18a NRSV). **Virginity** suggests holiness, a setting apart for future special use. In the old covenant this future is a woman's lifelong relationship with a man that images Israel's lifelong relationship with God (Ezek. 16:7–14) and produces the fruit of children of the promise to Abraham. In the messianic age it is either a lifelong relationship with another that images Christ's lifelong relationship with the church and honors the body that fulfills that promise (1 Cor. 6:13b–20; 7:12–16; cf. Eph. 5:29–32) or lifelong celibacy that honors the same body by concentrating one's love on the undivided whole (1 Cor. 7:25–35). Straddling these two dispensations, virginity is the unique state of the betrothed Mother of God, whose son is both the Spirit-anointed legal heir of Joseph, heir of David and Abraham (Matt. 1:16; Luke 3:23; cf. Rom. 1:3), and the eternally begotten Son of the Most High (Matt. 1:20–23; Luke 1:32–35; John 1:14; cf. Rom. 1:4). Mary embodies the virtues of both ages, which point from their different places in the Father's mystery to the lordship of her son and Lord and the glory of his body. Fornication signifies none of this. It acts as if our bodies were not from the Father, bought with the Son, or filled with the Holy Spirit (1 Cor. 6:19–20), but merely our own organs of pleasure, power, and self-replication. So "fornication sins against the body itself" (6:18b NRSV) in self-contradiction.

Faith The innocent **wife's** compensation for being maligned is her husband's loss of his prerogative to divorce. This implies that his prerogative disadvantages her. By withdrawing the option of divorce (Mark 10:10–12; 1 Cor. 7:10–11), Jesus commands a more equitable arrangement. He also sets a higher demand on all parties, to help marriages fulfill their original (Gen. 1:27 and 2:24 in Mark 10:6–9) and ultimate (Rev. 21:9–10) promise (→24:1–4).

Love But how then is a maligned **wife** to be compensated for her husband's false witness (5:20)? The New Testament church is worried less about compensating the wronged (1 Cor. 6:7–8) than sharing its alien righteousness. In fact, it is less invested in marriage in the first place and more invested in the coming age (1 Cor. 7). But it is still invested in family honor, now centered in the family of God (6:13b–20; →25:1–3). While it has not left behind the Torah's concern for interpersonal justice (1 Cor. 6:4; 7:35), its inner logic of chastity is no longer protection and punishment but restoration and loyalty. "You were bought with a price; therefore glorify God in your body" (6:20 NRSV).

Love The woman's sexual purity belongs not only to herself and her **father's house** but to all **Israel**. Sex is a political matter, not just a private one. In the new covenant this claim is extended to males, and sexual discipline is a criterion of church discipline (1 Cor. 5:3–5, 12)—since fornicators do not inherit the kingdom of God (5:11; 6:9–10).

Love "These are what some of you used to be" (1 Cor. 6:1, my translation). The church is a communion of sinning saints, whose integrity is constantly challenged. The **tokens of** its **virginity** are not its own virtuous past—it has none—but the signs of its unalterable righteousness: the blood of its paschal lamb (5:7) and the cleansing of its baptismal water (6:11). Only by appealing to this evidence can the church survive such challenges. The water and the blood, which are the Spirit's testimony (1 John 5:6–9), testify together to the righteous life that the Son shares with his church, vindicating and compensating the maligned **Father** who gave it (5:11) and challenging the challengers to retract their slander and embrace her as their own destiny (5:4–5).

> **22:22**If a man be found lying with a woman married to a husband, then they shall both of them die, the man who lay with the woman, and the woman: so you shall put away the evil from Israel (→5:18). **23**If there is a young lady who is a virgin pledged to be married to a husband, and a man find her in the city, and lie with her; **24**then you shall bring them both out to the gate of that city, and you shall stone them to death with stones; the lady, because she did not cry, being in the city; and the man, because he has humbled his neighbor's wife (→5:18; →5:21): so you shall put away the evil from your midst. **25**But if the

man find the lady who is pledged to be married in the field, and the man force her, and lie with her; then the man only who lay with her shall die: [26]but to the lady you shall do nothing; there is in the lady no sin worthy of death: for as when a man[+] rises against his[+] neighbor, and kills him[+], even so is this matter; [27]for he found her in the field, the pledged-to-be-married lady cried, and there was none to save her. [28]If a man find a lady who is a virgin, who is not pledged to be married, and lay hold on her, and lie with her, and they be found; [29]then the man who lay with her shall give to the lady's father fifty shekels of silver, and she shall be his wife, because he has humbled her; he may not put her away all his days. [30]A man shall not take his father's wife, and shall not uncover his father's skirt.

Faith Similar rules have abounded since antiquity among Israel's neighbors. This complex of laws pertains more to theft (→5:19; →5:21) than to adultery, rape, premarital sex, or incest as such. It regulates sexual plundering in order to protect the rights of **fathers** and husbands in patriarchal systems (cf. Lev. 20:10–21; →25:5–10). Moderns are tempted to dismiss or deplore these rules; but that response is shortsighted, for neither the systems nor the sins have disappeared from even the most formally egalitarian and feminist modern societies and social circles. They do not represent primitive and obsolete politics along a trajectory of social progress, but persistent features of human social structures. Ignore them or legislate them away in an egalitarian utopia and they flourish underground. The sexual maneuverings and contests of power from the patriarchal period (Gen. 12:10–20; 19:4–9; 20:1–18; 26:6–11; 29:1–31:55; 34:1–31; 35:22 [→33:6]; Gen. 38:1–26; 39:1–23; 49:3–4) to the time of the judges (Judg. 5:28–30; 11:37–40; 12:8–9; 14:1–16:22; 19:1–21:24; Ruth) and throughout Israel's monarchy (1 Sam. 18:27–29; 2 Sam. 3:12–16; 11:1–12:25; 16:20–23; 20:3; 1 Kgs. 2:13–25; 20:1–12; 2 Kgs. 24:13–16) testify to the social destruction that sexual rivalry causes (Prov. 6:32–7:27). Such power contests extend even to heavenly powers and principalities who would usurp their station and effectively plunder from God (Gen. 6:1–4; Jude 6–7). So it is providential that Moses acknowledges them to restrain abuses. Yet the days of and after Noah (Gen. 6:5–8; 9:4–6, 20–27) prove that the countermeasures of legal restraint and punishment, while temporarily effective against violence and sexual rivalry—and still necessary (Jude 11)—do not themselves justify. The powers and principalities must themselves be overcome (Eph. 6:10–13). Jesus overturns sexual strongholds throughout his life. He (apocryphally?) releases the adulterous woman from manipulation by the elders (John 8:7–10), condemnation by the law (Deut. 22:22–24 in John 8:5), his own just verdict (8:11), and her captivity to sin (8:11). Going to the heart of the matter, he deposes the violent and acquisitive hearts that the Torah restrains but leaves in place (Matt. 5:21–22, 27–30, 43–48). One comes to power in his order by forsaking, not acquiring, ordinary power over others (19:29–30).

Faith **Women** in this passage are truly marginal figures: as daughters (betrothed or not) they are pawns of their families, as wives they belong to their husbands, as conspirators they are punished, as innocents they are not penalized but not compensated, and as victims they are protected—if that is the right word (→22:13–21)—from having their rapists divorce them (cf. Exod. 22:16–17)! This disturbs contemporary sensibilities trained to focus on the victimized, marginal, and invisible. How are these passages anything but an indictment of the culture that they describe and a charge against the God who refuses to put an end to them? They do indict their culture (cf. Matt. 19:8), and ours. They also work from within that culture to raise a people for God and to bring about their salvation. Furthermore, God's salvation finds all of us, whose cultures are not so different as we sometimes imagine, in the position of this passage's women. The patriarchs were nobodies but for God's love (→7:6–8), and we are a nonpeople whom no legal claim but divine mercy alone has made God's people (→22:13–21). Remarkably, the rivalrous plunderers and plundered are only penultimate objects of YHWH's attention here. The ultimate objects are the enslaved, conspiratorial, victimized, marginal, invisible plunder—for "how can one enter a strong man's house and plunder his property, without first tying up the strong man? Then indeed the house can be plundered" (Matt. 12:29 NRSV) and the "property" can be freed from her tyrannical master, rehumanized, and empowered to reign along with her deliverer. Torah and gospel ultimately disarm and deprive these cultures of the very power that disturbs us here.

Love The church's life imposes Christ's royal ethic on the ethics of this age. The old is still discernible in the midst of the new: not abolished, but no longer dominant. Rather than a regulated acquisition of power, marriage in the kingdom becomes a means for disciples to remain righteous: "If someone thinks he is dishonoring his virgin, if he is passionate, and it is necessary, let him marry as he wishes" (1 Cor. 7:36, my translation). The gospel also renarrates adultery, rape, seduction, conspiracy, and politically motivated incest, rendering them unthinkable—not mainly as violations of a male neighbor's rights, nor even as subjugation of women's rights, but as strivings for power over others that are antithetical to Christ's kingdom (6:9–10). Indeed, even legal betrothal, marriage, and childbearing that are pursued for familial advantage become unfitting practices among its coheirs. Obeying the law of Christ yields not patriarchalism or feminism, not sexual repression or sexual liberation, not social status or artificial gender egalitarianism, but mutual submission (Eph. 5:21) in the will of YHWH (5:17).

Hope Moses's rules still restrain the saints, because the power of the flesh persists even when tamed under Christ's reign (Jude 4, 12–16). Even faithful Christians still encounter lust, heartbreak, frustration, loss, envy, manipulation, abuse, disillusionment, regret, and cynicism. Confession and baptism do not end sexual differentiation and competition, whose deeply biological character shows them to be good (if often abused) creations of God. But sexual competition is the ultimate state of neither human beings nor angels, for "in the resurrection they neither marry nor are given in marriage, but are like angels in heaven" (Matt. 22:30 RSV; →25:5–10). Here Jesus alludes to a new order of heavenly as well as earthly powers and principalities in an age when marriage and its cognates are fully and finally transcended. To anticipate this mysterious future the church is to "look forward to the mercy of our Lord Jesus Christ that leads to eternal life. And have mercy on some who are wavering; save others by snatching them out of the fire; and have mercy on still others with fear" (Jude 21–23 NRSV).

DEUTERONOMY 23

23:1 He who is crushed in the testicles, or has his penis cut off, shall not join the assembly of YHWH. **2**A misbegotten one shall not join the assembly of YHWH; even to the tenth generation shall none of his join the assembly of YHWH. **3**An Ammonite or a Moabite shall not join the assembly of YHWH; even to the tenth generation shall none belonging to them join the assembly of YHWH forever: **4**because they did not meet you with bread and with water in the way, when you came forth out of Egypt (→2:6–9; →2:26–30), and because Balak hired against you Balaam the son of Beor from Pethor of Mesopotamia, to curse you. **5**(Nevertheless YHWH your God would not listen to Balaam; but YHWH your God turned the curse into a blessing to you, because YHWH your God loved you.) **6**You shall not seek their peace or their good all your days forever. **7**You shall not abhor an Edomite; for he⁺ is your brother⁺ (→2:4–5): you shall not abhor an Egyptian, because you lived as a foreigner in his⁺ land (→10:17–22). **8**The children of the third generation who are born to them shall join the assembly of YHWH.

Faith "This is the gate of [YHWH]; the righteous shall enter through it" (Ps. 118:20 NRSV). This list of requirements draws a bright (if sometimes shifting) line between insiders and outsiders to God's **assembly**. However, genealogical realities are always more complex than genealogical ideals. Israel keeps finding itself portentously on both sides of YHWH's line, and outsiders keep showing interest in Israel's God. Jesus assimilates both outsiders and insiders. His identity incorporates the excludedness of his **Moabite** ancestor Ruth (Matt. 1:5) and his **misbegotten** ancestor Perez (1:3: Gen. 38:12–30; →25:5–10). Yet this ironically makes him a son of Judah as well as a successor of David and Solomon (Matt. 1:6; 21:9)—both of whom also enter oddly into the line of Israel's leadership. Jesus's time **as a foreigner** in **Egypt** (Matt. 2:13–15) and even his singleness—he reckons himself "a eunuch for the kingdom of God" (19:10–12, my translation)—suggest a distance from the established patriarchies who belong naturally to Deuteronomy's assembly. Yet in these very qualities he embodies Israel's exodus identity and his unbegetting divine sonship. The questioned paternity (Mark 6:3) of the Son of God (1:1) encapsulates this twofold identity, as the head of Israel's universal gathering who becomes salvation for all (Ps. 118:21) and who richly fulfills the prophecy that "the stone that the builders rejected has become the cornerstone" (118:22 in Mark 12:1–11 NRSV).

Faith A people who understands itself as Abraham's promised multitude will not generate a culture featuring eunuchs. Emasculation tells some other story than Israel's; indeed, the emasculation of Israelites means the humiliation of exile (Isa. 39:5–8). Yet in the anointed Son on whom God's mystery converges there is space for all peoples and cultures. "Who could have imagined his future?" (53:8 NRSV). The Ethiopian eunuch learns that the childless one **crushed** for Israel's iniquities "shall see his offspring, and shall prolong his days" (53:10 NRSV; cf. 53:7–8 in Acts 8:26–39). Humanity's eternal future does not issue from unforsaken sex organs but from baptismal water and a forsaken tomb. "Do not let the eunuch say, 'I am just a dry tree.' . . . I will give them an everlasting name that shall not be **cut off**" (Isa. 56:3–5 NRSV).

Hope **Edomites** are kin (→2:4–5), but they wear out their welcome (Ps. 137:7; Mal. 1:2–5). **Egypt** once hosted the Hebrews and its hospitality is returned, but one day Egypt will lie ruined with Edom (Joel 3:19). The privileges of international family and guests are conditioned upon continued faithfulness, not only in the old covenant but also in the new: "Note then the kindness and the severity of God: severity toward those who have fallen, but God's kindness toward you, provided you continue in his⁺ kindness; otherwise you also will be **cut off**" (Rom. 11:22 NRSV). Yet a new **way** offers the nations new opportunities to show hospitality: "Whoever gives you a cup of **water** to drink because you bear the name of Christ will by no means lose his⁺ reward" (Mark 9:41 RSV).

Hope Gathering before God happens by invitation only; by no act can outsiders qualify themselves. The gathering never loses its exclusivity, through no act of our own are we God's children, but only baptized into Christ (Gal. 3:27). Yet Israel's hospitable God invites all, even the unqualified, the inhospitable, and old enemies, into that baptismal unity (3:28–29).

Love Yet the term "exclusivity" is misleading. Entering the **assembly** (Greek *ekklēsia*) **of YHWH** means mainstream political participation in Israel. Many excluded Israelites are included in God's covenantal blessings: women and children, for instance. So while exclusion limits participation, it does not imply dissociation; eligibility is not equivalent to covenantal personhood; and even resident alien status is still status with God. Could these gradations of Israelite standing inform Paul's claims that believers sanctify their spouses and children (1 Cor. 7:14)? "It is to **peace** that God has called us" (7:15b NRSV margin) and to the possibility of sharing our hope with those with whom we live (7:16).

> **23:9**When you go forth in camp against your enemies, then you shall keep yourselves from every bad thing. **10**If there is among you any man who is not clean by reason of nocturnal emission, then shall he go outside the camp. He shall not come within the camp: **11**but when evening comes he shall bathe himself in water; and when the sun is down, he shall come within the camp. **12**You shall have a place also outside the camp where you shall relieve yourself: **13**and you shall have a trowel among your gear; and when you squat you shall dig with it and bury your excrement: **14**for YHWH your God walks in the midst of your camp, to deliver you, and to give up your enemies before you; therefore your camp shall be holy, that he[+] may not see an unclean thing in you and turn away from you.

Faith This is not standard military spit-and-polish, but a Levitical purity standard (cf. Lev. 15:16) applied to holy war (cf. 1 Sam. 21:2–6). God seems *literally* present in Israel's **midst**, so much so that the hygienic purity of Israel's **camp** is crucial to its military success. Only if God is truly present (→7:16–21) can Israel fight with God as its armory (→20:1–4). Places of YHWH's presence—pillar, camp, ark, tabernacle, temple, and finally the Messiah's eternal body—are YHWH's battle stations and must be treated as such.

Love "Where can I flee from your presence?" (Ps. 139:7 NRSV). The latrine?! The image of a God from whom we withdraw to take care of embarrassing situations is as charming as it is ridiculous. Yet, metaphysics notwithstanding, it is apt, for it honors the personal character of YHWH's relationships. People have faces and attentions that we turn toward and away from others. YHWH has a face too (→34:10–12). We **turn away** from our omnipresent God not just in betrayal or rejection but also in polite discretion, and God turns away not just in anger and condemnation (→32:19–21) but in the grace of giving us privacy. Our age's individualism turns privacy into autonomy, and its collectivism turns publicity into totalitarianism. This passage's earthy Israel and its **walking, delivering God** preserve both personal space and interpersonal space, for each absolutely depends on the other.

Hope Nothing **unclean** or accursed enters the new Jerusalem (Rev. 21:27; 22:3). That is an odd claim, coming as it does after the new earth is made and the polluted and condemned are consigned to the second death (21:1, 4–5, 8). The old distinctions are retained even after the reality that they distinguished is over.

> **23:15**You shall not deliver to his[+] master a servant who is escaped from his[+] master to you: **16**he[+] shall dwell with you, in your midst, in the

place he⁺ shall choose within one of your gates, where it pleases him⁺ best: you shall not oppress him⁺.

Hope Because relocation can be to anywhere in Israel, interpreters typically understand this rule to apply to (Gentile) refugees from outside. Israel is a place where only YHWH holds jurisdiction (→15:1–6), an earthly sign of heaven's kingdom. This makes it a refuge from principalities (→19:1–7), including Pharaoh (→5:12–15). **Deliverance** from foreign **servitude** is the narrative framework of the whole covenant (→6:21b–25).

Faith "Come to me, all you who are weary and heavy laden, and I will give you rest. . . . For my yoke is easy, and my burden is light" (Matt. 11:28–30, my translation).

Love This apparently innocuous rule launches a cosmic transformation. To extradite escapees to their **masters** would be **oppressive** obedience to foreign powers; to emancipate them by reforming other nations' social structures would be war (and hypocrisy); to enslave refugees in Israel would be exploitation. All would violate the scope of Israel's mission to enlighten the nations. Emancipation will not happen through simple abolition, because (regardless of governmental pretensions) powers are not simply abolished but must be confronted, warned, restored, and disciplined under YHWH's suffering lordship. While modern abolitionists try to overpower through revolution, protest, or military and legal coercion, the church's orders are to do it Christ's way, through subversive obedience (Eph. 6:5–9; Col. 3:22–4:1). The household of God is an asylum sharing the freedom it has received in its master (Isa. 61:1–2).

Love This rule obliquely promises an end to respect for Gentile slavery. What about slavery among God's own people? Release already makes the enslavement of Hebrews either temporary or volitional (→15:12–18), but Israel may still own Gentile slaves (→21:10–14). Philemon goes where Deuteronomy does not, freeing the slaves of the kingdom's heirs. It does so by the subversive obedience not of slaves but of fellow siblings (Phlm. 7) and partners (Phlm. 17) in the gospel. Human slavery ends in the ecclesial refuge of love backed by duty (Phlm. 8–9): "I preferred to do nothing without your consent, in order that your good deed might be voluntary and not something forced" (Phlm. 14 NRSV).

> ²³:¹⁷There shall be no prostitute of the daughters of Israel, neither shall there be a prostitute of the sons of Israel. ¹⁸You shall not bring the hire of a prostitute or the wages of a dog into the house of YHWH your God for any vow, for even both these are an abomination to YHWH your God.

Plain Opinions differ over whether these are sacred shrine prostitutes or ordinary prostitutes. They figure in pre-Israelite culture (Gen. 38:21–22) and persistently infiltrate Israelite culture (1 Kgs. 14:24), despite the efforts of the reforming kings Asa (15:12), Jehoshaphat (22:46), and Josiah (2 Kgs. 23:7).

Hope If this is a prohibition against all prostitution, it is strangely worded: it forbids *being* a **prostitute** rather than *engaging in* prostitution, and forbids it only of Israelites. These features suggest that the passage has a different fundamental goal than either allowing or banning prostitution. Like Deuteronomy's other instructions on how Israel is to remain Israel, these concentrate on forms of life arising out of its patriarchal order that directly affect Israelite identity and relationship with YHWH. For both **sons** and **daughters of Israel**, prostitution is inappropriate for reasons familiar from →22:22–30: it betrays relationships constitutive of Israel. Throughout the Torah's saga, sex is covenantal futurity. Sex for money or any other substitute perverts that divinely appointed purpose, bringing about a cursed rather than blessed future. Prostitution is the inglorious end of the godless (Job 36:13–15).

Hope Prostitution's indirect effects are disastrous too. **Prostitutes** share their own teleological ruination with their clients: "To keep company with prostitutes is to squander one's substance" (Prov. 29:3 NRSV). Patronage of prostitutes is the ruin of the foolish (Hos. 4:14). Prostitution, like adultery—and indeed promiscuity of all kinds—"increases the number of the faithless" (Prov. 23:28 NRSV). So the **hire** or gain from prostitution is wholly inappropriate as a worship offering, particularly one collateralizing a promise. (**The wages of a dog** is obscure, and the various responses are conjectural.)

Faith "Do you not know that whoever is united to a prostitute becomes one body with her? For it is said, 'The two shall be one flesh'" (1 Cor. 6:16 NRSV). A **prostitute** belongs to her or his many clients—thus to no one in particular. Promiscuity is thus destructive of identities, including national identity. In holy union, by contrast, spouses share themselves in life-giving mutual belonging (7:3–4). "Do you not know that your bodies are members of Christ?... Anyone united to the Lord becomes one spirit with him" (6:15–17 NRSV). (Paul's body/spirit distinction in 1 Cor. 6 anticipates 15:45's eschatological distinction between the first Adam's living soul and the last Adam's life-giving spirit.) If union with Christ and illicit sexual union contradict, marriage's compatibility with unity in Christ indicates that the two relationships are not only analogous but sacramentally participatory (→23:1–8). Human relationships mediate to all participants whatever constitutes both the persons and the relation: either the eternal *logos* in whom all things hold together or the transience of every substitute.

Love It is thus fitting that, as scripture repeatedly links dehumanizing sexual promiscuity to dehumanizing idolatry (31:16), so it links humanizing chastity—celibacy or marital fidelity—to humanizing worship. Contrast "Babylon the great, mother of whores and of earth's abominations" (Rev. 17:5 NRSV) with "a woman clothed with the sun, with the moon under her feet, and on her head a crown of twelve stars" (12:1 NRSV) and the groom's "bride [who] has made herself ready" (19:7 NRSV) to fulfill her eternal **vow**.

²³:¹⁹You shall not lend on interest to your brother⁺; interest of money, interest of food, interest of anything that is lent on interest: ²⁰to a foreigner you may lend on interest; but to your brother⁺ you shall not lend on interest, that YHWH your God may bless you in all you put your hand to, in the land you go in to possess. ²¹When you shall vow a vow to YHWH your God, you shall not be slack to pay it: for YHWH your God will surely require it of you; and it would be sin in you. ²²But if you shall forbear to vow, it shall be no sin in you. ²³What is gone out of your lips you shall observe and do as you have vowed to YHWH your God, a freewill offering you have promised with your mouth. ²⁴When you come into your neighbor's vineyard, then you may eat of grapes your fill at your own pleasure; but you shall not put any in your vessel. ²⁵When you come into your neighbor's standing grain, then you may pluck the ears with your hand; but you shall not move a sickle to your neighbor's standing grain.

Plain Some commentators massage the apparent double standard of **lending** to foreigners but not Israelites at **interest**, claiming that lending to Israelites in Deuteronomy's agrarian economy would typically cover dire emergencies, while lending to people from afar would tend to involve mutually beneficial business opportunities. But that humanitarian distinction is hard to maintain: **a foreigner** in the land and within one's gates may be even more vulnerable than a **brother⁺** (16:11). The distinction here between Israelites and foreigners mirrors the double standards in →15:1–6 and elsewhere and reflects Deuteronomy's primary interest to protect Israel's covenantal identity and integrity **in the land**. Moses is concerned about usury enslaving God's people, not other peoples. Deuteronomy is not out to change the world, at least not directly; it is out to protect Israel.

Faith These rules have an underlying commonality: do not take advantage of others' vulnerability—of those who lack, or the God to whom one binds oneself, or prosperous **neighbors**. Each prohibits the pressing of one's personal advantage. Exploiting one's advantage makes a relationship an exercise of power. But Israel has no power of its own to exercise, only grace (→8:17–18). God's people can be themselves only by bearing the kenotic love of God and neighbor. "Let each of you look not to your own interests, but to the interests of others. Let the same mind be in you that was in Christ Jesus" (Phil. 2:4–5 NRSV), who did not exploit his position but lived his lordship in humble servanthood of all (2:6–11; Mark 9:35), and whom God **blessed** with the highest name.

Hope The world trains us to gain all we can and protect all we have. While these rules protect Israel from abuses of self-interest, the Torah also calls us to more—to love the stranger God loves (→10:17–22). How can this covenant with its double standards help us do that? By calling Israel to a life whose necessary resources lie beyond it, the Torah calls Israel into a future of charity, trustworthiness, and hospitality where the resources to support them are at **hand** through faith.

Hope **Freewill** vows create accountability (Acts 21:23–26), with a variety of motives and effects. These motives hold mixed implications for discipleship. An *incentive* aims to induce God to do something in exchange for something God supposedly wants (e.g., Jephthah in Judg. 11:30–31). Either keeping or breaking this **vow** amounts to manipulation, whereas the spiritual fruit of joy, peace, and patience act out of *faith*. An *ultimatum* calls an external discipline on oneself (Jonathan in 1 Sam. 20:12–17; the psalmist in Ps. 137:5–6). Breaking this vow brings judgment, while the spiritual fruit of self-control acts out of *hope* rather than fear. Both these types of vow are better to **forbear**. The happiest of vows is a *resolution* that simply promises to do something right (Paul in Acts 19:21), because the force that fulfills it rather than fails it (1 Cor. 13:8a) can be the spiritual fruit of *love* (Gal. 5:22).

Love Sadly, the Messiah's universal communion misunderstood the point of the rule on **lending**, forbidding not just usury that exploits others' vulnerability but all charging of interest among Christians, even for investment purposes at rates that reflect money's true cost. Meanwhile medieval Jews developed halakic workarounds to allow legitimate business lending. Christian suspicion of financial trading and Jewish respect for the Torah's double standard backfired horribly as these two separate financial communities pressed their respective advantages over one another, intensifying mistrust and rivalry, with famously catastrophic consequences.

Love A kenotic church is to shine in the world like stars (Phil. 2:15). It honors Christ's eschatological standard for it, but it distinguishes itself from outsiders missionally rather than exclusively. It not only **lends** freely but gives as freely as it has received (Matt. 10:8). Its yes simply says yes, resolving and following through on its intentions according to its master's will (5:33–37). It neither hoards nor confiscates but accepts whatever its hosts offer with peace (10:9–13). Paul acknowledges that few Christians rise to this standard (Phil. 2:19–22), but he remains hopeful that Christ "will transform the body of our humiliation that it may be conformed to the body of his glory, by the power that also enables him to make all things subject to himself" (3:21; cf. 3:14–16).

DEUTERONOMY 24

24:1 When a man takes a wife, and marries her, then if she find no favor in his eyes, because he has found some unseemly thing in her, he shall write her a bill of divorce, and give it in her hand, and send her out of his house. **2**When she is departed out of his house, she may go and be another man's wife. **3**If the latter husband hate her, and write her a bill of divorce, and give it in her hand, and send her out of his house; or if the latter husband die, who took her to be his wife; **4**her former husband, who sent her away, may not take her again to be his wife, after she is defiled; for that is abomination before YHWH: and you shall not cause the land to sin, which YHWH your God gives you for an inheritance.

Love While commentators have found reasons to claim that this rule protects women—for example, from being pressured back to their first **husbands**—the point of the rule is not to protect wives or even husbands but the **land** (→11:8–15), from the **sin** of adultery (→5:18) under the guise of **divorce** and remarriage. **Or** in 24:3 shows that this scenario, like others, is illustrative rather than comprehensive. It presupposes the Hebrew practice of divorce and limits an abuse.

Faith "I hate divorce" (Mal. 2:16 NRSV). Divorce is a concession to Israel's hard-heartedness (Matt. 19:3–12). In fact, YHWH disregards this commandment (Jer. 3:1–2, 8–10), refuses to **send her out**, and even **takes** Israel **again** after she goes after false gods and tyrants. So the Torah cannot be the last word on an institution that images this relationship (Hos. 1:2). Jesus withholds its concession among his disciples and pours the Spirit into our hearts (Rom. 5:5) for the power to live by his commandments (Matt. 19:8–11). If his rules seem hard in biblical societies formed by Torah, they are harder—and more revolutionary—in a post-Christian West in which even fewer sexual and marital practices are considered defiling. They remind the forgetful that a marriage is a covenant: life-changing and life-making. It involves blessings and curses according to the faithfulness of its participants

(Deut. 28:1–6, 15–18). The import of marriage, underlined negatively here, is stressed positively in →24:5.

Hope A **marriage's** end is to be definitive. The remarried **wife** is free from her **husband**, forever. Thus the church that is taken from its former spouse—an authority of some other nation, or even the Torah—is free from the law of that spouse to belong to another (Rom. 7:1–6). To return to those earlier authorities after being **defiled** by Christ(!) would contradict the permanent effect of that union, making one's state worse than before (Matt. 12:43–45). What is old can be made new, but what is new is not made old again. So this passage foreshadows the pattern—what theology calls the order—of personal salvation. If baptism is an initiation into Christ analogous to marriage, there is no ecclesial act analogous to divorce—not even excommunication, for restoration after excommunication does not require or even allow rebaptism. The only act analogous to divorce is judgment: it is irreversible, it does not return the condemned to their old lives but to destruction, and it is the prerogative of Christ alone.

Love "It is well to remain as one is" (1 Cor. 7:26, my translation). The church leaves the old concessions in place in letting unbelieving spouses divorce believers, for "you were called to peace" (7:15, my translation), but among believers Christ's peace is best honored through contentment (2 Cor. 12:10; Phil. 4:11). This does not imply that Christian **marriages** are free from displeasure, offense, betrayal, or struggle, or that these pains are trivial—they are not—but that the gifts and fruit of the kingdom make them tolerable. The Spirit's strengthening makes both marriage and singleness more durable forms of life for weathering the fragility of their participants' hearts and strengthening them in turn. The gospel's aversion to concessions for hardness of heart is a gift to men as well as women, moving a culture with particular, imperfect, practices toward perfect holiness (2 Cor. 6:14–7:1).

> 24:5When a man takes a new wife, he shall not go out in the army, neither shall he be assigned any business: he shall be free at home one year, and shall cheer his wife whom he has taken.

Love The Torah puts the formation of a new family before the military needs of the whole people. This does not mean that marriage's goal is service to the state, but that the civil and familial spheres have their own interests and that neither is simply subordinate to the other. The newlywed **year** of a marriage is for each spouse's delight (→20:5–9) and perhaps the arrival of their first children. But marriage does not endlessly defer civil responsibilities. Life in God's covenant people involves an irreducible complex of blessings and goods that do not compete but coexist, as the seasons (Eccl. 3:1–8). Just so, life in the church does not reduce to worship, evangelism, childrearing, social justice, mission, or scholarship, or even a stable hierarchy of goods, but to each in its season.

Faith "Christ loved the church and gave himself up for her" (Eph. 5:25). The husband may not even volunteer, not for duty of any kind. This rule casts temporary exemption from military service as a sacrifice. Though a pleasant one, it will be dissatisfying to husbands eager to serve, who otherwise would be tempted to subordinate their families to the totalizing call of some other loyalty. Today this may be not only the tribe or state but business, ministry, a cause, or one's peers. He must sacrifice his ambition so that he does not sacrifice *her* to it.

Hope In Christ "all things hold together" (Col. 1:17 NRSV). Only by attending to all things in their proper significance do we learn which have lasting significance. Just one thing comes before all others, and it comes even before honeymoons: the banquet of the king (Luke 14:20), for he alone holds preeminence (Col. 1:18).

> **24:6**No man[+] shall take the mill or the upper millstone to pledge; for he[+] takes a life in pledge. [7]If a man[+] be found stealing any of his[+] brothers[+] of the sons[+] of Israel, and he[+] deal with him[+] as a slave, or sell him[+], then that thief shall die: so you shall put away the evil from your midst.

Hope An **upper millstone** is the lightest and most portable part of the mill assembly. Removing it disables the whole. Both of these offenses take a **life** (*nephesh*; →12:20–28) for improper gain. The egregious character of the latter crime brings out the subtlety of the former. The predatory lender takes away the "face" of the borrower—what the borrower needs to live. While this may be an inducement to pay, it induces such hardship that repayment may become even more difficult, even enslaving (which may be the lender's ulterior goal). It also depersonalizes borrowers, as if they are *merely* debt. The kidnapper does the same, without the legal pretext. Both are poignant violations of the Golden Rule (Luke 6:31). In the kingdom's economy, people are neither commodities nor mere means to commodities. With Babylon's demise comes the end of its merchants' "cargo of . . . **slaves**, that is, human souls" (Rev. 18:11–13 RSV).

Faith Joseph is so sold and **enslaved** (Gen. 37:28). Jesus is betrayed for money (cf. Zech. 11:7–14), falsely charged and convicted, and handed over to outlaws (Acts 2:23). Joseph's case is a conspiracy of his brothers; Jesus's is a conspiracy of his leaders. Though both sets of conspirators deserve Deuteronomy's harsh punishment, what comes at the moments they are convicted is extraordinary grace that frees even the captors from the **evil** that had led them to act. Joseph's and Jesus's mercy not only ends the injustices against them but opens Israel, both times, to a whole new future.

Love Deuteronomy remains focused on **Israel**, singling out the kidnapping of Israelites (→23:19–25; cf. Exod. 21:16). As some American crimes are federal offenses that involve additional jurisdictions and additional penalties, so the kidnapping of an Israelite *by* an Israelite is an even more profound offense of the covenant. Distinguishing this crime implies neither favoritism nor disregard of the land's beloved strangers (→10:17–22).

Love Many sins, when not appropriately punished, quickly multiply in ways that leave a people powerless to stop them. If kidnapping pays, it proliferates—as in lawless parts of the world today. A populace is unable to check its spread without decisive action by authorities. So Israel must **put away** these practices (→17:2–7), as the unleavened body of Christ must be preserved from uncontrollable contamination by sins of arrogance (1 Cor. 5:2) and must remain vigilant against their reintroduction at any time.

Love Remission of debts (→15:1–6) and limits on collateral put the health of the people of God before individual economic justice (here, the repaying of creditors). Modern foreclosure and bankruptcy laws do the same, limiting the power of capital to determine relationships. Indeed, "if he has wronged you at all, or owes you anything, charge that to my account.... I will repay it" (Phlm. 18–19 RSV; →24:10–15).

> **24:8**Take heed in the plague of leprosy, that you observe diligently, and do according to all that the priests the Levites shall teach you: as I commanded them, so you shall do. **9**Remember what YHWH your God did to Miriam by the way as you came forth out of Egypt.

Love All believers may be **priests** (1 Pet. 2:5), but not all are experts. Israel's priests have detailed guidelines on skin conditions, articulated in Lev. 13–14. Common Israelites need not become specialists on their own, but are to consult the **Levites**, Israel's public health authority. Since Levites are also spiritual authorities, teachers of Torah, they are in a position to diagnose a spiritually caused problem like **Miriam's** (Num. 12:10–15). Without their experience, Israelites are liable to falsely diagnose and mistreat. They might medicalize the spiritual or spiritualize the medical. Leaders in the kingdom too must be authorized, equipped, competent, and obeyed for their churches to be healthy. All four of these requirements are involved here.

Faith Do **as I commanded them** establishes a line of authority from YHWH through Moses and the priests to the people (→34:8–9). The **priests** are not to follow their own desires, but are under YHWH's orders. To obey them insofar as they are faithful to those orders is to obey YHWH. "All authority in heaven and on earth has been given to me. Go ... and make disciples ... teaching them to observe all that I have commanded you" (Matt. 28:18–20 RSV).

Hope Moses's warning about **Miriam** has an edge to it: she develops **leprosy** after she and Aaron speak against Moses (Num. 12:1). Could this be a veiled warning not only for the whole people to obey the priests, but also for the **priests** to remain obedient to Moses's orders? Any break in the chain of **command** will not only leave spiritual and physical conditions unaddressed, but also bring down new plagues that can be addressed only through the stringent words of new prophets (18:15–19). Conversely, as the prophet Elisha bypassed many of Israel's own sufferers but healed Naaman the Syrian who obeyed his strange advice (2 Kgs. 5:9–14), so skeptical insiders may find themselves put outside the camp like Miriam while their prophetic physician heals foreigners who do as he says (Luke 17:11–19).

Love If **leprous Miriam** is a type for skeptical Israel, then she is a type for the blemished church. We are bound to Moses's successor (→18:15–19) as our bridegroom and deliverer from **Egypt**; he has appointed our kin as agents to assist him as his teachers and interpreters; our failure to **heed** them has made us unpresentable, and our exclusion from the camp calls us to submit anew to his work (Eph. 5:27). How? Only by doing what Christ has **commanded** those agents for our sake—whether they are formal magisteria, pastoral or vocational or parental or peer teachers, or prophets with gifts of knowledge. This demands our discernment, but not (as we often imagine) our discretion.

> **24:10**When you lend your neighbor any kind of loan, you shall not go into his+ house to get his+ pledge. **11**You shall stand outside, and the man+ to whom you lend shall bring forth the pledge outside to you. **12**If he+ be a poor man+, you shall not sleep with his+ pledge; **13**you shall surely restore to him+ the pledge when the sun goes down, that he+ may sleep in his+ garment, and bless you: and it shall be righteousness to you before YHWH your God. **14**You shall not oppress a hired servant who is poor and needy, whether he+ be of your brothers+, or of your foreigners who are in your land within your gates: **15**in his+ day you shall give him+ his+ hire, neither shall the sun go down on it; for he+ is poor, and sets his+ heart on it: lest he+ cry against you to YHWH, and it be sin to you (Exod. 22:21–24).

Faith **Blessing** and **crying out** anticipate the covenant's blessings and curses (Deut. 28). Israel before YHWH is the hard-hearted creditor, who is also a massive debtor. Israel is also a forgiven debtor, who becomes a means of softening the hard-hearted. The discrepancy is resolved among those who pray as Jesus teaches, "Forgive us . . . as we forgive" (Matt. 6:12).

Hope Jesus riffs on the rule of prompt payment with a wondrous twist: all are paid (Matt. 20:8), but many workers *still* cry out, now against God's generosity (20:10–16). On the day when all are compensated, the "first" will receive what belongs to them and be sent away guilty, while the "last" will receive grace and stay for joy.

Love These **garments** are not collateral; they are basic comfort. Confiscation of necessities makes debtors' lives mere means of recovering debts (→24:6–7), a mild form of economically motivated torture and extortion. The church's fundamental debt is "to love one another" (Rom. 13:8a NRSV). This debt cannot be paid off or exacted through coercion. In the great reversal of the kingdom, it is the unforgiving who as the ultimate debtors will be handed over to torturers (Amos 2:6–8; Matt. 18:34–35). Here again Deuteronomy prohibits a cultural abuse in Israel that will be interculturally dissolved through the Torah-fulfilling (Rom. 13:8b) replenishment of messianic atonement.

Love The focus of this sequence of orders quietly shifts from not exploiting a poor man's[+] indebtedness to not exploiting a poor man's[+] merit. Exploitation is not structured into economic relationships in such a way that participants are caught in **unrighteousness**, but arises from evil hearts (Matt. 15:18–20). It is overcome by *respect* for all in fear and love of YHWH. Accordingly, Paul honors the spirit of the rule for a creditor not to invade a debtor's **house** in his correspondence with Philemon. He asks Philemon for Onesimus rather than demanding him when Philemon owes him his very self (Phlm. 10, 18). This is a splendid counterpart to →24:6–7, humanizing not only Philemon's relationship to Onesimus and Onesimus's relationship to Paul but Paul's relationship to Philemon.

Love A **pledged garment** must be returned nightly, inconveniencing the lender and embarrassing the debtor as a regular reminder of the need to repay. It blesses with the grace of comfort and the grace of gentle discipline. This makes a debtor's pledged garment a pointer to the Father's Spirit, our comforter (*paraklētos*; John 16:7) and critic (16:8). The kingdom's affliction "is for your comfort [*paraklēsis*] and salvation" and its comfort is "for your comfort you are experiencing by endurance of his sufferings that are also ours" (2 Cor. 1:6–7, my translation).

> **24:16**The fathers[+] shall not be put to death for the children, neither shall the children be put to death for the fathers[+]: every man[+] shall be put to death for his[+] own sin.

Plain This rule grants each Israelite **his** or her **own** standing. As an object of the covenant, a human being is not merely a part—of a tribe, lineage, class, or people—but a *person*. In its reaction against modern individualism, late modern theology can regard humanity as a collective in which identity, guilt, responsibility, virtue, and possessions are simply shared. Collective guilt and collective innocence haunt social-scientific politics. As God promises to spare a whole city for the sake of ten righteous individuals (Gen. 18:32), so Deuteronomy sets the covenant before not only *all* Israel but *each* Israelite, right down to its heart in the second-person-singular verbs of the Decalogue.

Love Israel's familial structure is double-edged. It is a fundamental network of sustenance, but also a network of suffering when its members fail. As other provisions throughout Deuteronomy protect the unfamilied from exposure (→24:17–22), this rule protects family members from guilt by association. By relativizing families, Deuteronomy makes room not only for persons but also for person-making relationships beyond the family. The household of God, built by the innocence of a single righteous one, reaches across familial and other boundaries to span all humanity.

Faith No one may bring an ancestral charge against Jesus or anyone else. The guilty verdict on his whole sinless life (Heb. 4:15) can only be a violation of Torah, and the crucifixion that follows is an abuse (13:13). Vindicated, appointed heir of all things (1:2), he has mercy on thousands (→5:8–10) of brethren[+] (Heb. 2:11–14) who live by faith (Hab. 2:4 in Heb. 10:38).

Hope What humans may not do, God reserves to himself[+]: to visit parents' guilt on **children** (Deut. 5:9–10). Sin *does* propagate from parents to children, spreading from the first transgressors down to all of us today (Rom. 5:12–14). Then why may humans not punish as God does? Perhaps because punishment-by-association pertains only to "those who hate" YHWH (Deut. 5:9), and only YHWH knows human hearts. Or perhaps because perpetuation of original sin ends in the fullness of time (Rom. 5:15–21; Ezek. 18; Jer. 31:29–30) so that all may be freed through repentance, "for I have no pleasure in the death of anyone" (Ezek. 18:32 NRSV). Or, as in the verses that follow, perhaps family is a penultimate human relationship, whose claims are real but not determinative: "No one who puts his[+] hand to the plow and looks back is fit for the kingdom of God" (Luke 9:62 RSV).

> [24:17]You shall not deprive the foreigner or the fatherless of justice, or take a widow's clothing in pledge; [18]but you shall remember that you were a bondservant in Egypt, and YHWH your God redeemed you there: therefore I command you to do this thing. [19]When you reap your harvest in your field, and have forgot a sheaf in the field, you shall not go again to get it: it shall be for the foreigner, for the fatherless, and for the widow; that YHWH your God may bless you in all the work of your hands. [20]When you beat your olive tree, you shall not go over the boughs again: it shall be for the foreigner, for the fatherless, and for the widow. [21]When you harvest your vineyard, you shall not glean it after yourselves: it shall be for the foreigner, for the fatherless, and for the widow. [22]You shall remember that you were a bondservant in the land of Egypt: therefore I command you to do this thing.

Hope The previous passage relativizes family relationships to protect insiders (→24:16). These rules join many others (→14:27–29; →16:9–12) in relativizing family to protect outsiders without strong enough families of their own. They protect by making Israel's story of **Egyptian** servitude a point of commonality with all of Israel's powerless. In humbling the house of Pharaoh and ending the lines of Canaanite kings, YHWH has not just exalted and preserved Jacob's clans but begun forging a new people whose identity transcends the familial (→5:14).

Faith The margins of the world's economy might be the center of the kingdom's. A jar in an anonymous **widow's** house sustains a mighty prophet (1 Kgs. 17:8–24), and another anonymous widow's mite from the far economic fringes of the Roman Empire dwarfs all the rest (Mark 12:41–44). This and many other negligible signs, including that of a fatherless Nazarene whose rights are trampled on in the course of a Passover festival, turn out to hold the key to God's redemptive work.

Love Bread, oil, and wine are staples. They are also the basic materials of Christian worship. The world's invisible ones **glean** the land's leftovers—its forgotten **sheaves**, stubborn **olives**, and late-ripening grapes. When they do, they gather the symbols of the discarded Anointed One who came to bring abundant life (→8:6–10). In commanding Israel to leave these crops behind, YHWH appoints a sign of the forsaken Son who comes to **redeem** all. Israel is not losing a little profit by letting go of these agricultural remnants; it is gaining its soul (Luke 9:25). (For an antithesis, →28:35–44.)

Love Torah distinguishes between persons (cf. Rom. 2:11), granting special protections to **widows** and the desperately poor. Is this favoritism? Moses claims the opposite: YHWH upholds justice for the least and provides for the destitute **foreigners** and orphans *because* he[+] shows no favor (→10:17–22). The ones YHWH blesses with prosperity are his[+] means of blessing sufferers, so that **all** who **work** in Israel are **blessed**. God's will is not just to bless or save or have mercy on some (John 1:7; 17:10; Acts 2; Rom. 11; 2 Pet. 3:4), but to choose some for the sake of all. This suggests a test for the righteousness, and even the political viability, of affirmative action and other special measures for particular categories of people: do they not hinder but advance the blessing of all?

DEUTERONOMY 25

25:1 If there is a controversy between men⁺, and they come to judgment, and the judges judge them; then they shall justify the righteous, and condemn the wicked; **²**and if the wicked one be worthy to be beaten, the judge shall have him⁺ lie down, and to be beaten before his⁺ face, according to his⁺ wickedness, by number. **³**Forty stripes he⁺ may give him⁺, he⁺ shall not exceed; lest, if he⁺ should exceed, and beat him⁺ above these with many stripes, then your brother⁺ should be shamed before you.

Plain The limit on **stripes** protects the dignity of yet another vulnerable outsider in Deuteronomy's social landscape: the wrongdoer. Deferring personal and civil standards of satisfaction to divine standards can help keep justice-seeking from metastasizing into vendetta and **judgment** into humiliation.

Faith Why spend half of this passage setting up the condition for the flogging? Because of the importance of due process. Corporal punishment is not to be a right of power—as it is when Pontius Pilate declares Jesus innocent and has him chastised anyway (Luke 23:15–16; John 18:38b–19:1). It is to be an exercise of justice. The stress on **righteousness** and **wickedness** suggests that the accuracy of the verdict, not the verdict itself, is decisive. So Paul's five floggings (2 Cor. 11:24) are juridical but not just. Like the prophets before them (Matt. 5:12; Acts 7:52), Jesus, **brother** of the crowds that turn on him, scorns the **shame** (*aischynē*; Heb. 12:2; cf. Deut. 25:3 Septuagint) of the cross that flagrantly violates YHWH's justice and ascends to his Father's commendation. All these are punished *outside* the law of Moses, not under it.

Love If Christian dissociation corresponds to Israelite stoning (→17:2–7), then milder Christian discipline corresponds to flogging. By whatever standards are appropriate to both the kingdom and its local culture, it is diligent to judge **wickedness** accurately, act publicly, punish without humiliating, and remind transgressors that they remain siblings. The antithesis is gossip—a far more common church practice that prejudges, whispers, shames, and shuns.

Hope In order not to abuse discipline, rabbinic halakah sets stringent restrictions on when penalties apply and draws back from applying full penalties (e.g., withholding one lash from the **forty**). In understandable reaction against centuries of horrifying abuses against our respective peoples, contemporary Jews and Christians are tempted to refrain from *all* ecclesiastical punishments. But yielding frustrates and even **shames** the victims who come forward for recognition of wrongs. This firm passage does not make judgment optional or punishment discretionary. However, every human community has its own setting and structure, and just discipline can take many forms besides corporal punishment. This is especially true in the kingdom healed by Christ's **stripes** to live for righteousness (Isa. 53:5 in 1 Pet. 2:24). Atonement revolutionizes the kingdom's discipline, though it does not eliminate the possibility of abuse: "If someone has caused pain, he⁺ has caused it not to me, but to some extent . . . to all of you. This punishment by the majority is enough for such a person; so now instead you should forgive and console him⁺, so that he⁺ may not be overwhelmed by excessive sorrow" (2 Cor. 2:5–7 NRSV).

25:4 You shall not muzzle the ox when he⁺ threshes.

Love YHWH sets his⁺ heirs over "sheep and oxen, and also the beasts of the field" (Ps. 8:6–7 NRSV), saying: "Let them have dominion . . . over the cattle" (Gen. 1:26 NRSV). Creation is a hierarchy in which inferiors are ends, not just means, and superiors are means, not just ends, and nothing is to be deprived of its share: "You cause the grass to grow for the cattle, and plants for humanity to cultivate, to bring food from the earth" (Ps. 104:14, my translation). Because the human mission is to herald and receive God's new creation, these creatures have a role in that mission. Their mundane harvests are YHWH's blessings of prosperity over covenantal Israel, whose firstfruits Israel offers back to God in gratitude (Deut. 18:3–4). So their humble share in those harvests is a share in the glory of the triune God. "The **ox** knows its owner" (Isa. 1:3 NRSV), and "every wild animal of the forest is mine, the cattle on a thousand hills" (Ps. 50:10 NRSV). So "praise [YHWH] from the earth, you . . . wild animals and all cattle!" (148:7–10 NRSV). All this teleology is a far cry from the human-centered utilitarianism of ancient Israel's pagan neighbors—and our contemporary economies. Conversely, God abhors golden calves (→9:15–17) and rescues cattle from futile lives threshing grain for Canaan's (→2:34–37) and Nineveh's (Jonah 4:11) idols, not just because God cares about God and Israel, but also because God cares for cattle.

Love Is this verse really directed "entirely for our sake" in the apostolic age? (1 Cor. 9:10 NRSV; cf. 9:9). Or does God care about animals too? Paul's rhetoric is like a rabbinic "if this, how much more that" (*qal wahomer*) comparison that does not empty this verse of its plain sense. This whole string of passages in Deuteronomy protecting the dignity of Israel's vulnerable makes room even for animals, for the one "dishonest in a very little is dishonest also in much" (Luke 16:10 NRSV). YHWH has not forged Israel to be a "largely holy" people, for there can be no such thing, but to share his[+] own perfect holiness (Lev. 11:44–45). If they compromise here, they will compromise with the stranger and the lonely, with one another, and with their redeemer. So there is no trade-off between wholehearted concern for God's covenant people then or now and consideration for their stock.

Faith How can this verse not be for Jesus's sake too? He separates the wheat from the chaff and gathers the grain in his granary (Matt. 3:12). His heavenly Father feeds him as he[+] feeds the rest (6:25), with material support from their common purse and others' hospitality. Yet the Son has additional food that his disciples do not at first discern: doing the Father's will and finishing his[+] harvesting. This harvest is its own compensation, for the work of sowing the good news of the kingdom and reaping its harvest pays off in shared joy (John 4:31–36). Yet more is gained than just joy: the Son receives all the Father has (16:15) and shares it in turn with his partners (16:23–24). This is a picture of healthy ministry: not a duty that feels burdensome, exploitative, or unsupported, but the privilege of reaping the fruit of another's labor and rejoicing together with all who have benefited (4:36–38; 17:13).

Hope "The one who plows should plow in hope and the one who **threshes** should thresh in hope of a share in the crop" (1 Cor. 9:10, my translation). Exploitation is heretical eschatology. It dissociates the temporal and eternal fulfillments that God has linked in the Messiah's advent, robbing both present and future activity of their true significance, then their power, then their reality. Such dissociation makes prosperity unsustainable: "Where there are no oxen, there is no grain; abundant crops come by the strength of the **ox**" (Prov. 14:4 NRSV).

> [25:5]If brothers dwell together, and one of them die, and have no son, the wife of the dead shall not be married outside to a stranger: her husband's brother shall go in to her, and take her to him as wife, and perform the duty of a husband's brother to her. [6]The firstborn whom she bears shall succeed in the name of his brother who is dead, that his name not be blotted out of Israel. [7]If the man does not want to take his brother's wife, then his brother's wife shall go up to the gate to the elders, and say: "My husband's brother refuses to raise up to his brother a name in Israel; he will not perform the duty of a husband's brother to me." [8]Then the elders of his city shall call him, and speak to him: and if he stand, and say: "I do not want to take her," [9]then his brother's wife shall come to him in the presence of the elders, and loose his shoe from off his foot, and spit in his face; and she shall answer and say: "So shall it be done to the man who does not build

up his brother's house." **¹⁰**His name shall be called in Israel, "The house of him who has his shoe untied."

Plain Removing the offender's **shoe** and **spitting** are obscure symbols whose meaning is clear enough: in a clever act of poetic justice, it ironically preserves the honorable **brother's** memory by publicly and memorably disgracing the name of the offending brother.

Faith This provision for polygamy in special circumstances (but →22:22–30) protects yet another voiceless and vulnerable group in Deuteronomy's patriarchal society: the heirless dead (cf. Judg. 21). YHWH commands that the closest family member intervene to produce a legacy that will perpetuate the **dead brother's name**. Until these have living advocates, YHWH is their special advocate; and until YHWH's will is done, their women plead on their behalf and civil authorities intercede and upbraid, so that the dead one "shall see his offspring, and shall prolong his days" (Isa. 53:10). It is an (admittedly odd) image of the Messiah's resurrection. The impossible justice that natural human structures can only approximate and anticipate, divine grace delivers: the Father brings life to the dead by intervening through another, his⁺ Holy Spirit, to retrieve the name of the forsaken and heirless Son (Phil. 2:6–11). God answers Jesus's need so rapidly that his ecclesial widow does not even have time to finish mourning him, let alone find a **stranger** to **marry**, before he is **raised** and his inheritance secured (Matt. 28:1–2).

Hope Because the **dead** man's **name** will not survive without his **brother's** co-operation, the passage exerts great rhetorical force on the uncooperative from all sides: YHWH, Moses, the widow, the **elders**, and all **Israel**. Yet the word of God "depends not on human will or exertion, but on God who shows mercy" (Rom. 9:16 NRSV). When **duty** and pressure fail, God can still rescue a whole tribe's name from obscurity—as God does for Judah in giving Perez to Tamar in spite of Onan's and Judah's resistance (Gen. 38). In doing so, God prevents a breach in the Messiah's genealogy (Matt. 1:3) and so preserves the future of all Israel. God goes to great lengths to guide and honor human agency, but is not finally frustrated by it.

Love What is causing the living **brother's** reticence? Fear for his own estate? Rivalry? Revulsion? Neglect? Self-centeredness? Grief? His own wife's jealousy? Or a combination? Whatever the reason, it is clear that Moses appreciates the sacrificial character of the surviving brother's duty. Protecting the vulnerable, living and **dead**, is risky, calling us even to leave father and mother and native land (Ruth 2:11). However, refusing to protect them is riskier. The next-of-kin who puts his family's inheritance above his duty to Ruth (4:6) dies nameless, while the good and faithful Boaz becomes the great-grandfather of David (Ruth 4; Matt. 1:5–6)—whose eternal **successor** risks and sacrifices everything for the sake of the lost. "Everyone who has left houses or brothers or sisters or father or mother or children or fields, for my name's sake, will receive a hundredfold and will inherit eternal life" (19:29 NRSV). Ecclesially as well as christologically, this passage's call to **build up the brother's house** anticipates what no earthly marriage can bring about (→22:22–30): a mutual, sacrificial love so radical that it yields what this whole section of Deuteronomy longs to see (Matt. 13:17)—community to the stranger, sustenance to the destitute, worship to the godless, and eternity to the dead. YHWH "is God . . . of the living" (22:32 NRSV; cf. Deut. 23:5).

> **25:11**When men strive together one with another, and the wife of the one draws near to deliver her husband out of the hand of him who strikes him, and puts forth her hand, and takes him by his private parts, **12**then you shall cut off her hand; your eye shall have no pity.

Plain The passage draws out a scenario that trains readers to sympathize with **the wife**—then delivers a shocking punch line that has left readers since the first rabbis grasping for ways to soften it. Even under these circumstances, her action is a grave offense, with the ring of a violated taboo.

Plain "I was afraid, because I was naked" (Gen. 3:10 NRSV). Many of the provisions preceding this rule share the theme of protection of the vulnerable. Now comes an uncomfortable reminder that the very feature that gives the most powerful members of Deuteronomy's patriarchal society their social strength—their manhood—also makes *them* vulnerable (→23:1–8). And it does not take a Freudian to notice the connection between male physiological vulnerability and male insecurity. For a **wife** to overpower another **man** in this way humiliates him, shames her, and even disrespects her **husband**. The peace of Israel's society depends upon female respect for men as well as male respect for women (→22:13–30). YHWH originally fashions skins for his+ fallen human beings to wear (Gen. 3:21), not to shield them from him+ (cf. 3:8) but to protect them from one another (3:7). This and Deuteronomy's other gender laws, lopsided and minimal as they are from our cultural and eschatological perspectives, go some of the way to discouraging the genders from humiliating one another.

Faith "If your right **hand** causes you to sin, **cut it off** and throw it away; it is better for you to lose one of your members than for your whole body to go away to Gehenna" (Matt. 5:30 NRSV margin). In expounding the Torah of his kingdom, Jesus can sound as drastic and even barbaric as the Torah of Moses. Powers, among them sexual powers as well as powers of aggression, are not trifles. The social, psychological, spiritual roots of sexual taboos are too powerful to be finessed away by conditioning, psychiatric therapy, social engineering, or even sexual revolutions. These powers must be met and overcome by the kingdom's greater power.

Faith A society that accommodates sexual anxieties can live in temporal peace. But it is trapped, bound to respect psychological qualities that are not God's intention for humanity. Structural sin is systemic adaptation to ways of life such as idolatry, slavery, and sexual oppression and perversity that fall short of God's glory. The Mosaic covenant does not surrender to structural sin, but it does not free from it. Male and female Israelites must still respect the curse that came from leading one another to disobey: her urge is to dominate her **husband**, and he rules over her (Gen. 3:16). The **pitiless** penalty for a **wife** touching another man's **genitals** to save her husband may hold back even worse consequences in Deuteronomy's culture, but it cannot be the last word from God on relations between the sexes. When a sinful woman weeps over Jesus's feet, wipes them with her hair, and kisses and anoints them, she breaks cultural taboo. Yet he receives these offenses as holy gratitude from a loving heart and forgives her (probably sexual) sins (Luke 7:36–48). His word breaks the taboos of sexual anxiety and the sinful structures that have held men and women at artificial distances from one another and restores peace (7:49–50).

Hope "I want you to be free from anxieties" (1 Cor. 7:32 NRSV). In the kingdom no curse reigns. We are free—not to serve our own compulsions for personal protection, pleasure, or power, but "to promote good order and to secure . . . undivided devotion to the Lord" (7:35 RSV). The church displays a new order of freedom among the genders in the midst of its sexually disordered societies that seems both dangerously casual to some outsiders and overly modest, even prudish, to others. To the discerning this demonstrates that its Lord is not a God of disorder but of peace (14:33).

Love "The wife does not have authority over her own body, but the husband does" (1 Cor. 7:4a NRSV). The condemned **wife** transgresses **her husband's** authority over her body by seizing another **man**. Sexual propriety in the kingdom is restored to God's original intentions (cf. Gen. 2:24 in 1 Cor. 6:16) of mutual matrimonial sharing and exclusivity: "Likewise the husband does not have authority over his own body, but the wife does" (7:4b NRSV). Husbands transgress their wives' authority over their bodies by seizing and preying upon others, by refusing to share themselves fully in mind, body, and spirit, and by putting themselves needlessly at risk—as the husband in Deuteronomy may have done by getting himself into a fight that tempts her to intervene.

> **25:13**You shall not have in your bag diverse weights, a great and a small. **14**You shall not have in your house diverse measures, a great and a small. **15**You shall have a perfect and just weight. You shall have a perfect and just measure, that your days may be long in the land YHWH your God gives you. **16**For all who do such things, all who do unrighteously, are an abomination to YHWH your God.

Plain This rule, the last of several chapters of regulations for ordinary life, addresses public and private fraud. Fraud preys upon yet another vulnerable group, to which even the strongest often unknowably (and ironically) belong: the ignorant. Fraud literally liquidates faith: it misrepresents in order to monetize another person's trust.

Faith "You know the commandments: . . . You shall not defraud" (Mark 10:19 NRSV). Our lives are full of examples of liquidated trust: hidden commissions, hidden taxes, exaggerated claims, misleading packaging, inflated rhetoric, empty threats, misleading statements, inferior customer service, disingenuous campaign promises, fine-print exclusions, tacked-on fees and surcharges, creative accounting, petty office theft, tardiness, and loafing on company time are so common and so costly that we are shocked and delighted when we *don't* find discrepancies between the nominal and the real. In his Markan exchange with the rich young man, Jesus interprets covetousness as fraud (→5:21). The two are naturally linked. If fraud misrepresents the truth to another, covetousness misrepresents the truth to oneself. One will naturally arouse the other. We certainly face, and regularly succumb to, our temptation to take a little extra from those we envy, and we soon rationalize it as a matter of justice. God names all this **unrighteousness**.

Faith Fraud offends both one's customer and God. Deuteronomy mentions no penalty for fraud, but Leviticus prescribes that the fraudulent should pay back what they owe plus one-fifth and offer a guilt offering to YHWH for forgiveness (Lev. 6:1–7). However, when Zacchaeus repays fourfold what he has defrauded, Jesus proclaims that salvation has come—without, here as elsewhere in the Gospels, demanding the required guilt offering (Luke 19:1–9). Why? Because Jesus is the Son of Man, both appointed to judge and sent to seek and save the lost (19:10). The sole criterion for forgiveness is his word. Zacchaeus's faith makes him not just a son of Jacob, but a son of Abraham who has found God's mercy (19:9; cf. 1:54–55; 3:8–9; 16:22, 25–31; Acts 3:25–26; 13:26).

Hope "The **measure** you measure will be measured back to you" (Luke 6:38, my translation). We who sacrifice trust for marginal gain enrich ourselves by impoverishing our relationships, above all our relationship with the **God** who sees our discrepancies between representation and reality and who knows our hearts. Such predatory self-promotion cannot **long** remain, but must end in the reign of the one who has put others before himself (Phil. 2:3–4). By announcing the approach of God's kingdom before the judgment, Jesus grants an opportunity for us to rebuild what had been torn down, saving both our ruined relationships and the people they involve. The dishonest but shrewd steward in his parable takes advantage of it: when he learns that judgment is upon him, he switches to converting dishonest money back into good will. Repentance regains trust, refunds relationships, and restores community with neighbors and God, that "they may welcome you into the eternal homes" (Luke 16:1–9 NRSV).

Love There can be no place for fraud in these eternal homes. Yet, preposterously, fraud infests the church. Wolves in sheep's clothing trade on Christ's name for unearned gain. "You yourselves wrong and defraud—and believers at that," says an incredulous Paul. "Do you not know that wrongdoers will not inherit the kingdom of God?" (1 Cor. 6:8–9 NRSV). Christian fraud tempts believers to fall back on two of the world's coping mechanisms: self-protection by litigation (6:1–6) and resignation to be victimized (6:7). While the latter is more ecclesiologically defensible than the former, Paul settles for neither. Instead he reminds the Corinthians that evil "is what some of you *used to* be. But you were washed, you were sanctified, you were justified" (6:11 NRSV). Paul never loses hope in his wretched churches or gives up disciplining us because he never loses confidence in the self-representation of the triune God in baptizing us in the Son and sealing us in the Spirit.

> **25:17**Remember what Amalek (Gen. 36:12, 15–16) did to you by the way as you came forth out of Egypt (Exod. 17:8–13); **18**how he met you by the way, and struck the hindmost of you, all who were feeble behind you, when you were faint and weary; and he did not fear God. **19**Therefore when YHWH your God has given you rest from all your enemies all around, in the land YHWH your God gives you for an inheritance to possess, you shall blot out the memory of Amalek from under the sky; you shall not forget.

Plain Deuteronomy supplies details for explaining why YHWH will fight this marauder people (Num. 13:29) until he⁺ blots out **Amalek's memory** (Exod. 7:14): they have preyed upon Israel's weakest stragglers. The reminder and its moral are a fitting end to a series of laws largely focused on protecting the vulnerable.

Plain In idiomatic context, to **fear God** is to "fear gods," to respect *any* consequences from heavenly powers of any kind. **Amalekites** are operating outside common decency. Like pirates or terrorists, their ethic is narrowly self-interested. Like Machiavellian regimes today, their success serves as its own justification, their defeat its own disproof.

Faith "O God, do not keep silence," the psalmist Asaph pleads concerning Israel's persecutors (Ps. 83:1 NRSV). Centuries in ghettos and then the Holocaust and unceasing jihad add urgency to the cry. Numbers 14:41–45 adds **Amalekites** to the Canaanites who intimidate and defeat Israel after Sinai (Deut. 1:44–45). That makes their humbling doubly unfinished business. The Amalekites are a chronic enemy and ally of enemies (Judg. 6:3–6, 33). In fighting them, though, Israel often shows itself to be *its* own worst enemy, weakening itself with disbelief (→1:43–45), idolatry (Judg. 3:12–14; 10:12–13), and greed (1 Sam. 15:4–9). Saul's plunder of the Amalekites is the basis of YHWH's rejection of him (15:10–29). David largely succeeds (30:18; 2 Sam. 8:11–12), but it is not until the days of Hezekiah that Simeonite clans destroy the Amalekites' last remnant (1 Chr. 4:41–43). Amalek is a particularly stubborn nuisance to Israel who exposes its weaknesses as well as testing its strengths and challenging God's faithfulness. Its defeat, then, is to be a warning to all nations, then and now, of that faithfulness (Isa. 45:22–23 in Phil. 2:10–11).

Hope Commentators rarely miss the irony of an order to remember to wipe out **Amalek's memory** (now read in synagogues before Purim every year!). What kind of memorial amnesia is this to be? Amalek is said to have engaged Israel hoping to exterminate the whole people (Ps. 83:7), perhaps to prevent the nation from settling as a rival. In the near term, Israel is not to forsake its divine eye-for-an-eye mission to retaliate (→19:15–21). Longer term, since this is embedded in a set of orders for Israel never to **forget**, Israel's **remembrance** consigns Amalekites to the eternal nonexistence of Israel's mortal enemies. Amalek's endless end anticipates the hell that awaits all who try to exterminate God's people and their memory (Ps. 83:4). Yet it also anticipates the unending frustration of YHWH's adversaries that drives them (even Amalekites! 83:7) to seek YHWH's name (83:16). Could Amalek's descendants repent of his enmity and leave his heritage to join all the other nations ransomed by the Lamb's blood (Rev. 5:9), who sing forever that "you alone, whose name is [YHWH], are the Most High over all the earth" (Ps. 83:18 NRSV)? Both ends would fulfill God's will and accomplish Israel's mission.

Love "First among the nations was **Amalek**," prophesies Balaam, "but its end is to perish forever" (Num. 24:20 NRSV). The utterly futile cause of persecuting the people of God must irreversibly change the persecutors. Yet the Spirit leads Asaph to foresee something more than just destruction for Israel's enemies (Isa. 60:1–3): a distant sense that the blood of the martyrs is the seed of the church. The duality of Ps. 83:16, in which persecutors are shamed in order to seek YHWH's name, mirrors Revelation's words of assurance to Christ's persecuted, as well as the unexpected sliver of cheer in the mourning of Babylon's merchants: "Rejoice over her, O heaven, O saints and apostles and prophets, for God has given judgment for you against her!" (Rev. 18:19–20 RSV). Perhaps the ray of light that has reached them through all their darkness causes the conversion that gathers the glory and honor of the nations into the new Jerusalem (Isa. 60:11 in Rev. 21:24–26). "The descendants of those who oppressed you shall come bending low to you, and all who despised you shall bow down at your feet" (Isa. 60:14 NRSV; cf. 45:23 in Phil. 2:10–11).

DEUTERONOMY 26

²⁶:¹When you have come into the land YHWH your God gives you for an inheritance, and possess it, and dwell therein, ²you shall take of the first of all the fruit of the ground, which you shall bring in from your land YHWH your God gives you; and you shall put it in a basket, and shall go to the place YHWH your God shall choose, to cause his⁺ name to dwell there. ³You shall come to the priest who shall be in those days and tell him, "I profess this day to YHWH your God that I am come to the land YHWH swore to our fathers to give us."⁴The priest shall take the basket out of your hand and set it down before the altar of YHWH your God. ⁵You shall answer and say before YHWH your God, "A wandering Aramean was my father; and he went down into Egypt, and lived there, few in number; and he became there a nation, great, mighty, and populous. ⁶The Egyptians dealt ill with us, and afflicted us, and laid on us hard bondage: ⁷and we cried to YHWH, the God of our fathers, and YHWH heard our voice, and saw our affliction, and our toil, and our oppression; ⁸and YHWH brought us forth out of Egypt with a mighty hand, and with an outstretched arm, and with great terror, and with signs, and with wonders (→6:21b–25; →34:10–12); ⁹and he⁺ has brought us into this (→3:12–17) place, and has given us this land, a land flowing with milk and honey. ¹⁰Now, behold, I have brought the first of the fruit of the ground, which you, YHWH, have given me."You shall set it down before YHWH your God, and worship before YHWH your God. ¹¹You shall rejoice in all the good that YHWH your God has given to you, and to your house, you, and the Levite, and the foreigner who is in your midst.

Plain The disasters in the final passage of the covenantal curses (28:58–68) correspond to the saving events recounted here, describing the decline, fall, and exile of Israel as an undoing of salvation history.

Faith This ceremony draws on a series of classic Deuteronomic connections that give Israelite faith its distinctive shape. As the solstices and equinoxes of the pagan solar year become feasts of the forerunner John the Baptist in the European liturgical calendar, so Canaan's agricultural cycle becomes a reminder of Israel's founding story, and exodus becomes the setting for Israel's present life in its present setting (→16:9–12). The striking narrative flow moves from **me** to Jacob, to the suffering Hebrews, to the exodus generation, to the conquerors, and finally back to **me**. The harvest introduces a story, and the story becomes a prayer. These words make the **basketful** of produce sacramental—an outward **sign** of inward grace that reaches from the historical past to include the present material world. All these elements anticipate the words of institution said over a meal that draw every new generation into Christ's exodus (Luke 22:14–20; cf. 9:31) "for our sins."

Hope Gerhard von Rad's influential Old Testament theology treats this ritual's epitome of salvation history as a yardstick of ancient Israelite faith. Less often appreciated is the way it measures the apostolic faith as well. The events recounted here dominate Stephen's remarkably uncompressed testimony in Acts 7:8b–45a. Rather than seeing Jesus as a mortal threat to the customs that Moses handed down (6:14), Stephen expects his audience to see the exodus paradigm in the events of Jesus's life, death, and resurrection. Their failure to respect his messianic refreshing of Torah places them not in the company of grateful Israelite witnesses such as this liturgy's farmer but among the prophets' stiff-necked persecutors (7:51–52; →18:15–19). Stephen's apologia draws on Deut. 33:2 Septuagint for his climactic and thoroughly Deuteronomic condemnation of covenant unfaithfulness (Acts 7:53), then adds an apocalyptic vision **before** the Son of Man standing ready to receive into his **inheritance** (7:56–60) those who **come to** it.

Love The **land** signifies the church (→11:8–15), and its fruit the Spirit's fruit (Gal. 5:22–24). We gather to offer and share **this** fruit through spiritual gifts (1 Cor. 12:4–11) and **rejoice** together (12:26). When we do, we always share an extremely compressed form of the Spirit's standard narrative testimony to the basis of our fellowship: "Jesus is Lord" (12:3). This passage's ceremony thus anticipates the creedally shaped liturgy and liturgically shaped creeds of Christian life.

Love **Levites** and **foreigners** have no share in the land, and (unlike during the Feast of Tents in 31:9–13) they participate only indirectly in this passage's confession. Yet they are full participants in the celebration, because by YHWH's grace they have a share in its blessings (→16:9–12). The church's sacrificial worship is to bless even those who do not so sacrifice.

> ²⁶:¹²When you have made an end of tithing all the tithe of your increase in the third year, which is the year of tithing, then you shall give it to the Levite, to the foreigner, to the fatherless, and to the widow, that they may eat within your gates, and be filled. ¹³You shall say before YHWH your God, "I have put away the holy things out of my house,

and also have given them to the Levite, and to the foreigner, to the fatherless, and to the widow, according to all your commandment you have commanded me: I have not transgressed any of your commandments, neither have I forgotten them: ¹⁴I have not eaten of it in my mourning, neither have I put away of it, being unclean, nor given of it for the dead (cf. 14:1; 18:1; Hos. 9:4; Jer. 16:7–8): I have listened to the voice of YHWH my God; I have done according to all you have commanded me. ¹⁵Look down from your holy habitation, from heaven, and bless your people Israel, and the ground you have given us, as you swore to our fathers, a land flowing with milk and honey."

Love Instruction—"law"—follows gospel: the firstfruits ceremony recounts the exodus from unrighteousness (→26:1–11), then the third-year tithe (→14:27–29) affirms the Torah of righteousness that allows Israel to remain in the **land** God has given. The one guards against forgetfulness of the founding events that have brought Israel to Canaan as God's showcase people, then the other resists the **transgressions** and neglect of **holiness** that threaten to compromise Israel's witness and send it, **unclean**, into exile (→26:16–19; →31:14–18). Reversing that coming catastrophe will mean a new gospel, of Jesus Christ. A new law, of Christ (→11:1–7), will follow it, marked by a celebrative responsibility that is honored by churches' own **tithes** and offerings to support the fellowship in its mission: "Bear one another's burdens. . . . All must carry their own loads" (Gal. 6:2–5 NRSV).

Love The focus on purity in 26:14, unusual in Deuteronomy, is fitting for the preparation and consumption of a **third-year tithe within one's gates**, in the absence of the priests who are experts in the proper procedures. Deuteronomy appreciates purity as God's concern for his⁺ people whether in the presence of priests (cf. 26:1–11) or away, and whether conquering (→23:9–14) or being settled in the land. Israelites may not compartmentalize their faith, living by clerical rules only when around clergy. Nor may Christians, whose Father sees and rewards in secret (Matt. 6:4, 6, 18).

Faith Other biblical teaching on tithes concentrates on tithes to the priests (Lev. 27:30–33; Num. 18:21–32; 2 Chr. 31:4–12; Neh. 10:35–39; 12:44; 13:4–14; Mal. 3:8–12; Heb. 7:5), not Deuteronomy's **third-year tithe** for outsiders within. This sets up Jesus's criticism of the scribes and Pharisees for tithing while neglecting the Torah's weightier matters (Matt. 23:23; Luke 11:42). As if restoring an institution after centuries of neglect, Jesus offers himself in fellowship to Israel's outsiders (Matt. 4:12–17; Luke 4:14–31).

Hope Charged to keep the **commandments**, the rich ruler answers Jesus, "I have kept all these" (Matt. 19:16–20 NRSV). His affirmation echoes this prayer of the upright Israelite. It is good enough for a **blessing from heaven** (cf. Ps. 102:19–22) on Israel and its **ground**; but this ruler still lacks God's final blessing *in* heaven (Matt. 19:21). To gain that, the disciple must **listen** anew **to YHWH's voice** and **do accordingly**. Jesus is no mere teacher of Moses (7:28–29). In his ascension and session he too **looks down** on his people (→11:8–15), delivering words of knowledge, call, and accountability for his disciples to obey (Matt. 28:20).

> **26:16**This day YHWH your God commands you to do these statutes and ordinances. You shall therefore keep and do them with all your heart and with all your self (→4:29–30). **17**You have declared YHWH this day to be your God, and that you would walk in his⁺ ways, and keep his⁺ statutes and his⁺ commandments and his⁺ ordinances, and listen to his⁺ voice (→18:15–19): **18**and YHWH has declared you this day to be a people for his⁺ own possession, as he⁺ has promised you, and that you should keep all his⁺ commandments; **19**and to make you high above all nations he⁺ has made, in praise and in name and in honor; and that you may be a holy people to YHWH your God, as he⁺ has spoken.

Faith Moses invites his audience to pause (or wake up?) and take stock. He has reminded Israel at great length of the shape of its covenantal life: God has taken this people under his⁺ governance to build them up not as just an exemplar but as his⁺ beloved son who **walks in his⁺ ways** (→8:1–5). Fifteen chapters of **statutes and ordinances** (cf. 11:32–12:1) are now concluded. They lay out a reciprocal relationship beautifully summarized here in three parallels: on the one hand, YHWH is Israel's God, Israel keeps the whole Torah, Israel heeds YHWH's voice. On the other, Israel is YHWH's people, Israel keeps the whole Torah, YHWH proclaims Israel's exaltation and sanctification. Moses's *summa* captures the marvelous essence of the covenant: Israel is God's pride and joy.

Hope If these words are sweet to Deuteronomy's implied audience, they are bittersweet to later ones. This passage connects Deut. 6–11 and Deut. 12–26 to the inaugurals of Deut. 27 and the blessings and curses of Deut. 28, but those conditionals and curses to come are stripped away here. It shines with sheer promise—or sheer delusion. After all, when are God's intentions for Israel ever actually realized? Life under Joshua is romantic but tenuous and uneven. Life under David and Solomon is glorious enough to enthrall practically every generation since, but under the surface it is troubled and precarious, and its glories are fleeting. And once Israel strays and crumbles, no civil restoration ever rises even to the Davidic monarchy's worldly respectability. Yet God foresees something better (Heb. 11:40). The perfecter of Israel's faith is its own author: its crucified and ascended king (12:2). In him alone Israel is truly **holy**, **walking** in God's **ways**, the **commandments** fulfilled, God's word truly **spoken** and heard (→27:9–10), Israel wholly God's **own**, and lifted up **above all nations** (→28:7–14). He alone has the **name** above all names (Phil. 2:9–11). The conditionals and curses that dominate the rest of Deuteronomy can fall away here because in the Messiah the covenant's promise is eternally secure.

Hope Moses insists that **this day** is different (→27:9–10). How? Hasn't the covenant been in effect since Sinai? It has, but its object—life in the land—is newly imminent. To enter the land is to enter the covenant's culmination (29:10–15; cf. Josh. 5:2–9). Other moments of realization, down to our own present day, are also called "today" (Ps. 95:7b in Heb. 3:7–4:11; →29:10–15). Each invites us to enter not only Joshua's rest but the eternal rest of the psalmist.

Love Those God has foreknown he[+] has glorified (Rom. 8:29–30). That transformation comes with Jesus Christ—him eternally foreknown, predestined, sent, vindicated, and glorified as the first of many—but it is already anticipated here in Israel's transformation from the least of **peoples** (→7:6–8) to the **holy** bearer of God's glory to the world.

Love Israel's Torah already anticipates and prescribes responses for a wide variety of sins, so Israel does not need to be sinless to **keep** Torah and deserve **praise** and **honor**. Nor does the church (1 John 1:8–10). It is not when Israel sins that it declines, for it sins constantly. It is when it no longer takes sin seriously. A suffering and disciplined church is already **a holy people**.

DEUTERONOMY 27

27:1 Moses and the elders of Israel commanded the people, saying: Keep all the commandment I command you this day. **2**On the day when you shall pass over the Jordan to the land that YHWH your God gives you, you shall set yourself up great stones and plaster them with plaster: **3**and you shall write on them all the words of this law when you have passed over; that you may go into the land YHWH your God gives you, a land flowing with milk and honey, as YHWH, the God of your fathers, has promised you. **4**When you have passed over the Jordan, you shall set up these stones, which I command you this day, in Mount Ebal (→11:26–32), and you shall plaster them with plaster. **5**There you shall build an altar to YHWH your God, an altar of stones: you shall lift up no iron on them (Exod. 20:25). **6**You shall build the altar of YHWH your God of uncut stones; and you shall offer burnt offerings thereon to YHWH your God: **7**and you shall sacrifice peace offerings, and shall eat there; and you shall rejoice before YHWH your God. **8**You shall write on the stones all the words of this law very plainly.

Plain Rabbis have struggled to resolve this passage's inconsistencies, and modern critics have struggled to reconstruct its redaction history. Both strategies tend to neglect the effect of the passage as it stands: to link in one monumental celebration (→27:11–14) the covenant's "yesterday, today, and forever" (Heb. 13:8)—the eve of Israel's crossing, **the day** of its crossing, and the legacy of its crossing.

Faith **Mount Ebal** in Shechem is central to Israel, at its east-west and north-south crossroads, and visible from most of Canaan. Israel's center is this relationship—not its fragile tribal confederation, destructible temple, fractious monarchy, or promised land. "What is the house you would build for me, and what is my resting place? . . . But to this one I look: the humble, contrite in spirit, trembling at my **word**" (Isa. 66:1–2, my translation).

Faith Are 27:1–8 and 27:11–26 parenthetical detours like →1:37–38 or →2:10–12? Only 27:9–10 maintains the flow of Deut. 26–28. This interruption distances the consequences of obedience and disobedience from the covenant itself, without detaching them. It trains us to celebrate the substance of the Torah with or without its blessings and curses (→26:16–19).

Faith Shechem is a portentous place. Both Abraham's altar at Shechem (Gen. 12:5–7) and Jacob's (33:18–20) are built before interruptions that threaten to derail Israel's making. Joseph is sold at Shechem (37:12–24), and his bones are ultimately buried there (Josh. 24:32). Shechem becomes a city of refuge (20:7; 21:21). Joshua convenes Israel there at the end of his life to renew the covenant after the conquests (24:1, 25). Abimelech (Judg. 9) and later Jeroboam (1 Kgs. 12:1) rebel there (cf. 12:16–19). The covenant at Israel's center is for keeping Israel centered.

Hope "Your statutes have been my songs wherever I make my home" (Ps. 119:54 NRSV). Inscribing the whole Torah on **stones** ensures that it is not left behind on the other side of **the Jordan** (→1:1b) like parents' directions after an adolescent is out the door. The covenant resides in Canaan, in what later becomes Samaria (→33:12–17). **Plastered** stones stand out especially from a distance. Yet plaster weathers and fades; stones in Canaan are not the Torah's permanent resting place. As Israel needs to carry the word of God in its memory (→32:44–47) as it crosses into the **land**, it will need to carry it into the kingdoms' separation, into exile, into tribulation, into the Greek tongue, and into the eschaton. "Not one letter, not one stroke of a letter, will pass from the law until all is accomplished" (Matt. 5:18 NRSV). And indeed, "in the fear of the Lord and in the comfort of the Holy Spirit" Judea, Galilee, and Samaria are reunified (Acts 9:31; cf. John 4:5–42).

Love Why is the new covenant not committed to writing as Moses's is? First, it is written on hearts, not **stones** (2 Cor. 3:3; cf. Deut. 9:9–11). Second, it is remembered through the Spirit rather than the letter (John 14:16; 15:26; 2 Cor. 3:6). Third, its feast is eucharistic (Luke 22:20; 24:35). It remains at the center of **the land** that is the church, taking the form appropriate to its context.

Love The **plain writing** of the Torah is readable by both the **elders** exhorting Israel to keep it and the priests officiating at the commemorative **altar**. Shechem is a location accessible to all the tribes. In every age gnostics have regarded Christ's true significance to be secreted away somehow and decipherable only by a spiritual, ecclesiastical, philosophical, or academic elite; but the Holy Spirit, the good news, the Bible, the creeds, and other monuments of the apostolic story are displayed in public, available to all, for the edification of all.

27:9 Moses and the priests, the Levites, spoke to all Israel (→1:1a), saying: Keep silence, and hear, Israel (→6:4): this day you have become the people of YHWH your God. **10**You shall therefore obey the voice of YHWH your God, and do his⁺ commandments and his⁺ statutes that I command you this day.

Faith Why **this day**? The Hebrews have been YHWH's people all along (Exod. 3:7; →26:16–19), and the whole Torah has been delivered since Sinai. Yet, because it is heard on this day as Israel's normative shape, this inaugural of life in the land is the defining moment that actualizes that longstanding relationship. We may read Ps. 2 similarly when the Father quotes it to his⁺ eternal Son at the Jordan: "You are my Son; today I have begotten you" (Ps. 2:7 NRSV in Luke 3:22; cf. Heb. 5:5). The event is a coronation—not an adoption—that later generations will recall as decisive (→27:11–14).

Faith God's **commandments** and God's **voice** agree, but here their messages are distinct. Tempted in the wilderness, Israel's Anointed One quietly keeps the commandments (→6:13–16; →8:1–5) and follows the Spirit's voice (Luke 4:1; cf. 4:15–18) and so qualifies to enter the land and redeem his fellow people of YHWH. "The law and the prophets were until John; from then the good news of the kingdom of God is proclaimed" (16:16, my translation). "Beginning with Moses and all the prophets, he interpreted to them the things about himself" (24:27 NRSV). The church honors all these words when leaders of the Jerusalem church interpret the Torah through the prophets in light of the gospel (Acts 15:13–21 on Deut. 14:2; Jer. 12:15; Amos 9:11–12; and Isa. 45:21).

Hope As it is not enough to heed only Moses *or* the prophets (Acts 24:14), so it is not enough to **hear** only the Spirit's written word *or* the Spirit's newly spoken word. Apostolic speech always continues to confirm and renew God's holy writings (28:23; Rom. 3:21–22). In every age the Spirit's wisdom is available to God's people in both forms, the written norming the spoken, the spoken enlivening the written, each one incomplete without the other (→18:15–19). As the scripture was speaking to Abraham (Gal. 3:8) and Pharaoh (Rom. 9:17), so Christ's mouth will be speaking to kings and governors at the end (Luke 21:12–15).

Love **The priests** join the elders in beginning to discharge their teaching office as **Israel** prepares for its inauguration (→31:9–13). They are stepping into their covenantal authority. That same intimidating task faces every new leader. "Do not say: 'I am only a boy'" (Jer. 1:7 NRSV). "Jesus said to him, 'Tend my sheep'" (John 21:16 NRSV). "These are the things you must insist on and teach. Let no one despise your youth" (1 Tim. 4:11–12 NRSV).

27:11Moses commanded the people the same day, saying: 12These shall stand on Mount Gerizim to bless the people, when you have passed over the Jordan: Simeon, and Levi, and Judah, and Issachar, and Joseph, and Benjamin. 13These shall stand on Mount Ebal for the curse: Reuben, Gad, and Asher, and Zebulun, Dan, and Naphtali.

¹⁴The Levites shall answer, and tell all the men⁺ of Israel with a loud voice,

Faith For solid critical reasons, scholars separate 27:11–13 from 27:14–26. What do the two mean together? As leaders from among the twelve tribes, the **Levites** are not outside the recipients of **blessing** and **curse**. Priests represent the people from within their midst (→10:6–11), and they represent YHWH as their inheritance (→18:1–8). Jesus is a priest of a higher order (Heb. 5:1–10) who truly belongs to both groups (1:8; 2:14–15).

Faith The words of the Torah shine from their bright plastered rocks below and in the midst of the tribes (→27:1–8), emanating both life and death (→30:17–20). **Gerizim** is southerly, greener, and closer to the place from which come the **blessings** from **Judah** on all Israel (cf. Gen. 49:8–10; Isa. 37:31–32; Zech. 2:12; Mic. 5:2 in Matt. 2:6; also Rev. 5:5; →33:7). (It is not grammatically clear, by contrast, whether **Ebal** delivers the curse or symbolically receives it.) The tribes of the **curse** are an unpromising group—the handmaids' sons (→33:20–25) and incestuous **Reuben** who lost his birthright (→33:6). Yet they also include brave (Judg. 5:13–18) and portentous **Zebulun**, which one day will receive universal significance through the Messiah who works there (→33:18–19). Through faith the cursed can be blessed, and by rejecting faith many of the blessed will find themselves cursed.

Hope Life-changing events are often enacted through drawn-out ceremonies that include a cluster of smaller components. Here, as Israel comes into its inheritance, after lengthy instructions and a history lesson but before final promises, warnings, predictions, and benedictions, the **Levites** begin to lead God's people in putting away private vices that will be hard for others to detect, let alone discipline (→27:26). The scene resembles the liturgical apotaxis of a new believer away from the devil and his⁺ works before the syntax that turns toward the altar and God's baptismal future (→11:26–32). Like the other interruptions in this chapter (→27:1–8), it cements another aspect of Israel's covenantal identity: its ultimate accountability for faithfulness in private. "You were ransomed from the futile ways inherited from your [fathers]. . . . Rid yourselves, therefore, of all malice, and all guile, insincerity, envy, and all slander" (1 Pet. 1:18–19; 2:1 NRSV).

Hope By separating the tribes on the two **mountains**, Moses stages a future sorting out of Israel into two groups, the one given eternal life and the other punishment (Matt. 25).

Love Our private sinning is still active sinning (→29:16–21). So all the people participate actively in this symbolic turning. It rouses us to affirm YHWH's conditional **curses** so that when we sin, we witness against ourselves and so affirm the goodness of the Torah that witnesses against us. "If I do what I do not want, I agree that the law is good. But in fact it is no longer I that do it, but sin that dwells within me" (Rom. 7:16–17 NRSV). Congregational participation in confession and absolution of sin is essential to keep holiness from appearing to be just one group's demand on another.

27:15"Cursed is the man⁺ who will make an engraved or molten image (→4:16–20; →9:12–14), an abomination to YHWH (→7:25–26), the work of the hands of the craftsman⁺, and set it up in secret (→13:6–11)." All the people shall answer and say: "Amen."

Hope What is a **secret** worshiper in a society but a secret agent? This person lives as if obedient to one power while serving another. A clandestinely idolatrous Israelite is living in the land of God's gifting, exalting a god that has given nothing. Such a testimony forfeits the blessing and invites YHWH to foreclose (→4:27–29). When Israel as a people surrenders to idolatry, the exile, captivity, and return that follow reassert YHWH's sole agency in giving Israel its life (Isa. 45) and the land its purity (Zech. 13:2–6).

Love YHWH's **secret** worshipers are secret agents too. Christians do not hide our loyalty so as to mislead others into trusting us under false pretenses. Covert Christians would testify to a Jesus who has withheld the gifts that he actually gives, which mark Christians as public signs of his reign.

Love **Amen**, or "let it be," receives a word as applying to oneself (Jer. 28:6; Luke 1:38). In **answering** the Levites, **all the people** take active ownership (→27:11–14) of the personal consequences of private sin. Israel's health does not depend on everyone being sinless (26:16–19), but on sins being policed and even self-policed. Healing, prophesying, conviction, and many other spiritual gifts work in the church's life not to prevent sin from happening but to cleanse what needs cleansing.

27:16"Cursed is the one insulting his⁺ father or his⁺ mother." All the people shall say: "Amen."

Love The text does not even exempt dishonorable parents (who are many) (→5:16). The **curse** is not on slander versus truth, but denigration versus respect (→21:15–21). Because YHWH blesses and curses across generations (→5:8–10), **insulting** in word or deed the generation that preceded us falsely asserts ourselves as the superiors and judges of our own being. Insulting our ancestors weakens the chain of blessing by which the promises come to us. Christ's forerunner turns children back to parents and vice versa to preserve the land from YHWH's curse (Mal. 4:6; Luke 1:17). Even Jesus the judge of all does not disrespect his parents (John 2:1–7). In Christ our parents are the fellow workers who hear and do God's word (Luke 8:19–21), whose spiritual gifts build us up into who Christ wants us to be.

27:17"Cursed is the one removing his⁺ neighbor's landmark." All the people shall say: "Amen." **18**"Cursed is the one misdirecting the blind on the way." All the people shall say: "Amen." **19**"Cursed is the one misjudg-

ing the foreigner, fatherless, and widow (→16:18–17:1; →24:17–22)."
All the people shall say: "Amen."

Hope "The land mourns" from greed and its crimes (Hos. 4:1–3, 8). **Curses** for moving a **landmark** are common in the ancient Near East, but the covenant supplies a distinctive context for them here. Deuteronomy has repeatedly insisted that the land is a blessing for *all*, including the land itself. To cheat one's **neighbor** out of his[+] inheritance turns the land from a gift into an acquisition and the neighbor from a fellow beneficiary into a victim (→19:14). To disinherit secretly or **misjudge** unfairly lives a lie by keeping up only the appearances of rejoicing together at celebrations, helping one another in daily life, and so on. "Shall not the land tremble on this account, and everyone mourn who lives in it?" (Amos 8:8 NRSV). It invites YHWH to disinherit offenders until all is lost (Zech. 7:8–14). Then grace will restore possession of "all things" to a remnant (8:12).

Faith To **misdirect** a **blind** person is sheer cruelty, with minimal risks since the victim cannot identify the sinner. Such hatred and contempt for the powerless **neighbor** is hatred and contempt for the God of Zion who "opens the eyes of the blind," "lifts up" the low, "loves the righteous," "watches over the **stranger**, . . . **orphan** . . . and **widow**"—and ruins the wicked (Ps. 146:8–9 NRSV). Jesus *grants* sight to show the blind **the way** and be discovered as Christ the Lord and healer, even when it exposes the blindness of the sighted and brings cruelty upon himself (John 9). He not only has YHWH's perception but the gifts to restore sight, fear, and love to the land of the holy (Lev. 19:14).

27:20"Cursed is the one lying with his father's wife, because he has uncovered his father's skirt." All the people shall say: "Amen." 21"Cursed is the one lying with any kind of animal." All the people shall say: "Amen." 22"Cursed is the one lying with his sister, the daughter of his father, or the daughter of his mother." All the people shall say: "Amen." 23"Cursed is the one lying with his mother-in-law." All the people shall say: "Amen."

Hope Incest, secretive because of its offensiveness and cultural taboos, also abuses patriarchal power and roles (→22:22–30). Israel's fathers are the channels of its future. Familial sexual sins are generally portrayed as capitulations to lust, with disastrous consequences for the extended family and all Israel (e.g., 2 Sam. 13:13). Like the other sins listed here, they bring exile (Lev. 18:6–30; 20:10–22). In the church, they ruin not just the people involved but the whole family of God (1 Cor. 5:1–6). They destroy trust and confuse, both when they remain secret and when they finally come to light. The damage is in neither the secrecy nor the publicity, but the acts themselves.

Love Bestiality is destructive of self, love, **animals** (→25:4), and covenantal life. It is mentioned along with incest in Lev. 18:23 and elsewhere, but that it is repeated here in such a brief catalog of private sins is a reminder that being the people of YHWH—and so properly imaging God as human beings—means representing

YHWH to all creation as well as one another, our creator, and ourselves. To violate any of these privileged relationships sets every relation wrong (Gen. 3), including Israel's relation to the land of promise, and restoration likewise restores *all* life and its interrelationships (Isa. 11:6–9).

> **27:24**"Cursed is the one striking his⁺ neighbor in secret." All the people shall say: "Amen." **25**"Cursed is the taker of a bribe to kill an innocent person." All the people shall say: "Amen."

Faith Land cries out from **innocent** blood (Gen. 4:10) and yields a **curse** upon those who sow it (4:11–12). Violence, retaliation, murder, and assassination are the most radical ways to disinherit (→2:16–23). A people of mutual enmity is no people at all (cf. 1 Pet. 2:10–11), especially not a people of this covenanting God (→5:17). Jesus's command to love enemies and pray for persecutors, known and unknown, offers restored fellowship to divided and cynical first-century Israel and even embraces the strangers who occupy it—at least among those who obey that command and accept the possibly bloody consequences for themselves (Mark 8:34–38). When Jesus is **stricken** and betrayed for money **in secret** (Zech. 13:7 in Mark 14:27, 48–49), his forgiveness ransoms many (10:45) to become a new priesthood among the still estranged (Zech. 13:8–9; 1 Pet. 2:9).

> **27:26**"Cursed is the one who will not confirm the words of this Torah to do them." All the people shall say: "Amen."

Faith This whole section of curses has concerned easily hidden sins. The priests' twelfth **curse** warns that *all* sins can be committed in secret (cf. Matt. 5:21–30). A dissenter in a community of faith can transgress quietly, secretly, or inwardly, even just by remaining noncommittal.

Faith In a classic Deuteronomic move (→5:21), the final **curse** is all inclusive. Having assented to a relatively easy series of commands, now Israel is forced to count the whole cost of its inheritance. It is prohibitive beyond the imagination of Deuteronomy's original audience: "[As many as] rely on the works of the law are under a curse" (Gal. 3:10 NRSV, which goes on to quote Deut. 27:26). The final curse's radical implications are not a later Christian imposition upon the **Torah.** The covenant's prohibitive cost is borne by the Righteous One who shares his inheritance with all who believe (→21:22–23). YHWH "was appalled that there was no one to intervene; so his⁺ own arm brought him⁺ victory, and his⁺ righteousness upheld him⁺.... He⁺ will come to Zion as Redeemer" (Isa. 59:16, 20 NRSV).

Love "Whoever keeps the whole law but fails in one point has become accountable for all of it" (Jas. 2:10 NRSV). This principle applies to more than just **Torah**; it applies to every law of liberty. The law of Christ's kingdom, to which all his disciples are subject, is wholly impartial love of neighbor (2:8). Its observance overthrows any judgment but divine mercy (2:12–13).

DEUTERONOMY 28

28:1 If you shall listen diligently to the voice of YHWH your God, to do all his⁺ commandments that I command you this day (28:13), YHWH your God will set you on high above all the nations of the earth: **2**and all these blessings shall come on you and overtake you if you shall listen to the voice of YHWH your God. **3**You shall be blessed in the city, and you shall be blessed in the field. **4**You shall be blessed in the fruit of your body, the fruit of your ground, the fruit of your animals, the increase of your livestock, and the young of your flock. **5**Your basket and your kneading trough shall be blessed. **6**You shall be blessed when you come in, and you shall be blessed when you go out.

Faith When Elizabeth blesses the **fruit** of Mary's womb, she acknowledges Mary's son to be a unique fulfillment of YHWH's covenantal favor on Israel (Luke 1:45) that makes Mary the mother of her Lord (1:41–43). Luke's other allusions—to the city of David, shepherds' fields and flocks, and voices from on high—in his nativity story artfully connect the mundane signs that God is blessing this faithful remnant with the extraordinary sign of Israel's Messiah (2:12, 34).

Hope A grateful believer might take one happy aspect of life—say, a happy family or a fulfilling career—as a sign of God's blessing. Israel's blessings, however, are comprehensive. Since Israel is immediately to be a society of **cities** and **fields**, agriculture and **livestock**, indoors and outdoors (→6:7–12), these reflect the wholeness of God's favor. Yet they also provide for the social change that is an inevitable consequence of blessing, which cannot help but alter the circumstances of the ones blessed. A people so favored will find itself **high above all** other **nations**, its power and sophistication growing with its population and wealth. So the blessing must apply in every new cultural and technological shift that it brings. Many national myths take a moment in history as a golden age and long for it to freeze into an eternity, but God wills a transformation still to come—and perhaps one that never stops transforming.

Hope The futures that will **overtake** Israel in this chapter sound like the heaven and hell of apocalyptic literature. Their descriptions seem to borrow from the exaggerated tropes of ancient Near Eastern treaties. However, Israel's terrible historical trajectory from the heights of the Solomonic empire to fracture, famine, and exile does not greatly exceed the rhetoric. Right from its patriarchal beginnings, Israel has been over its head in blessings and curses from YHWH. It is caught up in a process of cosmic reworking that goes far beyond the prosperity of a people and even the wealth of nations (→30:6–10). "May God be gracious to us and **bless** us and make his⁺ face to shine upon us, that your way may be known upon earth, your saving power among **all nations**" (Ps. 67:1–2 NRSV).

Hope "You prepare a table before me in the presence of my enemies" (Ps. 23:5 NRSV). Both the blessings and curses arrive in others' sight: Israel is lifted up above the onlooking Gentiles, and Israel is humiliated in the midst of empires. Annihilationists and universalists cannot conceive of heavenly joy in the presence of suffering, but it is a regular feature of the imagery of hope in Deuteronomy, the psalms, the prophets, and the apocalyptic literature of both Testaments. The others' presence turns blessing into honor and curse into shame. Are these elements concessions to a particular honor-shame society that are dispensable in other cultural contexts, or are they essential consequences of the obedience and disobedience of a humanity whose life is necessarily neighborly? Does Deuteronomy's juxtaposing of prosperity and suffering disturb us because it is obscene, or because we are either individualists or collectivists?

Faith God may grant prosperity and power, but not all prosperity and power is God's favor. The devil lifts Jesus **high above all the nations** and offers them in exchange for worship. Having heard the Father's voice at his baptism, Jesus determines to receive these things only as God's **blessing** upon Israel (→6:13–16).

Love This bright future can be secured only as Israel as a **nation** listens to YHWH (→26:16–19). Even when Jesus secures it as an individual, it can come to fruition only in a whole community. The church is the Father's necessary means of realizing his⁺ blessings on the Son. It is "the fullness of him⁺ who fills all in all" (Eph. 1:23 NRSV).

> ²⁸:⁷YHWH will cause your enemies who rise up against you to be struck before you. They will come out against you one way, and will flee before you seven ways. ⁸YHWH will command the blessing on you in your barns, and in all you put your hand to (12:4–7), and he⁺ will bless you in the land YHWH your God gives you. ⁹YHWH will establish you for a holy people to himself⁺, as he⁺ has sworn to you (26:18–19), if you shall keep the commandments of YHWH your God, and walk in his⁺ ways. ¹⁰All the peoples of the earth shall see that you are called by the name of YHWH; and they shall be afraid of you (2:25). ¹¹YHWH will swamp you with goodness (30:9), in the fruit of your body, and in

the fruit of your livestock, and in the fruit of your ground (→28:1–6; →30:6–10), in the land YHWH swore to your fathers to give you. [12]YHWH will open to you his[+] good storehouse in the sky to give the rain of your land in its season (11:14) and to bless all the work of your hand (2:7); and you shall lend to many nations, and you shall not borrow (→15:1–6). [13]YHWH will make you the head and not the tail, and you shall be above only, and you shall not be beneath, if you shall listen to the commandments of YHWH your God that I command you this day, to observe and to do (28:1), [14]and shall not turn aside from any of the words I command you this day, to the right hand or to the left (5:32), to go after other gods to serve them (6:14; 11:28; 13:1–2).

Plain Like a liturgical collect, this section summarizes earlier **blessings** by alluding to key passages from every major section of Deuteronomy and stressing YHWH as the one who ordains Israel's blessings. It is one of the punch lines of the book.

Hope Some of these **blessings** are fulfilled much earlier than others. The **striking** of Israel's enemies has already begun (→2:31–33), and under Joshua Israel will make definitive progress against them. Yet Israel will not enjoy worldwide glory until David and Solomon. Likewise, its Messiah reigns from birth (Matt. 2:2), but even after his coronation (Ps. 2:6–8 in Matt. 3:17) his enemies continue to **rise up** against him and strike (26:31). Even now the king waits for the subduing of all the kingdom's rebels and for **all the peoples** to **see** and **fear** him (24:14; 25:32).

Faith What does it mean to have all these **blessings**, including the blessing of being **above** all at the **head** of the world? Not the world peace and prosperous harmony that the modern left and right dream of. Not the royal glory that Moses's original audience imagines. Not the glory of Solomon, glory as the world reckons it; not even conventional heavenly glory along with worldly glory **beneath**, a generous measure of lordly prestige and a healthy measure of servantlike patronage. It means **only** baptism in the Messiah's victorious **name**, to **serve** God and live for many (Mark 10:35–45). Israel's ascent to glory is Christ's ascension and session: all that the Father lavishes upon the Son—power, life, harvest, rain, good work, wealth, and authority—concerns the kingdom's royal cross (10:32–34) from which he refuses to **turn aside**.

Love Revelation shows the church's enemies as a beast who is felled in **seven ways** by seven angels with seven plagues (Rev. 15:1–2; 16:19). The church likewise becomes an army of witnesses who conquer by following their leader (6:2; 19:11–14) in his suffering (3:5; 6:9–11). Both Testaments' apocalyptic prophecies accomplish a nearly perfect inversion of a covenantal "theology of glory" for the "theology of the cross" of the actual Israel, its Anointed One, and his church. This historical refusal of a covenantal "prosperity gospel" begs the question of the difference between the covenant's **blessings** and its curses (→28:15–19).

28:15 But if you will not listen to the voice of YHWH your God, to do all his⁺ commandments and his⁺ statutes I command you this day, all these curses (27:15–26) shall come on you and overtake you (28:45). **16**You shall be cursed in the city and you shall be cursed in the field. **17**Your basket and your kneading trough shall be cursed. **18**The fruit of your body, the fruit of your ground, the increase of your livestock, and the young of your flock shall be cursed. **19**You shall be cursed when you come in and you shall be cursed when you go out.

Plain This passage is a near mirror image of 28:1–6, lacking only a counterpart to God's promise of international preeminence. That is withheld in suspense, coming as a wrenching anticlimax at the chapter's end (→28:63b–68).

Faith If the covenant's blessings endure through every cultural circumstance (→28:1–6), its **curses** do too. Our era imagines social policy to be determinative for a people's future: if disaster strikes, policy is how we address it. However, *the* social act that leads any policy in Israel to succeed is obeying **YHWH's voice**. No other change—political reform, economic development, social revolution, not even the many policies in Deut. 12–26—can counter the covenant's curses on rebels; only repentance and restoration to fruitful obedience can accomplish it. YHWH will facilitate this on the day of deliverance by sending a messenger (Luke 1:67–79) to save from the coming wrath (Isa. 40:3–5 in Luke 3:3–9).

Hope "I am going to raise my hand against them, and they shall become plunder for their own slaves. Then you will know that [YHWH] of hosts has sent me" (Zech. 2:9 NRSV). Israel's future circumstances are not mere social dynamics as we commonly understand them. These blessings and **curses** are powers ordained by the Lord of hosts (Mal. 4:1–4; Jas. 5:4) to **overtake** God's people and bring them to repentance, with YHWH at their head like a general commanding troop movements.

Hope Theodicy treats natural evil and moral evil as problematic (though in different ways) for the righteousness of God. The covenant's **curses**—and the hellish future they anticipate—belong to neither of these categories; they *are* the justice of God on disloyal covenanters. Though horrific, and nearly as repugnant to God as the evils they address (Jonah 4:2, 9–11), they are good. This claim offends a common sense today that treats the objects of our desire as good and the objects of our revulsion as evil, as if human experience were the arbiter of good and evil. It is the very sense that leads Israel astray.

Love The New Testament displays a reticence toward **curses** that befits a messianic age where the Torah's blessings have **overtaken** its curses (→21:22–23). The church's mission is not to curse unbelievers (Luke 9:54–55) but to share Christ's blessings while warning of rejection's consequences (6:20–26): "Bless those who curse you, pray for those who abuse you" (6:28 NRSV). "Bless those who persecute you; bless and do not curse them" (Rom. 12:14 NRSV). "From the same mouth come blessing and cursing. My brothers⁺, this ought not to be so"

(Jas. 3:10 NRSV margin). Fruitless land "is worthless and on the verge of being cursed; its end is to be burned over. But we are convinced of better and salvific things for you, beloved, even if we speak thus" (Heb. 6:8–9, my translation).

> **28:20**YHWH will let loose on you cursing (Mal. 2:2; 3:9), confusion (→7:22–24; Isa. 22:3–4), and rebuke (Mal. 2:3; 3:11), in all you put your hand to do (Deut. 12:4–7), until you are destroyed, and until you perish quickly, because of the evil of your doings by which you have forsaken me. **21**YHWH will make the pestilence cling to you (Exod. 9:3, 15; Lev. 26:23–25; Num. 14:11–12), until he[+] has consumed you (→7:22–24) from off the land you go in to possess. **22**YHWH will strike you with consumption (Lev. 26:16), with fever (26:16), with inflammation, with fiery heat, with the sword (Deut. 20:13; →32:40–43), with blight, and with mildew (1 Kgs. 8:37–40); and they shall pursue you (→1:43–45; →28:45) until you perish. **23**Your sky that is over your head shall be brass and the earth that is under you shall be iron (cf. 8:9; Lev. 26:19). **24**YHWH will make the rain of your land powder (Exod. 9:8–9) and dust (Job 7:5); from the sky shall it come down on you until you are destroyed. **25**YHWH will cause you to be struck before your enemies: you shall go out one way against them and shall flee seven ways before them, and you shall be a horror among all the kingdoms of the earth (Deut. 3:21). **26**Your corpse shall be food to all birds of the sky and to the animals of the earth (21:23), and there shall be none to frighten them away (2 Sam. 21:10–14).

Plain This expansion on the **curses** of →28:15–19 inverts the expanded blessings of →28:7–14. It draws richly on imagery and terminology from throughout the Torah, as well as vassal treaties of a variety of neighboring cultures (→28:27–34), either to reinforce other warnings or to subvert what heartens elsewhere. The whole unit extends to 28:44 as both a threefold cycle of repeated plague, famine, and defeat and a loose chiasm of national frustration that centers in 28:30–33a. All these structures suggest a narrative progression: the first cycle introduces overwhelming military defeat, the second conquest and pillage (→28:27–34), and the third revolution (→28:35–44). The covenant's curses are the undoing of the defeat, conquest, and settlement by which Israel inherits the land.

Faith In Eden God curses the serpent above all **the animals of the earth** with enmity toward humanity, the woman with struggle against the man, and the man with frustration working the earth and eventual mortality (Gen. 3:14–19). All three elements are discernible in this passage's scavengers, armies, and inhospitable environment and plagues respectively. Faithless humanity's eviction from Eden foreshadows faithless Israel's eviction from **the land**, revealing Israel's inheritance of Canaan to have been a measured restoration of human obedience and service upon a renewed earth. What humans twice lose, Jesus twice recovers: his ministry of faithfulness to the Father is both Israel's messianic reclamation of the land and the last Adam's reclamation of paradise.

Hope In 28:27–28 seven more plagues follow the seven listed in 28:22. Heaven **lets loose** seven angels with seven plagues on the rebellious earth (→32:22–25; Rev. 15:1). Moses's warnings to Israel are the Spirit's warnings to the church. In every age **curses** visit rebellious servants, particularly those who exchange the good news for some other gospel (Gal. 1:8–9). Christ's triumph proves that the cursed do not jeopardize the inheritance itself, only their participation in it. "You have come to Mount Zion and to the city of the living God . . . and to the assembly of the firstborn who are enrolled in heaven. . . . See that you do not refuse the one who is speaking" (Heb. 12:22–25a NRSV).

Love Horror (*diaspora* in 28:25 Septuagint) connotes exile (Jer. 24:9; 29:18; 34:17; Ezek. 23:46), tying military disaster to Israel's political dissolution (→28:27–44). This chapter's curses are not just a heap of disincentives, but a web of consequences of a single overarching failure. YHWH is Israel's strength, joy, unity, justice, and legacy. To give up any of these is to give up YHWH and to give up all the rest. Churches that fall into unbelief are not just defeated by cunning powers and principalities but depressed, dispersed, and destroyed. "If they did not escape when they refused the one who warned them on earth, how much less will we escape if we reject the one who warns from heaven!" (Heb. 12:25b NRSV).

> ²⁸:²⁷YHWH will strike you with the boil of Egypt (Exod. 9:8–12; Deut. 7:12–15; 28:35), and with hemorrhoids (1 Sam. 5:1–6:18), and with the scurvy (Lev. 21:18–20), and with the itch, of which you cannot be healed. ²⁸YHWH will strike you with panic and with blindness and with confusion of heart; ²⁹and you shall grope at noonday as the blind one gropes in darkness (Job 5:13–14), and you shall not prosper in your ways (Deut. 4:40; 27:18); and you shall be only oppressed (Prov. 22:16) and robbed (22:22–23) always, and there shall be none to save you. ³⁰You shall betroth a wife, and another man shall take her; you shall build a house, and you shall not dwell therein; you shall plant a vineyard, and shall not use its fruit. ³¹Your ox shall be slain before your eyes, and you shall not eat of it; your donkey shall be violently taken away from before your face, and shall not be restored to you; your sheep shall be given to your enemies, and you shall have none to save you. ³²Your sons and your daughters shall be given to another people; and your eyes shall look, and fail with longing (Deut. 28:65) for them all the day; and there shall be nothing in the power of your hand. ³³The fruit of your ground and all your labors shall a nation you

do not know eat up; and you shall be only oppressed and crushed always, ³⁴so that you shall be mad for what you see with your eyes.

Plain Some blessings and curses in the Torah and the prophets (e.g., Exod. 23; Deut. 4; 7; Lev. 26; Jer. 5–7), and especially in this section, bear striking indirect resemblances to texts such as the Vassal Treaty of Esarhaddon §§37–42 (though what there is the work of four deities is here the word of YHWH alone). Though no specific line of influence among these texts can be definitely traced, the relationship confirms that many idioms in Deuteronomy were intelligible across regional cultures spanning centuries. This does not indicate, as some suppose, that YHWH just "stands in" for the gods who do the cursing elsewhere. Nor does it indicate that Israelite theology is simply of a genus of first-millennium, or even second-millennium, Near Eastern worldviews. Israel is not just a deity's Assyrian vassal in Deut. 28 any more than Israel is a deity's Hittite vassal elsewhere in Deuteronomy. Rather, Israel and its God are using cultural idioms to communicate. A real relationship expresses itself through ordinary language. Writers of biblical texts have always worked within their cultures' wide fields of images and genres, harvesting some and rejecting others, and refining everything they appropriate to suit it to the unique communications of a people chosen by its holy God to bear his⁺ incomparable message.

Faith Israel had once come into the prosperity of others (→6:10–12); weakened by plagues like the ones that broke the house of Pharaoh, it will now see its legacy taken over by **another**. In an obvious reversal of →20:5–9, the objects of Israelite hope fall into conquerors' hands. Perhaps this foretells King Shishak of Egypt pillaging all "the treasures of the house of [YHWH] and the treasures of the king's house," even "the shields of gold that Solomon had made" (1 Kgs. 14:25–26 NRSV). The Chronicler **sees** this humiliation as a partial and gracious reprieve (2 Chr. 12:9), but in Deuteronomy the spectacle induces despair—not because YHWH would actually give up his⁺ son⁺ (Hos. 11:8), but because Israel will have forgotten that its **power** lies not in itself, its possessions, or its position but only in the one who gives and takes away (Job 1:21). Jesus describes another comeuppance in his day: "What then will the owner of the vineyard do? He⁺ will come and destroy the tenants and give the vineyard to others" (Mark 12:9 NRSV). Like Job and Hosea, Jesus and his disciples retain their faith and hope through the disaster, but other leaders hear his prophecy of their displacement as a threat rather than an arrival of new grace and react defensively (12:12).

Hope Israel's **panic, blindness**, and **confusion** turn the conquest on its head. Zechariah senses here an inversion of God's will that will be rectified when powers of panic, blindness, and confusion again visit Jerusalem's enemies while YHWH watches over Judah (Zech. 12:4–6) and "the house of David shall be like God" (12:8 NRSV). Why? Because God's agents of discipline on unruly Israel often abuse their power and are disciplined in turn (e.g., Assyria in Isa. 10:5–19). Using vocabulary paralleled in this passage, Prov. 22 underlines YHWH's justice against bullies such as those who **oppress and rob** Israel here. YHWH "despoils of life those who despoil them" (22:23). So the covenantal saga extends beyond the immediate ramifications of infidelity to the punishment of Israel's chastisers and even ultimate deliverance for Israel.

Love This passage's cruel sequence of events is especially humiliating in the context of Deuteronomy's honor-shame society. Disciples and churches traveling along this chapter's trajectory of failure are dispirited, even as they **see** their rivals being emboldened. All parties are tempted to take this momentum as definitive. In an immediate sense they may be right: there may be **none to save** or **heal** a bewildered and desperate people from decline, ruin, and replacement. "I will come to you and remove your lampstand from its place, unless you repent" (Rev. 2:5 NRSV). Yet Christian history testifies to the limited power of the church's foes and to the real presence of the Spirit of the ascended Christ in the awakenings and revivals of faith that have carried the gospel across the world and down the centuries. The church in a particular nation may see the hard-won legacy of a millennium crumble in a generation, but even so Jesus's reign is proclaimed. "To everyone who conquers, I will give permission to eat from the tree of life that is in the paradise of God" (2:7 NRSV).

> 28:35YHWH will strike you in the knees and in the legs with a sore boil, of which you cannot be healed (Isa. 38), from the sole of your foot to the crown of your head (Job 2:7). 36YHWH will bring you, and your king whom you shall set over you, to a nation you have not known, you or your fathers; and there you shall serve other gods, wood and stone. 37You shall become an astonishment, a proverb, and a byword among all the peoples where YHWH shall lead you away. 38You shall carry much seed out into the field, and shall gather little in; for the locust shall consume it. 39You shall plant vineyards and dress them, but you shall neither drink of the wine nor harvest; for the worm shall eat them. 40You shall have olive trees throughout all your borders, but you shall not anoint yourself with the oil; for your olives shall drop off. 41You shall father sons and daughters, but they shall not be yours; for they shall go into captivity. 42All your trees and the fruit of your ground shall the locust possess (cf. 20:19–20). 43The foreigner who is in your midst shall rise above you higher and higher, and you shall come down lower and lower. 44He shall lend to you, and you shall not lend to him; he shall be the head, and you shall be the tail.

Plain Israel's **king** is useless in the crisis—not because Israel's monarchy as such is a failure to trust YHWH as king (as it is in 1 Sam. 8:7, 18; 12:13–25; 2 Kgs. 17:1–4), but because the king has failed to keep the covenant nearby and trust YHWH (→17:14–20). "They slaughtered the sons of Zedekiah before his eyes, then put out the eyes of Zedekiah; they bound him in fetters and took him to Babylon" (2 Kgs. 25:7 NRSV).

Faith The polytheistic world into which Israel has assimilated imagines YHWH to be, at best, one of a balanced assortment of forces for Israel to master or appease. But God refuses to be reduced to a spiritual ingredient in a formula for worldly success. As the third cycle of plagues incapacitates Israel, nature too revolts. Debilitated by angelic maladies and their own injustices, divinely broken and humiliated by rivals, and now ecologically crushed, God's people are victims of every circumstance. Israel still does not repent, but struggles to overcome with one of the last forces it can control—its own will to work—in vain. Meticulously, as if scientifically, God strips away every other aspect of Israel's strength until only one explanatory variable is left: his⁺ own favor. Suffering Israel will have "had no form or majesty that we should look at him, nothing in his appearance that we should desire him" (Isa. 53:2 NRSV). Only **leading** Israel **away** like a lamb (53:7) will reveal that YHWH's deliverance is the only way of restoration.

Hope Moses has charged Israel not to forget Sinai (→9:6–8) but to impress the covenant on itself (→6:7–9). Having shirked these responsibilities to serve other nations' **gods**, Israel now makes an ironic and unforgettable impression on all its conquerors. Whether in exaltation or condemnation, Israel cannot help but glorify YHWH: "What if God, desiring to show his⁺ wrath and to make known his⁺ power, has endured with much patience the objects of wrath that are made for destruction; and what if he⁺ has done so in order to make known the riches of his⁺ glory for the objects of mercy?" (Rom. 9:22–23 NRSV). Yet these two ways of glorification are unequal (→28:45–48): "If their stumbling means riches for the world, and if their defeat means riches of nations, how much more their full inclusion!" (Rom. 11:12 NRSV, adapted).

Love Bread, **wine**, **oil**—Israel's staples—now fail with the rest of its crops (but →8:6–10; →28:49–52). Churches in decline note a similar dearth of signs of God's favor (→24:17–22). How should such nonevents be interpreted? Some declare that God's special gifts of intimacy, new life, and power are gone forever. The more cautious among these are cessationists who deny certain charismata and antisacramental spiritualists who look suspiciously on material blessings; the reckless ones are abject defeatists and secularists. Others seek the old charismatic and sacramental gifts frantically and seize on any possible sign as a miracle, however implausible. The merely exuberant among these are "charismaniacs" (and "sacramaniacs" who presume to possess the regeneration that signs signify); the thoughtless ones are triumphalists. Both camps are in for surprises, because the weakening of Christ's body is neither permanent nor so easily reversed.

Love The third cycle of plagues brings a social revolution from within which Israel is powerless to stop. **Foreigners** in the land, meant to be blessed through Israel's kindness (→10:17–22) and to rejoice with God's people (→16:13–15), now **rise above** their cursed masters and the impotent **king** and displace them. "The falling and the rising of many in Israel" is "a sign [of contradiction] . . . that the designs of many hearts will be revealed" (Luke 2:34–35, my translation): such unlikely power in Israel's midst does not bless Israel and bring it joy, but provokes national embarrassment, envy, and resentment. Similarly, new subcultures rise within and without the new Canaan of Christianity (→11:8–15): new religious movements, spiritual and ideological transplants, secular movements, suppressed folk traditions, cults of personality, upstart denominations, and reactionaries. Unless the weakened remnant correctly diagnoses the problem, it is likely to pursue the same wrongheaded responses—utilitarian tactics, power alliances, willful ignorance, wishful thinking, and so on—that weakened it in the first place.

> **28:45** All these curses shall come on you, and shall pursue you and overtake you until you are destroyed, because you did not listen to the voice of YHWH your God, to keep his[+] commandments and his[+] statutes that he[+] commanded you (28:15); **46** and they shall be on you for a sign and for a wonder, and on your seed forever. **47** Because you did not serve YHWH your God with joyfulness and with gladness of heart for total abundance, **48** therefore you shall serve your enemies whom YHWH shall send against you, in hunger, and in thirst, and in nakedness, and in total want (28:57); and he[+] shall put a yoke of iron on your neck until he[+] has destroyed you.

Plain A further—and perhaps later—expansion of the **curses** ends the chapter. It is not a later event in a sequence running from 28:15 to 28:68, but an extraordinarily ugly detail from the scene already sketched in 28:15–19 and again in 28:20–44.

Faith "It is easier for a camel to go through the eye of a needle than for someone who is rich to enter the kingdom of God" (Mark 10:25 NRSV). After plenitude and power drown out the **voice of YHWH**, horrific destitution and slavery will restore Israel's hearing (cf. 2 Chr. 12:5–8). Bitter servitude will remind God's people of the lesson they ought to have learned forever from the **signs and wonders** on Egypt and Canaan's dispossessed: the inhumanity of power for power's sake, against which YHWH eternally sets his[+] face. Only in God's company is it possible for wealth to coexist with trust (Mark 10:26–31).

Hope The **curse** to be **destroyed** sits uneasily alongside the curse that remains **on** Israel's **seed forever**. As Adam hears a glimmer of hope in God's curse on his wife and the serpent—that each would attach to *descendants*—and realizes the woman will live (Gen. 3:20), so we can also hear the faintest promise in the midst of damnation. Israel's judgment ends not in total destruction but in "the destruction of its flesh for the salvation of spirit" (1 Cor. 5:5).

Love The first are now last (Mark 10:31). The **curses** that **overtake** Israel (→28:1–6; →28:15–19) have been **pursing** it since it turned aside from YHWH in its time of plenty. The afflictions that now overwhelm it were once distant, even imperceptible threats—but no less real. "You say, 'I am rich, I have prospered, and

I need nothing.' You do not realize that you are wretched, pitiable, poor, blind, and naked. . . . I reprove and discipline those whom I love. Be earnest, therefore, and repent" (Rev. 3:17–19 NRSV).

> ^{28:49}YHWH will bring a nation against you from afar, from the end of the earth, as the eagle swoops (32:11); a nation whose language you shall not understand; ⁵⁰a callous nation, that shall not respect the person of the old, or show favor to the young, ⁵¹and shall eat the fruit of your livestock, and the fruit of your ground, until you are destroyed; that also shall not leave you grain, new wine, or oil (→24:17–22; →28:35–44), the increase of your livestock, or the young of your flock (7:12–15), until they have caused you to perish. ⁵²They shall besiege you in all your gates (12:15), until your high and fortified walls come down, in which you trusted, throughout all your land; and they shall besiege you in all your gates throughout all your land, which YHWH your God has given you.

Faith Israel's enemies are portrayed as predatory aliens, not unlike the goblins and orcs of Tolkien's Middle Earth. This makes them more terrifying—and sets up the scandal of the next passage in which a desperate Israel preys on its own children.

Faith Israel stupidly **trusts** not in YHWH who scales and fells the walls of its enemies (3:5; Josh. 6) but **in the walls** themselves. "Fool! This very night your soul is required of you; and the things you have prepared, whose will they be?" (Luke 12:20 RSV). YHWH is Israel's only reliable fortification (Ps. 18:2).

Faith God's people are at this point so foolish that they would not know their savior if he appeared in their midst. "There was a little city with few people in it. A great king came against it and **besieged** it. . . . Now there was found in it a poor wise man, and he by his wisdom delivered the city. Yet no one remembered that poor man. So I said, 'Wisdom is better than might; yet the poor man's wisdom is despised, and his words are not heeded'" (Eccl. 9:14–16 NRSV).

Love Imagery from elsewhere in Deuteronomy—for example, the **eagle**, **fruit**, staples, **increase**, **gates**, **land**—that connoted blessing here signifies catastrophe. "All to whom God gives wealth and possessions and whom he⁺ enables to enjoy them, and to accept their lot and find enjoyment in their toil—this is the gift of God" (Eccl. 5:19 NRSV). Imperial Israel's wealth makes it a rich target for marauding empires. Prosperity tends to weaken the faith of disciples, who increasingly imagine themselves strong and self-reliant, even while attracting predators whose schemes make vigilant trust all the more urgent. "There is an evil that I have seen . . . : those to whom God gives wealth, possessions, and honor . . . yet God does not enable them to enjoy these things, but a stranger enjoys them" (6:2 NRSV).

Love The specificity and determinacy of this section's warnings, along with stylistic differences and other oddities such as its description of Deuteronomy as a book

(→28:58–68), suggest that these verses may be interpolations from an Assyrian or Babylonian context when the covenant's curses have come to pass. If so, then this passage would be less for encouraging preventative obedience than for discerning the times. For instance, the past few centuries saw these curses literally fulfilled in the wholesale confiscation of church property. Among the most famous examples, rulers in Scandinavia, Switzerland, and England dissolved their monasteries in the sixteenth century. Socialists nationalized ecclesiastical property in the Soviet Union and its client states, in Mexico following the revolution of 1910, and elsewhere. Often these churches held extraordinarily wealth but not the trust of many of their own members. They had come to view themselves with the same false assurance as Israel's and Judah's hollow monarchies.

Hope As elsewhere (→25:17–19), a thin ray of light shines in the enveloping darkness: **the land** remains YHWH's gift to tortured and overrun Israel.

Hope If 28:49–68 is a later reflection on Israel's terrible future, the lack of a similar expansion on the blessings of 28:1–14 is a poignant omission. The monarchy's fleeting moments of glory apparently do not warrant such a treatment. The prophets can only anticipate its requisite joy. In the Bible this passage's counterpart lies only in the New Testament, in the joyful relief of the witnesses to the resurrection of Jesus and those who believe their word. The apostolic age is 28:1–14's missing expansion.

Hope "With stammering lip and with alien tongue he[+] will speak to this people" (Isa. 28:11 NRSV). Someday the alien will be the Holy Spirit, and the unintelligible **languages** those of the kingdom's angelic messengers of restored love, grace, and fellowship (Isa. 28:11–12 in 1 Cor. 14:21–22) with **the end of the earth** (Acts 1:8).

> 28:53You shall eat the fruit of your own body, the flesh of your sons and of your daughters (Lev. 26:29), whom YHWH your God has given you, in the siege and in the distress with which your enemies shall distress you. 54The eye of the man who is gentle among you and very sensitive shall be evil toward his brother, and toward the wife of his bosom, and toward the children he has remaining, 55so that he will not give to any of them of the flesh of his children whom he shall eat, because he has nothing left him, in the siege and in the distress with which your enemy shall distress you in all your gates. 56The eye of the gentle and sensitive woman among you, who would not adventure to set the sole of her foot on the ground for gentleness and sensitivity, shall be evil toward the husband of her bosom, and toward her son, and toward her daughter, 57and toward her afterbirth that comes out from between her legs, and toward her children whom she shall bear; for she shall eat them for total want

secretly, in the siege and in the distress with which your enemy shall distress you in your gates.

Faith YHWH has set Israel "in the center of the nations" (Ezek. 5:5 NRSV), but Israel has come to think of itself as the center of all creation and has abandoned its deliverer to strike out on its own. Alone and overwhelmed, starving Israel now outdoes its predators in its ruthlessness. Consuming its own future in order not to surrender its sovereignty to armies sent by YHWH reveals the depth of Israel's mistrust of everyone but itself. "Parents shall eat their children in your midst, and children shall eat their parents; I will execute judgments on you, and any of you who survive I will scatter to every wind" (5:10 NRSV).

Faith The passage does not really focus on the horror of cannibalism, but uses the horror of cannibalism to expose the selfishness of the people's hearts. Indeed, devoting four verses to distinguishing men from women highlights the distance in these people's most intimate relationships. The one who in Genesis sees "flesh of my flesh" (Gen. 2:23) now sees simply **flesh** for his own flesh; the mother of the living (3:20) now lives on what she mothers. The hearts of the starving Israelites are as **evil toward** their immediate family as **toward the children** they consume. This is not just "rejecting my ordinances and not following my statutes" (Ezek. 5:6 NRSV; cf. 5:5–10); it is reverting to inhumanity. Imaging a God who sacrifices his[+] only Son for *others*' sake entails asceticism, not craven self-preservation (Gen. 22:1–19). Hungry after a second forty-day fast, Moses stays centered on his people's welfare rather than his own (→9:18–21). Hungry after forty days of fasting, Jesus refuses to turn stones into bread, out of his regard for the Father and Israel's lost sheep (Luke 4:3–4; →8:1–5). Indeed, he offers his very **flesh** as bread from heaven to raise up in the Spirit all the Father gives to him (John 6:30–51, 63).

Hope "The chastisement of my people has been greater than the punishment of Sodom, which was overthrown in a moment, though no hand was laid on it" (Lam. 4:6 NRSV; cf. Deut. 4:9–10). Yet Israel's chastisement is also greater in another respect: it holds open the prospect of reprieve, repentance, and recovery. "The punishment of your iniquity, O daughter Zion, is accomplished, he[+] will keep you in exile no longer" (Lam. 4:22 NRSV).

Love Israel's straits strip away every empty pretense of culture and morality until this idolatrous people resorts to sheer savagery. The enemy's anonymity respects the perpetuity of these curses. Most biblical references to cannibalism under siege concern Nebuchadnezzar II's siege of Jerusalem in 589 BC, but 2 Kgs. 6:24–32 relates an anecdote from the ninth-century northern kingdom. This passage's depravity is not a unique development in human history but a persistent human condition. Civilization is a veneer, underwritten by material prosperity and propped up by the constant threat of rulers' violence. These two things are providential gifts from God. They need only be withdrawn momentarily for human life to descend into a living hell (Jer. 19:9). This is as true in Christian eras and contexts as elsewhere. The Wars of Religion (in which siege sometimes led to cannibalism), the Reign of Terror, American slavery, the barbarity of World War I, the Shoah, communist and postcolonial genocides and terror-famines, riots and crackdowns, human traffickers and their clients, thugocracies of every kind—all provide a parade of occasions to reflect on the character of the unsupported human heart. "Because the people have forsaken me, and have profaned this place by making offerings in it to other gods . . . and because they have filled this place with the blood of the innocent. . . . So will I break this people and this city" (19:4–11 NRSV).

Love Does the church figurally suffer this curse too? So-called Christian pluralists who reduce dogma to opinion and are "spiritual but not religious" spurn our ancestral tradition and radically privatize both our own faith and others'. By leveling all supposedly religious claims we neglect the spiritual ills of not just the stranger but the neighbor, spouse, and sibling. We suppress apostolic witnesses whose universal claims threaten us. We withhold the covenant from our own children by twisting it into a matter of personal preference. We make all these sacrifices to hold onto the absolute sovereignty of our individual consciences. In all these ways and more we exhibit the same narrowness of heart that manifests itself so repulsively when under literal siege.

> 28:58If you will not do all the words of this law that are written in this book, that you may fear this glorious and fearful name, YHWH your God, 59then YHWH will astound by your afflictions and the afflictions of your seed, great and lasting afflictions and severe and lasting sicknesses. 60He+ will return to you all the diseases of Egypt you were afraid of, and they shall cling to you. 61Also every sickness and every plague that is not written in the book of this Torah YHWH will bring on you, until you are destroyed. 62You shall be left few in number, whereas you were as the stars of the sky in multitude (1:10; Gen. 15:5; 22:17; 26:4), because you did not listen to the voice of YHWH your God. 63aAs YHWH rejoiced over you to do you good and to multiply you, so YHWH will rejoice over you to cause you to perish and to destroy you.

Faith Deuteronomy 28's final section rehearses the grand proposition of the covenant's curses: if Israel refuses to obey, it will be uncreated and salvation history crossed out, line by line, until Jacob is again wandering and **few in number** (26:5). The same message is delivered, more reassuringly, by the Messiah, whose life and death make him worthy of glory: "If you conquer, you will be clothed like them in white robes, and I will not blot your name out of the book of life" (Rev. 3:5 NRSV).

Hope Israel first saw **the diseases of Egypt** poured out on the Egyptians while it was spared; when the **plagues** return Israel will suffer as surrounding nations gape. This is more than poetic justice; it declares YHWH's **glorious and fearful name** to Israel and all the earth (Isa. 10:22–23).

Hope Could YHWH really **rejoice over** beloved Israel's destruction? Especially in our time the notion suggests a sadistic God who is as happy to victimize Israel as to bless it. A church that took this seriously would be roundly condemned as a den of fundamentalistic haters. However, the claim is important and even redemptive. Sinners are tempted to leverage God's pity into tolerance for their sins. But that only compounds the problem of disobedience. A critical factor of producing true repentance is for the transgressor to learn that justice is more important, and even more satisfying, than postponing suffering and prolonging an untenable status quo. Modern Christianity's common reticence to accept this feature of God's love for the world suggests that we may especially need its bitter medicine. "Alas, alas, the great city. . . . Rejoice over her, O heaven, you saints and apostles and prophets!" (Rev. 18:19–20 NRSV). This relief is not the sadistic pleasure of harming innocents, for which God is cursing Israel (Deut. 27:17–19, 24–25; Jer. 19:6–9). And it remains inferior to God's far greater joy in forgiving the penitent (30:9): "It is better to suffer for doing good . . . than to suffer for doing evil. For Christ also suffered for sins once for all, the righteous for the unrighteous, in order to bring you to God" (1 Pet. 3:17–18 NRSV).

Hope After every destructive **plague** has passed, a remnant of Israel remains. YHWH can overthrow whole cities and whole generations at once, so this outcome must be intentional. The purpose of the curse is not to break God's promises to the patriarchs, but to continue remaking Israel as "a holy people" *in* fulfillment of those promises (→7:6–8).

Love Moses's discourse is now a **book of Torah** (→17:14–20; →29:16–21). This is commonly taken as a sign of a much later date for the passage and even the whole of Deuteronomy. Whatever the term might indicate about Deuteronomy's tradition-history, it shows the durability of Moses's words, even across the epochs. From Joshua's generation to Josiah's (2 Kgs. 22:8–13) to Jesus's and especially to ours, whether as an address, recitation, scroll, codex, or hypertext, Deuteronomy's words **cling to** us and work in the power of the eternal Spirit to discipline every audience. "These things came about with [Moses's generation] as a type, but were written for our admonition on whom the ends of the ages have come. So let the one who appears to have stood watch out that he[+] not fall" (1 Cor. 10:11–12, my translation).

Love "For this reason many of you are weak and ill, and some have died" (1 Cor. 11:30). The church withers under God's judgment. God breaks off unbelieving branches (Rom. 11:20), cuts down fruitless trees (Luke 13:9), and cuts off those who do not "continue in his[+] kindness" (Rom. 11:22 NRSV). While **Egypt** loses only(!) its firstborn in its most terrible **plague**, YHWH piles further sufferings on his[+] beloved people, even sufferings not recorded, to **destroy** them. This curse forecasts a precipitous decline in Christian faith where God is not obeyed, feared, and glorified. Whole families, local churches, and church traditions can **perish** to the gospel. This is not merely because of the church's internal weakness, though that can be an important factor, but also because of gathering forces from without.

Many Christian sufferers are quick to characterize their predicaments as spiritual attacks, but Deuteronomy reminds us that it might be God who is on the offensive. Persecution and plague call for opposite responses—perseverance in the face of persecution, but repentance in the face of punishment—so discernment is a critical task and a necessary spiritual gift: "If we judged ourselves, we would not be judged" (1 Cor. 11:31 NRSV). A prime resource for training in discernment is of course familiarity with the biblical stories of Israel, Jesus, and the church. By **listening** to them we come to know ourselves, our Lord, and our times.

> [28:63b]You shall be plucked from off the land you go in to possess. [64]YHWH will scatter you among all peoples, from the one end of the earth even to the other end of the earth; and there you shall serve other gods that you and your fathers have not known, wood and stone. [65]Among these nations you shall find no rest, and there shall be no resting place for the sole of your foot: but YHWH will give you there a heart of worry, and exhaustion of eyes, and desperation of self. [66]And your life shall hang in suspense before you; and you shall fear night and day, and shall have no assurance of your life. [67]In the morning you shall say: "I wish it were evening!" and at evening you shall say: "I wish it were morning!" for what your heart fears and what your eyes see. [68]YHWH will return you to Egypt in ships, by the way I said you would not see again, and there you shall sell yourselves to your enemies as male and female slaves, and there will be no buyer.

Faith Israel wanted self-reliance and power. Empires wanted the fruit of Israel's blessings. Israel wanted the nations' **gods** and ways. Empires wanted Israel's land. Only two things remain unwanted at the denouement of this long tragedy: Israel, unfit even for the **slave** labor that Pharaoh once coveted, and **YHWH**, forsaken by his[+] heirs and by the nations whose sages once sought their kings' wisdom. Both rejections anticipate the rejected Messiah. As the exiles have **no resting place**, so "the Son of Man has nowhere to lay his head" (Luke 9:57–58 NRSV).

Hope God has forbidden Israel to go on **the way** back to **Egypt** (→17:14–20). Does Moses contradict God by foretelling its travel along that way? Rather, he shows the nihilism of disobedience. Sin is a contradiction of God and all God has made. It destroys more than just its perpetrators and victims; it annihilates whole futures. Monarchical Israel's stubbornness brings about an alternative future— really a nonfuture—that, while foreseen by God, is neither God's design nor Israel's true future (Hos. 11:1–11). As if shifting time into reverse, the covenant's curses press Israel back to an existence even more tenuous than the patriarchs—nervously sojourning in Egypt (Gen. 20:1–11), respecting household **gods** (31:19), at a fraction of their former number (46:27). The reference to **ships** indicates a very different return to Egypt than ever before: piloted by foreigners, led by no one, as haggard passengers rather than a tribal army or even a starving clan, with no Jordan, Sinai, or dry Sea of Reeds to mark their regress, literally and figuratively at sea—though not without God's word (→30:11–16). If restful Israel in **the land** (→5:12–15) symbolizes YHWH's blessing of all creation (Gen. 1:1–2:4), its **restless** Diaspora symbolizes YHWH's curse of uncreation upon all who have sinned and fallen short of God's glory (Rom. 3:23). Israel **sees** itself made **fearful**, discontented with each **night and day**, deformed, diminished, and **scattered**, resigned to perpetual work for its enemies. The Hebrews finally get their wish in the wilderness to **return to Egypt** (Num. 11:4–6): the remnant left behind in Judah following the Babylonian exile flees there out of fear of Babylon (Jer. 43:5–7; 2 Kgs. 25:26)—and, in the punch line of the chapter, the refugees' desperate offer to **sell themselves** finds **no buyer**. Israel is unmarketable even as slaves, unfit even for the bottom of a social order, placeless and classless, *tohu wabohu* ("formless and empty"; Gen. 1:2). Yet this humbled ending (2 Kgs. 25:27–30) is also a beginning, setting the stage for a new Israel to arise (Ezra 1). The story is not quite blotted out (→28:58–63a; →29:22–24); Israel's *theologia gloriae* has been crucified and buried so that a *theologia crucis* might rise in glory (→28:7–14).

Love A dead church is ready for revival when it knows it is dead, realizes its own strength is broken, has exhausted every temptation to fall back on some other source of **life** and **assurance** than the giver of life and assurance, accepts its death as judgment not victimization, and sees no alternative but to return to the judge for clemency. Like the prodigal son (Luke 15:17–19), by the final verse of this tortuous chapter Israel is finally ready. With some exceptions, the church of Jesus Christ is not. Revival has come not to the disciples with the most spiritual and material assets but to those who have most urgently sought God's face: monastic communities, seekers of Pentecostal and charismatic renewal, open *and* diligent students of the word of God (many are one but not the other), and servants whose ministerial careers in churches, mission fields, and marketplaces have failed. "Fool! What you sow does not come to life unless it dies" (1 Cor. 15:36 NRSV).

DEUTERONOMY 29

29:1 These are the words of the covenant YHWH commanded Moses to make with the sons⁺ of Israel in the land of Moab (1:5; 2:18), besides the covenant he⁺ made with them in Horeb (5:22).

Hope The Masoretic Text and Septuagint make this verse the conclusion to Moses's second discourse, which began at 4:44. English Bibles have **these words** introduce his third discourse (29:2–31:6). The verse bridges the terms of the covenant and Israel's hope of understanding it and succeeding. It places Deuteronomy's series of Mosaic addresses in proper eschatological trajectory: (1) reviewing the past with a view toward the present, (2) living in the present with a view toward the near future, and (3) enduring the near future to await the far future (→32:44–47).

29:2 Moses called to all Israel, and said to them: You have seen all YHWH did before your eyes in the land of Egypt to Pharaoh, and to all his⁺ servants, and to all his⁺ land; **3**the great trials your eyes saw, the signs and those great wonders. **4**But YHWH has not given you a heart to know, and eyes to see, and ears to hear, to this day. **5**I have led you forty years in the wilderness: your clothes have not grown old on you, and your shoes have not grown old on your feet. **6**You have not eaten bread, neither have you drunk wine or strong drink, that you may know that I am YHWH your God. **7**When you came to this place, Sihon the king of Heshbon (2:24–37) and Og the king of Bashan (3:1–11) came out against us to battle, and we struck them: **8**and we took their land and gave it for an inheritance to the Reubenites and to the Gadites and to the half-tribe of the Manassites. **9**Keep therefore the words of this covenant, and do them, that you may prosper in all you do.

Faith To whom is Moses talking? His present audience has seen the wonders of **Heshbon** and **Bashan** with their own **eyes**, but not those of **Egypt**. Yet they are enough. Seeing just one work of divine power usually opens us to whole galleries of wonders we have not personally experienced, and we "see greater things than these" (John 1:50 NRSV). To see one is in a sense to **see** them **all** (21:25).

Faith Deuteronomy's later audiences have not **seen** even the wonders of the conquest. We may only **hear** and repeat the testimony of eyewitnesses (→26:1–11; Luke 24:48; Acts 1:8). Yet Moses points out that Israel's generations have been oblivious to it anyway. Without the gift of sonship (John 8:42–47) that bestows **eyes to see** (9:39), **ears to hear** (Luke 14:35), and minds to understand (24:45), we see no **signs**, hear no word of YHWH (Jer. 6:10; Ps. 19:3 Masoretic Text), and **know** no shepherd's voice (John 10:3–4).

Hope Some read **to this day** only as "before the day of Moses's speech." Yet even if that is appropriate (cf. 34:6, 10), Moses's claim still anticipates a gift long after Torah (→30:6–10). Deuteronomy 28's trajectory of rise, decline, and exile foretells an Israel that is elect and, given the knowledge of YHWH in Torah, still cannot understand the significance of its own witness (Isa. 44:18; Ezek. 12:2–3). "God gave them a sluggish spirit, eyes that would not see and ears that would not hear, down to this very day" (Rom. 11:7–8 NRSV quoting Deut. 29:3 and Isa. 29:10). Only with a new mind and new senses can we put away our falseness (Jer. 5:20–31) and keep ourselves from idols (1 John 5:21). "On that day the deaf shall hear the words of a scroll, and out of their gloom and darkness the eyes of the blind shall see" and sanctify YHWH's name (Isa. 29:18 NRSV; cf. 29:23; Matt. 6:9).

Love God has been teaching Israel what every evangelist of the "prosperity gospel" forgets: that the miracles themselves are not Israel's success, only its foundation. **Forty years** of trials (→8:1–5) have made Israel experienced in grace so it can become a new and different people that **knows** YHWH to be our **God** (→6:4). From the wilderness's spiritual food and drink and every other providence, Israel is to learn that **I am YHWH** (5:6); and learning this lesson is to make them into a people who **prosper** in God's kingdom (4:32–40). Because the prosperity gospel is so seductive, God will have to keep instructing from Egypt, through the wilderness, on the east bank, in the land, in global exile, and in the Messiah's regathering, discipleship, and fellowship; and even then, the last judgment will reveal many who never learned the Torah's lessons (Luke 16:31).

Love Moses has already charged Israel to remember (→6:10–12; →8:11–14a; →8:19–20). Here he charges Israel to obey in order to **know**. Revelation is not yet reception; obedience is not necessarily appreciation; knowledge is more than rote memory. A people can see and even relate something we do not understand, perpetuating the unintelligible through mnemonic traditions until it is either finally forgotten or finally grasped. Indeed, we pass holy scripture from generation to generation even as it eludes us. Understanding is a task that lies beyond Deut. 4's demonstration, Deut. 6's transmission, Deut. 8's remembrance, and even this chapter's obedience. All are necessary elements in forging and maintaining YHWH's relationship with the people he⁺ has chosen to light the world.

> **29:10**You stand this day, all of you, before YHWH your God; your heads, your tribes, your elders, and your officers, even all the men[+] of Israel, **11**your little ones, your wives, and your foreigner who is in the midst of your camps, from the one who cuts your wood to the one who draws your water, **12**that you may enter into the covenant of YHWH your God and into his[+] curse (→29:16–21) that YHWH your God makes with you this day, **13**that he[+] may establish you this day to himself[+] for a people, and that he[+] may be to you a God, as he[+] spoke to you and as he[+] swore to your fathers, to Abraham, to Isaac, and to Jacob. **14**Not with you only do I make this covenant and curse, **15**but with the one who stands here with us this day before YHWH our God, as well as the one who is not here with us this day.

Love The whole spectrum of covenantal participants, from its elites to its "guest workers," attests to the catholicity of the local church. **All**—not just the powerful and famous—are heirs of the promise and **Abraham's** offspring (Gal. 3:29). Moses even includes generations who do **not stand with them**, while rather laboriously maintaining his focus on those who do. Israel's fullness remains on the way for every new covenantal generation of Jews and of the Gentiles in their service; yet its focus is always on those who are in the position to hear and respond (→31:24–30).

Faith The inclusivity of Moses's claim is logistically baffling. How can **foreigners** be **Abraham, Isaac, and Jacob's** offspring? How can God **covenant** with people who do not yet exist? How can the covenant apply to Gentiles for whom its terms do not apply? There are a number of possible solutions (→29:16–21), but the answer God eventually supplies is christological: "As many of you as were baptized into Christ have clothed yourselves with Christ" (Gal. 3:27 NRSV). As eternal object of the covenant (→8:1–5), Jesus mediates its divine fellowship to all who share his grace and Abraham's faith (Rom. 4:16–18). He holds in himself all its diversity in unity. As the terms of the common covenant are different for leaders, men, children, wives, and foreigners, so the ways are distinct in which past and future, Jews and Gentiles, slaves and free, males and females (Gal. 3:28a) are included in the covenant's ratifiers; yet these have their common focus in him: "All of you are one in Christ Jesus" (3:28b NRSV).

> **29:16**For you know how we lived in the land of Egypt, and how we came through the midst of the nations through which you passed; **17**and you have seen their abominations, and their idols, wood and stone, silver and gold, which were among them. **18**There might be among you man or woman (13:1–5) or family (13:6–11) or tribe (13:12–18) whose heart turns away this day from YHWH our God, to go to serve the gods of those nations; there might be among you a root that bears gall and wormwood (Lam. 3:15); **19**and when such a one hears

the words of this curse, he⁺ might bless himself⁺ in his⁺ heart, saying: "I shall have peace, though I walk in the stubbornness of my heart, to destroy the moist with the dry." ²⁰YHWH will not pardon him⁺, but then the anger of YHWH and his⁺ jealousy will smoke against that man⁺, and all the curse written in this book shall lie on him⁺, and YHWH will blot out his⁺ name from under the sky (Deut. 9:14). ²¹YHWH will set him⁺ apart to evil out of all the tribes of Israel, according to all the curses of the covenant written in this book of the Torah (→28:58–63a; →29:25–28).

Hope The previous passage includes both outsiders and future generations in the **covenant**. Moses now begins to explain the secret (→29:29) of how this is to come about: through its **curse**. In Deuteronomy's earlier contexts, rebellion threatens to stall YHWH's redemptive purpose, as if sinners could hold God's will hostage by not cooperating. The threat is graver when rebellion spreads to the whole **nation** and disciplinary practices alone can no longer heal or protect. "Their **root** will become rotten, and their blossom go up like dust; for they have rejected the instruction of [YHWH Almighty], and have despised the word of the Holy One of Israel" (Isa. 5:24 NRSV). Moses's concluding sermon promises release from slavery to self-centered **stubbornness**, by refusing to grant unbelief even its power to frustrate others. A path through wholesale apostasy is ironically the way out of the impasse between this stiff-necked people and their **jealous** God. Israel will **go** to the **gods** of the nations, and in reaction to the consequences of its arrogant apostasy, witnesses from the nations will come to Israel (→29:22–24) and receive its God.

Faith Apostasy is here portrayed as self-realization. The **cursed** one **self-blesses**, self-assures, self-justifies, and ultimately self-condemns. Self-centeredness is the ultimate form of exceptionalism, setting oneself above (or below) all others. Moses insists that there is no exceptionalism in Israel's impartial God (→10:17–22) for any individual or group that forgets the **covenant** (→4:21–24). In fact, even God is unexceptional in holiness: the worthy Son submits to the Father, follows the Spirit, and obeys Israel's written **Torah**.

Love Moses has repeatedly addressed inward rebellion, as bringing about **curses** when it is still private (27:15–26) and punishments when it comes to light (→13:12–18). The topic reemerges in this chapter's context of renewal. Respecting catholicity in a context of freedom of conscience is a lasting dilemma. Should the people of God be *restricted*, to include only those who want to belong to it, or should it be *restrictive*, including some who do not? Deuteronomy commands both—disciplining with a measure of tolerance to chasten rebels, as well as cutting them off to stop their offenses from spreading. Christian life honors this complexity by **setting apart** both sin and sinner with means of conviction to identify the problem, with practices of penitence to restore health, and with the last resort of excommunication to protect the uncompromised.

Love The one who **blesses himself**[+] and is **blotted out** is named in 28:20 as a **man**, but can also be a **woman**, a **family**, or a whole **tribe** that judges itself exempt from the covenant's curses and free to pursue its own desires. So this passage pertains not only to apostates such as Ahab and Jezebel but to the tribes that are lost to Israel through syncretism. All these "lost sons" are significant in Israel's secret future course—even those of the new covenant: Simon the Magician, a baptized believer, remained "in the **gall** of bitterness" even after seeing the Holy Spirit received in Samaria (Acts 8:23 NRSV).

> **29:22**The generation to come, your children who shall rise up after you and the foreigner who shall come from a far land, shall say— when they see the plagues of that land and the sicknesses with which YHWH has made it sick, **23**and that the whole land of it is sulfur, salt, and burning, that it is not sown or bears, or any grass grows therein, like the overthrow of Sodom and Gomorrah, Admah and Zeboiim, which YHWH overthrew in his[+] anger and in his[+] wrath—**24**even all the nations shall say: "For what has YHWH done thus to this land? For what is the heat of this great anger?"

Love Rehearsing Israel's destruction from the perspective of those who **see** it adds an important—and redemptive—element of shame to the guilt and suffering in Deut. 28 and to the heavy conscience from Deut. 32. Asking the meaning of Israel's suffering in terms of God's **anger** is a project of theodicy. But this passage's descendants and witnesses do not ask questions with the accusatory tone of much contemporary theodicy. Rather than placing the burden of proof on God for an explanation that satisfies interrogators' prior convictions, these inquirers simply ask **what** the events are **for**, inviting an interpretation. The common query of these very diverse peoples is open to a wider variety of answers—including surprising answers that can turn them into a community of common assent to the God of the sufferers. Both ways of theodicy begin with our incredulity, but only one can lead us out of it.

Hope Admah and Zeboiim are "cities of the Plain" overthrown along with **Sodom and Gomorrah**. Israel is overthrown by the **sulfur** and fire of God's judgment (Gen. 19:24) and the **salt** of both foreign armies' scorched-earth tactics and its own attachments (19:26). Yet despite the imagery (or perhaps honoring it, since God rescues Lot's family; 19:29; →2:6–9), disaster at home and abroad will not end the generations of Israel, and its spectacle will draw wonderers who **come** from afar to **see** (→29:16–21). And when God's deliverance of his[+] wretched people converts **the whole land's** sterility into fecundity and converts Israel's shame into good news, that good news of God will thus be heard not only among the sufferers' descendants but also received by witnesses from **all the nations**. First the prophets, then the apostles, testify to the revelation that God's **great anger** is preliminary to God's greater mercy (→30:1–5). "How can I make you like **Admah**? How can I treat you like **Zeboiim**? My heart recoils within me; my compassion grows warm and tender" (Hos. 11:8 NRSV; cf. 11:1 in Matt. 2:15).

Faith "Now is the judgment of this world; now the ruler of this world will be driven out. And I, when I am lifted up from the earth, will draw all people to myself" (John 12:31–32 NRSV).

> **29:25**They shall say: "Because they forsook the covenant of YHWH, the God of their fathers, that he+ made with them when he+ brought them forth out of the land of Egypt, **26**and went and served other gods and worshiped them, gods they did not know, that he+ had not given to them: **27**therefore the anger of YHWH was kindled against this land to bring on it all the curse that is written in this book; **28**and YHWH rooted them out of their land in anger and in wrath and in great indignation, and cast them into another land, as at this day."

Faith Now Deuteronomy's grand thesis is finally grasped, its central lesson learned—but by a very unlikely set: a still-dispersed Israelite remnant in pilgrimage to its ruined homeland, along with God-fearers from all nations. Such an achievement makes it possible for YHWH to open the next chapter in its saga of cosmic salvation-history (→30:1–5). "Parthians, Medes, Elamites, and residents of Mesopotamia, Judea and Cappadocia, Pontus and Asia, Phrygia and Pamphylia, Egypt and the parts of Libya belonging to Cyrene, and visitors from Rome, both Jews and proselytes, Cretans and Arabs—in our own languages we hear them speaking about God's deeds of power" (Acts 2:9–11 NRSV).

Hope While these students of history seem to arrive at this conclusion themselves, in fact **they** have an interpreter. The nations and generations to come understand what Israel's suffering means only because they have a **book** (→28:58–63a; →29:16–21) on hand to consult. Holy scripture *as such* plays an integral part in the working out of God's mysterious eschatological plan for the world through Israel. "Faith comes from what is heard, and what is heard comes through the word of Christ" (Rom. 10:17 NRSV on Isa. 52:7, as commentary on Deut. 29–32).

Love The dynamic of learning through others' disasters, fundamental to the exodus story, frames all of Deuteronomy's addresses. It is basic to the logic of wisdom literature from Proverbs to Ecclesiastes to Job and the proclamation of the prophets—complemented, happily, by the dynamic of learning through others' blessings (e.g., Jer. 31:10, in which the nations witness Israel's scattering and regathering). This continues in the messianic age (Rom. 11:11–12). Believers have repeatedly reacted to decadent Christianity with revival movements that rejuvenate and spread the faith. God thus uses the most private of sins (→29:16–21) to spur the most public of revolutions.

Faith God **gives gods** to peoples? Statements early in Deuteronomy are sometimes understood that way (→4:16–20), but such an interpretation is unthinkable, especially in this context. Serving and trying to manipulate lesser powers is repulsive because it is antithetical to God's eternal purpose of peace, unity, and mutuality in heaven and on earth. Yet God does give gifts worthy of worship: the Father through the Spirit gives the Son, the Son gives the Father's Spirit, and the Son in the Spirit gives the Father—first to Israel, then to all nations, so they will know and be known to YHWH. Idolatry is the sin of preferring the gifts of God to their giver.

> **29:29**The secret things belong to YHWH our God; but the things that are revealed belong to us and to our children forever, that we may do all the words of this Torah.

Hope This chapter has been a tantalizing *apokalypsis* ("revelation") into the surprising course of the promise in the life of settled and uprooted Israel. Learning a bit of its shape can tempt knowers to jump ahead of—or just out of—our actual place in the story, a temptation not far from the elitism and rank speculation of gnosticism. Baroque end-times scenarios, presumptuous church-growth techniques, ulterior manipulations of the Jewish people, Constantinian power plays and alliances, and "reconstructive" transmogrifications of apostolic doctrine all shorten the time frame of our trust: **forever**. Moses's admonition eternally distinguishes *gnōsis* ("knowledge") from gnosticism. What God requires of us is not strategizing as if we were clairvoyants, but trustful constancy in the face of persistent mystery. "Blessed is that slave whom his⁺ master will find at work when he⁺ arrives" (Matt. 24:46 NRSV).

Faith This constancy does not, however, bind *God* to perpetual stasis; the covenant's terms can be made new with a change in priesthood (Heb. 7:12), and God's will can be activated upon the death of the one who made it (9:15–17; →6:21b–25; →24:1–4).

DEUTERONOMY 30

30:1 When all these things (→4:29–30) have come on you, the blessing and the curse I have set before you, and you shall call them to mind among all the nations where YHWH your God has driven you, **2**and shall return to YHWH your God, and shall obey his⁺ voice according to all I command you this day, you and your children, with all your heart and with all your self, **3**then YHWH your God will restore you (Ezek. 16:53) and show you love (Deut. 13:17), and will return and gather you from all the peoples where YHWH your God has scattered you. **4**If your outcasts are in the uttermost parts of the heavens, from there will YHWH your God gather you, and from there he⁺ will bring you back: **5**and YHWH your God will bring you into the land your fathers possessed, and you shall possess it; and he⁺ will do you good, and multiply you above your fathers.

Hope **Outcasts in the heavens?** What may originally be hyperbole in fact describes just what is to happen. "Elijah is indeed coming first to restore **all things**" (Mark 9:12a NRSV), yet all nations "will see 'the Son of Man coming in clouds' with great power and glory" (13:26 NRSV; cf. 9:12b). "Then he will send out the angels, and **gather** his elect from the four winds, from the ends of the earth to the ends of heaven" (13:27 NRSV). The parousia is the consummation of Israel's restoration from the heavens, the earth, and under the earth; and Jesus, having dwelt in all three (Acts 2:22–36), is the common agent and focus of the reunion of all God's scattered ones in all these domains (Phil. 2:10; Rev. 5:13).

Faith Moses's syntax can help us appreciate one of Jesus's most perplexing claims: "This generation will not pass away until **all these things** have taken place" (Mark 13:30 NRSV). Moses's **you** in this passage cannot refer to only one generation, but includes all those who have traveled parts of Israel's journey in a blessed life that surpasses all earlier stages. Yet every audience in every age and every nation is *the* generation that receives his words to do them. How can settled generations, exiled ones, and their **children** all be restored to a life **above** every predecessor's? Only by the radical **restoration** of resurrection—through which generations survive even the passing away of heaven and earth (13:31) and are brought together as one assembly. Jesus is not mistaken, as some have supposed. Nor is he counting the years since Israel's or Jerusalem's twentieth-century political rebirth. He is preaching apocalyptic Torah.

> [30:6]YHWH your God will circumcise your heart and the heart of your seed to love YHWH your God with all your heart and with all your self (6:5), that you may live. [7]YHWH your God will put all these curses (→28:58–63a) on your enemies and on those who hate you, who persecuted you. [8]You shall return and obey the voice of YHWH and do all his+ commandments I command you this day. [9]YHWH your God will make you plenteous in all the work of your hand (→14:27–29), in the fruit of your body, and in the fruit of your livestock, and in the fruit of your ground, for good; for YHWH will again rejoice over you for good (→28:58–63a), as he+ rejoiced over your fathers (→1:8), [10]if you shall obey the voice of YHWH your God, to keep his+ commandments and his+ statutes that are written in this book of the law, if you turn to YHWH your God with all your heart and with all your self.

Faith **Your fathers** is sometimes read as settled Israel's obedient early generations, but in Deuteronomy it typically refers to Abraham, Isaac, and Jacob—a meaning suited to the inclusive **you** of this chapter (→30:1–5). **Circumcision** dedicates one's **seed**, rather graphically, to a perpetual patriarchal covenant (Gen. 17:9–14; →10:12–16). Circumcision of the **heart**—the source of life and the engine (cf. Ps. 38:10) of the blood that holds that life (→12:20–28)—dedicates the whole of one's life to that Abrahamic covenant of faith (Gen. 15:4–6). Each circumcision honors and deepens the other.

Hope As Israel returns, the earlier promises of **fruitfulness** return (→28:1–6; →28:7–14)—with one significant difference: YHWH, not Israel (cf. 10:16; Jer. 4:4), will **circumcise** its **heart**. Only then will the greatest commandment become practical and feasible (→6:5). "If we love one another, God lives in us, and his+ love is perfected in us" (1 John 4:12 NRSV). Significantly, this circumcision happens late in Israel's process of reconciliation, after being returned, convicted, and made repentant (→30:1–5). That suggests sanctification rather than faith or justification. **Love** is **fruit** not of the flesh but of the Spirit (Gal. 5:22) who is given to abide in us (1 John 4:13, 16b). If the church in its failure can reap the covenant's bitterest curses (→28:63b–68), then in restoration it can receive anew the perfecting flow of the Spirit through circumcised hearts and fruitful lives. The Torah's far promises describe the opportunities open to us who live at the ends of the ages (1 Cor. 10:11). When we read its blessings, we might invert

Paul's warning about its curses: "If you think you are *falling*, watch out that you *may stand*" (cf. 10:12).

Hope As the covenant's **curses** do not annul its blessings, so its blessings do not abolish its curses. Instead, they shift those curses to the **enemies** and **persecutors** of God's eschatological regathering. This promise suggests the traditional hell of real suffering (→25:17–19; →28:1–6) rather than the empty hell of universalism.

> ³⁰:¹¹For this commandment I command you this day is not too over-whelming for you, nor is it far off. ¹²It is not in heaven, that you should say: "Who shall go up for us to heaven, and bring it to us, and make us to hear it, that we may do it?" ¹³Nor is it beyond the sea, that you should say: "Who shall go over the sea for us, and bring it to us, and make us to hear it, that we may do it?" ¹⁴For the word is very near to you, in your mouth, and in your heart to do it. ¹⁵Behold, I have set before you this day life and good, and death and evil, ¹⁶in that I command you this day to love YHWH your God, to walk in his⁺ ways, and to keep his⁺ commandments and his⁺ statutes and his⁺ ordinances (→10:12–16), that you may live and multiply, and that YHWH your God may bless you in the land you go in to possess (4:1; 8:1).

Plain These verses are conventionally read as Moses's affirmations of the ease and practicality of Torah observance. But 30:11's **commandment** is grammatically broader than 30:16's **commandments and statutes and ordinances**. Moreover, the conjunction *ki* (**for**) suggests a connection with the preceding verses and their eschatological scenario: God will give **you** perceptive eyes and ears and circumcise your heart, and you will love God wholly and obey, and God will rejoice for your good, all *because* **the word is near you to do it**. The word's power to release Israel from exile is already and always at hand, in the commandment itself. "When [YHWH] roars, his⁺ children shall come trembling from the west" (Hos. 11:10 NRSV).

Hope Who shall go up? echoes the scene at the base of Horeb when YHWH speaks to a terrified Israel from **heaven** (4:36). **Who shall go over?** is reminiscent of exiled Israel piloted across the sea to sell itself (28:68). One question looks fearfully forward to God's dwelling place above, the other regretfully back to the tabernacle and temple of God's dwelling place before. Both are cries of desperation. In fact, both carry a note of unbelief that shirks responsibility by looking for some deliverer to **make** Israel **hear** and act. Instead, Moses assures of a God ever present and powerful in the **word** of Israel's **mouth and heart**, whatever its circumstances. Paul honors precisely this sense of the verse in locating it in Israel's eschatological context—where, dispersed and domi-nated, having tried to establish its own righteousness and stumbled over Zion's cornerstone (Isa. 28:16 in Rom. 9:30–33), Israel might suddenly suspect that God has abandoned it and either look in vain for a way to restore itself or wait in vain for some other deliverer. Faith's righteousness already perceives that way, but it is not a foreign or coercive one: it is Israel's own (11:1–2) word of the Messiah who himself has already overcome every distance Israel may think lay between them (Deut. 30:12–13 in Rom. 10:5–10). His ascension is not their abandonment, for Jesus is Lord; the crucifixion is not his defeat, for God has raised him from the dead (10:9); his message is not an exotic perversion but the prophets' good news (Isa. 53:1 in Rom. 10:14–17). So the word of faith on Israel's lips and heart is **nearer** and more powerful than ever, and able as always to save (Rom. 10:8 on Deut. 30:14). Paul's treatment is brilliant and sensitive apostolic exegesis.

Faith Jesus is thus the ultimate referent of Moses's **word**. He alone bridges even vaster distances than even those **overseas** or to **heaven**: the distances between **God** and **us**, **good** and **evil**, and **death** and **life**. This is not a journey into the **overwhelming** or the esoteric, but a straightforward accounting of how the Messiah has answered God's promises to Israel. "He who descended [into the lower parts of the earth] is the same one who ascended far above all the heavens, so that he might fill all things" (Eph. 4:10 NRSV; cf. Rom. 11:36).

Love **Life and good** and **death and evil** are conventionally opposed as mutually exclusive alternatives between which Israel chooses. Yet Deut. 28–33 repeatedly foretells *both* evil and good, death and life for Israel. This prediction should be tremendously reassuring in retrospect, for it shows that **the word is near** regardless. That word strengthens faith's righteous ones to walk in YHWH's ways and love him[+] wholeheartedly (30:6), but it also turns and restores the wayward by awakening **love** that then **walks** and so finds its faith along the way. These effects tend to confute synergistic theologies that bind God's power to cooperative human righteousness, as well as monergisms that rob divine action of its genuine human responsiveness (→30:17–20). Yet they confirm the Reformation's conviction, which these synergisms and monergisms are both trying to protect, that the word belongs to the *esse* of the church.

> [30:17]But if your heart turns away, and you will not hear, but shall be drawn away and worship other gods and serve them, [18]I declare to you this day that you shall surely perish (→8:19–20); you shall not prolong your days in the land you pass over the Jordan to go in to possess. [19]I call heaven and earth to witness against you this day (→4:25–26) that I have set before you life and death (→30:11–16), the blessing and the curse (11:26–32; 28:1–68): therefore choose life, that you may live, you and your seed; [20]to love YHWH your God, to obey his[+] voice, and to cling to him[+] (→4:3–4; →11:22–25); for he[+] is your life and the length of your days; that you may dwell in

the land YHWH swore to your fathers, to Abraham, to Isaac, and to
Jacob, to give them.

Faith In this, the third discourse's penultimate passage, Moses crystallizes chapters
of pleas, rules, promises, threats, and hints into one basic challenge. Here the plain,
christological, eschatological, and ecclesiological senses of the text converge onto
one ever-present existential point. The word's tenacious nearness ($\rightarrow$30:11–16)
does not imply a fate that overpowers Israel's **choice**, but respects the freedom it
bequeaths to Israel to **love** and **obey** and thus **live** as God intends (Josh. 24:14) as
a servant in God's triune project of cosmic restoration. To abuse that freedom still
brings **death**, though not a death that finally frustrates the will of the one rejected.
To walk in it yields the eternal life of **dwelling** in fellowship with Abraham's dead
and living **seed** (Gal. 3:15–18; cf. Rom. 4:16–17; $\rightarrow$5:16), who Augustine noted
is "'the way, and the truth, and the life'; that is, you are to come through me, to
arrive at me, and to remain in me" (John 14:6 in *On Christian Doctrine* 1.34).
"Whoever follows me will never walk in darkness but will have the light of life"
(John 8:12 NRSV). This life is not the mere extension of lifespan, for Israel's
length of days is YHWH himself⁺. It is exalted and superabundant life (10:10;
$\rightarrow$7:12–15), divine life, life together, eternal life.

DEUTERONOMY 31

31:1 Moses finished speaking these words to all Israel. **2**He said to them, "I am one hundred twenty years old this day, I can no more go out and come in, and YHWH has said to me, 'You shall not go over this Jordan.' **3**YHWH your God, he+ will go over before you; he+ will destroy these nations from before you, and you shall dispossess them. Joshua shall go over before you, as YHWH has spoken. **4**YHWH will do to them as he+ did to Sihon and to Og, the kings of the Amorites, and to their land when he+ destroyed them (→3:21–22). **5**YHWH will deliver them up before you, and you shall do to them according to all the commandment I have commanded you (e.g., 7:2–5; 12:2–3). **6**Be strong and courageous, do not fear or dread them: for YHWH your God, he+ it is who goes with you (→1:29–33); he+ will not fail you or forsake you (→4:31)." **7**Moses called to Joshua, and said to him in the sight of all Israel, "Be strong and courageous: for you shall go with this people into the land YHWH has sworn to their fathers to give them, and you shall cause them to inherit it. **8**YHWH, he+ it is who goes before you; he+ will be with you, he+ will not fail you or forsake you; do not be afraid, neither be dismayed."

Faith This passage is the real denouement of 29:1–31:6. It is a moment that Moses seems to have been dreading: he makes it a postscript attached to his **finished** words. He pleads his own frailty (→1:9–14; but →34:5–7) rather than YHWH's proscription (→1:37–38), as if trying to reassure himself of the rightness of his retirement. Yet he ends fittingly: not with a thundering rhetorical climax that glorifies his own ministry but with a formal resignation that stresses **YHWH's** singular glory and publicly endorses **Joshua's** succession. True servants of God's kingdom admit, however reluctantly, that they—we—"must decrease" while "**he** must increase" (John 3:30).

Hope YHWH is constantly reassuring believers in a time of transition that a new age that is beginning is not to be worse than the old (→1:20–21). "Why are you **frightened**, and why do doubts arise in your hearts? . . . I am sending upon you the promise of my Father" (Luke 24:38, 49, my translation).

Love Now that **Moses** has done **all** he was ordered to do, he says in effect, "[I] have done only what [I] ought to have done" (Luke 17:10 NRSV), "I have kept the faith" (2 Tim. 4:7 NRSV), "I do not count my life of any value to myself, if only I may finish my course and the ministry that I received from the Lord Jesus, to testify to the good news of God's grace" (Acts 20:24 NRSV). Israel honors him by taking his word not as false modesty but as sound doctrine, wholeheartedly following their new anointed leader, and imitating the old one.

Love YHWH has charged **Moses** to strengthen **Joshua** (→1:37–38; →3:28–29). This he now does, by **strengthening** the people along with him. We love and serve Christ when we love and serve one another (John 13:34–35; Matt. 25:40), and vice versa. Yet Moses maintains a decisive distinction between Joshua and Israel; Joshua will cause **them** to inherit. Absent such a differentiation, Israel will be headless and soon falter. Leadership distances one from even the people one represents (→1:9–14). The same dichotomous unity describes the differentiated head and body of Messiah. Its dichotomy owes to the singularity of Christ's ascension and session, its unity to the fellowship of the Holy Spirit. A pneumatic Chalcedonian Christology grounds accurate ecclesiology and healthy church polity.

> **31:9** Moses wrote this Torah, and delivered it to the priests, the sons of Levi, who bore the ark of the covenant of YHWH, and to all the elders of Israel. **10** Moses commanded them, saying: "At the end of every seven years, in the set time of the year of release, in the Feast of Tents, **11** when all Israel has come to appear before YHWH your God in the place he+ shall choose, you shall read this Torah before all Israel in their hearing. **12** Assemble the people, the men and the women and the little ones, and your foreigner who is within your gates, that they may hear, and that they may learn, and fear YHWH your God, and do all the words of this Torah; **13** and that their children (6:7), who have not known (→6:20–21a), may hear, and learn to fear YHWH your God as long as you live in the land you go over the Jordan to possess."

Hope "Turn my heart to your decrees. . . . It is good for me that I was humbled, so that I might **learn** your statutes" (Ps. 119:36, 71 NRSV). It is appropriate that the scripture resides next to **the ark**, in YHWH's **chosen place**, and in the custody of his priests (Deut. 31:25–26), for it is a (not *the*) liturgical mediatory of God's life-giving presence: through its rendition **all** who **come** and **appear** before YHWH **hear**, **learn** to **fear** and **know** their **God**, **do** his+ will, and **live**. The written Torah accompanies the tables of the Decalogue in the ark as Israel enters the land (→5:22; →10:1–5; →31:24–30). Its public reading, though, is overshadowed by the likelihood (→30:17–20) and certainty (→31:14–18) of mass apostasy. While Israel loses the tables and ark, it holds onto **this Torah**—which accompanies it into exile, in Diaspora, back into the land, and in its apostolic regathering. Torah is to be **read** not *because* Israel fears God, not as an expression of piety, but *so that* Israel **fears** God, as a foundation for piety. "The unfolding of your words gives light; it imparts understanding to the simple" (Ps. 119:130 NRSV). The word's alien power to create is most evident where Israel's **children** had **not known**: when Josiah's servants discover the neglected book of the law (2 Kgs. 22:10–23:25), when Nehemiah and his teachers explain it to a colony of returned exiles (Neh. 8), when Jesus teaches as if at his Father's own subversive **Feast of Tents** (John 7:1–31; →16:13–15), and when Jesus explains the things pertaining to him "in all the scriptures" (Luke 24:27 NRSV)—all these surprised audiences react similarly: "Were not our hearts burning within us while he was talking to us on the road, while he was opening the scriptures to us?" (24:32 NRSV).

Love Deuteronomy 31's apparently jumbled structure realistically conveys the complexity of this transition of leadership. Every Israelite line of authority has converged on **Moses**; but that has been a temporary arrangement, and it is ending. He is not an earthly king who fathers a dynasty of supreme successors (→17:14–20), but a servant handing over to God what has been entrusted to him. So he **writes** the covenant he has received and **delivers it** to the **priests** and the other tribes' **elders** to keep and use; he yields executive authority to Joshua; and he arranges for **all** its subjects' educations, including **women**, children, and resident aliens (→29:10–15). All these trustees share custodianship over Israel's identity. With this Deuteronomic constitution and its array of old and new institutions, God is constituting his⁺ people, reshaping them out of what they had been in Egypt and in the wilderness. It is not around the ephemeral figure of Moses that they are constituted, but around the **covenant**. Nor can a church owe its identity to some equally ephemeral figure, however towering—Augustine, Gregory the Great, Thomas Aquinas, Martin Luther, John Calvin, Menno Simons, John Wesley, or even Peter or Paul—but the **living** Christ alone.

Love Here all these custodial responsibilities are focused on written Torah. Some traditions interpret **Torah's** written form and priestly custodians as signs that the Bible is only for specialists. Catholics argued this particularly insistently in the heat of the Reformation. However, as the **Feast of Tents** is explicitly for everyone, so is holy scripture. It is not just for clergy (the **priests**) to understand and interpret to the ignorant. It is not just for leaders (the **elders**) to use in directing the masses. It is not just for the powerful (the males of 16:16–17) to maintain dominance. It is not just for the literate (the readers) or the mature (the adults) for whom its **words** are most clear. It is not even just for Israel's tribes as their exclusive commitment. These scriptures are catholic, universal; they indwell ecclesial structures in order to assimilate all who gather into the whole people of God, so that "there shall be no poor with you" (15:4). Their place in the liturgy of a major feast suggests a participatory style of **assembled** worship, celebratory in character, multicultural and intergenerational in form, and biblical in content (Neh. 8).

Love "The table is prepared. . . . In the name of Jesus Christ, you are forgiven." The sabbatical (15:1–6) **Feast of Tents** (16:13–15) is a fitting context for a massive Torah performance. As that harvest festival both celebrates God's bounty and frees Israel's poor for a fresh economic start in their ancestral homes, so the **covenant** supplies the significance of both the past's and the future's claims on the present. Without it the meanings of harvest, release, fellowship, and worship drift from their covenantal definitions over to the participants' unformed imaginations and unstable cultural conventions. Any such liturgy of celebration and release—which for Christians happens weekly as we celebrate Christ's provision together and release one another through his atoning grace—holds together when it devotes considerable time and energy to biblical catechesis: to the service of the word that precedes the service of the table. "Guard your steps when you **go to the house of God. To draw near to listen** is better than fools' sacrifice, for they do not perceive evildoing" (Eccl. 5:1, my translation).

> **31:14**YHWH said to Moses, "Behold, your days approach that you must die. Call Joshua, and present yourselves in the tent of meeting, that I may commission him." Moses and Joshua went and presented themselves in the tent of meeting. **15**YHWH appeared in the tent in a pillar of cloud, and the pillar of cloud stood over the door of the tent. **16**YHWH said to Moses, "Behold, you shall sleep with your fathers (→32:48–52); and this people will rise up (→4:21–24), and play the prostitute (→23:17–18) after the strange gods (32:12; →32:15–18) of the land (→5:7; →6:13–16) where they go to be among them, and will forsake me, and break my covenant that I have made with them. **17**Then my anger shall be kindled against them in that day, and I will forsake them, and I will hide my face from them (→22:1–4), and they shall be devoured, and many evils and troubles shall come on them (→28:15–19); so that they will say in that day, 'Have not these evils come on us because our god (→31:19–23) is not among us (→1:41–42)?' **18**I will surely hide my face in that day for all the evil they shall have worked, in that they are turned to other gods.

Faith The narrative moves to a final scene that echoes the patriarchs' farewells in Genesis—but then YHWH preempts the ceremonies with a surprise **appearance** and special announcement. Though God's words repeat many of the themes that **Moses** received on Sinai forty years ago, they are not simply a rehash of earlier Deuteronomic material but a new prophecy (to Moses alone?), from a **cloud** reminiscent of Horeb (→5:22) and the wilderness (1:29–33). The warning, of an *inevitable* rebellion against YHWH in Moses's absence that brings about a fatal estrangement, reframes all of Deuteronomy's earlier provisions, command-ments, and promises. They have always sounded a slim but real chance of blessing and coaxing and threatening Israel into willing faithfulness. Now, at the last mo-ment, God snatches even this faint hope of an "if" from Israel and from Moses. The **covenant** will be not merely violated but **broken**. Israel is not marching to glory; Israel is a dead man walking. Moses is now a Jeremiah, an Isaiah, a Joel—a prophet of sure disaster. When Jesus's disciples are on the verge of appreciating him as the Anointed One, he too dashes their unrealistic expectations of what is coming: "The Son of Man **must** undergo great suffering, and be rejected by the elders, chief priests, and scribes [and the apostles, we learn later], and be killed" (Luke 9:22 NRSV; cf. Mark 8:31). It is a turning point in the Gospels, giving "Jerusalem" the ominous quality that YHWH's epiphany to Moses here gives **the land** and giving the cross its character as the normative shape of Christian life as exile from the world (8:34).

Hope "You will all become deserters" (Mark 14:27 NRSV). YHWH's announce-ment changes the mission inalterably. **Moses** and **Joshua** must prepare a people now effectively guaranteed to **forsake** God for **strange gods** and to be forsaken in return (→32:19–21). We rarely conceive of service in this way. We prefer to act as if Deuteronomy ended at 31:15—as if the future were open for success and our efforts would encourage that success. Yet God calls the prophet like Moses (→18:15–19; →34:10–12) to a ministry like Moses, and his disciples share in that ministry. The calling of a prophet of the persecuted kingdom of God is to lead God's people not *around* certain failure but *through* it into God's deliverance.

Love "The very commandment that promised life proved to be death" (Rom. 7:10 NRSV). The scene atop Horeb (9:15–17) repeats, with God interrupting his[+] own grave business to warn **Moses** of a rebellion already underway. In this respect forty years have changed nothing (→9:22–24). This dispels a widespread illusion that circumstances alone impair human goodness. The **evil** heart that produced the golden calf is not merely a product of its Egyptian environment, because the generation raised in freedom is plotting the same kind of **uprising** once it enters Canaan. Changing this takes a change of heart (→30:6–10; Rom. 5:5), not just a change of context. But then why bother issuing rules when they will be broken? Why bother trying to obey them? Because "the law is spiritual; but I am carnal" (7:14 RSV). "The commandment is holy and just and good" (7:12 RSV). The law of the Spirit remains the shape of our righteousness in the freedom that Christ has won (8:2–4). Obedience precedes disobedience in the law because obedience succeeds disobedience in the gospel.

31:19Now therefore write this song for yourselves, and teach it to the sons[+] of Israel. Put it in their mouths, that this song may be a witness for me against the sons[+] of Israel. 20For when I shall have brought them into the land I swore to their fathers, flowing with milk and honey

(→32:10–14), and they shall have eaten and filled themselves, and grown fat (→32:15–18), then will they turn to other gods, and serve them, and despise me, and break my covenant. ²¹When many evils and troubles have come on them, this song shall testify before them as a witness; for it shall not be forgotten out of the mouths of their seed. For I know what they are thinking of doing this day, before I bring them into the land I swore." ²²So Moses wrote this song the same day and taught it to the sons⁺ of Israel. ²³He commissioned Joshua the son of Nun and said: "Be strong and courageous, for you shall bring the sons⁺ of Israel into the land I swore to them: and I will be with you."

Hope That God foresees Israel's rebellion raises the classic issue of divine foreknowledge. Has YHWH **known** of Israel's apostasy all along, or has YHWH gauged the people's internal response to Torah? Deuteronomy suggests both kinds of insight. While they remain distinct, they have more in common than we sometimes appreciate. Each threatens certain views of human freedom, and philosophical theologians are right to characterize the relationships among God, powers, humanity, and the rest of creation with extreme care and sensitivity to the ways each may be distorted. However, each kind also threatens certain views of human goodness to which we are proudly attached. Our sinful self-deception blinds us to the obvious, making the knowable—whether in the human heart or in the course of human events—appear unknowable. God is free from that distorted perception and thus knowledgeable in ways that are mysterious, and seem **despicable**, to treasonous imaginations. "Truly I tell you, one of you will betray me, one who is eating with me. . . . It is one of the twelve, one who is dipping bread into the bowl with me" (Mark 14:18–20 NRSV).

Hope Habakkuk's vision "speaks of the end, and does not lie" (Hab. 2:3 NRSV). The narrative elements of the song mentioned here build God's case against Israel and refute Israel's self-serving account that its God (or **gods**, depending on how paganly one interprets *elohay* in Deut. 31:17) might be at fault for its **troubles**. Committing this lawsuit to prophecy (cf. Isa. 30:8) allows God's future judgment on unrighteousness to be mediated early, pricking the consciences of sinners while they can still repent. Jesus's complaint on the cross turns this act on its head, building his case against humanity's abandonment, refuting his enemies' self-serving theories that their condemnation of him is just (Matt. 27:49), and pricking the conscience of one such sinner on the spot (27:54).

Love Unusual terms in 31:16–21 parallel the language of Deut. 32's song. Whatever the tradition-history of both, the text as it stands suggests that God is supplying either the images for Moses to use in composing the song or this text for Moses to write down. (Deuteronomy finds it remarkable that **Moses** [and **Joshua**? →32:44–47] **writes this song** on **the same day**, suggesting an artistic role, not merely a secretarial one.) Deuteronomy concretizes the covenant, and more broadly the word of God, in a range of cultural forms as broad as the life of the covenant's people. It becomes familial customs, political institutions, liturgical traditions, written scriptures, sacred time and space, military doctrine, a whole tribe's liturgical life—and works of popular culture. These last efforts are sometimes disparaged by the custodians of the word's other forms, but here they are such an urgent need that God and Moses apparently put off Joshua's ordination to finish the task of **writing** and **teaching** the same day. We theologians may scoff at our students' Christian T-shirts, but there are occasions when a T-shirt speaks more powerfully than a syllabus. And if a T-shirt, how much more a song.

Faith Heaven and earth testify (→4:25–26), the people testify (→27:15), Moses testifies (→8:19–20), the book testifies (→29:16–21; →31:26), and someday Israel's own conscience, informed by a long experience with **this song, will testify**. Among all these witnesses only the song **will not be forgotten** or silent (Ps. 19:3), because poetic memory will have internalized and preserved it in the midst of all Israel's **troubles**. Folk wisdom can be among the most durable of human traditions: more resilient than airtight arguments, more convincing than painstakingly documented academic research, more memorable than childhood catechisms, more vivid than personal experience, more entertaining than elegant sermons, more respected than pedigreed authorities, and more cherished than holy writ. Only when the gospel becomes folk wisdom is it truly learned.

Faith After the digression and its awful news of certain failure, **Moses** returns to **commissioning** and **encouraging Joshua** with the same confident language as before (→31:1–8). YHWH's assured presence with Joshua sounds absurd after the doom of future abandonment. The juxtaposition is in fact a mysterious sign of what Luther called God's "alien righteousness": God's perseverance in the face of human *as well as* divine abandonment. The most radical dialectic of presence and dereliction is the cry of Joshua's namesake, "My God, my God, why have you forsaken me?" (Ps. 22:1 NRSV in Matt. 27:46). The forsaken conqueror later assures those who had deserted him and would surely fail him again, "**I am with you** . . . to the end of the age" (28:20 NRSV).

> ³¹:²⁴When Moses had finished writing the words of this Torah in a book until their end, ²⁵Moses commanded the Levites, who bore the ark of the covenant of YHWH, saying: ²⁶"Take this book of the Torah, and put it by the side of (→5:22) the ark of the covenant of YHWH your God (→31:9–13), that it may be there for a witness against you. ²⁷For I know your rebellion and your stiff neck: behold, while I am yet alive with you this day, you have been rebellious against YHWH; how much more after my death? ²⁸Assemble to me all the elders of your tribes and your officers (29:10) that I may speak these words in their ears, and call heaven and earth to witness against them (→4:25–26). ²⁹For I know that after my death you will utterly corrupt yourselves and

turn aside (9:12) from the way I have commanded you, and evil will happen to you in the end, because you will do what is evil in the sight of YHWH, to provoke him⁺ to anger (9:18–21) through the work of your hands (24:17–22)."³⁰Moses spoke in the ears of all the assembly of Israel the words of this song, until they were finished.

Hope **Moses** now reveals to all Israel the certain downfall that God revealed to him. Remarkably, he does not place that apostasy in some far future long after the glorious reigns of David and Solomon, but in the aftermath of his own **death** (cf. 31:16). The far future is in some sense happening now, in the hearts of his contemporaries. It is only the **evil** consequences that are postponed. Moses's apocalyptic foreshortening of time only intensifies our appreciation of the grace YHWH displays in being with Joshua as he enters the land (→31:19–23) while Israel is **turning aside**.

Faith As **Moses** teaches Israel his **song** as a witness, so Jesus has a final and similar lesson for his followers on the night he is betrayed (Mark 14:22–25). His ordinance keeps his story alive, and ready to remind us of our stubborn sin in the face of God's even more stubborn grace, and available so that through it we might recognize him when he appears (Luke 24:30–35).

Faith In Deuteronomy, **Torah** ("instruction") refers to the words of the covenant. Yet Moses has already written down those words and given them to the priests and elders (31:9). The duplicate account shows scripture's multiple roles in the life of God's **stiff-necked** chosen people. It teaches generations to "learn to revere YHWH" (31:12–13). But it also **witnesses against** their **rebellious** hearts and lives. This complex role of justifying and accusing somewhat resembles Calvin's doctrine of the three uses of the law: goad to civil righteousness, tutor driving us to Christ, and rule of life. Duplication also allows the **song** to be folded into the Torah's corpus along with Moses's narrative preamble, the Decalogue, the statutes, and the blessings and curses. It is as if Moses calls Israel back the same day to repeat and expand all he has already said. Jesus does the same on the night he is betrayed when he tells the disciples, "Rise, let us be on our way" (John 14:31 NRSV), then teaches and prays for three more chapters. It is not sloppy editing on the evangelist's part, but an intensifier that sets Jesus's last words along "the way" of his people's undoing and remaking. Like John 15–17's warning, call, and promise, Moses's song of Israel's destruction and renewal is not a postscript (as Deut. 33's blessings and Deut. 34's tag are), but the punch line at the **end** of the **covenant**.

Faith If **Moses's** living presence is what has been holding Israel's **corruption** in check—already a reasonable inference from what happens while he is away on Sinai (but →9:12–14)—then what **rebellious** humanity really needs is not just a **Torah** or a **song** but a prophet like Moses (18:15–19) who somehow never **dies** and never leaves. Israel receives just this in the gift of the Holy Spirit of the risen and ascended Son. The Spirit's indwelling sets aside Deuteronomy's warnings of separation's consequences insofar as we remain in perpetual contact with the prophet like Moses, while the warnings stand as revelations of who we are apart from that gracious presence.

Love The people of God walk into the land under a death sentence of their own making. The sin in the stubborn hearts of **Moses's** audience (to which →29:10–15 adds future generations), soon realized in **the work of their hands**, is what will destroy Israel in the **end**. Every new act of rebellion begets its own trajectory of self-destruction for future generations to inherit (→5:8–10). The fellowship of saints is thus a fellowship of suffering others' transgressions. Yet every new act of righteousness begets *its* own trajectory of new creation as YHWH blesses love to the thousandth generation (→5:8–10), making his+ fellowship of suffering also a fellowship of healing. "The judgment following one trespass brought condemnation, but the free gift following many trespasses brings justification" (Rom. 5:16 NRSV).

DEUTERONOMY 32

32:1 Give ear, you heavens, and I will speak.
　　Let the earth hear the words of my mouth.
2My doctrine shall drop as the rain.
　　My speech shall condense as the dew,
as the small rain on the tender grass,
　　as the showers on the herb.
3For I will proclaim the name of YHWH.
　　Ascribe greatness to our God!

Faith Canaan's topography makes the **heavens** the only reliable source of water for agriculture (→11:8–15), and YHWH is the only reliable rainmaker (→11:16–21). Moses's teaching is not only *like* water in giving life, it is like Canaan's **rain** in being the only source of life. Indeed, the figural water of Moses's words is the covenant he has collected from heaven, by which Israel believes and so receives the literal water that grows its produce. And in worshiping Baal, the Canaanite lord of rain, apostate Israel will ditch it all to chase after a mirage.

Hope Moses's audience is universal creation—not only **heaven** and **earth** but all their hosts (Gen. 2:1; Ps. 33:6). This familiar image (→4:25–26) is appropriate for introducing a song of universal and ultimate import (→32:40–43). For many years Moses's good news will go unappreciated by some of its own preachers (Rom. 10:18) even as its reach extends to the heavenly places and all nations.

Hope The cycle of rain imagery, from **rain** to **dew** to **small rain** to **showers**, foreshadows the saga of Moses's influence on Israel. In Egypt, on Sinai, and now on Moab, Moses's communications have been copious and penetrating. But that stage has now ended, and by turning aside from Moses's Torah Israel will soon be suffering from doctrinal drought and theological famine. His legacy will appear to be lost. Yet invisible remnants will survive in Israel (1 Kgs. 19:18) that gradually **condense** on its conscience into perceptibility. As a *bat qol*, a "still small voice" (19:12 RSV), God's powerful word is easy to overlook or ignore, but it gradually increases to nurture the tender growth of faithfulness in the prophets of exile and return, and then bursts anew from the clouds of **heaven** as the people finally recognize YHWH in their words of renewal, remember the Torah, restructure their lives according to it, and await the pouring out of God's own living water on all flesh (Joel 2:28–32 in Acts 2).

Love The **naming** of God's greatness is the burden of Moses's song; YHWH's worthiness is Moses's grand lesson for Israel. Every turning aside represents a new failure for us to **ascribe greatness** to the God of Israel. We take God's majesty as partial, imaginary, past, distant, irrelevant, or malicious—thus defining his[+] greatness in some way other than the specific shape of his[+] disciplining mercy—and then we suffer the curses of not having taken this lesson to heart. Biblical worship is thus the lifeblood of the living church.

> [32:4]The Rock, his[+] work is perfect,
>> for all his[+] ways are justice:
> a God of faithfulness and without iniquity,
>> just and right is he[+].
> [5]He[+] ravaged, for him, not, his[+] children, their blemish.
>> They are a perverse and crooked generation.
> [6]Do you treat YHWH so,
>> foolish people and unwise?
> Is he[+] not your father who has bought you?
>> He[+] has made you, and established you.

Plain The meaning of 32:5a is perplexing. Even the referent of **not** is uncertain. Such incoherence in the heart of a song's thesis would be more frustrating if the sense of the immediate context and the whole song were not so clear. In this line the song's major themes are all present, lacking only intelligibility. Robert Alter offers an especially attractive guess: "Did he act ruinously? No, his sons' the fault" (2004: 1039).

Hope These verses state the song's thesis. It may be framed as a "prophetic lawsuit"; Israel would then be the defendant and the heavens and earth a jury. Like the director's commentary on a film, it offers an authoritative perspective back onto events with which the audience is already assumed to be familiar. In its absence, Israel's tragic future will be interpreted self-servingly by the parties involved: Israel will indulge in victimization, trusting the accursed and overlooking or impugning God. Israel's enemies will indulge in triumphalism, trusting in power and glory and vilifying the weak. Onlookers will fail to appreciate the conflict's relevance to them (→32:26–31), maintaining neutrality. These continue to be predominant responses to conflict in our culture. That our habits would cause us to miss the significance of Israel's story reveals our depravity and shows the lasting necessity for God to make known the truth. Later apocalyptic, including Revelation's account of the battle between the beast and the Lamb, has the same functions.

Faith We know the existential satisfaction of being vindicated of others' slander. But YHWH's purpose here is redemption, not self-satisfaction. As the plaintiff as it were, YHWH's thesis is positive as well as negative. Israel's future course confirms the **perfect ways** that Moses already announced and Jesus will define: YHWH disciplines Israel as a father his son (→8:1–5), bringing us in the Spirit to the Son's perfection.

Love Christians tempted to triumphalism, victim-glorification, and neutrality can recall that Jesus takes up YHWH's old case on his own behalf in calling his own disciples a "faithless and perverse generation" when a demon intimidates them (Matt. 17:17 NRSV; cf. Deut. 32:17). In Christ, both Israel's saga and our **Rock's** saga were *and remain* ours.

> **32:7**Remember the days of old.
>   Consider the years of many generations.
> Ask your father⁺, and he⁺ will show you;
>   your elders, and they will tell you.
> **8**When the Most High gave to the nations their assignment,
>   when he⁺ separated the sons of Adam,
> he⁺ set the bounds of the peoples
>   according to the number of the gods.
> **9**For YHWH's portion is his⁺ people.
>   Jacob is the lot of his⁺ inheritance.

Faith The Masoretic Text reads "the sons⁺ of Israel" instead of, with the Septuagint and Qumran, "the sons⁺ of the gods." The latter is probably more original (Job 1–2; Sir. 17:17) and better fits the storyline. God has achieved supremacy on behalf of his⁺ people against the opposing powers of the peoples (→32:26–31; →32:36–39). God accomplishes this by consigning humanity to our own refusal to acknowledge and serve him⁺ (Rom. 1:20–25), so that human beings *are* numbered by the false gods we construct. The gods are real powers in this sense (cf. Ps. 82)—strongholds of rejection. Salvation-history is YHWH's victory over the powers, conceived through **Jacob's** election as **YHWH's portion** and realized once and for all in Christ. "There are many gods and many lords—but among us one God, the Father, from whom are all things and for whom we exist, and one Lord, Jesus Christ, through whom are all things and through whom we exist" (1 Cor. 8:5–6, my translation). "Sons⁺ of Israel" takes a shortcut to the song's outcome (32:39).

Hope El Elyon, **the Most High**, is the old Canaanite name for the high god above all gods (Gen. 14:18). The name's use here is sometimes read as a sign of the song's antiquity. Regardless of its age, it fits the narrative: God's boast about a rebellious nation won back over from impotent rivals. YHWH is no regional or **national** deity but great beyond Canaan (Mal. 1:5). The song's testimony of the ascension of the God of Israel to absolute supremacy over all others (Isa. 45:20–25 in

Phil. 2:5–11) can terrify those who do not appreciate its substance, which is the rescue of all **the peoples** through God's self-sacrifice in the Lamb (Rev. 5:6–14; →32:32–35), but it inspires joy in those who do (→32:40–43).

Love The evidence of **the days of old** lingers in the far reaches of our memories, repressible but not erasable (→31:19–23). The **elders** are those most likely to remember (→8:11–14a; 2 John 1–6). Moses is the elder par excellence. When wondering about the significance of their encounters with Jesus, the apostles "inquire . . . of bygone generations" (Job 8:8–10 NRSV) by reviewing the scriptures (e.g., John 2:17). Their new scriptures are the key for *our* consideration of the Spirit's moves then and ever since. Elders and parents in the church have the experience and bear the responsibility of mediating the **many generations** to the Father's youngest children, so they do not act in their predecessors' ignorance (Titus 1:5–9).

> **32:10**He⁺ found him in a desert land,
>> in the waste howling wilderness.
> He⁺ surrounded him; he⁺ cared for him.
>> He⁺ kept him as the apple of his⁺ eye.
> **11**As an eagle that stirs up her nest,
>> that flutters over her young,
> he⁺ spread abroad his⁺ wings, he⁺ took them,
>> he⁺ bore them on his feathers.
> **12**YHWH alone led him.
>> There was no foreign god with him.
> **13**He⁺ made him ride on the high places of the earth.
>> He ate the increase of the field.
> He⁺ caused him to suck honey out of the rock,
>> oil out of the flinty rock;
> **14**butter of the herd, and milk of the flock,
>> with fat of lambs,
> rams of the breed of Bashan, and goats,
>> with the fat of the kernels of the wheat.
>> Of the blood of the grape you drank wine.

Faith That YHWH **found** Jacob in the **wilderness** suggests a new beginning, perhaps after the golden calf or Kadesh-barnea, on the way into Canaan. It may also recall others: the days of creation; God's postlapsarian grace on Eden's exiles leading to the choice and blessing of Abraham, Isaac, and Jacob; the rescue of abandoned Joseph and the sheltering of his brothers' families in Egypt for Jacob's sake; and YHWH's retrieval of Israel, starting with Moses on the run in Midian, back into Egypt to lead his⁺ people out of it and into the promised land. Beyond the books of Moses it resembles the return of exiled and then Diaspora

Israel—and especially the baptism, wilderness temptations, and powerful early ministry of Jesus, as well as the Spirit-baptism and prosperity of the church in the early chapters of Acts. Jesus's parable of the lost sheep (Matt. 18:10–14) plays out over and over in every new mercy on the wanderer.

Hope This passage moves from gracious rescue in the midst of death (32:10a), to loving nurture in safety (32:10b–11), to miraculous support through lifeless things (32:13), to abundant life through sacrificial life (32:14). At the center of this resurrection is **YHWH alone** (32:12). The progression resembles Paul's account of the world's maturation through promises in infancy (Gal. 3:15–18), ruling principles (*stoicheia*; 3:19–4:3) in childhood, adulthood through adoption into the risen Christ (4:4–31), to the full life of the Spirit (5:1–26)—all for "the Israel of God" through Christ alone (2:15–21; 6:2, 14–16). "You know no God but me, and besides me there is no savior" (Hos. 13:4).

Love All the costly blessings of **honey, oil, butter, milk, fat,** and **blood** (→8:6–10) are lavished on Israel by its sacrificial Father, who spared not even his[+] only Son (Rom. 8:32). The song's jarring sudden use of **you** reminds all later audiences that we are among YHWH's beneficiaries. If Israel's settled generations had appreciated and understood these chapters of their history—if they had really learned to see hermeneutically through this song and never forgotten—then they would not have gone wrong later. We need the same doxological training, lest ingratitude and forgetfulness cost us the love the church had at first (Rev. 2:4). As that Son signifies the Father's new generosity by eating and drinking, so the church appropriately celebrates his sacrifice with feasting (→16:13–15).

> [32:15]But Jeshurun grew fat, and kicked.
> You (→32:10–14) have grown fat.
> You have grown thick.
> You have become thickheaded.
> Then he forsook God who made him,
> and lightly esteemed the Rock of his salvation.
> [16]They moved him[+] to jealousy (→4:21–24) with strange gods.
> They provoked him[+] to anger with abominations (→7:25–26).
> [17]They sacrificed to spirits, nongods,
> to gods that they did not know,
> to new gods that came up recently,
> whom your fathers did not dread.
> [18]Of the Rock who begot you, you are unmindful,
> and have forgotten God who gave you birth.

Faith Now God's blessings meet resistance, and this story of mercy takes the familiar, awful turn of all its types and antitypes (→32:10–14). Sometimes the resistance is external, in the hearts of those it intends to help indirectly—as in the persecutions of Joseph's brothers, Pharaoh, Jesus's opponents, and the church's enemies. Here it is internal, in the **forsaking** hearts of direct beneficiaries. Grace's ultimate opponent is common to both: the powers of sin, death, and the devil.

Faith Creation and redemption—two possible referents of the multivalent narrative of →32:10–14—are here unified through parallelism. They are discrete aspects of one grand economy. Much supposedly ecumenical theology forgets this. A healthy "theology of creation" is not more inclusive, pluralist, or non-sectarian than a healthy "theology of redemption"; creation is the foundation of redemption, redemption the perfection of creation, YHWH the triune creator and triune redeemer, Jesus Christ the firstborn over all creation and firstborn from the dead (Col. 1:15, 18).

Faith Both the use of **Jeshurun** ("upright") (cf. 33:5; →33:26–29), a term of affectionate pride (Isa. 44:2), and the move from paternal (Deut. 32:6) to maternal imagery intensify the sense of betrayal and insult. Ignoring and forgetting a mother is a heartbreaking dishonor (→5:16). These devices also imply an even deeper loss of consciousness of self. Israel is not just orphaning itself from its source; in abandoning its ancestry it is unjustifying itself, estranging itself, forgetting itself, caving into its concupiscent appetites, losing its soul. Its idolatry is the outward manifestation of its inward self-destruction.

Hope For landed Israel to pursue a different future with **new gods** when its present is so blessed (→32:10–14) is absurd. It can be made to seem reasonable only by reinventing the past—by renarrating present circumstances and ignoring the elders who know otherwise. While God is away, the serpent tempts the first humans in Eden to renarrate God's abundance as scarcity (Gen. 3:1) and pursue the one future forbidden to them (→4:16–20), bringing greater scarcity than they could imagine (Gen. 3:17–19). Israel's nonsensical move to idolatry will yield the same harvest of dust (Deut. 32:22). Drawing on the prophets' images of that failure, Jesus describes the institutions of unbelieving Israel of his day—and his own irresponsible disciples after his ascension—as a fruitless vineyard, a barren fig tree, a nonperforming investor, and drunken and abusive stewards. Idols are not involved, but the foolishness, the breach of trust, the psychological denial, and the consequences are the same.

Love Identifying demonic **spirits** with **nongods** as well as unknown and **new gods** poetically juxtaposes the insubstantial and substantial aspects of evil. (So do ethical dilemmas concerning meat offered to idols [1 Cor. 8] and apocalyptic prophecies of the terrifying rise and amazing dissolution of powers that stand against God's agents [Dan. 7].) It also poses God's solution to their problem. Evil's strange apparitions, like the demons of the Gospels and the present day, are fearsome only insofar as we defer to them. *We* who bear God's image hold the power they crave. They have no real power but what they trick us into handing over. As we grant it, they become real and powerful, dominating and abusing us and further consolidating their rule. The natural power of God disarms them (Col. 2:13–15) and exposes their bluster as a smokescreen hiding wretched, cowering nobodies

(→32:36–39). For Israel to fall for their lies after meeting YHWH in Egypt and on Sinai is inexcusable, let alone for Christians to do so after witnessing the power of the cross and the resurrection on top of all that had come before.

> **32:19**YHWH saw and detested
>> the aggravation of his[+] sons and his[+] daughters.
> **20**He[+] said: I will hide my face from them.
>> I will see what their end shall be;
> for a mixed-up generation they are,
>> children with no faith in them.
> **21**They have made me jealous with a nongod.
>> They have angered me with their vanities.
> I will make them jealous with a nonpeople.
>> I will make them angry with a foolish nation.

Faith These verses are the key to interpreting God's actions in the rest of the song. God's initial reaction (32:20) seems distanced, **hiding** and peeking as faithless Israel reaps what it has sowed. However, it immediately develops into an active campaign to punish Israel (32:21) and ultimately right the wrong. It is as if Israel has multiple relationships with God, so that withdrawing God's protective presence exposes Israel to a different, disciplining divine presence. Lutheranism develops this relational complexity into its dialectical *simul iustus et peccator*, Calvinism into its distinction between God's passive and active reprobation, Wesleyanism into distinctions of grace, Barth into the Father's dual election of Jesus Christ, and so on. Pauline eschatology does not quite fit into any of these systems because it better retains this passage's subtle narrative shape. The *deus absconditus* of 32:20, unpacked in the account of God's furious withdrawal before his[+] own energized foreign armies in →32:22–25, becomes the *deus revelatus* of 32:21, unpacked in God's enlightenment of those confused nations in →32:26–30. The cycle destroys all unbelief, ushering in all faith (Rom. 10:4).

Hope What is going on when Israel embraces new gods that turn out to be **nongods** (→32:15–18) and **vanities** (Eccl. 1:2; 12:8)? Moderns know the pattern well: a new era is declared in which the old rules no longer apply. Perhaps the Enlightenment has supplanted the Dark Ages. Perhaps a republican *novus ordo seclorum* in America has ended the reign of kings. Perhaps socialist utopias abolish the satanic mills of industrial capitalism. Perhaps the sixties have liberated young people from the oppressive mores of squares over thirty. Or perhaps a new economy dispels the old rules that asset prices ought to reflect actual earnings. In any event, this shift soon leads to a mania whose internal momentum seems for a time to vindicate the prophets of change. The old is denigrated and abandoned and the innovation is vested with godlike revolutionary power. Sometimes the change lasts—because there was real substance to the forces that led to it. But when the manic energy outruns the underlying substance, or when euphoria is all there was to begin with, the powers falter and the unsustainable revolution collapses back on itself in a panic. "Consider the work of God; who can make straight what he⁺ has made crooked?" (Eccl. 7:13 NRSV).

Love YHWH will go on to describe his⁺ people's destruction (→32:22–25) in terms reminiscent of the covenant's curses. But how can that treatment **make them angry** with **jealousy**? It cannot—so the succeeding passage does not merely amplify this one. Israel's men and women have provoked their father (→32:4–6) by preferring nonentities. The poetic justice here must take the analogous form of God turning to nobodies with the grace earlier shown to his⁺ **children**. In the Gentiles' embrace of Jesus, the Apostle Paul perceives the fruit of this divine vengeance on Israel's obstinacy (32:21 in Rom. 10:19). The weapons of God's recompense are the nations' tears of joy and tongues of praise (11:11). When grace's beneficiaries turn the love of their Rock into the love of nothing, the Rock turns their love back to him⁺ (11:12) through the love of others. The song's prophecy of destruction comes to fruition then in the persecuted church (11:25–26). This of course honors the objective from the beginning—to make many nations through Abraham (Gen. 17:5 in Rom. 4:16–17).

> ³²:²²For a fire is kindled in my anger,
>> burns to the lowest Sheol,
> devours the earth with its increase,
>> and sets the foundations of the mountains on fire.
> ²³I will heap evils on them.
>> I will spend my arrows on them.
> ²⁴They shall be wasted with hunger, and devoured with burning heat
>> and bitter destruction.
> I will send the teeth of animals on them,
>> with the poison of crawling things of the dust.
> ²⁵Outside the sword shall bereave,
>> and in the rooms, terror;
> on both young man and virgin,
>> the nursing infant with the gray-haired man.

Faith Suffering believers often say or hear that God is punishing them (Job 5:17; John 9:2; Jas. 1:12–16). Passages such as this seem to support such claims. When Israel's armies presumptuously went up against the Amorites in God's absence (Deut. 1:43–45), they were routed. The judgment was God's, but the means of judgment were natural. After worse offenses, the natural **evils** that have always surrounded Israel—fickle weather, wild animals (Ps. 22:20–21), and foreign powers—now become YHWH's own weapons of discipline (Deut. 28:49–52). Having acted like Canaanites, God's children are now treated as Canaanites. These threats are only continuing to do what they always do; but now they do it to a newly exposed people. In Deuteronomy's view that makes them agents of wrath, like the forces that wiped out the Horites and Avvim in Canaan (→2:16–23). Setting the connection between suffering and punishment in the heart of Israel's folk wisdom (→31:19–23) keeps that conviction alive in an era when there is no other way to penetrate Israel's confused conscience. If Job's friends, Jesus's opponents, and James's readers—and many counterparts in today's churches—are wrong to identify suffering directly and uncritically with sin, we can be too quick to dismiss any connection equally uncritically, along with the transforming discipline suffering might train us to seek.

Hope God promises seven wrathful plagues (→28:20–26) on his⁺ sons and daughters (→32:19–21). Does family betrayal justify familial violence? It has seemed so in many cultures even to this day—and the Torah does command the civil stoning of a stubborn and disobedient son (→21:15–21). Many instinctively draw back from identifying with this reaction, mindful of the child abuse, spousal abuse, and even honor killings it seems to imply. However, this passage fits none of these categories. First, the Pentateuch characterizes God's treatment of sinners outside the covenant no less violently (Gen. 6:7; Exod. 12:29–30; Deut. 2:20–23). The Pentateuch's overall picture (excepting perhaps the patriarchs) is one of divine and covenantal impartiality (→1:15–17a; →29:16–21), neither singling out family for special punishment nor sparing them. Second, this chapter's familial language is not the *basis* for punishment but only highlights the depth of Israel's betrayal. Third, a just action cannot be abusive, and abuse cannot be just. Careless use of our culture's terminology can prejudice our biblical interpretation. Finally, God does not suddenly become a **devouring fire** in a flash of anger, as many detractors and popular interpreters suppose; that would make sin, judgment, and salvation all functions of an anthropomorphic divine psychology. Fire—Holy Spirit—is who God has been all along (→4:21–24), and God persistently and uncompromisingly confronts unholiness, even to the last (Heb. 12:29; →10:12–16).

Love The natural afflictions in this passage do not spare the weak, strong, **young**, or old; the demographic spectrum of terrified mourners is comprehensive, stretching from society's strongest to its most defenseless. This proves that "no flesh will be justified in his sight" (Rom. 3:20, my translation). The thesis shocks our cultural sensibilities. We would at least spare **infants** the guilt of their generations until some age of accountability. But Deuteronomy does not know a dignity inherent to humanity that is only lost through deeds, let alone gained through them. Nor does it know a radical individualism that isolates every human being from every other. It knows only a *theologia crucis* (→28:7–14): the salvation of an abiding personal relationship with YHWH offered in a hostile and fallen world and mediated through the covenantal faith of a whole people—which is just what Jesus offers in sharing with us his one baptism for the forgiveness of sins.

32:26I said: I would scatter them afar.

I would erase their memory among men[+];

27did I not fear the provocation of the enemy,

lest their adversaries should judge wrongly,

lest they should say: "Our hand is exalted,

YHWH has not done all this."

28For they are a nation void of counsel.

There is no understanding in them.

29Oh that they were wise, that they understood this,

that they would consider their latter end!

30How could one chase a thousand,

and two put ten thousand to flight,

unless their Rock had sold them,

and YHWH had delivered them up?

31For their rock is not as our Rock;

our foes (cf. Isa. 1:24) are judgments.

Hope The story suddenly shifts from conventional curses on misbehavior to YHWH's perspective on the matter. Now we learn what Moses omits from his intercessory exchange on Sinai (→9:18–21): that God is sparing Israel to rescue his[+] reputation among Israel's enemy (Exod. 32:7–14). Restoration is not demanded by God's love or compassion (→28:58–63a), let alone Israel's or humanity's intrinsic worth, "but for the sake of my holy name, which you have profaned among the nations" (Ezek. 36:22–23 NRSV). Destroying the nation entrusted with YHWH's historical **memory** would expunge God's own reputation and give interpretive free rein for Israel's **adversaries** to glorify themselves and their nongods. Israel's apostasy leaves God in the spectacular dilemma of having to tolerate either one intolerable people or another. The only ways out are to annihilate all of them— hardly a reputation builder—or to make them both tolerable and gain universal glory in the **end** (→10:17–22). It is for the rescue of God, not just ourselves, that we pray when we ask that our Father's name be hallowed (Matt. 6:9).

Faith When does Israel ever fall to a foreign army that is orders of magnitude smaller? Biblical and intertestamental literature record no such defeat. The image is probably different: an Israel so weakened and intimidated that masses flee before only a few soldiers. For someone with the requisite memories or knowledge of the covenant (cf. Lev. 26:8), this reversal of Gideon's lopsided victory against the Midianites (Judg. 7:19–23) suggests just how far Israel has wandered from its old protector. If "**one** of you puts to flight **a thousand**, since it is [YHWH] your God who fights for you" (Josh. 23:10 NRSV), then such a dramatic turnaround implies that YHWH is fighting *against* Israel (Isa. 30:17). However, this is not something the enemy's pagan logic can perceive. Polytheism sees not power withdrawn, but weakness overpowered—an inferior force overcome by some superior force, presumably the victor's deities. God's own judgment will be taken (as it often is!) as a warrant for blasphemy. YHWH will have to change course yet again (30:18–26) to prove that the Rock of Israel is not like these other lesser powers (→32:39).

Plain The last line is obscure, but the literal translation offered here plausibly fits the context of condemnation of the enemy's boasts. Confused Israel's hostilities toward its confused conqueror not only represent YHWH's judgments on Israel but also portend judgments on the conqueror. This is a familiar theme in the Old Testament that is picked up in the New: "Why do the nations conspire, and the peoples plot in vain?" (Ps. 2:1 NRSV).

Faith The true resolution of Deuteronomy's eschatology thus comes into view: God will end Israel's scattering in a way that corrects both Israel's confusion and that of its oppressors. This will happen not with destructive weaponry but with the gift of counsel. "The Spirit of [YHWH] shall rest on him, the spirit of **wisdom** and **understanding**, the spirit of **counsel** and might, the spirit of knowledge and the fear of [YHWH]" (Isa. 11:2 NRSV). The anointed heir of YHWH's memory will bring these **enemies** to agree that YHWH alone is **exalted**. "You are worthy . . . for you were slaughtered and by your blood you ransomed for God saints from every tribe and language and people and nation" (Rev. 5:9 NRSV).

Love Undiscerning Israel, spared for the sake of its own judge, will carry God's truthfulness until discernment dawns. While Christian communities have been quick to discount and even excommunicate other Christian communities—and often for compelling reasons!—generations later it has usually turned out that God has not abandoned the abandoned after all. Keeping dead churches and heretical splinter groups around as unlikely resources of the Spirit's renewal may be one of the more surprising ways God sanctifies his[+] name over and against all rivals.

> 32:32For their vine is of the vine of Sodom,
>   of the fields of Gomorrah.
> Their grapes are grapes of gall,
>   their clusters are bitter.
> 33Their wine is the poison of serpents,
>   the ruthless venom of asps.
> 34Is it not laid up in store with me,
>   sealed up among my storerooms?
> 35Vengeance is mine, and recompense,
>   at the time when their foot slips (cf. Ps. 121:1–4),
> for the day of their calamity is at hand.
>   The things stored up for them shall hasten.

Hope "Take from my hand this cup of the wine of wrath, and make all the nations to whom I send you drink it," YHWH tells Jeremiah (Jer. 25:15 NRSV). The enemy's deadly **wine** is the cup of God's judgment (Jer. 25:15–16; Ezek. 23:31–34), which now passes from Israel to the nation with which God has punished it. If God has not spared his[+] own people from condemnation, surely God will not spare others (Jer. 25:29). The image of Lot's fruitful plain (Gen. 13:10–12) ruined along with Sodom and Gomorrah (19:24–25) foretells the end of the idolaters' arrogance: they will not hold the lush land promised to Israel (Deut. 32:13–14) but will gain only fire and brimstone. This is the treasure from the master's **store-rooms** that the Messiah's prophetic scribes bring (Matt. 13:52): the awful, good news of a heavenly kingdom **at hand** (4:17) that harvests the righteous and will cast the evil into the fiery furnace (13:47–50).

Faith Astonishingly, the Messiah receives this very cup from his Father and drinks it (Matt. 26:27–29, 39). The Son of God does not remain above the fray but enters into it—and not only as David's successor (Rom. 1:3) or Jacob's (9:4–5), but Abraham's (4:19–25) and Adam's (5:12–21). "The kingdom suffers violence" (Matt. 11:12, my translation) as Jesus absorbs the punishment of a confused alien nation on his own confused nation's zealotry, condemning both and winning a new start for all. His entry into the barren lands of fallen peoples proves to be the greatest **calamity** for the powers he **ruthlessly** casts out (4:10–11; 8:16; 24:7, 29–30). It accomplishes God's sweetest **vengeance** on evil: overcoming it with good (Rom. 8:37–39; Deut. 32:35 in Rom. 12:14–21).

Love The present form of this destruction of nations is the church. It blesses, passes, and drinks Jesus's cup, sharing in his blood (1 Cor. 10:16). We bear YHWH's **recompense**—in the uncompromising word of the kingdom's apostles and prophets, in the baptism of death and resurrection that we offer God's enemies, in the broken flesh and spilled blood of Christ that we eat and drink in order to pass with him from death to eternal life (John 6:53–58), and in every other act by which we receive and give the wrathful grace of the God of Israel. The church also looks rather like arrogant Israel and its arrogant enemies (cf. Rom. 12:16). It often abuses what worldly power it has and strives for more (cf. 13:1–2), curses its persecutors (cf. 12:14), jockeys for social status and claims wisdom that it lacks (12:16), and repays evil for evil (12:17). In these failures it too bears the wrath of God—incurring the divine judgment of literal swords (13:2–4) as **galling** divine judgment that helps renew its mind (12:2). The terrible renewal of the world described in the song of Moses is both the vocation and the chastising of the body of Christ.

> 32:36For YHWH will judge his[+] people,
>   and take satisfaction (Isa. 1:24) on his[+] servants,
> when he[+] sees that their power is gone,
>   no longer bound or loosed.
> 37He[+] will say: Where are their gods (Ps. 135:5),
>   the rock in which they took refuge;
> 38which ate the fat of their sacrifices,
>   and drank the wine of their drink offering?

Let them rise up and help you!
Let them be your protection.
[39]See now that I, even I, am he[+],
there is no god with me.
I kill, and I make alive.
I wound, and I heal.
There is no one who can deliver out of my hand.

Hope The pronouns **you** and **they** in 32:38 show that God still regards Israel's idols not as its own **gods** but as its enemies'. The nongods of nonpeoples do not belong to the people of this God (→32:15–18). So the undoing of Israel's abandonment of its befriending God cannot come in God's abandonment of Israel, but only in God's stark refusal to be abandoned—his[+] abandonment of our abandonment. Even in judgment, God will continue to have Israel as **his[+] people**. "We do not yet see everything in subjection to him[+]. But we see Jesus . . . crowned with glory and honor because of the suffering of death, so that without God he might taste death for everyone" (Heb. 2:9, my translation).

Faith The relentless use of the first-person singular in 32:39 resembles the dominance of God's first-person agency in eschatological prophecies such as Ezek. 36:22–28. Is Israel then inevitably cast in a supporting role? Surprisingly, no, for the story's messianic twist also places the first-person pronoun in the mouth of a Son of Man (Rev. 1:13) who is both subject and object of Deut. 32:39–40's supremacies: "Fear not, *I am* the first and the last, and the living one; *I* died, and behold *I am* the living one to the ages of ages, and *I* hold the keys of death and the grave" (Rev. 1:17–18, my translation). Jesus is both giver and receiver of death and life. He is both powerless and almighty, offering and offerer, healed and healer, wounded and wounder, delivered and deliverer, servant and Lord. The covenant's dialectics of judgment and mercy, death and life, dread and love, and subject and object all resolve in him (Isa. 45:21–24 in Phil. 2:9–11).

Love The first line is more ambiguous than many translations admit: God may be vindicating and having compassion, or God may be judging and avenging. (The Septuagint has God judging and being called on or comforted.) Retaining the ambiguity extends the tone of severity from the previous passages to the end of the song, while keeping alive the hint of mercy that begins in 32:26. Psalm 135:14 quotes Deut. 32:36a in a doxological context: God's supremacy over all gods and condemnation of idolatry are why Israel should rejoice. When the line retains its note of judgment rather than its conventional rendering, the whole psalm takes on the same sense of dread. Praise does not arise just out of loyalty and gratitude to a God who has looked after us (cf. Luke 7:47); praise arises also out of dread of a God who puts an end to our gods, our magic, and every other nonpower we cherish (cf. Acts 19:13–20). Much theology in the developed world's declining Christian traditions has labored to finesse the covenantal harshness of God, but the holy duality of divine mercy and divine strictness is basic to the narrative logic of this paradigmatic eschatological text, and the Christian churches growing in and from the southern hemisphere tend to appreciate its place in the apostolic faith. The fear of God is not immature, evil, or outmoded. Condemning it as emotional manipulation, shrugging it off as fundamentalism, or dismissing it as the relic of the Dark Ages turns the God of Israel into a god who does not exist—a nongod whose help is worthless and who is destined to fail and fade away—and turns the church that believes in that god into a **helpless, powerless**, vulnerable, useless thing. As this song is directed toward an Israel learning a bitter lesson that the nations' **gods** have provided no **refuge** or **protection**, and the psalm is directed toward an Israel that needs to remember that lesson forever, so both texts are for Christian communities who stand (→32:32–35) in the same positions.

Love The word for Israel's **power** is *yad*, which literally means "hand." Israel's paralyzed hand contrasts absolutely with the **hand** of YHWH, from which **no one can deliver**. Yet while Israel in humiliation is **no longer bound or loosed** (my translation of a difficult idiom; cf. 2 Kgs. 14:26), no longer good for either service or freedom but redundant, Christ's gift of binding and loosing (Matt. 16:19) restores usefulness for both through the authorized action of his apostles. The keys of the kingdom open up to us a new life of fruitfulness as God's free servant people.

> ^{32:40}For I lift up my hand to heaven,
>> and say: As I live forever (→32:36–39),
> ⁴¹if I whet my glittering sword,
>> my hand take hold on judgment,
> I will render vengeance to my adversaries,
>> and will recompense those who hate me.
> ⁴²I will make my arrows drunk with blood.
>> My sword shall devour flesh, with the blood of the slain and the captives,
>> from the head of the leaders of the enemy.
> ⁴³Heavens, rejoice with him⁺,
>> bow down before him⁺, all gods (Ps. 97:7b),
> O nations, rejoice with his⁺ people,
>> let all sons⁺ of God exult;
> for he⁺ will avenge the blood of his⁺ sons,⁺
>> and render vengeance to his⁺ adversaries,
> requite those who reject him⁺,
>> and will ransom his⁺ land his⁺ people.

Hope The climax of the song in 32:43 has notorious textual difficulties. The reconstruction here is not of some original text but a synthesis of the Septuagintal, proto-Masoretic, and Essene text traditions current in the first century. Each of these brings resolution to major themes of the song: heaven and earth (and all their hosts) as the song's audience called to ascribe greatness to God (32:1–3), God's fatherhood of Israel as his⁺ portion amid all the nations and their gods (32:4–9) and God's gift of abundant life in the land (32:10–14), Israel's (and its enemy's) unjust rejection of him⁺ (32:4–6, 15–18), and God's just requital (32:4–6) through a pagan enemy (32:19–21) and subsequent correction of the misconceptions of both Israel and the enemy (32:26–31). No one text tradition captures the whole—which may explain why competing traditions had arisen by the time of Messiah's advent. The mingling of images in this patchwork of original phrases, translations, euphemisms, and glosses reflects the involvement of every agent in this cosmic saga. "With all wisdom and insight he⁺ has made known to us the mystery of his⁺ will, according to his⁺ good pleasure that he⁺ set forth in Christ, as a plan for the fullness of time, to gather up all things in him, things in heaven and things on earth" (Eph. 1:8–10 NRSV).

Faith In our debates over canonicity, Protestants often champion critical texts that strive to reflect their original written forms, while Catholic and Orthodox traditionalists often champion the forms that have developed over centuries of Israel's and the church's life. One leads into an unrecoverable past, the other into an indeterminate future. Both of these stable opposites miss the most common dynamic in the New Testament's use of Old Testament texts: "Christ has become a servant of the circumcised on behalf of the truth of God in order that he might confirm the promises given to the patriarchs, and in order that the Gentiles might glorify God for his⁺ mercy. As it is written" (Rom. 15:8–9 NRSV). Jesus fulfills the scriptures as they *are* written—as they are when they encounter him in his concrete historicity—not as they once might have been or someday might be. Paul uses Deut. 32:43 Septuagint to appreciate the significance of the Gentiles' turn to Messiah in the face of Israel's—temporary—rejection (Rom. 15:10) because Jesus has fulfilled the Septuagintal Deut. 32:43. Indeed, Jesus has fulfilled the Septuagintal, Qumranic, *and* proto-Masoretic forms of 32:43: he announces his victory to the powers in the heavenly places (1 Tim. 3:16), godlike "sons of God" (1 Pet. 3:19 on Gen. 6:1–4; *1 Enoch* 9:10; 10:11–15), God's chosen (e.g., Abraham in John 8:56–58), and all nations (Matt. 24:14; 25:32; 28:19). Jesus does not simply meet a standard given in autographs, established by magisteria, or blundered into by meddling scribes. Nor do texts matter simply because they happen to map onto Jesus's earthly and heavenly career. Rather, the textual word and the incarnate Word truly interact, in the concrete inspired forms they have been taking in real historical space and time, the Son defining the canon and the canon defining the Son. This codeterminative space and time include the Word's preexistence and eternal life, so original forms and final forms of the texts still matter. Yet Christ *came* to fulfill the scriptures (Matt. 5:17, aorist tense), and *did* fulfill the scriptures in his audiences' hearing (Luke 4:21, perfect tense), so the historical scriptures of Jesus and the historical Jesus of the scriptures are forever central to one another's character.

Hope What God starts, God finishes. **If** in 32:41 can be understood conditionally, but it can also mean "when," "whenever," and even after an oath an emphatic negative—"I will not." In context, the word connotes God's determination to follow through in judgment. The song's ending fanfare does not eclipse the bloody, gory imagery of **vengeance** that so dominates the whole song; it follows from it. All the cosmos rejoices at the carnage. Can it be good to **rejoice** in **adversaries'** destruction? We do it all the time in society when an enemy's demise serves our sense of justice; but is it holy? Academic theology has increasingly abandoned these images as revolting and unworthy of God. Their place here in the heart of Deuteronomy proves that when we reject them, we are indulging in the old heresy of Marcionism, a form of gnosticism that arranges qualities in a hierarchy and excludes the "lower" ones from the high God's essence. In Deuteronomy these qualities belong to the High God himself[+], not some imaginary subordinate (→32:7–9). Yet even Deuteronomy glimpses only hints of how deep God's identification with vengeance really is. Faith is not an exercise in mass insensitivity to sufferers, because faith trusts the God who satisfies justice by taking on the **hatred**, **captivity**, and injury of heirs and enemies in his own **flesh** and **blood** (→32:32–35). The passion sets Jesus on all three sides of the dispute of this song: he is the Lord suffering on behalf of both treasonous Israel and conniving Rome. God's way of vengeance is the way of the cross. The song's rough justice is intuitive enough to survive in an Israelite remnant's faded memory and fallen conscience, but ambiguous enough to anticipate the surprising redemptive destruction that the rejected Messiah actually brings. So this text legitimately calls us to embrace God's costly joy (Luke 6:22–23) by first **rejoicing** with Elizabeth and Mary in the good news of the world's undoing (1:41–55), answering our hesitations with Zechariah's trust that through Christ's work "we, being rescued from the hands of our enemies, might serve him[+] without fear" (1:74 NRSV), and sharing Simeon's hope that Christ's surprising career will purify our consciences (2:34–35) of both the cheap hatred of enemies and the cheap grace of lenience. "The heavens and the earth, and all that is in them, shall shout for joy over Babylon; for the destroyers shall come against them out of the north, says [YHWH]. Babylon must fall for the slain of Israel, as the slain of all the earth have fallen because of Babylon" (Jer. 51:48–49 NRSV; →25:17–19).

Love The nominative first-person pronouns of 32:39–42 (→32:36–39) drive the possessives in 32:43. In love, in judgment, and in forgiveness God acts toward us for God's sake. The song resolves all tension between the two, for they are one in redemption's triune economy. "He[+] leads me in paths of righteousness for his[+] name's sake" (Ps. 23:3 RSV).

Love "Ransom his[+] land his[+] people" is ungrammatical Hebrew. Most translations render these awkward words "cleanse his[+] land of his[+] people," which would read slightly differently in Hebrew. It is a stretch, but an intriguing one, to consider the construction as an appositive: "God's land, God's people." Not only are these two appropriate aspects of God's one atoning ransom—to **ransom** the **land** apart from the **people** or vice versa would betray the patriarchal promises—but such a cleansing is a particularly sweet form of vengeance on God's enemies. Finally, it suggests the very ecclesiological identification that Jesus will make in describing his church as receiving Canaan's blessings in his new covenant (→11:8–15). God's purification of the holy land is God's purification of the holy church.

> ^{32:44}Moses came and spoke all the words of this song in the ears of the people, he and Joshua the son of Nun. ⁴⁵Moses made an end of speaking all these words to all Israel; ⁴⁶he said to them, "Set your heart (→6:6) to all the words I testify to you this day, which you shall command your children to do, all the words of this Torah. ⁴⁷For it is no vain thing from you; because it is your life, and through this word you shall prolong your days in the land you go over the Jordan to possess."

Faith After all these hours of exposition, after delivering tantalizing promises and blood-curdling curses, after outlining responsibilities in every realm that matters most to us, from the familial and personal to the liturgical, political, and economic—and all of this framed by Israel's stunning military victories and forty years of penitence for not having paid attention earlier—it seems inconceivable that Israel should treat **this Torah** from Sinai as a trifle! Yet the people soon turn aside from it and forget (cf. 5:32–33). More egregiously, in our day churches and theological schools train believers to treat **this word** as a plaything, as an irritant, as a tool of oppression, as too demanding and obscure, as irrelevant, as a mine for simplistic proof-texts, as obsolete, as an object of fascination but not commitment, and as a relic **from** a primitive and extinct culture. Jesus, by contrast, clings to Deuteronomy as his **lifeline** when he faces the devil's temptations in the wilderness (→6:13–16; →8:1–5).

Hope "Do this, and you will live" (Luke 10:28 NRSV). **Torah** as **life** means much more than just obeying rules in order to thrive. Moses's first address reviewed the past with a view toward the present; his second shifted to life in the contemporary present with a view toward the near future; his third prepared Israel to endure the near future in order to await the far future (→29:1). Life has gone from being a new start in Egypt to an immediate future in the land (4:1), to the extension of generations (4:9–10), to days of blessing (5:33), to a risk of loss (28:30, 66), to a choice (30:19), to a doom (32:25), and finally to an eternal gift (32:39, 43). To take this past, present, and future life to **heart**—not just the exhortations and conditionals that suggest a potentially bright future but the doomsaying of the song too, with all that it reveals about our character—is what it means to remain ourselves through the whole wrenching process of life, death, and resurrection. Israel's epic identity, from its primordial past to its sanctified future, is held within the consistency of Torah, which is the consistency of God's will to prosper it (Jer. 29:11–14).

Love "Do not despise [YHWH's] discipline or be weary of his⁺ reproof" (Prov. 3:11 NRSV). Deuteronomy has already narrated Moses's delivery of the song

(Deut. 31:22, 30) and the Torah (29:1; 31:1). Not only are Moses's words repetitive (→6:1–3), but the account of him repeating them is repetitive! Deuteronomy does not stake the covenant's future on rhetorical beauty, cleverness, logic, or existential relevance. It does adopt some of these strategies, of course; but it is not confident that the message's own truthfulness or esthetics will be enough to win it a persistent hearing in Israel. Indeed, **Joshua** the deliverer now joins **Moses** as teacher. Deuteronomy labors to inject the word of God into Israel's stubborn consciousness through sheer exposure. Then why does the whole Bible not drive itself into our heads in the same way? It may be that the softened consciences and heightened sensitivities that can receive more subtle messages are the fruit of Deuteronomy's rhetorical brute force (→29:2–9). What feels mind-numbing at the time turns out to have been mind-awakening. As children endure the repetition of parents, teachers, and elders and as new Christians endure the repetition of liturgical texts, Bible memory verses, and standard catechisms, so Moses's Torah tutors us in order to give us the capacity to learn.

> [32:48]YHWH spoke to Moses that same day, saying: [49]"Go up into this mountain of Abarim to Mount Nebo, which is in the land of Moab that is over against Jericho, and see the land of Canaan (→3:26–27), which I give to the sons[+] of Israel for a possession. [50]And die on the mountain where you go up and be gathered to your people, as Aaron your brother died on Mount Hor (cf. 10:6) and was gathered to his people; [51]because you trespassed against me in the midst of the sons[+] of Israel at the waters of Meribah of Kadesh, in the wilderness of Zin, because you did not sanctify me in the midst of the sons[+] of Israel. [52]For you shall see the land before you, but you shall not go there into the land I give the sons[+] of Israel."

Faith Moses implies in →1:37–38 that he is banned from entering the land because he shares responsibility for Israel's response to the spies' report. The current passage, like Num. 20:1–13, appeals to the incident, many years after Kadesh-barnea, of Moses striking the rock disrespectfully at **Zin**. It is possible to read Deut. 1:37 as a parenthetical insertion alluding to that future event in order to identify Moses with the generation from Egypt rather than the generation that inherits Canaan under Joshua. A more popular explanation takes the two accounts as simply reflecting two different traditions. Either strategy leaves readers of Deuteronomy in its canonical form with a similar interpretive question: what is the effect of having both 1:37 and 32:51, at nearly the bookends of Deuteronomy? There Moses is excluded for Israel's sake, amidst passages showing Israel's political vulnerability; here he is excluded for the sake of God's holiness, following a passage stressing the spiritual perversity of **Israel's** children. The first account highlights Israel's unreadiness to believe, the second the impossible standard of **sanctification**. The combination shows us two dimensions of authority, political and spiritual. Each is dependent on the other; success depends on both. The impossible, indispensable demands of both anticipate the "Joshua" to come: Jesus Christ, king of the Jews and high priest of the Father, sage of Israel's wisdom and prophet of the Spirit.

Faith **Moses** is to ascend by way of the **mountain of** the **Abarim**, a pun on "Hebrews" and a cognate of "beyond" (cf. 1:5), two bitter verbal reminders of what he is missing by having to stay on the mountain. Yet it is on a mountain not far away that Moses returns to greet the Messiah who will lead a new exodus (Luke 9:28–31)—an honor not bestowed on those Israelites who died natural deaths at home with their people. By accepting the unusual death commanded for him in this unusual place, Moses becomes a type and an encourager for the one who ascends the Mount of Olives to face his time of trial (22:39–40) and bring all Israel home with him.

Hope For God to exclude **Moses** from the land after more than forty years of constant service because of just one brief failure seems petty, insensitive, and even vindictive—a stumbling block for faith. At a deeper level, like many such stumbling blocks, it is a memorable sign of the character of God's kingdom. Admission into the land is neither the wages of a worthy life of service nor the casual gift of a prosperity gospel. To enter Canaan is a generation's vocation. Events show that Moses and his generation are simply not (or no longer, anyway) right for it. So the task falls to children as successors (→1:37–38). The pattern recurs here and there: **Aaron** to Eleazar (Num. 20:23–29), Eli to Samuel, Saul to David, Elijah to Elisha, John to Jesus (cf. Matt. 11:11–12), and Paul to Timothy. Succession implies no necessary disrespect on the one succeeded—only that God's servants are not interchangeable, so they may need to decrease and increase as their qualities and broader circumstances dictate. The saga of the song of Deut. 32 shows just how catastrophic it is for unready people to inherit a critical mission. "New wine must be put into fresh wineskins" (Luke 5:38 NRSV).

Love This brief passage stuffs additional locations into the sparer account in Num. 27:12–14, filling God's penultimate words to **Moses** (cf. Deut. 34:4) with memories and lost dreams of his years of service since Egypt—as well as the ancestral memories and burning dreams of his children in exile in every age. In an act of great and surely painful trust, Moses obeys YHWH and relinquishes his office and his dream (→34:5–7). Many servants of Christ ruin our career legacies by failing to do so when our time is up. We convince ourselves that we are indispensable to God, that we deserve rewards in this age as well as the next, that we can compensate for our faults, that we have been misunderstood. Moses stands as the patron saint of all who face these temptations. If he can stand aside as his kin prepare to enter their future of joy, betrayal, and death—separated with cruel irony from his kin in order to be **gathered** to generations who had not received what was promised (Heb. 11:39)—then surely we can stand aside in the assurance of Israel's risen and ascended Lord of lords (11:40–12:2).

DEUTERONOMY 33

³³:¹This is the blessing, with which Moses the man of God blessed the sons⁺ of Israel before his death. ²He said:

YHWH came from Sinai,
  and rose from Seir to them.
He⁺ shone forth from Mount Paran.
  He⁺ came from the ten thousands of holy ones
  from the south of the slope for him.
³Yes, he⁺ loves peoples.
  All his⁺ saints are in your hand.
They sat down at your feet;
  each receives your words.
⁴Moses commanded us a Torah,
  an inheritance for the assembly of Jacob.
⁵He was king in Jeshurun,
  when the heads of the people were gathered,
  all the tribes of Israel together.

Plain As do key texts in Deuteronomy (e.g., →26:1–11) and the book as a whole, these verses narrate a definitive future through the defined past. **Moses's** blessing on the tribes begins with a reminder of all they have **received**—which is nothing besides the covenantal promises, provisions, and traditions of **Torah**, Israel's title deed.

Faith In this briefest of retirements **Moses** does the last thing he can: he caps off his life like Jacob the patriarch (Gen. 49). The time is past for leadership, discipline, instruction, and even intercession. All this **man of God** has left is his relational *memory* of Israel's children and YHWH, his *will* to bless each through the other, and the *intellect* to embody all this as a powerful word of **blessing**. His last testament is an act of mediated creation.

Faith The places all lie in the region of Sinai or the Negev. *Riveboth kodesh* (**ten thousands of holy ones**) either figurally or literally describes heaven. The obscure phrase rendered **south of the slope** might refer to Pisgah (→3:12–17; 4:49). Identifying this event with the **Torah's** delivery and God's royal command of the tribes, as the next verses do, makes speaking the word a martial act. The rider's sword is also the church's sword (Eph. 6:17). Israel is a conquering army insofar as it arms itself with its king's words. The proud name **Jeshurun** recalls Israel's glory days (→32:15–18). They will return when YHWH comes again from heaven: "Then I saw heaven opened, and there was a white horse! Its rider is called Faithful and True, and in righteousness he judges and makes war. . . . From his mouth comes a sharp sword with which to strike down the nations" (Rev. 19:11, 15 NRSV).

Love A part of this passage, 33:4, has become a traditional Jewish catechetical text. Befitting a final **blessing** on a **gathering** of **tribes**, the thrust of Moses's benediction is intensely ecclesiological. The blessings that follow apply to some, but the consequences affect all. "To each is given the manifestation of the Spirit for the common good" (1 Cor. 12:7 NRSV). The common good is not the ultimate reason for the gifts, but reflects their healthy incorporation into the missional life of God. Entrusted with the **inheritance** of God's **words**, from Moses's **Torah** to Jesus's gospel, YHWH's **saints** from among all the world's **peoples** are **assembled** into the **king's** army and tasked with the king's mission. Conversely, as the schism of Israel fatally weakens **the sons+ of Israel** until they are reconstituted in exile, so failure in any sector of the church becomes a fatal vulnerability for the whole (11:30).

Hope For all their similarities with **Jacob's** blessings, **Moses's** blessings are much more positive. Jacob's reflect the lasting shock of a father who learned late in life (cf. Gen. 47:28) that almost all his heirs have been scoundrels. So his **blessings** are **words** of painful truth-telling. Moses has been confronted almost daily with the destructive habits that Israel inherited in four centuries of slavery, meditating long on blessings and curses delivered on Sinai and now facing the prophecy of his people's certain apostasy. Whereas Jacob's warnings counterbalance the unconditional patriarchal promises for his sons' tenuous future in Egypt, Moses's words are contrasting words of hope that counterbalance Deuteronomy's earlier curses and the song's disastrous future in and around Canaan. They reveal the passionate desires of Moses's heart, which contrast remarkably with Jacob's. Yet for all their differences, both of these old men bless their people out of faith in God's grace alone to carry them through the dark times ahead.

Hope All *whose* **saints** are in *whose* **hand**? These opening verses feature the shifts of subject and object that are common in Deuteronomy, but here they come with confusing swiftness. **Moses** speaks for Israel and then for God, to God and then to his audience, of a beloved people and of all **peoples**, sometimes within the same sentence. Here it is almost as if he were delivering charismatic words of knowledge, moving fluidly in and out of a prophetic consciousness as the Spirit's voice and Moses's voice indwell one another in perichoretic unity. It is an encouraging sequel to Deut. 32: the song's breach between God and Israel, haunted on both sides by the forsaken and crucified Messiah (→32:36–39; →33:8–11), is supplanted with unity. Israel's better future is life-giving fullness in the Spirit. "If while we were enemies we were reconciled to God by the death of his⁺ Son, much more, now that we are reconciled, shall we be saved by his life" (Rom. 5:10 RSV).

> ³³:⁶Let Reuben live, and not die;
> but let his men be few.

Hope "Many of the first shall be last" (Matt. 19:30, my translation). The tribe of **Reuben** is perilously exposed—across the Jordan, vulnerable, a firstborn pushed to Israel's margins (e.g., Judg. 5:15–16) and eventually overcome by Moab. In Genesis this owes to Reuben's sleeping with his father's concubine (Gen. 49:3–4 on 35:22), a theft that invites death (Deut. 22:22–30). Moses concedes Reuben's penalty in the second half of his brief blessing (which some translations hide by translating *vav* as "nor"), yet reaches beyond it in willing **life** for the tribe. Deuteronomy never underestimates the consequences of sin, but in hope it steadfastly refuses to grant them finality.

Love **Reuben's** low numbers really are a blessing if they represent a restraint on sin in Israel. Paul echoes Moses's dialectic of hopeful discipline on Reuben in his treatment of the Corinthian churchman who sleeps with his father's wife. His arrogant flesh is to be destroyed that his spirit might one day be saved (1 Cor. 5:5)—removed to east of the Jordan, as it were, but not consigned to outer darkness; quarantined in order to contain the contagion and someday eliminate it.

> ³³:⁷This is for Judah. He said:
> Hear, YHWH, the voice of Judah.
> Bring him in to his people.
> With his hands he contended for himself.
> You shall be a help against his adversaries.

Faith Jacob's word for **Judah** is glorious and remarkably messianic (Gen. 49:8–12). Moses's is more restrained and even plaintive, as if he senses this "lion's whelp" will feel forsaken and look more like a lamb slain; but it remains confident. Judah soon inherits Joshua's unfinished business, fighting the Canaanites on the nation's behalf (Judg. 1:1–20) in a challenge that grows over centuries to unmanageable proportions. However, Moses's confidence is vindicated. In every nation the Lion of Judah conquers alone (Rev. 5:5–9; cf. Gen. 49:9) and wins a kingdom of priests who conquer behind him (Rev. 5:10; cf. Gen. 49:8). Jesus the son of Judah (Heb. 7:14) "was heard because of his reverent submission . . . having been designated by God a high priest according to the order of Melchizedek" (5:7, 10 NRSV).

Hope Moses's blessing on **Judah** envisions an eschatological fusion of the covenant's curses and the song's tribulations on the one hand and the patriarchal promises and covenant's blessings on the other. God will bring Judah **in to his people** in a disastrous (cf. Jer. 25–28) and ultimately triumphant (cf. Jer. 29–31) campaign. The final restoring of Judah's and Jerusalem's fortunes (Joel 3:1; cf. 2:28–32 in Acts 2:16–21, 39) begins in Israel's restoration to the land (anticipated in Isa. 37:31–32; 44:26; 65:9), proceeds in the Son of Man's first advent (Matt. 16:13–17), and culminates in his last (24:30–31).

> **33:8**Of Levi he said:
> Your Thummim and your Urim are with your godly one,
> > whom you proved at Massah,
> > with whom you strove at the waters of Meribah;
> **9**who said of his father, and of his mother, "I have not seen him";
> > neither did he acknowledge his brothers,
> > nor did he know his own children:
> for they have observed your word,
> > and keep your covenant.
> **10**They shall teach Jacob your ordinances,
> > and Israel your Torah.
> They shall put incense before you,
> > and whole burnt offering on your altar.
> **11**YHWH, bless his substance.
> > Accept the work of his hands.
> Strike through the hips of those who rise up against him,
> > of those who hate him, that they not rise again.

Hope Jacob's blessing on **Levi** (Gen. 49:5–7) sounds more like a restraining order than a benediction. Yet his condemnation is a blessing after all, for the intervening centuries discipline Levi's passions. His children confine their violence to sacrificial liturgy (Deut. 12:15–19; 18:1–8), and they practice holy war armed only with the horn and the ark (31:25; Josh. 6:6–7). Where once Levi's blind loyalty to the family name had cost the family its peace (Gen. 34:25–31), his tribe's loyalty to YHWH above even their **brothers** and **children** has pacified God and proven them fit for service in the place of YHWH's choosing (Exod. 32:25–29). **They will teach** the **word** of God in Israel and herald the coming of a new family of those named not for kinship (Luke 1:59–63) but for obedience to the word they will hear (8:20–21).

Love Levi receives a blessing filled with allusions that puzzle Deuteronomy's later audiences. These may refer to lost traditions, for example, about some special Levitical role at **Massah** and **Meribah** (cf. Exod. 17:1–7) that inaugurates its priesthood. The Levite Asaph's Ps. 81 is a similar remembrance of YHWH's past faithfulness in Egypt, on and under Horeb, and at Meribah. Paul appeals to the same constellation in telling the Corinthians not to desire evil (1 Cor. 10:6) or provoke YHWH to jealousy (10:21–22) but to endure every test in faith (10:13).

We serve as priests, and because the righteousness that qualifies us to serve is not our possession, it will still conquer even when we fail it.

Faith The shifts in pronouns here (→33:1–5) set a peculiar distance between the **Levites** (**they** in 32:9b–10) and a godly one (**he** in 32:8b–9a and 32:11) before God (**you** throughout). The identity of the two is real but problematic. Levites, namely Moses and Aaron, are judged and disciplined at Massah (Num. 20:12). Moses strikes the rock, and Aaron shares his punishment for obscuring God's holiness—an egregious failure for a clan charged to manifest that holiness in Israel's midst. Their sin is the Levites' sin, and it still weighs on Moses's conscience. He does not understand himself or his tribe to be YHWH's **godly one**. Who then is he who is **proven** at Massah and **striven** against at Meribah? The only one vindicated at that place is the one standing on the rock (Exod. 17:6): the stricken Christ who followed Israel in the wilderness (1 Cor. 10:4). He is the Son whom the Holy Spirit leads into the same temptation to doubt God's providence, who there first exercises his appointed priestly office (Ps. 2:7, reverberating in Luke 4:9–11; cf. Heb. 5:5–10), and who remembers **Torah** and so defeats the enemy (Luke 4:12–13; →6:13–16). Jesus is the defenseless but faithful one **accepted** and delivered from his opponents into the Father's eternal security. Through trust in his **work** the Levites can become obedient and the tribe's priestly identity fully reconciled to itself: "A great many of the priests became obedient to the faith" (Acts 6:7 NRSV).

Love The priests rely on **Urim** and **Thummim** somehow to discern the will of God in dilemmas (1 Sam. 14:41). These belong to the **godly one** who discerns with the eyes of the Spirit (Isa. 11:2–4 in Rev. 5:6) who judges the world (John 16:8–11). He will bequeath his Urim and Thummim on his church by sending his Spirit and giving the Spirit's gifts of discernment (John 12–15; cf. 1 Cor. 12:4–11).

Hope Simeon is included in Jacob's blessing on **Levi** (Gen. 49:5) and not mentioned in this chapter's list—a beneficiary with all of **Israel**, we may hope, of Levi's blessing and intercession even though excluded from its Levitical office (Ezek. 48:24).

33:12Of Benjamin he said:
The beloved of YHWH shall dwell in safety by him+.
He+ covers him all the day long.
He dwells between his+ shoulders.
13Of Joseph he said:
His land is blessed by YHWH,
for the precious things of the heavens, for the dew,
for the deep that couches beneath,
14for the precious things of the fruits of the sun,
for the precious things of the growth of the moons (Gen. 37:9–10),
15for the chief things of the ancient mountains,
for the precious things of the everlasting hills,

¹⁶for the precious things of the earth and its fullness,
   the good will of him⁺ who lived in the bush.
Let this come on the head of Joseph,
   on the crown of the head of him who was separate from his brothers (Gen. 37:7–8).
¹⁷The firstborn of his herd, majesty is his.
   His horns are the horns of the wild ox.
   With them he shall push all of the peoples, to the ends of the
   earth:
They are the ten thousands of Ephraim.
They are the thousands of Manasseh.

Faith Rachel's two sons and Jacob's favorites are central figures in the story of the young family's deliverance in Egypt (Gen. 39–47). Jacob had held onto his **beloved Benjamin** during the brothers' original forage for food, "lest harm befall him" (42:4, my translation), and blessed his kidnapped son with a predator's liberty (49:27; cf. 37:33). Moses's blessing honors both wishes by setting Benjamin in a secure central location in Canaan in and under YHWH's midst. By the same fraternal love with which **Joseph** pulls Benjamin from his starving father's false security into the sustenance that God has prepared for them in Egypt (42:15–20), Andrew brings Simon to the Messiah with whom he is **dwelling** and to a rock-solid future **covered** by the Lamb of God (John 1:35–42).

Hope Moses's blessing on **Joseph** practically reproduces Jacob's (Gen. 49:22–26). Both recall the dreams of preeminence that alienated Joseph's **brothers**. Here Joseph even gains the striking image of the burning **bush** (Exod. 3:2) as a land indwelt by God for the sake of God's people. The homage all pay to Joseph in Egypt (Gen. 41:39–45, 57) is eternalized as a rich heritage in Canaan's fertile **hills** (Deut. 11:11; →32:1–3), in which Joseph becomes the preeminent tribe in the north. "There is no one who has left house or brothers or sisters or mother or father or children or fields, for my sake and for the sake of the good news, who will not receive a hundredfold now in this age—houses, brothers and sisters, mothers and children, and fields, with persecutions—and in the age to come eternal life" (Mark 10:29–30 NRSV).

Love Jacob adopts **Ephraim** and **Manasseh** as his own sons in Gen. 48:13–20, raising second-born Ephraim to prominence (→1:37–38) and making him multitudinous in the earth as "a fullness of nations." Ephraim and Manasseh are situated on either side of Shechem and Mounts Ebal and Gerizim (→11:26–32; →27:1–8; →27:11–14), a region that becomes Samaria. These people infamously assimilate Assyrian culture or are dispersed in exile (many Persian Jews claim Ephraimite ancestry). This reversal appears to frustrate Moses's promise, but in reality it echoes the drama of Joseph's own life. Fittingly, Persian Parthians are the first named Diaspora hearers of the apostles' preaching at Pentecost (Acts 2:9), and it is in Samaria that the gospel first crosses from ethnic Israel to the nations and ultimately **to the ends of the earth** (1:8; 8:4–8). In the Gospel of John this happens (4:39–42) when Jesus stops to rest at "a Samaritan city called Sychar, near the plot of ground that Jacob had given to his son **Joseph**" (4:5 NRSV; cf. Josh. 24:32). God grants Moses's wish for Joseph and his sons in the church catholic, "the fullness of him who fills all in all" (Eph. 1:23 NRSV). As Jacob's twelve sons rarely lived up to their obligations as their ancestors' descendants (even Joseph was a spoiled young tattletale), so the church has rarely lived up to its obligation to be Moses's blessing on Joseph, Israel's other tribes, and all the families of the earth. It is incumbent on the church not to be a curse on Israel or anyone else, but to be an honor to Joseph and a disciple of his way of reconciliation.

> **33:18**Of Zebulun he said:
> Rejoice, Zebulun, in your going out;
>> and Issachar, in your tents.
> **19**They shall call peoples to the mountain.
>> There they will offer sacrifices of righteousness,
> for they shall draw out the abundance of the seas,
>> the hidden treasures of the sand.

Hope A frustrated Leah regards **Issachar** as Jacob's "wages" to her for giving Rachel her aphrodisiac mandrakes (Gen. 30:14–18), but she considers **Zebulun** a "gift" (30:19–20). The gift outlasts the reimbursement: Zebulun remains a significant Israelite legacy, whereas Jacob destines Issachar to fade into obscurity (49:13–15). Matthew loads the story of Jesus's move to "Capernaum by the sea, in the territory of Zebulun and Naphtali" (Matt. 4:13 NRSV) with eschatological significance. His arrival fulfills Isa. 9:1–6's prophetic vision of Israel's emancipation through the gift of a son: "Land of Zebulun, land of Naphtali, on the road by the **sea**, across the Jordan, Galilee of the [**peoples**] **Gentiles**—the **people** who sat in darkness have seen a great light" (Matt. 4:14–16 NRSV, adapted). In Matthew's very next passage, walking by the sea, Jesus proves it: he enlists its fishermen to harvest people (4:18–22), then leads crowds from Galilee to Judea to beyond the Jordan (4:25) and even up a **mountain** (5:1) to call them to light the world (5:14) through a **sacrificial** pursuit of God's **righteousness** (5:6; 6:33). Returning to Capernaum, he brings joy to a centurion who comes **out** to meet him and to his servant confined at home (8:5–13). On another day at the seaside (13:1–2), with his parables of the field, the pearl, and the net (13:44–50), Jesus invites his followers to **draw out** the **hidden** but **abundant treasures** of his kingdom. These multiple echoes train us to appreciate Christ's advent as finally unlocking the promise in Moses's blessing to Zebulun. "They **rejoice** before you as with joy at the harvest" (Isa. 9:3 NRSV).

Love The pilgrims from these two tribes (as well as Ephraim and Manasseh) who participate in Hezekiah's Passover after the temple's restoration gain God's favor, even though they celebrate the festival unclean (2 Chr. 30:18). They **rejoice**

(30:25) that God imputes **righteousness** to their **sacrifices** because they have "set their hearts to seek God" (30:19–20 NRSV). The kingdom's trustee-beneficiaries gather from a motley assortment of tribes even less remarkable than these undistinguished Israelites, full of joy and grateful simply to be cleansed and justified by grace through faith (Matt. 8:1–4).

> ^{33:20}Of Gad he said:
> Blessed the enlarging of Gad.
>> He dwells as a lioness,
>> and tears the arm, yes, the crown of the head.
> ²¹He provided the first part for himself,
>> for there a ruler's allotment was
>> when the heads of the people gathered (cf. Septuagint).
> He executed the righteousness of YHWH,
>> his⁺ ordinances with Israel.
> ²²Of Dan he said:
> Dan is a lion's cub
>> that leaps out of Bashan.
> ²³Of Naphtali he said:
> Naphtali, satisfied with favor,
>> full of the blessing of YHWH,
>> possess the west and the south.
> ²⁴Of Asher he said:
> Asher is blessed with children.
>> Let him be acceptable to his brothers.
>> Let him dip his foot in oil.
> ²⁵Your bars shall be iron and bronze.
>> As your days, so your strength will be.

Plain If **Bashan** refers to **Dan's** general vicinity, rather than the place of the metaphorical **lion's** lair, then here Moses is blessing Dan's eventual **leap** of relocation (Josh. 19:47; Judg. 18). Bashan also recalls Og's defeat (Deut. 3:3–4; cf. Ps. 68).

Hope Eventually situated in fertile country west and south of the sea of Galilee, **Naphtali** enjoys a worldly comfort that reflects YHWH's **favor**. This goodness takes its place alongside the expanses of **righteous Gad**, the numbers of **acceptable Asher**, the prowess of **Dan** and many other **strong** tribes, and the various blessings of the others in a whole spectrum of temporal and eternal grace. Deuteronomy's grand vision is neither an indulgent worldliness nor an ascetic otherworldliness, but the difficult realization of a sustainable covenantal order through which all the nations and all Israel will perceive the glory, judgment, and hand of YHWH (Ezek. 39:21–40:4).

Love Some of the church's diversity is rarely celebrated. The last four names to be blessed are the handmaids' tribes. These children are pawns of two sisters' patriarchal rivalry. They are even named for the status they lend their mothers' jealous ladies (Gen. 30:1–13). These are inauspicious beginnings, and the tribes enjoy undistinguished legacies. All four stand on Mount Ebal for the curse (→27:11–14). Jacob's blessings on the two firstborn stress their aggression (Gen. 49:16–19), while he bestows a servant's blessing on each second-born son (49:20–21). It would be easy for these tribes to consign themselves to outsider status and internalize both the resentments of the women who used them against one another and the rejection of the father who never loved them as his own. But Moses tempers **Gad's** and **Dan's** aggression into strength with a measure of glory and deepens **Naphtali's** and **Asher's** servanthood into blessed prosperity. What the flesh had separated, the covenant has joined together and built into a considerable legacy in which all the tribes significantly contribute. As members of Israel, all twelve have been emancipated and brought into God's life-giving covenant, and all now receive YHWH's blessing. Favor is not just for the wives' sons or the few luminaries who would crowd out the rest in our winner-takes-all world. Now the present humiliation of the last-blessed does not earn or even justify solidarity or exaltation in the future, as Marx and his liberationist disciples have wished; as this chapter poignantly shows, that is not the way that either God's world or God's kingdom works. Yet, as the least in Israel-according-to-the-flesh (Rom. 9:3), these four tribes may better appreciate the kingdom's opportunity to become greatest in all of eschatological Israel (11:26; cf. Ezek. 48:32–34; Rev. 7:5–6) by taking on Christ's even more radical servanthood (Mark 9:33–37). The church's many Gentiles who cannot even boast in minimal tribal status can follow them and boast in our crucified Lord (Rom. 5:1–5, 11; cf. 3:27; 2:17–24; 11:17–18).

Faith **Asher** is the least of the least on Moses's list. In one of many lovely touches in Luke, it is Anna, a worshipful aged widow of Asher's tribe—least of the least of the least—who comes to the Christ **child** at his dedication and first shares the news of her distant cousin from Judah "to all who were looking for the redemption of Jerusalem" (Luke 2:38 NRSV).

> **33:26**There is none like the God of Jeshurun,
>   who rides on the heavens for your help,
>   and in his⁺ majesty on the clouds.
> **27**The eternal God is a dwelling place,
>   everlasting arms underneath.
> He⁺ thrust out the enemy from before you,
>   and said: "Destroy!"
> **28**Israel dwells in safety;
>   the fountain of Jacob alone,

in a land of grain and new wine.
>   Yes, his[+] heavens drop down dew.
[29]Blessed are you, Israel.
>   Who is like you (4:7), a people saved by YHWH,
>   the shield of your help,
>   the sword, your majesty?
>   Your enemies shall capitulate before you (Gen. 27:29).
>   You shall tread on their backs (Job 9:8).

Faith At the blessing's conclusion the metaphors mix and collide—**rider, dwelling place, arms, destroyer, shield, sword**—as Moses struggles to describe Jeshurun's indescribable God. Is this benefactor the same figure as the terrible judge of Deut. 28 or the jealous YHWH of Deut. 32? What conqueror is the very sanctuary he[+] guards? Following the curses' precise threats and the song's doomsaying, the finale of Moses's glowing benediction has an air of unreality. Is any god *at all* **like** this? Or is Israel's heavenly rescuer a fantasy like all of history's other faded deities? Generations have withered waiting for **Jeshurun's** God to ride to their rescue, and Deuteronomy's critical contemporary readers have often come to treat YHWH as a product of a culture's customs of wishful poetic imagination—a figure that has tragically failed to materialize in times of greatest need. In recent contemporary theology these metaphors have been segregated into two camps, sometimes characterized by gender. These characterizations rarely respect the complexity of Deuteronomy's whole picture. Blessed Israel is not to prefer either its "feminine" nurturer or its "masculine" aggressor, for all these qualities characterize the ferocious lover and the tender fire whom the Hebrews have come to know by invitation. Moses's expectation is neither wishful thinking nor cynicism, neither fantasy nor paranoia. It is hopeful desire informed by historical realities—both the signs of deliverance and sustenance and the wonders of wrath and rejection that have filled Israel's past four decades. The incomparable one is a God who punishes Israel *and* who saves it, who curses *and* blesses it, who stops his[+] ears *and* who hears and answers. The Baptist and the apostles will recognize this mysterious figure in the tender, ferocious face of Jesus son of Mary: not as a manifestation of only *some* of these qualities, the more holy or reasonable or palatable or intriguing ones, but as one in whom "all the fullness of God was pleased to dwell" (Col. 1:19 NRSV). His ascension, session, and return make him the Son of Man coming on the **clouds** in glory (Acts 7:55–56; cf. Luke 21:27 and 22:67–70).

Faith All the varieties of the land's bounty mentioned earlier (8:7–9) narrow down to two archetypical goods, **grain and new wine** (cf. Gen. 27:28b), which are juxtaposed to the **shield** and **sword** of **Jeshurun's** salvation. The two sets of images merge in the Messiah's self-offering; the fruit of conquest becomes the means of conquest. So broken bread and poured out wine become the elements of Christian remembrance of God's faithfulness to realize the deepest sense of Moses's words. "This cup that is poured out for you is the new covenant in my blood. But see, the one who betrays me is with me, and his hand is on the table. For the Son of Man is going as it has been determined, but woe to that one by whom he is betrayed!" (Luke 22:20–22 NRSV).

Hope Some variety of the root *'vn* ("abode") is often substituted for the Masoretic Text's *'ayin*, **fountain** or well, on the grounds that it makes more sense. The two words' connotations overlap in any case. The **fountain of Jacob** can also connote the Fountain Gate of Jerusalem, prominent in the city's postexilic restoration (Neh. 12:37)—as well as Jacob's well, where Messiah promises restoration of Israel's worship in Spirit and truth (John 4:6; →33:12–17). Both signal the approach of the age in which **Israel dwells** in temporal as well as eternal security.

Love This summary blessing has no counterpart in Gen. 49, where Jacob only blesses his sons individually. Instead it echoes Isaac's blessing of Jacob in 27:27–29. Centuries of slavery, exodus, and wandering have brought **Jacob's** fractious children together. While they remain distinctly named and distinctly blessed, their past has become a common one, and they face the future together. In the land, tribal selfishness will lead to division (Judg. 5:14–18; 20:1–25), and tribal division will lead to schism and ruin (1 Kgs. 11:9–13). But the eschaton will bring reconciliation and reunification. The unity of the apostolic church is to signify that **blessed** wholeness (Luke 6:20–23), for the coming Jerusalem "has a great, high wall with twelve gates, and at the gates twelve angels, and on the gates are inscribed the names of the twelve tribes of the Israelites. . . . And the wall of the city has twelve foundations, and on them are the twelve names of the twelve apostles of the Lamb" (Rev. 21:12–14 NRSV; cf. Ezek. 48:30–35).

DEUTERONOMY 34

34:1 Moses went up from the plains of Moab to Mount Nebo (→32:48–52), to the top of Pisgah, that is over against Jericho. YHWH showed him all the land of Gilead, to Dan, **²**and all Naphtali, and the land of Ephraim and Manasseh, and all the land of Judah, to the hinder sea, **³**and the South, and the Plain of the valley of Jericho the city of palm trees, to Zoar. **⁴**YHWH said to him, "This is the land I swore to Abraham, to Isaac, and to Jacob (→1:8), saying: 'I will give it to your seed.' I have caused you to see it with your eyes, but you shall not go over there."

Plain "I have finished the race, I have kept the faith" (2 Tim. 4:7 NRSV). Deuteronomy's final chapter is not the postscript it might seem to be. Heeding God's command to ascend and die at the threshold of his people's homeland may be **Moses's** most difficult task. It recalls Abraham's climb on his way to sacrifice his only son (Gen. 22:2) and contrasts absolutely with cursed Israel's pursuit of self-preservation at all costs (→28:53–57). Moses's climactic act as a prophet of Israel is to walk the covenant's talk. His faithfulness protects the inheritance promised to the patriarchs' little ones (→1:39) and "all who have longed for [the Lord's] appearing" (2 Tim. 4:8 NRSV).

Faith "The devil took him to a very high mountain and **showed him all** the kingdoms of the world and their splendor" (Matt. 4:8 NRSV), but God "tempts no one" (Jas. 1:12–16). YHWH shows **Moses** not faltering kingdoms but heritable **land**, not ephemeral power given on condition of fealty but sheer promise. As Moses remains on the **mountain** to die, so Moses's successor and Israel's truest **seed** (→5:16; →30:17–20) does not grasp at what is forbidden (→6:13–16) even when it is in reach.

Hope **Dan** (→33:20–25), **the hinder sea** (Mediterranean), and **Zoar** are not literally visible from **Pisgah**. If **Moses** sees them, YHWH must be **showing** him a vision perceptible only with **eyes** of hope. Then why must Moses climb the **mountain** to see this supernatural vision? Why not see the whole view "from below"? Because hope sees through the visible **to** the invisible. It is not blind faith or obvious inference but insight grounded in experience. We see the compatibility of the visible with the invisible only as we walk in the visible and sense the approach of the invisible (Heb. 2:6–9). Then we can witness, not just conjecture, that God the Father Almighty is maker of "all things visible and invisible."

Love Like **Moses**, we have been given a vision of an imminent future. "We do not yet see everything in subjection . . . but we do see Jesus" (Heb. 2:8–9 NRSV). We can die in frustration at what we do not have (12:25) or continue to wait with a life of mutual love (13:1). "Let us then go to him outside the camp and bear the abuse he endured. For here we have no lasting city, but we are looking for the city that is to come" (13:13–14 NRSV).

> ³⁴:⁵So Moses the servant of YHWH died there in the land of Moab, according to the word of YHWH. ⁶He was buried in the valley in the land of Moab over against Beth Peor: but no man⁺ knows of his tomb to this day (→1:1b; →2:10–12). ⁷Moses was one hundred twenty years old when he died: his eye was not dim, or his natural force abated.

Faith Does God euthanize **Moses**? The evidence is ambiguous. Moses claims fatigue (→31:1–8), yet he has just climbed a mountain. God has commanded him, "Die on the mountain," but this is as much a **word** concerning *where* to **die** as a command *to* die. He is still sharp and fresh, yet he has reached the full number of days God has decreed (Gen. 6:3). Beyond the evidence, though, the question itself is foreign to biblical categories. Hellenized cultures like our own can think of human life as having its own momentum—a life force or an immortal soul or some other quality we possess—that must be cut off by natural or artificial causes. By contrast, Hebrew scriptures describe limited providential sustenance: "He⁺ might reach out his⁺ hand and take also from the tree of life, and eat, and live forever" (Gen. 3:22 NRSV). "My spirit shall not abide in [*adam*] for ever, for he⁺ is flesh" (6:3 RSV). "When you take away their breath, they die and return to their dust. When you send forth your spirit, they are created" (Ps. 104:29–30 NRSV). So our suspicions are misplaced. Moses has simply reached the good end of a good and full life, his mission accomplished. Neither euthanasia nor **death** by natural causes is a fitting description for Moses's end. Perhaps the old word *exspirare* ("expire") best honors it. Moses's last breath foreshadows the expiring of another **servant of YHWH** who dies according to God's word (Luke 9:44). Rome does not seize Jesus's breath from Israel's crucified king; he commends his spirit to his Father (23:46). A servant can die a good death at any time—young or old, in sickness or in health, through violence or in peace (2:29)—simply by yielding life back to God in the same trust with which the disciple has come to receive it.

Faith The long life of **Moses** dominates Stephen's speech, which follows the later tradition of trisecting Moses's full life into forty-**year** epochs: the first in the house of Pharaoh (Acts 7:20–22), the second in Midian (7:23–29), and the third in the wilderness (7:30–44). Each age is a kind of exile whose significance Moses's contemporaries do not discern. The first yields the wisdom of the Egyptians (7:22), the second two sons (7:29), and the third the tent of witness (7:44). Stephen compares these heritages favorably to Solomon's harvest in the land: magnificent but unheeded wisdom, an incompetent successor Rehoboam, and an impressive but immovable house (7:47–50). It becomes clear over the course of Stephen's argument who better resembles the Righteous One who has come, and who better resembles his betrayers (7:51–53). The Son of Man does not sit on a manufactured throne like Solomon the monarch, but stands in God's presence like Moses the lawgiver (7:54–56).

Hope Joseph's bones will rest in Canaan like those of his father (Gen. 50:13; Josh. 24:32), but not **Moses's**! His fellow Levites may not carry his body across the Jordan, but must leave his body in the Transjordanian territory near the tribes of Gad and Reuben. They follow his example of obedience, resisting familial pressures that are stronger than we can probably imagine, and Moses is **buried** (not necessarily by God; the verb may be functionally passive) down from the mountain and across from **Beth Peor** (→3:28–29) where he has delivered his Torah (4:46). This is an appropriately Levitical end to Moses's journey, as for brother Aaron's (10:6; →32:48–52). In a priestly tribe with no inheritance but YHWH (→18:1–8), Moses belongs wherever God is—and God is everywhere along the way to eternity (John 14:6). It is also an encouraging sign for Israel, for honoring YHWH's exile of Moses's body shows his people appropriating their old leader's hope.

Hope "Why do you look for the living among the dead?" (Luke 24:5 NRSV). **Moses's** body remains unavailable for **human** purposes either of veneration or desecration. That is as it should be: Moses's relics should not distract attention from his towering legacies, the Torah and its people. Yet this does not mean that the dead are alone or abandoned; far from it. The church is the assembly of the living and the dead. Angels of YHWH may know Moses's **tomb** and guard it against the slanders of kings (Jude 8–9; cf. Dan. 10:21) until the day of Moses's reappearance in the Messiah's presence (Matt. 17:3) to testify along with his prophetic counterpart Elijah, who has been safely hidden above. It would not be the only time for such heavenly vigilance: the angel of YHWH at Jesus's empty tomb intimidates its sentries into deathly silence (28:2–4), then sends the pilgrims away from Jesus's obsolete grave with news of his resurrection and his return to Galilee to rejoin them among the living (28:5–7).

Love Moses has lived an apostle's life: being sent more than sent for (1 Cor. 1:17), on the move rather than settling in (16:5–9), and sowing more than reaping (3:6). Some of Deuteronomy's audiences share Joseph's honor of being gathered to their fathers in the promised land, or even Joshua's or Ephraim's honor of being buried in his own territory; but many more share Moses's more humble honor of being gathered on the way back. The church can rest anywhere, because it hopes in "the communion of saints, the resurrection of the body, and the life everlasting." Yet YHWH's deliverer has himself been delivered ever since being sent on the water and drawn out into the house of Pharaoh; YHWH's emancipator knows his own freedom from slavery. We all know salvation as a past as well as future blessing, so "we wait for it with patience" (Rom. 8:25 NRSV).

> **34:8**The sons[+] of Israel wept for Moses in the plains of Moab thirty days (26:14): so the days of weeping in the mourning for Moses were ended. **9**Joshua the son of Nun was full of the spirit of wisdom; for Moses had laid his hands on him: and the sons[+] of Israel listened to him, and did as YHWH commanded Moses.

Faith The generation that was deaf to **Moses** (29:3) listens to **Joshua**. The work of Joshua's commissioners, YHWH and Moses, is paying off. Perhaps this new patience and self-control are spiritual fruit of **Israel's** grief and days of reflection in the wilderness (Eccl. 7:1–4).

Faith The measure of **Israel's** fidelity to **Joshua** is Israel's fidelity to the covenant. "Not everyone who says to me, 'Lord, Lord,' will enter the kingdom of heaven, but only the one who does the will of my Father in heaven" (Matt. 7:21 NRSV).

Hope Death remains an enemy even when we obey God (1 Cor. 15:26). So **Moses** receives a mourner's kaddish of the same duration that anyone should, from Aaron (Num. 20:29) to an enemy of Israel (Deut. 21:10–13). Death reigns (Rom. 5:14) in spite of God's royal power, and that makes weeping an act of faith (John 11:35; 12:9–11). Yet, in stark contrast to the land of pyramids that Israel left behind, God's limit on death's reign places a limit on believers' sorrow (1 Thess. 4:13–14). When the time for **mourning** has **ended**, God sends his[+] renewing **spirit** (Ps. 104:30; Ezek. 37:5) and **Israel** returns to pursuing the mission that will transcend every mortal generation—until the generation arrives that survives death itself (Mark 13:30–31). Then death, and death alone, will be denied the dignity of mourning (Isa. 25:8 and Hos. 13:14 in 1 Cor. 15:54–57; Rev. 21:4).

Love In Numbers, **Joshua's** spirit (Num. 27:18) makes him an appropriate candidate for **Moses** to authorize (27:15–23). In Deuteronomy, receiving Moses's authorization fills Joshua with **the spirit of wisdom**. The two accounts could be carefully reconciled grammatically: for instance, it could be that only at his commissioning does Joshua's spirit fill him or yield wisdom. Yet the disparity between them is instructive. In Numbers, receiving God's anointing is not the same as gaining authority. Common church experience confirms this: we all know authorized leaders who lack the requisite spiritual gifts for their vocations (→32:26–31), and we know rank-and-file who are providentially equipped for powerful leadership service in the kingdom but outside formal ecclesiastical hierarchy. In Deuteronomy, placing a candidate of integrity in a position of authority creates the conditions for leadership and its constitutive skills to emerge. We also know many rank-and-file who have risen to the occasions of leadership being thrust upon them. Either way, the king's gifts and the king's offices coincide only when leaders discern and obey God's call, as Moses and Joshua both have here. And only then are God's people well led, mindful, and obedient. It is in this exact pattern that the young Jerusalem church appoints Stephen, "a man full of faith and the Holy Spirit" (Acts 6:5 NRSV), to the diaconate.

> **34:10**There has not arisen a prophet since in Israel like Moses, whom YHWH knew face to face, **11**in all the signs and the wonders YHWH sent him to do in the land of Egypt, to Pharaoh, and to all his servants, and to all his land, **12**and in all the mighty hand and in all the great terror Moses worked in the sight of all Israel.

Love From his birth to his death, **Moses's** whole life has been a great **sign** and **wonder** of salvation. His towering legacy leaves Israel in the position only to remember and reflect upon what has happened **in its sight**. Many prophets to follow will proclaim deliverances they are not **sent** to enact. So this passage's note of witness is an appropriate fermata to leave ringing in our ears. After the Messiah redeems all God's people from the principalities of sin and death and the powers of the kingdoms of this world, Israel will find itself in the very same position of watching, waiting, and reflecting: "Be alert; I have already told you everything" (Mark 13:23 NRSV).

Hope This epitaph is sometimes used in rabbinic Judaism to assert the absolute priority of Torah over all other authorities. Yet the Deuteronomistic narrator leaves room for other incomparables: on one unique day of battle, YHWH heeds Joshua's human voice and stops the sun (Josh. 10:14). Solomon receives matchless wisdom (1 Kgs. 3:12), and his glorious throne is unparalleled (10:20). Josiah turns to YHWH like no other king (2 Kgs. 23:25). So Deuteronomy's last words do not foreclose even brighter futures. They make **Moses** exemplary in enjoying the kind of trust that leads repeatedly to advents of the genuinely new.

Love Deuteronomy's poignant end is the Holy Spirit's cry for YHWH to answer the covenant's extravagant promises. As YHWH heard Israel's cry in Egypt (Exod. 3:7), so YHWH has heard and answered the Deuteronomist in granting new "deeds of power, wonders, and signs" (Acts 2:22 NRSV; cf. Joel 2:30 in Acts 2:19) to the one like **Moses** he[+] **raises** up (3:22–26). The messianic exodus (Luke 9:31) brings captives freedom (Isa. 61:1–2 in Luke 4:18–19) in all the world (4:21–27) in a new and everlasting Canaan (→11:8–15) under a new covenant (Luke 22:20). Messiah's **signs and wonders** are also the signs and wonders of his servant church (Acts 5:12–16). Truly YHWH knows the suffering of his[+] people (Exod. 3:7). Through the grace of the Father's anointed, crucified, and risen Son, all nations in all **lands** have entered into this story of Moses. The Spirit's cry is still being answered every time the Son's disciples extend the Father's mercy (Luke 6:35–36).

Faith Athanasius characterizes God's redeeming act of salvation in the Word's incarnation as twofold: inhabiting human life to reverse corruption, and showing humanity the invisible God to end ignorance (*On the Incarnation* 16). **Moses's** epitaph appeals to both these elements: **face-to-face** divine fellowship, and spectacular death-defying liberation. These two aspects, revelation and atonement, necessarily come from the same deliverer. Moses's **knowledge** of almighty God manifests itself **in all the** terrifying **signs and wonders** of his work. Yet the "latter prophets" from Samuel to John the Baptist who foresee restoration without enacting it do not share the same intimacy with God. Only one prophet's career is like that of the once incomparable Moses (→18:15–19)—the one in whom we see the Father himself⁺ (John 14:1–14).

Faith What happened to all the commandments? The instruction that dominates Deuteronomy is hardly discernible in this epitaph. That is because Deuteronomy's core is in the midst of the narratives of **Moses** that surround it. Torah is discipline for a chastened people (→5:4–6) to display YHWH's glory before all nations (→4:5–8). The Pentateuch's structure shows that Israel was not made for the covenant, but the covenant for Israel (cf. Mark 2:27). This further suggests that the prophet like Moses is lord of the covenant (cf. 2:28).

Love Egypt's prominence here is striking. Until now Deuteronomy has paid much more attention to the wilderness wonders. Now these last words step back and set Deuteronomy, and thus Israel's future, in the Pentateuch's greater narrative frame. Egypt has been a constantly recurring theme ever since Abram's and Sarai's journey to Egypt in Gen. 12:10. As Passover never forgets, so Deuteronomy never leaves Egypt behind—not least because Egypt also lies ahead (→28:63b–68). Nor do Christians forget in our remembrance the Roman cross on which the world's paschal lamb was slain, for crosses lie ahead for his followers too (Mark 8:34). God's way forward does not escape these nations, or any nation, but leads through them all (13:9–10) that God's holy name "may be proclaimed in all the earth" (Rom. 9:17 NRSV).

Faith Of course, we followers can cross into only one place at a time—starting with whichever place God has set before us. And now it is time to cross (Josh. 1:1–2).

BIBLIOGRAPHY

Alter, Robert. 1981. *The Art of Biblical Narrative*. New York: Basic Books.

———. 1985. *The Art of Biblical Poetry*. New York: Basic Books.

———. 2004. *The Five Books of Moses: A Translation with Commentary*. New York: Norton.

Beckwith, Roger T. 1990. "Formation of the Hebrew Bible." Pp. 39–86 in *Mikra: Text, Translation, Reading, and Interpretation of the Hebrew Bible in Ancient Judaism and Early Christianity*. Edited by Martin Jan Mulder. Minneapolis: Fortress.

Bockmuehl, Markus. 2006. *Seeing the Word: Refocusing New Testament Study*. Grand Rapids: Baker Academic.

Braaten, Carl, and Christopher R. Seitz, eds. 2005. *I Am the Lord Your God: Christian Reflections on the Ten Commandments*. Grand Rapids: Eerdmans.

Brenneman, James E. 2004. *On Jordan's Stormy Banks: Lessons from the Book of Deuteronomy*. Scottdale, PA: Herald.

Brown, William P., ed. 2004. *The Ten Commandments: The Reciprocity of Faithfulness*. Louisville: Westminster John Knox.

Brueggemann, Walter. 2001. *Deuteronomy*. Abingdon Old Testament Commentaries. Nashville: Abingdon.

Clines, David J. A. 1978. *The Theme of the Pentateuch*. Sheffield: Continuum.

Cowles, C. S., Eugene H. Merrill, Daniel L. Gard, and Tremper Longman III. 2003. *Show Them No Mercy: Four Views on God and Canaanite Genocide*. Grand Rapids: Zondervan.

de Lubac, Henri. 1998. *Medieval Exegesis*, vol. 1: *The Four Senses of Scripture*. Translated by Mark Sebanc. Grand Rapids: Eerdmans.

Fishbane, Michael. 1985. *Biblical Interpretation in Ancient Israel*. Oxford: Clarendon.

Friedman, Richard Elliott. 2001. *Commentary on the Torah*. San Francisco: Harper.

Hammer, Reuven, ed. and trans. 1986. *Sifre: A Tannaitic Commentary on the Book of Deuteronomy*. New Haven: Yale University Press.

———, ed. 1995. *The Classic Midrash: Tannaitic Commentaries on the Bible*. New York: Paulist Press.

Hays, Richard B. 1989. *Echoes of Scripture in the Letters of Paul*. New Haven: Yale University Press.

———. 1996. *The Moral Vision of the New Testament: A Contemporary Introduction to New Testament Ethics*. San Francisco: Harper.

Heschel, Abraham Joshua. 2005. *Heavenly Torah as Refracted through the Generations*. New York: Continuum.

Magonet, Jonathan. 2004. *A Rabbi Reads the Bible*. New edition. London: SCM.

Nelson, Richard D. 2002. *Deuteronomy*. Old Testament Library. Louisville: Westminster John Knox.

Newbigin, Lesslie. 1982. *The Light Has Come: An Exposition of the Fourth Gospel*. Grand Rapids: Eerdmans.

O'Keefe, John, and R. R. Reno. 2005. *Sanctified Vision: An Introduction to Early Christian Interpretation of the Bible*. Baltimore: Johns Hopkins University Press.

Olson, Dennis T. 1994. *Deuteronomy and the Death of Moses: A Theological Reading*. Minneapolis: Fortress.

Payne, David F. 1985. *Deuteronomy*. Daily Study Bible. Louisville: Westminster John Knox.

Polzin, Robert. 1993. *Moses and the Deuteronomist: A Literary Study of the Deuteronomic History*, vol. 1: *Deuteronomy, Joshua, Judges*. Bloomington: Indiana University Press.

Provan, Iain, V. Philips Long, and Tremper Longman III. 2003. *A Biblical History of Israel*. Louisville: Westminster John Knox.

Rowe, C. Kavin, and Richard B. Hays. 2007. "What Is a Theological Commentary?" *Pro Ecclesia* 16:26–32.

Seitz, Christopher R. 2004. *Word without End: The Old Testament as Abiding Theological Witness*. Waco: Baylor University Press.

Steinsaltz, Adin. 1976. *The Essential Talmud*. Translated by Chaya Galai. New York: Basic Books.

Tigay, Jeffrey H. 1996. *Deuteronomy*. JPS Torah Commentary. Philadelphia: Jewish Publication Society.

Work, Telford. 2002. *Living and Active: Scripture in the Economy of Salvation*. Grand Rapids: Eerdmans.

SUBJECT INDEX

Aaron, 122, 123, 127, 131, 143, 217, 298, 299, 304, 313, 314

Abraham, 29, 37, 42, 44, 65, 68, 75, 76–77, 82, 84, 85, 98, 106–107, 115, 118, 121, 124, 129, 136, 165–166, 187, 195–196, 202, 208, 228, 237, 238, 262, 268, 271, 284, 288, 292, 295, 311, 316

Adam, 36, 68, 80, 90–91, 193, 211, 248, 252, 283, 292, 312

adultery, 67, 84, 204, 205, 211, 214

Amalek; Amalekites, 229–230

Ammon; Ammonites, 44, 45–46, 49, 52, 53, 207

Amorites, 27, 29, 31, 32, 34, 39, 46, 48, 49, 50, 51, 52, 62, 72, 103, 186, 272, 288

apocalyptic, 17, 66–67, 89, 116, 128, 175, 177, 184, 185, 188, 201, 232, 244, 245, 268, 279, 282, 286

Aquinas, Thomas, 21, 274

Augustine (of Hippo), 21, 109, 146, 178, 271, 274

baptism, 26, 38, 45, 49, 50, 67, 68, 78, 129, 138, 142, 143–144, 166, 196, 202, 203, 205, 208, 215, 239, 244, 245, 289, 292

Baptist, John the, 83, 126, 140, 232, 240, 309, 316

Barth, Karl, 120, 287

Beth Peor; Baal Peor, 58, 59, 60, 62, 72, 312, 313

Bible (see *scripture*)

blood, 38, 60, 63, 83, 105, 140, 142, 143, 149, 161, 163, 168–169, 179, 180, 181, 188, 190, 191–192, 200, 203, 230, 242, 256, 268, 282, 285, 291, 292, 294, 296, 309–310

Caleb, 31, 35–36, 38

Calvin, John; Calvinism, 21, 26, 38, 274, 279, 287

cherem, 39, 49, 109, 148

children, 13, 30, 36, 37, 42, 59, 61–62, 66, 67, 71, 77, 78, 81, 82, 92, 94, 97, 98, 114–115, 131–132, 134, 141, 142, 150, 153, 160, 164, 187, 193, 194, 202, 205, 207, 208, 215, 219, 220, 240, 254–255, 256, 264, 266, 267–268, 269, 273, 274, 284, 287, 288, 297, 298, 299, 303, 305, 310

communion, 55, 60, 122, 139, 142, 163, 192, 203, 232, 237, 255, 275, 279, 292, 309–310

confession, 39, 62, 67, 95, 109, 119, 181, 182, 188, 191–192, 205, 239

David, 36, 53, 62, 68, 69, 75, 95, 100, 106, 171, 194, 202, 207, 225, 229, 234, 243, 245, 249, 279, 292, 299

despair, 34, 53, 84, 91, 111, 115, 119, 249

divorce, 84, 192, 194, 203, 205, 214, 215

Eden, 121, 147, 198, 247, 286

Edom; Edomites, 26, 42, 44, 48, 207–208

Eucharist (see *communion*)

exegesis, 18, 20–23, 36, 38, 270

family, 30, 37, 42, 54, 61–62, 67, 81, 82, 83, 86, 88, 90, 95, 100, 109, 133, 136, 146, 147, 157, 164, 165, 173, 174, 179, 182, 193, 194, 195, 198, 203, 205, 215–216, 219, 220, 225, 241, 255, 264, 289, 303, 306

fear, 13, 25, 28, 31, 32–33, 42, 44, 46–47, 49–50, 51, 55, 62, 66, 75, 79, 84, 91, 92, 94, 98, 99, 101, 104, 107, 108, 112, 123, 128, 129, 135, 138, 145, 146, 153, 154, 155, 160, 161, 169, 170, 171, 177, 183, 185, 193–194, 196, 206, 213, 219, 225, 229, 237, 241, 245, 256, 257, 258–259, 269, 272, 273–274, 286, 290, 291, 293–294, 296

Feasts (cultic), 113, 163–166, 232, 273–275

forgetting; forgetfulness, 41, 44, 61, 62, 63, 65, 69, 97, 98, 111, 113, 114, 116, 119, 135, 138, 146, 229, 230, 233, 251, 263, 285, 286, 297, 316

fornication, 60, 67, 84, 88, 202–203

four-fold sense, 18–20, 23–24

genealogy, 49, 82, 171, 194, 207, 225

Gnosticism, 25, 47, 96, 143, 173, 237, 266, 296

greed, 43, 56, 86, 104, 115–116, 158, 175, 199, 229, 241

halakah, 100, 101, 113, 201, 213, 223

holiness, 31, 54, 61, 64, 66, 79–80, 100, 105, 119, 121, 124, 135, 142, 143, 146, 148, 150, 151, 152, 153, 161, 166, 174, 175, 191, 202, 209, 215, 224, 232– 233, 234, 235,

SCRIPTURE INDEX